Windows to the Past

200 Years of Perinton, New York, History

Front cover photos (l. to r.):
Conover Farm house, see page 27
Canal photo, see page 59
James Hannan
Lucretia Packard Hannan

Back cover (clockwise from top):
Fairport High School Baseball team, 1907, see page 229
American Can Co. office, see page 99
Fred Potter in a buggy
Midvale School

Windows to the Past

Jean Keplinger

Mountain Air Books
Rochester, New York

Mountain Air Books
Scott Krause
1045 University Ave., Ste. #2
Rochester, NY 14607
585-442-9468

ISBN: 978-0-615-56237-7

ACKNOWLEDGMENTS

Without the dedication, research, and organization of the historians who preceded me in the office of Perinton historian, Susan Roberts, Helen Butler, Alta Fisher, and Charlotte Clapp, this book would not have been possible. It also would not have been possible without the support and encouragement of James Smith, Town Supervisor, and the Town Board. Thank you.

Many thanks are also owed to all those who have contributed articles, family histories, stories, and photos to this office. Marjorie Snow Merriman is one of those whose attention to detail, indexing skills, and personal stories have added immeasurably to the preservation of local history. Thank you to the readers of my columns whose positive comments over the years helped me to consider doing this book. Thank you to Scott Krause for being a patient and immensely helpful editor, making suggestions and putting up with my omissions and changes, and to Janet Northrup for proof reading. Finally a profound thank you to my husband Bill for carefully reading every column, making suggestions, asking questions, and editing as only an English teacher can do.

Jim Smith, Town Supervisor

When most of us think of Perinton, we think of rolling green hills and the attendant physical beauty of our town. But, that is simply the canvas upon which the rich and exciting history of Perinton has been painted. The artists have been the people of our community, from Glover and Johanna Perrin to present day residents. They are the people about whom the stories are told and retold, the community portrait that is drawn one brushstroke at a time.

We have been blessed to have a succession of dedicated Town Historians who have done a wonderful job of chronicling Perinton's growth and maturation. Jean Keplinger, as the latest in that lineage, has done an exemplary job of selecting stories for this volume that convey the two centuries of accomplishments that have truly made our wonderful community what it is today.

I trust you will enjoy reliving our past as much as our ancestors enjoyed creating it!

Yours,

Jim Smith

This book is a compilation of columns written and published in the *Fairport-East Rochester Post* from 1998 through 2010 that attempt to give a picture of 200 years of community history. While many topics are covered, by no means does this book claim to have written about all the people, organizations, and events in Perinton and Fairport.

Table of Contents

A BRIEF HISTORY of PERINTON and FAIRPORT

Oliver Phelps and Nathaniel Gorham purchased 2.6 million acres of land in the wilderness of Western New York in 1788 with the intent of selling the 102 thirty-six square mile sections. The area had rich soil and abundant water power, both essential in luring farmers from the rocky hills of New England to the western frontier. William Walker of Canandaigua purchased a 36 square mile township and hired his brother Caleb and his cousin Glover Perrin to survey the land and divide it into 66 equal lots. The area was known as Township 12, Range 4, in the governmental unit of Northfield.

Glover Perrin, his family, and his six siblings and their families settled in the same area, which became known as Perinton, when it was officially established by the New York State Legislature on May 26, 1812. Other settlers soon followed, as word of the area's good farming traveled back east. Between 1800 and 1814, the Perinton census showed a growth in population from 71 to 821 people.

Because the earliest settlers were farmers, they settled in the flat areas of the town that were easily cleared, specifically in Egypt and Perinton Center (the area along Ayrault Road between Moseley and Turk Hill Roads). Other settlers located near the area's streams, where they built mills. Early commercial ventures also included blacksmith shops, taverns, and inns. On April 6, 1813, the first town meeting was held in Cyrus Packard's tavern in Egypt, which was thriving as a stagecoach stop between Canandaigua and Rochester. Many of the current and future leaders of the town lived and farmed in Egypt, including Packard, who was elected Perinton's first supervisor.

By the 1820's, things were changing as the Erie Canal opened up western New York. The Village of Fairport, an approximately one square mile parcel within the Town of Perinton, was drained of its unhealthy swamps by the new canal, and the north-south route through the village served as a natural highway for farmers to bring produce to the canal. The result was a booming canal town which eventually eclipsed the hamlet of Egypt as well as the surrounding canal settlements of Knapp's Bridge, Fullam's Basin, and Hartwell's (Bushnell's) Basin. Cyrenus Mallett moved from Egypt and built a popular hotel on the canal, one of many that, along with numerous canal stores and barns, lined the new route. Political power also moved to the village as town meetings were held in Fairport starting in 1827. In 1829, the Post Office moved from Fullams' Basin to the Village of Fairport.

From the 1840's to the 1950's, Perinton's history was primarily the history of Fairport, which was incorporated as a village in 1867 with its own governing body. The village was not only an active canal port, but also developed into a booming industrial town, echoing a trend that was occurring nationwide. As a result of the availability of cheap and easy transportation, which by the 1850's included the railroad as well as the canal, companies like the DeLand Chemical Company and the Cobb Preserving Company grew and thrived. DeLand Chemical produced saleratus, known today as baking soda, which it marketed nation-wide. It was eventually succeeded by the Fairport Vinegar Works, which developed pectin, sold as Certo, used in the jelling process. Cobb Preserving, the forerunner of the American Can Company, was one of the first companies to perfect the use of the open-top sanitary can, thereby greatly increasing the safe use of factory-canned goods. The Trescott Company developed fruit grading and packing systems that revolutionized the wholesale grocery business. Taylor's Oil of Life and Crystal Rock Mineral Water, catering to the late nineteenth century demand for cure-all "patent medicines," were both produced in Perinton and shipped across the country.

Services, including a fire department, a public library, street lighting, and parks, enhanced the life of the town and village. A number of schools, churches, and cemeteries served the growing community. The philanthropy of the early industrialists like the DeLands, Taylors, and Potters contributed to many of those services. In addition, residential areas, with homes built in a variety of architectural styles, were built around the thriving village center.

The town, outside of the Village of Fairport, remained essentially rural until the 1950's. Maps of the late nineteenth and early twentieth centuries show many family farms with names like Spruce Grove Farm and Grand View Farm. It was not until the suburban boom of the 1950's and 1960's that the farms began to disappear. Today, although farms still exist in Perinton, that former farmland supports not only suburban subdivisions, but also office and industrial parks, an impressive number of parks and open spaces, and a trail system of approximately forty miles. An Historic Preservation Ordinance, passed by the Town of Perinton in 1987, exists to protect the town's historic areas and buildings. The Village of Fairport has also changed significantly over the last 100 years. In the late 1960's and early 1970's the old canal town buildings were torn down and replaced with the Village Landing and Packett's Landing complexes, which do maintain the ambiance of a canal village. In addition, Fairport has developed its canal frontage allowing it to capitalize on the recreational aspects of the canal that have superseded its commercial use.

The community looks to the future with the goals of maintaining reasonable growth and preserving both its rural and canal town heritage.

- I -
Early Neighborhoods and Pioneer Settlers

The people who first settled what became the town of Perinton came by wagon, on horseback and on foot to clear and cultivate their own land and establish institutions of government and community in the western wilderness.

The Phelps and Gorham Purchase and the Northfield Area

How did the lands in Western New York become organized for white settlement? Who were the original owners and how did Oliver Phelps and Nathaniel Gorham purchase the land? How were the towns in this area first organized?

Before the coming of the white man, members of the Iroquois nation lived on the land that is now Perinton. The Iroquois nation had been allies of the British during the Revolution, but the Treaty of 1783 ending the war made no provision for them vis-à-vis their land. Further confusing the land issue was the fact that both Massachusetts and New York claimed the lands of Western New York. Eventually the two states signed treaties that gave governmental control of the land to New York, but reserved preemption rights (title rights and the right to sell) for Massachusetts. Between 1783 and 1788 a number of treaties for land were made with groups from the Iroquois nations, and in addition, several private organizations conducted negotiations for land. It was a treaty made in 1788, however, that for all intents and purposes stripped the Iroquois nations of their claims to over two million acres of Western New York land.

In early 1788 Massachusetts granted Oliver Phelps and Nathaniel Gorham and their partners the right of purchase to 6 million acres of Indian land in Western New York. In the summer of that year, a council was to take place in the city of Geneva between the Indians and the various groups who sought their land. After several disputes and misunderstandings, the council was finally held at Buffalo Creek, the Indian town at the present city of Buffalo, in July of 1788. Among those present were the Rev. Mr. Kirkland, appointed by Massachusetts to oversee any treaty; a number of interpreters; chiefs of the Onondagas, Cayugas, and Mohawks; Joseph Brant; John Butler; members of the Seneca Nation; and of course Oliver Phelps and others who were interested in purchasing the land. The resulting deal, which cost £2,100 (about $5,000) in New York money, about one-half cent per acre, essentially cleared any Indian title to 2.6 million acres of land and opened the door to white settlement. The boundaries of the tract reached from the Pennsylvania border in the south to Lake Ontario in the north, and from the Genesee River on the west to Seneca Lake on the east.

Surveyors quickly created 102 approximately thirty-six square mile "townships," which were then sold to settlers and speculators. In 1796 the name "Northfield" was given to a 220 square mile area that would become Webster, Penfield, Perinton, Irondequoit, Brighton, Pittsford, Henrietta, and the eastern portion of the city of Rochester. In 1808, for some reason, the name was changed to "Boyle."

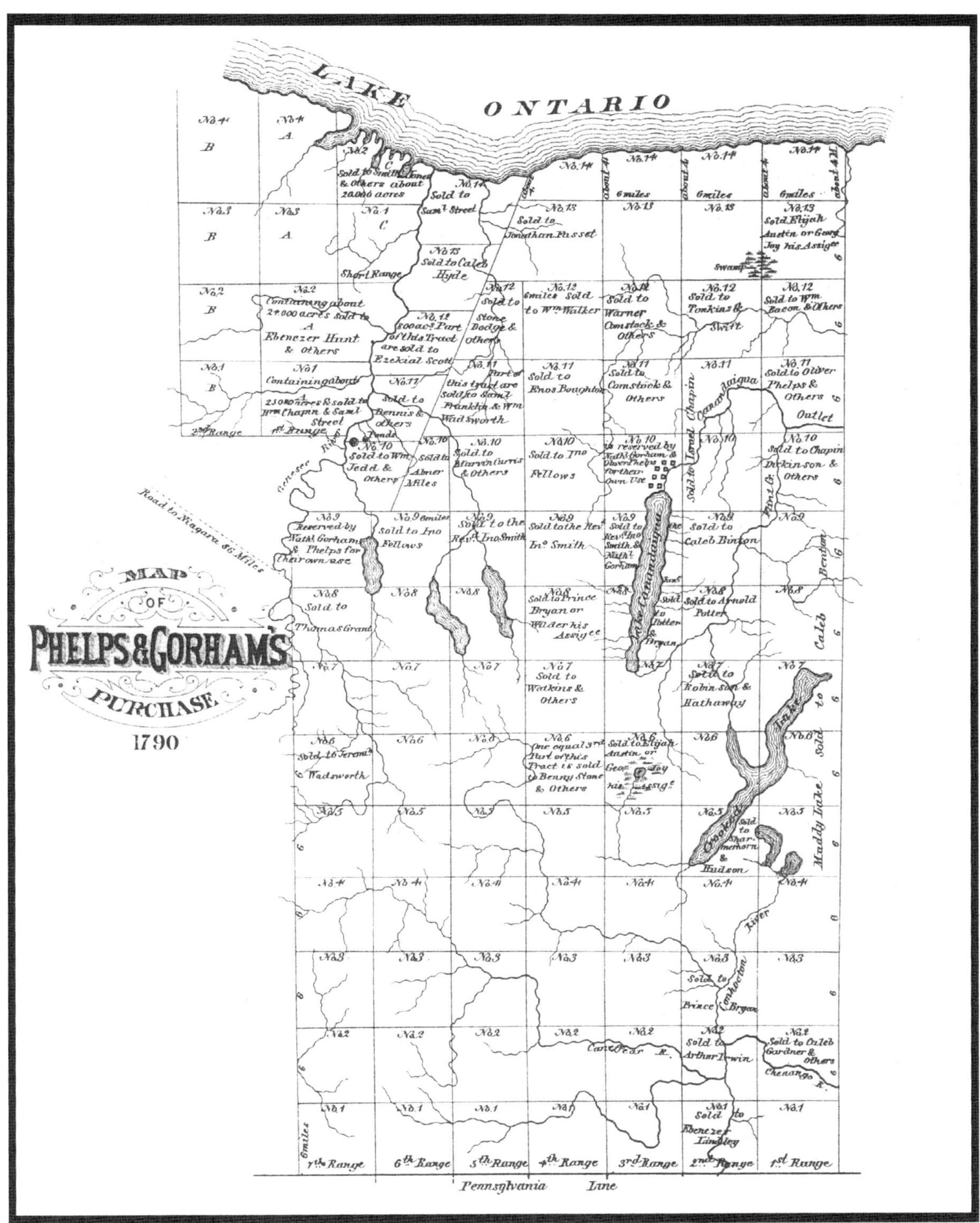

Land division map showing Perinton-Township #12

Both sales and settlement of the Northfield area were rapid. While the 1800 census showed a population of only 398, the subsequent (1810) census showed a population of 2,360. The area called Boyle was bought up by a number of different investors and settlers. General Jonathan Fassett of Pittsford, Vermont, purchased Township 13 in 1790 for about $4,160, had it surveyed and resold it. Eventually the parcel was purchased by Daniel Penfield, and in 1810 the town separated from Boyle and became the town of Penfield. Another of the individual purchasers was William Walker, who bought Township 12 (Perinton) for £1,056 in August of 1789. Walker, his brother Caleb, and his cousin Glover Perrin, surveyed the land into 54 lots of approximately 320 acres each and another dozen of somewhat larger size in the western part of the town near Irondequoit Creek. Perrin remained as the first settler in town and gave his name to the community, which was established in 1812. Townspeople from Lenox, Massachusetts, bought the tract that became Brighton in 1814. The town of Pittsford was purchased by the Association of Stone and Dodge, a family group from Washington County and was also incorporated as a town in 1814, taking its name from the Vermont hometown of local war hero Caleb Hopkins.

The part of Boyle that would become Henrietta, Irondequoit, and Webster was deeded in 1790 to Robert Morris, financier, for a cost of about six cents an acre. Morris sought buyers in England despite laws that forbade foreign ownership of land. To avoid the law, the three buyers, Sir William Pulteney, William Hornby, and Patrick Colquhoun, sent Charles Williamson to the U.S. to become naturalized and act as agent. A number of subsequent transactions occurred, but in 1818 the town of Henrietta was incorporated, named after the daughter of Sir William Pulteney. Township 14, which became the town of Irondequoit in 1839, was, of the towns created from Boyle, the least hospitable. Areas were subject to sand storms from the wind off Lake Ontario, and the glaciers had left huge granite boulders on the land; however, the areas at the south end of the town were excellent for farming. Caleb Lyon was the first one to purchase land in what would become in 1840 the town of Webster, named after Daniel Webster.

Thus, by 1840, the original Northfield/Boyle area had been settled and organized into the towns that are recognizable today. The remainder of the Phelps and Gorham purchase was developed in much the same way. Within two years of the purchase, by 1790, all 102 townships had been sold, 50 to individual buyers and the rest to Robert Morris. The nation was on its way west.

The Perrin Family

William Walker purchased Township 12 of the Phelps and Gorham Purchase and hired his son Caleb and his nephew Glover Perrin to survey the land into sixty-six lots. Subsequently Glover purchased 160 acres in Lot 46, which included the area from today's Ayrault Road to south of Pittsford-Palmyra Road and from Moseley Road westward about half way to Kreag Road. Before returning to Rehoboth, Massachusetts for his wife Johanna and their belongings, he built a log cabin on Ayrault Road just west of Moseley Road.

Travel to the wilderness of western New York was difficult. People tended to travel in early spring when frozen ground made travel a bit easier, and even then, foot, wagon, or horse were the only available methods. It is known that the Perrins left Rehoboth, Massachusetts, in the early spring, arrived in Canandaigua in the early summer of 1790 and reached their Perinton cabin in late summer. Because Johanna was the only white woman in the area for their first two years, she was an object of fascination for the local Native American population, many of whom would come to her door. Since Glover was often away on surveying business, these visits, although friendly, frightened her as she remembered stories of Indians burning homes and barns in her native Rehoboth.

Within two years other members of the Perrin family began to arrive in the town. Like many of the early settlers in the area, they came from Massachusetts towns near Boston like Rehoboth, and from towns in the Berkshires like Lenox and Adams. In 1792, Glover's brother Jesse, his wife Abigail, and their family settled in a cabin on Moseley Road. They were followed in 1800 by Abner Wight and his wife Huldah Perrin Wight, Edward and Lydia Perrin, Ezra Perrin, Jacob and Elizabeth Perrin, Asa and Rebecca Perrin, and Daniel and Nancy Perrin. They all had families, but Abner and Huldah's son Asa was the first white child born in Perinton who lived to grow up. These families settled in the vicinity of Glover's cabin, on Moseley and Ayrault Roads, thus forming Perinton Center, the first settlement in the town of Perinton.

The Perrins were, needless to say, active in town affairs. Early in the first decade of the nineteenth century, Glover and Jesse cleared land for Perinton Center Cemetery, located on Ayrault Road. The graves of Jesse and his family are located there. The two men purportedly planted Perinton's first apple orchard at the corner of Ayrault and Turk Hill Roads. The first meeting of the Congregational Church took place in Jesse's house on Moseley Road in the early 1820's. Glover, Jesse and their brothers, Asa, Edward, and Ezra, all served as highway commissioners. One or another of them at times also served as juror, school commissioner, assessor, overseer of the poor, and fence viewer.

Glover and Johanna built a new frame house on Moseley Road in the vicinity of Georgetown Commons in 1806. It was not, however, enough to ease Johanna's depression, which was probably a result of her isolation and the death of her only child, as well as of the difficulty of living on the frontier. Subsequently, Glover and Johanna moved to the village of Pittsford where he ran a popular tavern. His license states that he was "of a good moral character and of sufficient abilities to keep an inn or tavern" and that "an inn or tavern is absolutely necessary at the place where he proposes to keep a tavern for the actual accommodations of travelers...." Glover died in 1830 and soon thereafter Johanna married the Rev. Andrew Huntington. She died in 1842 and is buried along with both husbands in Pittsford's Pioneer Cemetery.

Glover and other family members wanted the town where he and his family had first settled to be called Perrin's Town; however, the State legislature had different ideas and enacted the following on May 26, 1812:

> *"Be it enacted by people of the State of New York, represented in the Senate and Assembly, that from and after the first Monday of April next, all that part of the Town of Boyle, in the County of Ontario, foresaid known, and distinguished by the township number 12, in the fourth range of townships in said county, is hereby erected into a separate town by the name of PERRINTON; and that the first town meeting shall be held at the house of Cyrus Packard, in said town."*

In those early years, spelling was not standardized and the name of the town was spelled with either one or two r's, and sometimes as Perrington. By the middle years of the century, for the most part, the second r had been dropped, and the spelling was more or less standardized to "Perinton."

While some members of the first generation of Perrins are buried in Perinton, many of their children, seeking more land, moved further west in the 1820's and 1830's, settling in Michigan and Ohio. There is a Perintown, Ohio, named for Glover and Jesse, and numerous Perrin streets and roads throughout the Midwest. The last Perrin in Perinton was James, a cooper and a canal boatman who lived here until 1872. Perrin Street in Fairport village was named for him.

Perinton Center and its Pioneers

Perinton Center was one of the earliest areas of settlement in what would become the Town of Perinton. It surrounds the intersection of Turk Hill and Ayrault Roads and extends westward to the site of Martha Brown School and southward toward Pittsford-Palmyra Road. Glover and Jesse Perrin both settled in that area and Perinton's first road was the path that connected their two cabins. By 1805, Ayrault Road west of Turk Hill had been laid out, and by 1811 Turk Hill Road had been laid out from the town's north line to its south line.

Among the early settlers, in addition to the Perrin families, was the Arnold family. In 1811, Isaac Arnold purchased sixty acres of land in Perinton Center for $240 and built a public house or inn. Originally the inn was run by Lyman Tripp, another settler, but as business began to grow, Isaac himself took over. Records show that he held a license for keeping an inn from 1822 to 1829. As was common practice in early settlements, the local inn was also the center of public discourse and action, and, not surprisingly, was the site of town meetings from 1827 to 1829. Arnold's tavern still stands on the northwest corner of the Ayrault-Turk Hill Road intersection.

Isaac Arnold and his family were Quakers from Rhode Island. Isaac served in the War of 1812 and was subsequently very active in town affairs, holding a variety of positions between 1813 and 1826, such as poundkeeper, clerk, overseer of highways, and fenceviewer. In addition to his duties as innkeeper, he made wooden churns and apple grinders for cider making. Isaac and his wife Abigail Wilbur had seven children, one of whom, Thomas Henry, lived for a number of years on his South Main Street farm in the house currently known as the Arnold-McDonough house (# 224). Darius Arnold, Isaac's brother, also lived in Perinton, and was active in town affairs, serving as overseer of highways, fenceviewer and poormaster. He was married to Joanna Slocum, whose four brothers, Amasa, Elisha, Benjamin, and Smith were early settlers in the Perinton Center area as well. Amasa was married to Darius' sister Anne. A search of local cemeteries reveals the graves of Thomas Henry and his wife Marietta in Greenvale Cemetery and Darius Arnold's wife Joanna and five of their children, as well as Darius and Isaac's mother Lavinia in Perinton Center Cemetery.

Isaac Arnold's tavern, Northwest corner of Turk Hill & Ayrault Roads

The Benjamin Slocum family came from Adams, Massachusetts and settled on a parcel of land purchased from William Walker, the first owner of land in Perinton. They paid $1,170 for 320 acres on the west side of Turk Hill Road between Ayrault and Pittsford-Palmyra Roads. In 1804, Benjamin and his four sons, the aforementioned Amasa, Elisha, Benjamin, and Smith, along with Amasa's wife Anne Arnold and daughter Amy, moved to the new farm. The move did not begin auspiciously as the small cabin in which they took shelter burned on their first night. Samuel Bennett, another early pioneer in the area, took them in until they could build log houses. The Slocum men were active in Perinton affairs and served in such positions as School Commissioner, Overseer of Highways, Fence

Viewer, and Town Clerk. Amasa was the first elected town clerk in Perinton, and he was also interested in the area's business beyond his farm. As such he took boats through the canal, one of which transported 130 bushels of potatoes, twenty barrels of pork, thirty barrels of flour, and twenty barrels of whiskey from Wayneport to Brockport for Darius Arnold, his brother-in-law and fellow pioneer. The Slocum farm boasted the first orchard in town and perhaps a cemetery as well, which is said to have been located on the southwest corner of the Ayrault-Turk Hill Road intersection. However, there is no longer any evidence of a cemetery in that location. The Slocum farm remained in the family for over sixty-five years. Although Smith Slocum and his wife Elizabeth are buried in Perinton Center Cemetery, other members of the family are buried in unmarked graves, after the custom of the Quakers, in Farmington's Friends' Cemetery.

Samuel Bennett, who had housed the Slocum family on their arrival in Perinton Center, had come to Perinton in 1795, after purchasing 320 acres in the Ayrault-Turk Hill Road area. He was a Revolutionary War veteran, a survivor of British prisoner-of-war camps, and, more importantly, a blacksmith, an essential trade in any settlement. Known for his ingenuity and his ability to make the best use of scarce iron, he first set up his business under a tree with a sign reading "Horses shod unless the weather be rainy." A devout Baptist, Bennett was instrumental in the founding of several churches in the area and was also one of the trustees of the new Perinton Center Cemetery. Samuel and his wife Paulina died in 1819 while on a visit to Cayuga county where they "took the fever." They had two daughters, one of whom married Benjamin Slocum, thus adding another pioneer family connection.

By the 1820's, Perinton Center was a thriving community with an inn, a blacksmith, a school (District School #3 located on Turk Hill Road between Ayrault and Pittsford-Palmyra Roads), a cemetery (Perinton Center Cemetery across from Martha Brown School), and a number of successful farms. Along with the hamlet of Egypt, the community was growing.

The Hannan Family

For nearly a century and a half, the intersection of today's Routes 250 and 31, known as Hannan's Corners, was farmland. In the first decades of the nineteenth century, James Hannan purchased 160 acres there and soon added 100 more. At least a portion of that land remained in the Hannan family until the late 1960's.

James Hannan was born in Florida, Montgomery County, and came to western New York with his friend David Cady (or David's brother, Lovejoy), around 1810 to clear their newly purchased land. Clearing his heavily wooded land with an ax and oxen, Hannan developed into a proficient woodsman. However, he did have time to ride into Egypt to court Cyrus Packard's daughter, Lucretia. They were married April 9, 1811, and moved to a log cabin on the newly cleared land at Hannan's Corners. While James served in the War of 1812 on the Niagara frontier near Fort Erie and also on the Genesee River when Sir James Yeo was bombarding the area, Lucretia was left with the running of the new farm, which she did admirably well.

Over the subsequent twenty years, the Hannans increased the size of the farm and Lucretia became known as an exceptional spinner, weaver, and cook. They had ten children, five of whom lived to adulthood and only three of whom were long-term survivors: Susan, Julia, and Jesse. By 1838, a frame house had replaced the log cabin. That house stood until it was razed during the construction of Perinton Hills Mall. James was active in the town, serving as fenceviewer and highway overseer. He lived a long active life, dying on October 7, 1871, at eighty-six. His wife Lucretia had died the previous year, in 1870, at age eighty-one.

Jesse Briggs Hannan, the only surviving son, in addition to teaching for a short time, ran the farm for his father and mother for a number of years before their deaths. He, too, was active in the town of Perinton, serving as Supervisor and Chairman of the Board of Supervisors. In 1885, at the age of fifty-three, he married Alice Yale of Pittsford, who was twenty years his junior. Their daughter Stella was born in 1887 and their son Jesse on June 2, 1888. Tragically, Jesse Sr. never knew his son. Nineteen days (or fifteen or sixteen) before his birth, he was working in the barn with one of the spirited horses he loved and was kicked in the abdomen, an injury which proved fatal the next day. He was fifty-six years old. His young widow rented the farm to the William Bulmans and moved into the village of Fairport to raise her two children.

1877 Etching of the Hannan farm

In 1905, at the age of seventeen, despite not having any education or experience in farming, Jesse took over the running of the farm. He did, however, have the help of four hired men. In spite of the hard farm work, Jesse apparently had time for himself, because three years later he eloped with Lucille Parce of Fairport. She was the daughter of Walter Parce, founder of East Rochester, and Carrie Higbie of Penfield. The young couple was married in Batavia and went off to honeymoon in Niagara Falls. Their families learned of the elopement by telegram. "We were married in Batavia at 5 p.m. today. Will be home in about two weeks. Love, Lucille and Jess." Upon their return to Perinton, the newlyweds moved into the family farmhouse with mother Alice and sister Stella. Stella would remain in that house until her marriage in 1915 to Howard Whitman, after which they built their own house next door.

Jesse and Lucille Hannan were successful dairy farmers and active members of the community. They were members of the Congregational Church, and Jesse also belonged to the Masons. Following in the political footsteps of his father, Jesse served as Town Supervisor from 1924 to 1935. He oversaw the adoption of some of the first zoning ordinances and planning regulations in the county. During the depression, with the WPA providing jobs, three water districts were established and water lines constructed. He also began a cooperative agreement with Monroe County for highway maintenance. He served the county as Treasurer from 1935 to 1936 and then as Director of Social Services from 1936 until his retirement in 1953. Lucille Hannan served the community for a number of years as the matron of the Monroe County Hospital and Home, a place that she referred to as "the county's greatest friend of old people." Her husband said of her, "She can't help but have their confidence....She is the kindest, yet shrewdest, woman in the world, and that's why the county is lucky to have her in the position she is in."

Jesse and Lucille had four children, Walter Parce, Lucy, Marguerite, and Jesse Briggs, Jr. Both sons joined their father in running the farm and were active in the Grange and the Monroe County Farm Bureau. Marguerite Hannan Antell, a well-known ceramist, and her husband Robert, are known in Perinton for having conceived and built the "Mushroom House" which is located on Park Road near Powder Mill Park. Their house was subsequently purchased by Steven Whitman, a cousin, and his wife Christine.

In the early 1950's the Hannan farm was recognized as a "Century Farm," as it had been in the same family for well over 100 years. After the death of their father in 1961, Parce and Jesse continued to run the farm despite the pressure of the growing suburbs and a devastating barn fire that destroyed a $10,000 barn. However, in the late 1960's, bowing to the advancing suburbs and the difficulty of maintaining a relatively small dairy business, the family sold the property, which was subsequently developed as Perinton Hills Office Park.

The Hamlet of Egypt

The hamlet of Egypt has been a part of Perinton since the 1790's, which qualifies it as one of the town's oldest settlements. In a certain sense, Egypt mirrors the history of the area as it developed from a pioneer agricultural settlement, to a village, to a suburban part of a twentieth and twenty-first century community. Recognizing that, the Town of Perinton designated the hamlet of Egypt as an historic district in 2001.

The Ramsdells and the Packards were among the earliest white families to settle in the area. Thomas Ramsdell purchased 320 acres of land in 1802 in the part of Perinton that would become known as Egypt and built a house at what would become 7516 Pittsford-Palmyra Road. In 1807 he sold 197 acres of that land to his son Gideon who was both a surveyor and a teacher in Macedon and who built his house on Mason Road (173). The Cyrus Packard family also purchased land in Egypt and Cyrus opened a tavern there in 1806. Settlers were drawn by the fertile soil and the abundant water supply, and the area became not only a significant agricultural settlement, but also an important stagecoach village.

Egypt was known for its excellent agriculture and bountiful harvests, even in the years of "no summers" in the early decades of the 1800's, which were probably caused by an erupting volcano in the South Pacific. According to some stories, the name "Egypt" derives from the Bible story of the Israelite migration into Egypt, a land of abundance, to escape famine in their own land.

The Egypt of the early 1800's was the center of commerce and politics in Perinton. There was Roswell Everett's tannery, Daniel Whitman's blacksmith shop, a school, a Methodist church that served as both a social and religious gathering place, a cemetery, three popular taverns, and a grist mill, in addition to its homes and farmsteads. Egypt was about half way between Rochester and Canandaigua on the main stage route, making the "honorable business" of running a tavern lucrative and popular. Cyrus Packard's tavern was the site of Perinton's first town meeting on April 6, 1813, when Packard himself was named Perinton's first Supervisor.

Old Route 31

According to various accounts, the tavern was later moved to the Ranney property and partly incorporated into the barn which burned in 1918. In 1950, Leander Conover of Mason Road recalled a large hollow filled with stones which was uncovered every time it was plowed. This, he felt, was the cellar hole of the old tavern. Packard also ran a store and the grist mill.

Oliver Loud, who moved to Egypt in 1806, owned and operated a tavern in the area of today's Town Centre Plaza. Apparently, lumber was so scarce at the time that he had to use boards from his wagon for the cabin. He built a second, larger tavern in 1825. The two-story structure with its ample porches served not only as a tavern and inn, but also as a store, a mail drop, a salesroom for traveling salesmen, a place for transient shows, and a courtroom where Loud's father-in-law, a justice of the peace, attempted to settle arguments among hot-headed canal workers. During the Civil War, after training at the Methodist Church, troops naturally went next door to the tavern to relax. Loud's Tavern was used by various owners as a tavern and hotel up to the turn of the twentieth century. In 1985, the building was moved to Bushnell's Basin where for a time it became a twenty-first century version of a tavern and inn, before being converted into a private residence.

Olney Staples ran the third and largest tavern in the hamlet, which was located in the vicinity of the Quailbush subdivision. Its size, location, and facilities, particularly its stable and change of horses, made it particularly attractive to the stage line, splitting the twenty-five mile six-hour trip between Palmyra and Rochester in half. The building itself was a frame structure with a deep rubblestone foundation. An eight-foot square ash bin in the basement held up fifteen-inch square hand-hewn beams. Each room had 8x 8 foot or 8x 4 foot square posts in the corners, and the floorboards were twenty inches wide. The rafters were secured with 12 inch wooden pegs to the 9 inch square ridgepole. Six fireplaces heated the rooms. As with most taverns, the first floor included a tap room, as well as a ladies' parlor, a dining room, and a kitchen. The second floor had a 12 x20 foot ballroom and guest bedrooms. A ghost was said to haunt the northwest guest room, until it was discovered that the "ghost" was the wind across the top of a bottle lodged in a window frame in the room.

Staples' Tavern

Because the taverns were not only places to eat, drink, and sleep, but were also places where the local people could meet and discuss politics, business, and the other issues of the day, it is not surprising that the three tavern owners themselves were active in the community. Cyrus Packard not only served as Perinton's first supervisor, but was also at various times Assessor and Commissioner of Highways. Oliver Loud was Overseer of Highways and School Inspector. Staples served as Commissioner of Highways and School Commissioner.

Unfortunately, most of the commercial buildings that marked those early days of Egypt are gone. However, the farmhouse at 7516 Pittsford-Palmyra Road that belonged to the Thomas Ramsdell family and that was built around 1815 is still standing and qualifies as being Perinton's oldest residence. It is one of only several Federal style buildings in the town. Gideon Ramsdell's house also still stands, as does another early 1800's farmhouse. Both are on Mason Road, at 173 and 353, respectively. Two other houses, 7339 and 7215 Pittsford-Palmyra Road, were probably built in the 1820's.

The coming of the Erie Canal in 1825 brought significant changes to the hamlet of Egypt. No longer was commercial activity tied to a stage route; commerce and travel now centered around the new canal, several miles to the north in the village of Fairport. While the hamlet did not lose its identity as a community, its growth was slowed, and it ceased being the center of business and politics.

Trolley stop on Pittsford-Palmyra Road in Egypt

The subsequent years of the nineteenth century saw Egypt continue to thrive as an agricultural community anchored by the Ramsdell farms on Mason and Pittsford-Palmyra Roads, small businesses and stores, the church and school, and a growing number of residences along Loud, Mason, and Pittsford-Palmyra Roads. Gideon Ramsdell's home on Mason Road was purportedly a station on the Underground Railroad and also a place where Tonawanda and Buffalo Indians encamped during the summer months. Philemon Austin built his house at 7420 Pittsford- Palmyra Road and manufactured pumps. The house at 353 Mason Road, which was built in 1820, had an iron foundry where the Lapham family manufactured "Egypt Plows." The next family to live there, the Conovers, added to the house in 1860 and ran a farm and a creamery there. Several other houses, including 30 Loud Road, built in 1840 by a member of the Loud family, and 7596, 7383, 7489, 7725 and 7752 Pittsford-Palmyra Road, built between the 1830's and the 1870's, add to the area's mid-nineteenth century architectural legacy. The building that formerly stood on the corner of Loud and Pittsford-Palmyra Roads, known as Nelson's Store, was constructed during this period and served both as a store and a post office. It continued as a store and a gas station through much of the twentieth century and was eventually razed as part of the Route 31 expansion project early in the twenty-first century.

Other structures in the hamlet date from the early decades of the twentieth century. District #4 School (also known as the Fairport Grange), at 7700 Pittsford-Palmrya Road, was built in 1908 of molded concrete, a popular, inexpensive, and durable product that was popular at the time. Now serving as an office, it is a wonderful example of how an older building can be adapted for today's use. At the west end of the hamlet at 7200 Pittsford-Palmyra Road is Robinson's Garage. Built in 1924, it is a reminder of those days when family-operated gas stations and repair shops were common and an important part of the community. In addition, several homes on the north side of Pittsford-Palmyra Road reflect the Colonial Revival style popular in the 1930's and 1940's.

Egypt was linked to the rest of Perinton by the Rochester, Syracuse, and Eastern Interurban Trolley, which began operating in 1906. Coming into Perinton from East Rochester, the trolley line was carried across Baird Road on a bridge, went through what is today BOCES I into the village of Fairport where it ran along the north side of the canal. Crossing at Turk Hill Road, running south behind the Perinton Town Hall and Community Center and then east to Egypt, where it crossed Pittsford-Palmyra Road and continued on to Syracuse. The Egypt Fire Hall is located on the site of the former Egypt trolley stop. The ten trolley stops within Perinton served to connect outlying areas like Egypt with the center of activity in the village of Fairport.

Canning factory

Around the turn of the century, Egypt became one of several food processing centers in Perinton. At the corner of Loud and Pittsford-Palmyra Roads, Frank Monihan and John Martindale opened a small evaporating plant or dry house, which dried and sold local produce. By 1904, they had developed a working system of canning those products, and the Egypt Canning Company was born. In the early years, the local farm women would take the vegetables and fruits from the fields and orchards, prepare them at home, and then deliver them to the factory ready for the canning process. By 1908, the company had added automatic machinery and had enlarged the facility. The business was incorporated in 1916 and became known as Comstock Canning Company. Growing through the 20's, 30's, and 40's, by 1957 the company joined several other canners to form Comstock Foods. The company provided regular employment for many Egypt area residents as well as for seasonal migrant workers and by the 1950's was pumping $300,000 into the local economy, canning, among other things, applesauce, sliced apples and beans.

The latter part of the twentieth century into the beginning of the twenty-first brought further change to the hamlet of Egypt, not all of it positive. Although Comstock Foods (the former Egypt Canning Company), a division of the Borden Company in the 1960's, and a division of Curtice-Burns in the 1970's, was processing up to 200 tons of beans per day and employing about 255 seasonal workers during that period, its future was uncertain. Eventually, as a result of consolidation and reorganization, the Egypt plant was closed for good in 1982. Today, portions of the plant have been demolished. The water tower, however, a recognizable visual sight, remains. Towers of that type were common fixtures in most towns and villages and Egypt's tower is the only one that remains in Perinton.

The old Staples tavern, in the vicinity of today's Quailbush subdivision, was torn down, and Oliver Loud's tavern was moved from the current site of the Town Centre Plaza to Bushnell's Basin. Traffic increased on Route 31, but there were few reasons to stop in the old hamlet that was increasingly surrounded by suburban subdivisions. On the other hand, several new buildings were constructed to house a variety of businesses. Perinton's hikeway-bikeway trail, using the old Rochester-Syracuse and Eastern trolley bed, became part of the hamlet. In the late 1980's and 1990's, with a growing interest in historic preservation, and after Perinton had enacted an Historic Preservation Ordinance, the Ranney house and barns at 7516 Pittsford-Palmyra Road were designated historic landmarks, as was the old schoolhouse/grange further east at 7700 Pittsford-Palmyra Road. In 2001, the Hamlet of Egypt was designated an historic district. Two more houses, 7752 and 7725

Pittsford-Palmyra Road were added to the list of Perinton's landmark homes in 2001 and 2002 respectively.

The old Nelson's Store, unfortunately beyond repair, was razed in order to align Loud and Mason Roads in conjunction with the Route 31 expansion project. The Ramsdell-Ranney property has become part of adjacent Northern Nurseries, thereby saving Perinton's oldest frame house and preserving a segment of the area's agricultural heritage. Egypt Park, Lollypop Farm, the hikeway-bikeway and sections of the Crescent Trail offer recreational opportunities in the area.

Nelson's Store

The Historic Architecture Commission, using the town's Egypt Subarea Plan formulated in 2003, which provides development guidelines, works with developers to insure that new structures are appropriate to the historic nature of the area. The challenge for the future will be to allow development while insuring that the small scale rural ambiance of the hamlet is preserved. In any case, the hamlet of Egypt, Perinton's first area of settlement, is very much alive and well in the twenty-first century and will likely continue to reinvent itself as it has so many times in the past.

The Packard Family

The Packard family arrived in this country in 1638 from England aboard the *Diligent of Ipswich.* Samuel, his wife Elizabeth, and their daughter Elizabeth first settled in Hingham, Massachusetts, and eventually in old Bridgewater where they built a homestead. In 1682, he and his four sons were among the eighty proprietors in the town, and Samuel is said to have built the first mill in the town.

About 100 years later, Samuel's great great grandson Cyrus built a mill in the hamlet of Egypt in the town of Perinton, New York. Cyrus's father had been the first of the family to move west. He purchased 640 acres in Western New York and moved there from Cunningham, Massachusetts, in 1791 with his wife and family, but he did not stay, soon returning to Massachusetts. However, his three sons, Cyrus, Bartimeus, and John, returned to the area, arriving in Macedon by oxcart in February 1793. Bartimeus stayed in Macedon, John continued on to Michigan, and by 1806, Cyrus had settled in Egypt.

Cyrus Packard was born February 26, 1771, in North Bridgewater, Massachusetts. He married Sally (Sarah) Pullin in January 1789. Since their daughter, Lucretia was born the following September in Phelps, Ontario County, apparently they were living in Western New York at the time. Sally died shortly thereafter and Cyrus married Leah Beal sometime between 1790 and 1794. By 1806, having found fertile farmland in the Egypt area, Cyrus and his neighbor, Thomas Ramsdell, had become large landowners and successful farmers. The Packard property was on the south side of what is today Route 31.

Cyrus Packard's tavern

In addition to farming corn and other grains, and building and running a grist mill, Packard also ran a tavern and a store. Since Egypt was about halfway between Rochester and Canandaigua on the main stage route, inns, taverns, and stores did a good business. In those days, the tavern was the center of activity in a community. It was where business decisions were discussed and made and where issues of political importance were decided. Often the local tavern or inn also served as the courthouse. Perinton's first town meeting was held in Packard's tavern with Cyrus serving as the first Supervisor. Oliver Loud's tavern down the road, which opened at about the same time, between 1806 and 1812, offered space for the local courtroom. Packard's store provided travelers on the stage route with needed goods. According to some sources, it also provided a measure of respectability that operating a tavern did not.

The Packard family was active in community affairs. In addition to serving as the first Perinton Supervisor, Cyrus was, at various times, assessor, Justice of the Peace, School Commissioner, Overseer of Highways, Fence Viewer, Election Inspector, and Constable. His wife Leah was one of the original nine people who met at Jesse Perrin's house to organize the First Congregational Church in 1824.

Leah and Cyrus Packard had eight children between 1794 and 1816, but it is Lucretia, the daughter of Cyrus and Sally, about whom there seems to be the most information relevant to Perinton. Lucretia, being bright and having a good head for business, most likely helped her father run his store and tavern, and probably learned a good deal about both politics and business in the process. McIntosh's *History of Monroe County* notes that she was an "exceptional spinner, weaver and cook, all of which work was executed with ease and expedition." It also notes that her education was excellent and that "no modern speller could stand before her at the spelling-school." She was also an accomplished horsewoman, apparently breaking a colt that had thrown one young man, a member of the Ramsdell family of Egypt. She could often be seen riding along the trails between Egypt and Canandaigua. After teaching in the Perinton Center school on Turk Hill Road, she married James Hannan and moved to a log cabin on a farmstead in an area known an Antioch or Hannan's Corners at what is today the intersection of Routes 31 and 250. Lucretia Packard Hannan took care of the farm during James' absences and over the years bore and raised ten children, five of whom survived childhood.

Cyrus Packard died at the age of fifty-five and is buried in Perinton Center Cemetery. After his death, his widow Leah and several of the children moved to Michigan. Lucretia is the only other member of the Packard family to be buried in Perinton. She died at the age of eighty-one and is buried in Perinton Center Cemetery with her husband and other members of the Hannan family who in the tradition of those early settlers did much to serve the community.

Ramsdell–Ranney Homestead

One of the oldest surviving pioneer farmsteads ... one of four houses in Perinton with Federal architectural features ... an outstanding example of an intact nineteenth century pioneer farmstead... Perinton's oldest frame house. All of these phrases describe the house that was built sometime between 1818 and 1820 on the main coach road between Palmyra and Rochester for the Thomas Ramsdell family.

The two-story post and beam house at 7516 Pittsford-Palmyra Road has clapboard siding and a rectangular main block with a long gabled rear wing. The six-over-six double hung windows, symmetrical facade, and center entrance are Federal features, while the cornice returns and the temple-style front porch with its paneled columns are Greek Revival. The north wing of the house contains original twelve-over-twelve windows. In addition, the northernmost section of that wing may well have been a woodshed which was later finished off for a hired hand.

The significance of the property was enhanced by the two historic agricultural outbuildings, to the east of the house. The smaller of these two barns, which unfortunately had to be razed in 2006, had a high stone foundation and was used for grain storage, probably corn. The larger barn has a gambrel roof, which was the dominant barn form by the late nineteenth century. The surviving two buildings with their surrounding trees form an integrated whole, which are representative of Perinton's agricultural past.

Ramsdell-Ranney house circa 1900

Thomas Ramsdell purchased Lot 22, a total of 320 acres, in what was then called the Town of Boyle, in 1802. He built his house on what would become the Palmyra-Rochester coach road, the regular stage and mail route to Rochester. Three taverns, (one of which, Packard's, hosted Perinton's first town meeting), a stage depot, a tannery, blacksmith shops, a foundry, and a wagon shop were among the commercial establishments that made this area the center of activity and government in early Perinton There Ramsdell and his wife Hannah raised six children and successfully farmed his 320 acres. Indeed, it was due to Thomas Ramsdell and other successful farmers like him who were able to harvest corn in 1816, the "year without a summer," that the name "Egypt," after the Biblical Egypt that provided food for the famine-stricken Israelites, was given to the area. Thomas, like other members of his community, was active in public service. He served as Overseer of Highways, Poormaster, and Commissioner of Highways. He was active in the Northfield Congregational Church and also donated land for the Mason Road Cemetery and the First Methodist Society's church.

Gideon Ramsdell, Thomas' son, was given 192 acres north of his father's house on what is now Mason Road. Gideon and his wife, Hannah, were Quakers, following beliefs which surely influenced their generosity toward runaway slaves and Indians. Their house, sometimes referred to as "Ramsdell's Castle" because of its size, sits on the west side of Mason Road. It is a rambling wood frame clapboard house, and is said to have been one of the stops on the Underground Railway. Not only did Hannah and Gideon freely offer food and shelter to runaway slaves, but they also allowed Tonawanda and Buffalo Indian groups to camp for the summer on part of their property. Gideon's son Jeremiah, also a Quaker, lived with his grandfather Thomas and was the last member of the Ramsdell family to live in the farmstead on Pittsford-Palmyra Road. In 1862 he sold the property to Hiram Ranney.

The Ranneys were also successful farmers, and were active in the social and political life of Perinton for more than eighty years. Hiram Ranney, his son Roswell, and his grandson Hiram served as Overseers of Highways, election inspectors, and school trustees. They were members of the Grange, the Masons, and the First Congregational Church. When Hiram, the grandson, died in 1945, his obituary referred to him as a "specialist in his chosen profession of farming...(held) in high esteem by his neighbors." Nellie, Hiram's widow, continued to live in the house for many years followed by David, her son, who owned the house until it was sold in 2000. The new owners of the property proposed to open a restaurant in the old house and build several other buildings that would house small retail shops. Unfortunately the project never came to fruition and the house sat empty for the ensuing six years. Northern Nurseries, which had previously purchased the large barn and adjacent property, eventually purchased the house and the remainder of the property. The house has been restored and is used as an office. The development has kept intact one of Perinton's oldest landmark.

The Lapham-Conover Farm

The Hamlet of Egypt was long an agricultural community, home to pioneer families such as the Ramsdells and Ranneys. It was also home to the Lapham and Conover families, long time residents who lived in the farmhouse at 353 Mason Road.

The farmhouse itself was apparently built in two parts, the south section having been built sometime during the first two decades of the nineteenth century and the north section in the 1860's. The south part, with its front-facing gable, features narrow clapboards and 6 over 6 windows. Originally the entrance hall led to a front parlor and a kitchen. A brick wall between the two rooms suggests the existence of a chimney and a fireplace. Stairs lead up to two bedrooms. The basement displays hand-hewn beams and joists with mortise and tenon joinings and a gravel floor. The north section includes two entrances with double Roman-arched lights and a wider clapboard finish. The addition included a newer kitchen and a large dining-living room on the first floor, a bedroom on the second floor, and an attic with an ocular window which was reached by ladder. Before the advent of modern central heating, the house was warmed by stoves and the kitchen cook stove. Water was obtained from two pumps, one near the front porch and the other in the kitchen, which pumped water from the basement cistern. Indoor plumbing and running water were added in the 1940's. A gabled barn and a shed-roofed chicken coop remain of the outbuildings. Others have burned or been torn down.

In 1791 John Clark purchased Lot 22 and several other lots from William Walker, the original surveyor, of what would become the Town of Perinton. He subsequently sold 320 acres to Thomas Ramsdell, one of Egypt's pioneer settlers, in 1802. There is evidence that he built the south portion of the house at 353 Mason as well as the house at 7516 Pittsford-Palmyra Road. Both Mason and Pittsford-Palmyra Roads were laid out in the early years of the nineteenth century, in 1816 and 1803 respectively. Ramsdell soon sold the house and a portion of his property to the Lapham family sometime during the second decade of the nineteenth century and it remained in that family until the late 1850's or early 1860's.

Pazzi and Bethany Foster Lapham lived both in Dutchess and Albany Counties and Pazzi is said to have been in the same Masonic Lodge as George Washington. Their son Fayette is said to have been named for Lafayette as father Pazzi was sitting in the lodge with both Washington and Lafayette while he was awaiting the birth. Due to the untimely death of his parents, Fayette was raised by his sister and his paternal aunts in the Mason Road house. It is not clear why or how they came to live in the house that was at the time owned by the Ramsdells.

Conover house on Mason Road early 20th century

Eventually, Fayette married Lucy Ramsdell, Thomas' daughter and, after living for a while in a small house on Pittsford-Palmyra Road that became the office for the Egypt Packing Company, purchased the Mason Road house and fifty-eight surrounding acres in 1822. He and Lucy had four children; however, she died soon thereafter and Fayette remarried (three times). He was active in the community as a member of Egypt's First Methodist Church (located on Pittsford-Palmyra Road), and a charter member of the Fairport Grange. His son Nathan inherited the property, and before moving to Michigan, operated a grist mill and a foundry that made "Egypt Plows" near the stream south of the house.

For some years after the Lapham family's departure the house had a number of owners. In 1868 Van Rensselaer Conover purchased the property and the family would keep the house until late in the 1950's. The Conover family had come to the Genesee country in 1815 and purportedly were pioneers in the driving of cattle and sheep overland to eastern markets. Van Rensselaer and his wife Cynthia Dunham probably added the north wing of the house and apparently used the bedroom for orphans that they took in to work the farm and the attic room to house a hired man. Van Rensselaer's son Leander Asher and grandson Leander E. carried on the farm. Grandson Leander and his wife ran a popular creamery business, selling a quart of cream for fifty cents. Leander was active in the Grange and in the First Congregational Church and was also a Justice of the Peace. The family name appears on Perinton maps dating from the 1850's.

The last member of the Conover family to live on Mason Road was Ella Conover Weirich who died in 2009. She lived in a house on the southern edge of the farm property that she and her husband had built in the 1950's on land given her by her father. She recalled cows grazing on the land now developed as Conover Crossing and of course she remembered when there were no subdivisions at all. She talked about playing in the barn, fishing in the stream, picking berries, collecting eggs, and keeping a pet hen. There were Native American flints to collect from the pasture, cold walks to the Egypt school (now offices across from the Victor-Egypt Road), and rides on the Rochester, Syracuse, and Eastern Trolley from the stop near the Egypt Fire Hall. Nelson's Store, Rush's Meat Market, and the canning factory, whose odor permeated the neighborhood, were part of the Egypt "downtown."

Today both the Ranney and Lapham farmsteads continue to be part of the community. The old trolley bed is a well-used hiking and biking path and the Egypt school is an office building. The old canning factory remains as well. And, despite changes, the Hamlet of Egypt continues to endure.

Early Settlement on Baird Road

The history of the Baird Road area between Fairport Road Whitney Roads parallels that of Perinton itself, first as a pioneer community, then as a rural, farming community, and finally as a residential area, a "trolley subdivision." This community included a schoolhouse near the Old Rochester Road (Fairport Road) which was established in 1815; the site of one of Perinton's first mills, built in 1810; a federal-style house built in the 1860's; a stone railroad underpass built in the 1850's; the site of Rochester, Syracuse, and Eastern trolley stop #11; and a number of small middle class homes, all over fifty years of age.

The Northrup family was the first to settle in the area. Isaiah Northrup built a sawmill on Thomas Creek in 1810. Peter Ripley and Joseph Richardson followed suit. The Northrup site can be found on the property at number 2729. Northrup's mill was sold several times and was used as a grist mill, a plaster mill and a flour mill well into the 1880's. Another sawmill was built by Ebenezer Lewis in 1817 on the east side of the road. A group of properties formed around this mill in the 1830's and was referred to as the "Northrup Settlement."

Farms provided produce and part time work for area residents. In 1866, the Northrup lands were sold to Alonzo Cook, who farmed and sold produce for a living. The land was subsequently sold to J.J. Richards, who operated it as Sunnyridge Fruit and Berry Farm. The family ran the farm until 1906. The Wilbur and Hawkins farms bordered Thomas Creek. Herman Steffen owned the farm house at number 2783 and built greenhouses there in 1912. Herman's son George expanded the farm and grew squash, which he sold to a baby food manufacturer. He also grew tomatoes, raised bees, and grew chrysanthemums, which were sold at Hart's Flower Shop in Rochester. During World War II, George employed German POW's from Clyde. When field work was slow, he had them painting his house. However, when a neighbor, who was supposed to do the painting, complained that the POW's could not do work which could be done by available Americans, the work stopped. The Steffen land was sold in 1960 and became Island Valley Golf Course. The greenhouses were demolished in 1968. The Dannenburgs at number 2758 grew cherries, pears, and apples. They also raised annuals in their greenhouses. Their house was torn down in 1970.

The New York Central R.R. underpass was built in the 1850's. It is, of itself, an historic structure, as it indicates the importance of the railroad to the development of the area. It also has the distinction of being one of the last narrow, one lane underpasses in the county. Mass transit, however, in the form of an interurban electric trolley line, the Rochester, Syracuse, and Eastern, significantly changed the nature of the community. In 1906 this line opened from Macedon to Rochester, and the era of suburban development began. Stop #11 was located just south of the N.Y.Central line, convenient to the new Midvale subdivision, and really established Baird Road as a residential area.

Carl Patterson, who purchased the Sunnyridge Farm in 1906, and George Higbie, who owned a substantial piece of property adjacent to the trolley line, were responsible for starting suburban development in the area. Within ten years, Patterson had subdivided and sold his land to new homeowners, and also to the two small farms owned by the Steffens and Dannenburgs. The six houses that he built on the ridge were relatively small, averaging around 1500 square feet, but were on two acre lots. Most were in the bungalow style popular between 1930 and 1950 with porches, dormers, clapboards or shingles, and large yards which dropped off toward Thomas Creek. The houses appear today much as they did then, except that the trees are bigger. George Higbie advertised his Midvale subdivision in a flyer with the question "Why not live in a park?" A prospective buyer could choose from several price lists, and for only ten dollars down be guaranteed a site with running water, graded streets, side walks, and more.

Many of the people who settled in the area were of German ancestry, and held jobs in the East Rochester car shops or the piano works. Because of the new Rochester, Syracuse, and Eastern trolley

Old Baird Road

line, the commute was easy, and residents could enjoy "country living" after a long day at the factory. A former resident recalls, "Papa would be up early, sometimes 5 o'clock, to work in his garden. He could tell by the change in the water pressure from his hose that Mama had started his breakfast, and would come in to eat before catching the trolley to work. He had a wonderful garden." The local store at the north end of the district, Fish's store, provided groceries and other goods. The farms provided seasonal work for the children and women who needed it. The Midvale School, located at the south end of the district was not only the educational center, but also the community center.

The Midvale School was built in 1883 as a two-room school. All the children from Baird Road and Midvale Drive attended. The maintenance and support of the school involved the entire community, as did the various school functions. The annual Harvest Dinner would draw all the families in the area, who would each contribute a dish to pass. The school was enlarged in 1926 with the addition of three new classrooms and a new front entrance. In the 1940's a basement lunchroom was built and hot lunches were provided. Classrooms in the school were used until 1955. Today the schoolhouse is an office building.

The house at number 2677 is different from the others on the street. It was built in the Italianate style in 1869, making it the oldest house on the street. It was also first located on the east side of the road. When it was threatened with demolition by the construction of the trolley, the structure was moved across the street. Since it was impossible to then turn the house around, the back of the house is now the front and the original front facade faces the creek.

The Rochester, Syracuse, and Eastern trolley shut down in 1936, finished off by the Depression, the automobile and the bus. The earthen abutments, however, can still be seen just south of the railroad overpass. Between the 1960's and the 1980's, the road was rerouted and a number of structures on the street were demolished. The one hundred and ten year old Osburn house at number 2698 was torn down as well as the former Steffen house at #2783. In 1970, the Dannenburg house and barns were torn down and the fill was used to modify the course of Thomas Creek to facilitate the building of the BOCES center.

Today Baird Road between Fairport and Whitney Roads still preserves a sense of community. Mature trees shade the homes and buffer the noise of traffic. The large yards sloping down to Thomas Creek maintain a sense of openness and serve as a reminder of the early mill era. The buildings are anchored on the south by the brick schoolhouse and on the north by the oldest house in the district. This cluster of homes surrounded by open spaces is a microcosm of Perinton history and the future will no doubt add another chapter to the history of the area.

The Baird Family

Although Baird Road was first settled by the Northrup family, it was eventually named after the family who owned large amounts of farmland in the area. Beginning in the 1820's and extending through most of the nineteenth century, Bedent Baird and his sons Byron, Burrett, and David farmed land that extended between Baird and Nine Mile Point Roads.

Bedent Baird, born in Monmouth, New Jersey, to a Scottish immigrant family in 1819, moved to Perinton with his wife, Catherine Quackenbush, of Montgomery County. According to *Landmarks of Monroe County*, published in 1895, Bedent had been a man of "unusual mental attainments, (who) became in mature years an important social and political factor in Perinton." The notation also describes Baird as having superior mathematical skills, a conclusion based on papers from 1802. Bedent and Catherine had eight children: David, Burrett, Harriet, Samuel, Catherine, Ursula, Helen, and Byron. The 1820 census records show Bedent and Catherine as already having four children, three daughters and one son, under ten years of age. The school rolls of 1831-2 indicate that they had five children in school.

2414 Baird Road

Apparently, Bedent Baird worked for others in the 1820's, as he did not purchase his own land until the 1830's. The 1836 and 1843 tax records show ownership of 125 acres between Baird and Nine Mile Point Roads. The 1852 map shows two houses, one on Nine Mile Point and one on Baird Road. The 1872 map shows three houses, two on Baird and one on Nine Mile Point Road. Since that map notes the Nine Mile Point Road house as owned by "Mrs. Baird," the two houses on Baird Road, identified as being those of "B. Baird and B. Baird," most likely were those of sons Byron and Burrett. Notes on one of the Baird Road properties further indicate that the first building was a log cabin, probably built by Bedent around 1830 when he purchased the property. The log cabin was soon replaced by the first section of what would become a fourteen room three-section farmhouse which still stands at 2414 Baird Road. Bedent's son Byron and his wife Imogene also lived in the house. The 1855 New York State census gives details of the farms. One of the Baird Road farms is listed as having a cash value of $12,200. It produced 390 bushels of winter wheat and 900 bushels of oats. Two cows produced 200 pounds of butter and thirteen sheep produced forty pounds of wool. There were, in addition, five horses and one pig under six months. The farm also produced barley, corn, and potatoes.

Bedent Baird held several positions in the Town of Perinton. In 1823, 1825, and 1827, he is listed as an Overseer of Highways and a Fence Viewer. He was also listed as a juror several times. Bedent died at the age of seventy-eight on December 22, 1868. His wife, Catherine, continued to live in the family homestead until her death in 1871.

Of the eight Baird children, David, Byron, Burrett, Helen, and probably Catherine remained in Perinton. Samuel studied law and lived in Watertown and later in Lowell, Washington. Byron and Burrett continued to farm the family property. David married Almeda, Helen married John Hayes of Perinton, Catherine married William Mead, and Ursula married Jacob Brown of Penfield. There were four grandchildren mentioned in Bedent's will, all of whom were Catherine's children. David's will mentions a daughter Hetty.

By 1895, only two of Bedent Baird's children were still living: Samuel of Washington and Byron of Perinton. Byron had combined his and his brother Burrett's and his mother's property to create "Grandview Farm," 177 acres which stretched between Baird and Nine Mile Point Roads. It is on the 1902 Perinton map.

Like many successful farmers, in his later years Byron retired "in town," moving to Fairport. He died in 1910 and is buried with his mother and father and several other members of his family in Mt. Pleasant Cemetery.

- II -
FARMS, FARMHOUSES, AND FARM FAMILIES

From its beginnings until the suburban development beginning in the 1950's, Perinton was an agricultural community. Many families owned significant amounts of land and as farmers contributed greatly to the growth and success of the community. This chapter features a number of these families.

The Aldrich Family

The first members of the Aldrich family arrived in Massachusetts in the 1660's. About one hundred and thirty years later, the first Aldriches appeared in western New York. In the 1790's, Leonard, Stephen, Brice, and Ahaz were farming in the Farmington-Macedon area. Asa and Abraham purchased 270 acres in Macedon in 1801, and in 1802, Solomon and his son Adolphus walked the 260 miles from Ashfield, Massachusetts, to Macedon to visit the relatives and assess the possibility of moving west permanently. Apparently Solomon was impressed with the substantial log houses, fertile soil, ample water, and free life of the frontier and decided to return home, sell many of his possessions and move west.

Solomon and his wife, Susan Walkup, and their eight sons and one daughter loaded a feather bed, some crockery, kettles, gridirons, and the family Bible onto a wagon to be drawn by a yoke of oxen and set off to walk west. They purchased land in Macedon from Benejah and Hulda Aldrich, built a log cabin with a roof of elm bark, floors of split logs, and a door of hewed planks. The cabin had one tiny window which was covered with oil paper in the summer and furs in the winter. The chimney was made of mud, straw, and sticks. Solomon and his sons cleared the land and planted corn as their first crop. The subsequent abundant harvest proved to them that the decision to come west had been a good one.

S. Aldrich House, Pittsford-Palmyra Road

Solomon, however, sold his Macedon land in 1805 and purchased 360 acres in Perinton near the county line in Lot 3. He built his log cabin on a hill two miles east of Egypt and with help of his sons, cleared and farmed the land. In addition to farm work, the male members of the family also helped lay out the Rochester Road (Route 31). He also found time to be active in local politics, serving as a juror and as a poormaster. Solomon Aldrich died in 1839 at the age of 78. The land was divided between Adolphus and George, two of his sons. Other sons had moved further west and one, David, had moved to Coburg, Canada.

Adolphus Aldrich farmed the eastern section of the family property. He married Jane Van Duzer in 1812, and after serving in the War of 1812, he returned to his 143 acres where he and his wife remained for the rest of their lives. Like his father, Adolphus also served his community as a juror and an Overseer of Highways and a Fence Viewer.

George Aldrich farmed the western portion of the family property. He and his wife, Mary Potter, raised two sons, Adelbert and Josiah, in a log cabin on that property. Both sons were educated in the local schools. Josiah, well-versed about herbs and folk medicine, expressed an early desire to become a physician, but could not be spared from work on the farm. Throughout his life, however, Josiah managed to find a variety of ways to serve his community. He delivered mail to Wayneport for twelve years, was a Justice of the Peace for twenty years, served as town supervisor in 1866 and as Town Justice for several terms. He was also the local printer for the Know-Nothing Party in the 1850's. Married three times to Margaret Wood, Samantha Springer, and to Julia Potter (who survived him), Josiah lived his entire life on the family farm, dying in 1903.

Aldrich Road, laid out in 1820, is named for the family and lies on the western boundary of George Aldrich's property. The Aldrich name appears on the 1852, 1858, and 1872 maps of Perinton.

The Ayrault Family

In 1831 John Ayrault purchased land in Perinton from Hezekiah Petterson along the eastern section of what was then called Wapping Road. The farm, where John and his heirs worked the land for the next 120 years, eventually covered more than 300 acres, and the road was renamed Ayrault Road.

The Ayrault family were descendents of French Huguenots Pierre Ayrault and Francoise de Boylon, who had come to America in 1687 together with Pierre's two brothers and their families, and settled in Wethersfield, Connecticut. John, born in 1787, was the son of Nicholas, a Revolutionary War veteran. Apparently, Nicholas went west and left his five children with their grandfather, James, who raised them on his farm in Sandisfield, Massachusetts, and saw that they were educated. James was a member of the Massachusetts legislature and was said to have been "a trusted leader in the affairs of town and state." John managed his grandfather's farm, and in 1817 married Hulda Smith, "who for 7 winters and 10 summers had taught school in her native state." In that same year he was asked by his grandfather to drive a herd of cattle to the western New York estate of General William Wadsworth. John and Hulda, who regarded the journey as a wedding trip, were impressed by the fertile land and abundant water in the Genesee valley and decided to settle there. They purchased land in the town of Leicester where they lived for six years before moving to Caledonia where they remained for another eleven years. John was a successful farmer; Hulda taught school and raised a family.

In 1831 when John moved to the large farm in Perinton, his family included his wife and seven children. Three other children, Miles, Louise, and Huldah had died before the move. The seven grew up in Perinton and were educated at the Macedon Academy. The farm itself, which was in the vicinity of the present Fairport High School, extended from Wapping (Ayrault) Road north to the canal. The 1836 tax records indicate that the property was worth $8400. By 1855 it was worth $24,000. Records also show that in addition to a large frame house, the Ayraults owned 48 cows, 8 horses, 5 mules, 17 sheep, 182 chickens and an ox. They sold apples, butter, and cheese, and ran a cider and a fulling mill. Obviously John Ayrault was a prosperous and versatile landowner. In addition, he was a prominent member of the Monroe County Agricultural Society, an excellent judge of livestock, and a respected judge at local and state fairs. It was said of him that he was "benevolent; his ideas of right and justice were pronounced; his opinions were strong and decided and his counsel was often sought. In politics he was a Whig and later a Republican. . . ."

Ayrault and Jensen families

There are number of anecdotes about the property and its other uses. Although members of the Presbyterian Church, the Ayraults encouraged other church groups to use their woods for picnics. There was a good stream there, which not only was good for picnickers, but was also used by canal boats to replenish their water supply. One record states that "the church bells were ringing in the nearby village of Perrington (sic) when about 100 canallers of all sects gathered by Ayrault Woods to hear the Wembly Brothers" who conducted Sunday services up and down the canal. At another time, it was reported that gypsies were camping in the Ayrault orchards. In 1905 it was reported that a natural gas well being drilled on the property had reached 2,000 feet. (There does not, however, seem to be any subsequent report of natural gas actually being found.) At one point a skeleton, thought to have been a dinosaur, was uncovered. Indians lived in the woods during the summer and made black ash splint baskets, which they sold in town. Apparently a group of those Indians was eventually moved to the Tonawanda reservation.

After John died in 1861, his son Allen bought out the other heirs and continued to run the farm. Allen was married to Lavilla Smith, daughter of Eleazer Smith, an early Perinton resident. The 1902 map shows the 313 acre Ayrault Stock Farm, which Allen ran successfully until his death in 1910. Allen's three children, John Winthrop, Edith, and Allen inherited the property. John Winthrop and his wife Kate Mauer Staley took over the house and the farming chores, but John died an untimely death in 1925 after his car skidded into a trolley. His stepson, Jay Staley, and his wife Virginia continued to work the farm, which remained in the family until it was sold to Pierce Titter in 1951, thus ending 120 years of Ayrault family ownership.

Ayrault farm wagon, with steam tractor in background

Ayrault homestead

The former farmland now supports suburban housing tracts as well as Fairport High School and its surrounding playing fields. Ayrault Road, however, reminds us of the 120 years of successful farming that took place there and the important place that agriculture has had in Perinton's heritage.

The Budlong Family

The Budlong family first arrived in New England in the 1650's. Descended from John Budlong, the sole survivor of an Indian attack that killed the rest of the Budlong family in 1675, Milton, the son of John and Zilpha Ladd Budlong of Schuyler, New York, was the first of the Budlong family to come to Perinton. He walked to western New York with his possessions (consisting of a coat, $25, and two shirts) tied up in one of his two shirts on his back, supposedly walking barefooted to save his one pair of shoes. He went to work for his uncle, Samuel Ladd, cutting wood.

After two years working for his uncle and one year back in Schuyler, Milton returned to Perinton and married Clarissa Shumway, daughter of Isaac and Patience Pratt Shumway. They were able to purchase twenty-five acres of land at 17 ½ cents an acre from a Mr. Stone and several years later another eighty acres from Asa Randolph in Lots 3 and 4 in the northeastern part of Perinton. By 1830 with the help of friend, Ralph Lister, who had noticed Budlong's "energy and economy," he decided to get into the cattle business.

Milton Budlong proved to be a resourceful businessman and farmer. In 1833 he made his first cattle drive to the market at Albany. In 1840 he drove over 600 head to market. The drovers had to work hard to keep the cattle out of any fenced cultivated areas since there were fines for allowing livestock to wander into those areas; however, area boys looked forward to helping with the drive. While they had to walk all the way to Albany, they were able to ride home on the wagons that had carried feed for the animals. In addition the trip gave them a chance to see new areas and meet new people.

Apparently, Milton was quite successful with his cattle drives since each year he sold between $20,000 and $25,000 worth of cattle and by 1850 was worth $10,000, a significant sum for the times. His land holdings eventually included 415 acres in Rush and over 600 acres in Perinton. His Perinton land straddled the road that would eventually be named Budlong Road (now Perinton Parkway) and an etching in the 1877 *History of Monroe County* shows a prosperous-looking house surrounded by a number of outbuildings and barns. The road had originally been laid out in 1815 to connect the end of Quaker Road in Macedon to the recently completed Macedon Center Road

Milton and Clarissa raised a family of seven children who lived to adulthood: Schuyler, Isaac, Levi, Rena, Louisa, Elvira, and Zylphia. In addition to caring for a family, and tending to their acreage, both found time to be active in the Free Will Baptist Church (today's Fairport Community Baptist Church). Milton also served his community as a juror and as Overseer of Highways and a Fence Viewer.

Today the Budlong property is being used for a very different purpose. Sometime after the family left Perinton, a good quality of gravel was found on the farm. Tons were trucked away leaving craters that eventually filled with water becoming deep ponds. Eventually the land was deemed suitable for a landfill and tons of waste were trucked in to fill in the areas from which the gravel had come. In the 1970's, the landfill area was taken over by Waste Management and the facility became known as High Acres Landfill. The over 1,000 acres of Waste Management property also include Little League baseball fields and a 250 acre wildlife refuge with trails and ponds. Much of the rest of the former Budlong Property has been developed as an industrial park.

Budlong Farm etching

Carter Road

Carter Road, in Perinton's northeast corner, was first settled in the 1820's. It is named for Miles Carter, who moved there in the early 1830's after purchasing sixty-three acres from a gentleman by the name of Park Brown. After the coming of the canal, Carter Road, along with Fellows and Fairport-Webster Roads, became main routes for farmers bringing their produce to market. With settlement came a schoolhouse and a cemetery. This rural area also featured at various times a clay brick-making business, tobacco crops, and several distilleries. Today, Carter Road maintains a rural character and is the site of two homes that have been designated as Perinton landmarks.

In 1875, in a show of wealth and prosperity, Richard Woolsey built a large brick farmhouse at 4692 Carter Road that stands on a knoll and overlooks the surrounding countryside. It was the second house to be built on the site. The property includes mature maple trees, a large gable barn with a gambrel wing, a concrete block silo, a carriage house, and a stone smokehouse.

The main house is a striking, mostly Italianate, brick structure. Its arched double doors with their stained-glass panels led neighbors to nickname the house "Woolsey's church." The sixteen-room house is constructed in a cross-gable style, with peaks or gables on all four sides and windows of Italianate style. High in each gable end are small round-arched windows with stone lintels and keystones. The larger main windows repeat the same details. Sometime around 1900, porches were added to the north, west, and south sides of the house. Their styling is Greek Revival, as they all have Ionic columns with cast concrete pedestals. At about the same time, an east wing was added that was used as a cottage cheese factory. It included a coal room and an indoor privy. That wing eventually became an entryway.

4394 Carter Rd. *4692 Carter Rd.*

The interior of the house has been lovingly and beautifully cared for. The main doors open onto a hallway with a sweeping staircase. The room to the left has elegant glass-fronted built-in bookcases. All the rooms have a spaciousness enhanced by the high ceilings and long windows. No longer referred to as "Woolsey's Church," it was renamed "Toad Hill" by subsequent owners after they found hundreds of toads on the property.

The former "Pleasant View Farm" or "Esten-Wahl Farm," the second of Carter Road's designated landmark homes, is located to the north of Toad Hill. Probably the second structure on the property, the house first appears on the 1858 Perinton map and is a clapboard vernacular farmhouse with some Italianate detailing. It has a two-storied front gable and side wing, with a smaller rear gable. The property includes a large gambrel barn with a corn crib that has been used as an apartment. A twentieth century garage, a pool, and tennis courts complete the site.

The land was farmed by the Esten family for three generations. The 1858 Perinton map notes that the property is that of G.W. Esten. Subsequent maps of 1872 and 1902 also show George Esten as owner. John Wahl purchased the property in 1908, hence the name "Esten-Wahl." Reminiscences of George Whitfield Esten, son of the first owner, include the following anecdotes. "The squirrels were so thick in the woods at the rear of the farm that the boys of the family were given warming pans to bang with a stick and they marched up and down frightening away the squirrels." Just north of the Esten property, Carter Road curves to the east, and Esten notes, " ...Thus was formed a triangular piece on which were two distilleries ... Byron Woolsey's grandfather helped erect the distillery. Men met, chose sides to see which side would be raised first. The last log was just being placed when it caught Mr. Woolsey on the head and he was instantly killed. Forty years later when the building was torn down, his grandson found the blood stains still on the log." Byron Woolsey's father, Richard, would build the brick farmhouse that is today "Toad Hill."

Former owners have found shards of china and glassware outside what used to be the pantry. The story is that one of the Wahl women got tired of taking care of it all and simply threw dishes and glassware out of the window.

Carter Road and its designated landmarks preserve distinctive nineteenth century architecture as well as intact rural settings, both of which are significant parts of Perinton's early agricultural heritage.

Carter Road tobacco

Tobacco Sheds on Carter Road

The Diedrich Family

For many Perinton families, cutting the yearly Christmas tree at Normandie Farms on Howell Road was a tradition, and for two generations of Diedrichs working that farm was also a tradition.

In the late nineteenth century a number of German immigrants settled in the Rochester area and often met for social occasions and reunions. At one event in Hilton, Bertha Steffen, the oldest daughter of Fred and Minnie Steffen of Perinton, met William Diedrich. The two were married December 12, 1906, and moved to the Steffen farm on East Whitney Road. William helped Fred on his 200 acres, ten of which were muckland that produced, among other crops, celery, onions, and carrots. Bertha and Minnie took care of the many household chores such as serving breakfasts of fried salt pork, fried eggs, potatoes and bread to the family and the hired hands. Their son Norman was born there in 1908.

By 1910 William and Bertha were able to purchase their own farm of forty-two acres on Howell Road where, shortly thereafter, Bertha gave birth to a daughter, Iona. The farm had few conveniences. The family used an outhouse, carried water in from the well, and heated the house with a coal stove. Lighting was from kerosene lanterns. There was no refrigeration so pork was smoked, salted or made into sausage, and beef was only available in the cold weather when a frozen carcass could be kept in the barn. Chicken was regularly available.

The Diedrichs added to their farmstead when they purchased an additional twenty-four acres across the road. The family raised tomatoes for the canning factory, and hay, oats, wheat, and vegetables for the public market. They also kept several horses, a few cows, and some chickens. Norman enjoyed the wheat harvest, finding it the "cleanest, most pleasant joy on the farm," and he allowed that the hay harvest "wasn't bad."

Norman and Iona walked the three-quarters of a mile to school, probably District School #5 on Carter Road, until a lady in Fairport let them use her Canadian pony (about two-thirds the size of a regular one) in exchange for its care. For seventh and eighth grade, they drove the pony and a buggy the four miles into the village of Fairport and, as promised, took care of the pony, which meant bringing a bag of hay and a sack of oats to school and feeding the pony at noon. By their junior and senior years, they were driving a car (an Oakland) to school. After high school, Iona graduated from the Rochester School of Commerce and worked for the Mechanics' Institute (RIT), the Pierce Oil Company, and Nance's Mustard before joining Rochester Instrument Systems. At the same time she continued to be involved with the family farm and with the Grange. Norman also graduated from high school and became fully involved in the family farm business, which at that time involved a number of greenhouses where the family raised tomato plants. Over the years, the Diedrich farm produced over a million plants each year for the canning factories. Norm would be involved in farming for the next 60+ years.

During his grade school years, Norman had begun hunting and trapping, an activity he engaged in for most of the rest of his life. The sale of a muskrat for $1.50, found while cutting firewood, started him on what turned out to be a well-paying sideline. As a senior in high school one February he "conveniently caught the chicken pox" and made up to $40 a day trapping and selling muskrat pelts. At the age of eighteen he purchased his first car, a Chevrolet, with $750 in muskrat money. In his later years, Norman would range much further afield for his hunting.

While coming home from the public market one day, probably in 1930, Norman Diedrich met an acquaintance and "the prettiest girl I had ever seen." Norman and Florence Button, who was from Wellsville and a Pittsford school teacher, were married on June 23, 1931, the groom's twenty-third birthday. The newlyweds build a house on Howell Road family property. The house was a two-story colonial with gumwood trim and hardwood floors that left them owing $1,500 to the bank, which they paid off the following year.

In their early years together Florence continued teaching school and Norman tended to the tomato plants and the chickens. Their diet was supplemented by Norman's trapping and hunting skills which added deer and rabbit to the table. Income was supplemented by trapping and selling fox pelts (until the bottom fell out of the market and the pelts brought only fifty cents apiece).

Norman and Florence Diedrich

By the mid 1930's two daughters, Joyce and Sylvia, had joined the family, and the Diedrichs continued to supply area canneries with tomato plants. When Norman's draft number came up at the beginning of World War II, he was sent home with orders to continue to produce his 1.5 million tomato plants for Egypt's Curtis Canning Company. In the 1950's, Gerber Baby Food Products contracted with the Diedrichs to grow fifty tons of Boston Marrow Squash at $20 per ton. That crop served the family well until the price dropped to $12 a ton. At that point they stopped planting squash and decided to plant Christmas trees instead, a crop for which they would become well-known. By the early 1950's the nursery stopped growing tomato plants, as the price was declining, and started to grow and sell bedding plants. Within ten years, petunias, pansies, and impatiens (Florence's specialty), were selling to retailers from as far away as Watertown.

The bedding plant business eventually led to the creation of Bedding Plants, Inc., an organization of growers from around the country which served as a clearing house for all sorts of information related to the cultivation of bedding plants. Norman served three terms on the Board of Directors and saw the organization become known world-wide, traveling to Europe, New Zealand, and Australia. The need for top soil for the plants led the Diedrichs to purchase a 45-acre plot of land on the edge of Fairport village. They trucked a good amount of the soil to their farm, cleared the trees from the land and planted successful crops of wheat, squash, and beans on twenty acres of the land. This plot was eventually sold and developed as Fairport Manor.

The Normandie Farm's Christmas tree business thrived, with up to twelve varieties of trees (which took twelve to fifteen years to mature). At the height of the business, the length of Howell Road was full of parked cars on December weekends and over 3,000 trees were sold during the season. Where the first 500 trees sold for between $1.50 and $4.00, in the last few years trees sold for $20 and $30 each. Florence also made wreaths, sometimes 400-500 per year.

The growing seasons for bedding plants and Christmas trees complemented each other. Bedding plants needed care from late winter to late spring; trees were fertilized and trimmed in summer and harvested in November and December. This schedule allowed time for the Diedrichs to travel and for Norman to hunt in places near home like the Adirondacks, and as far afield as Alaska and Africa.

Returning to his love of hunting, Norm Diedrich traveled the country and the world in search of all sizes of game. For over ten years, he hunted moose in Ontario, bringing home at lease half a moose each year and claiming that moose "is better eating than beef." After Ontario Province banned American hunters, Norman looked to Alaska. He flew to Fairbanks and then to a camp about 200 miles from Prudhoe Bay (shortly after oil had been discovered there). The camp was equipped with three tents, one for sleeping and eating, one for outfitters, and one for provisions. His first quarry was a Dall ram, then a caribou. The ram's head was stuffed and kept as a trophy. It was not, however, his last trophy.

In 1971 at the age of sixty-three, he arrived in Churchill, Manitoba, to hunt polar bear. From there he set out for Coral Harbor and then went off by sled with two Eskimo guides to seek his prey. After ten days out and surviving snow and wind, Norman was rewarded with a ten year old polar bear, whose skin (and head) was made into a rug. Subsequent trips to Alaska and Wyoming brought more caribou, moose, and elk which provided both meat and trophies. In their seventies, both Norman and Florence traveled to Africa. While there, he collected Cape buffalo, zebra, and eight other trophies. By this time, they had put an addition on the house just for the trophies.

Norman and Florence loved their community. Norman served Perinton as Town Councilman from 1948 to 1959. He also was a member of the Fairport Grange, the Rotary Club (with seventeen years of perfect attendance), and was a Mason.

The Diedrichs closed their greenhouses in 1985, but continued to grow and sell Christmas trees until 1994. Having probably spent more than half his life outdoors, Norman did not want to see his land sold for development. As a result, in 1992, the Diedrichs agreed to sell the land to the Town of Perinton. Part of the land will remain open and part will be developed into a park.

At the end of his book of reminiscences, *One Man's Life in the 1900's* (from which much of the information for this article has come), Norm Diedrich says, "The tree plantation and the greenhouses, along with my other endeavors made a little empire that it was fun to manage, but finally my knees gave out, and it was sad to see it all crumble; however, it has been a long and happy life and I wouldn't change it for anything I see now. After living in our house for over sixty years, we sold it to our grandson, Bruce Yoder, and moved to a good apartment complex [the Highlands], where we get good food and are comfortable."

Florence Button Diedrich died in 2003 and was followed in 2005 by Norman at the age of ninety-six.

Early Perinton Ellsworths

William Pratt Ellsworth shouldered his knapsack and began the trek west from Florida, New York, to Perinton where two of his former neighbors, James Hannan and Lovejoy Cady, had purchased 160 acres. An ambitious 21- year-old looking for new opportunities, he went to work on the Hannan and Cady farms and eventually married Cady's daughter Irena. They "began their life together in a part of the house of James Hannan." After six years, they decided that more opportunities existed west of the Genesee and bought a farm in the Holland Purchase at Ridgeway on Oak Orchard Creek. They moved themselves and all their belongings in an ox cart and settled down to begin a new life. Unfortunately, it was not a successful move. William developed a serious case of malaria, probably from the mosquitoes that bred "like bees" in the low scummy water of the creek. Irena and William returned to Perinton in 1832 and purchased land from Samuel Hanford in Perinton Center (in the vicinity of today's Ayrault and Turk Hill Roads). Here they finally began to establish what would become known as the "Ellsworth Homestead."

Ellsworth Homestead

William Ellsworth was an excellent farmer. He began to clear the land of trees and the ever-present stones. Corn grew well in the newly-opened areas, as did wild strawberries, making the air "sweet with the fragrance of crushed fruit." As more land was cleared, he planted wheat, which was cradled, cured, flailed by hand, and then carried to Albany by ox cart to obtain the best price. There is also some evidence that he grew tobacco.

Ellsworth was also a good businessman. While early fences were built from the many stones removed from the fields, by the 1840's, fences were made entirely of rail and zigzagged across the landscape. Later those fences were replaced with plane board ones, all of which needed caps to hold the sections firmly together. William made and sold thousands of these caps. He also ran a tannery and a kind of bank. As there was no bank in the area, he purchased a safe, loaned people money at a reasonable rate, and placed important deeds, notes, and papers in his safe. It was known as Ellsworth's Bank. Over the years, the property was filled with a number of structures including, besides the farm house, a barn, sheds, cider mill, cheese factory, bee houses, and poultry sheds.

Hattie & Herbert Waite Ellsworth

Irena was significant in her own right. She had received a good education and ran a school across the road from her house. Unusual for a woman, she was adept at drafting and was in demand locally for such services, especially for the construction of mills. She was also a surveyor and could use a cross-bow. William and Irena had six children, two of whom, James Byron and David Henry, lived to adulthood.

James Byron married Mary Theresa Yale. They lived and farmed in Perinton, raising a family of eight. Mary Theresa also taught music.

After Mary's death in 1876, James married Sarah Mina Stone and the couple raised another nine children. Sarah outlived James, who died in 1921, and married George Bulman, a retired farmer.

For the first eighteen years of his life, James' and Mary Theresa's son Lincoln Ellsworth lived and worked on his grandfather William's farm. Later on he worked at Maple Grove Farm, another of the Ellsworth family farms, located in the vicinity of today's Perinton Wegmans. He married Jessie MacMillan, daughter of James McMillan, who owned property near the Maple Grove Farm. They raised five children. Lincoln was very interested in machines and built one of the first steam engines in town. Eventually he moved to Rochester and opened a bicycle shop. At first he sold the high-wheeled ones, but eventually he turned to the new lower bikes, developing the safety brake. He was a frequent lecturer and demonstrator of the new bicycles, winning prizes for his designs. He continued this work for about nine years before returning to Perinton and the family farm, where he remained until his death in 1941.

William, Irena, James, Mary Theresa, Lincoln, and Jessie are all buried with many other Ellsworths in Perinton Center cemetery. The farm on the corner of Ayrault and Turk Hill Roads remains in the Ellsworth family and is still under cultivation.

The Ketchums of Ketchum Road

Today's travelers from Bushnell's Basin to Victor drive on Route 96, Pittsford-Victor Road. One hundred years ago this was known as Ketchum Road, most probably named after the Ketchum family who owned several farms in the eastern part of Bushnell's Basin.

A variety of sources, including maps and census and land records, provide some answers as to who the Ketchums were. The family was in Ipswich, Massachusetts, as early as 1635, appearing in Rensselaer, New York, about one hundred years later, and finally showing up in Perinton in the early 1800's.

Land records indicate a number of transactions involving members of the Ketchum family. In 1829, Thomas and Mary Leggett sold 332 acres of land in Lot 49 (in the Bushnell's Basin-Route 96 area) to fifty-two-year-old Joseph Ketchum and his son Daniel. They added another thirty-two acres to their property in 1832. By the mid 1830's, both Seymour and John Van Ness Ketchum had purchased property in the same area. John Van Ness probably acquired land from his father Joseph.

Ketchum Road near Matthews farm

Census records shed some light on each of the families. The1850 census lists Joseph as living with his son Joseph and daughter-in-law Lucy. By that time Daniel had moved to Webster. The 1855 census lists another son, William, his wife Emiline, along with a widowed daughter Sarah and her son Melvin joining Joseph in the household. Joseph died in 1856, and yet another son, Cornelius, inherited the property and lived on the site with his wife Caroline and their children Elvira, Edward, and Clayton. They appear in the 1865 census records. After Cornelius' death in 1874, Caroline continued to live on the property with her daughter Elvira and her grandson Elington. She and her daughter are listed in the 1900 census, as is their son Andrew and his family, who probably ran the farm after Cornelius' death.

Ketchum-Matthews barn

John Van Ness Ketchum is listed in the 1850 census with his wife Alma and his children Erasmus, Mary, and Charlotte. He also shows up in the 1855, 1865, and 1875 census records. By 1865 his household consisted of his wife, sons Darwin and Franklin, daughters Mary, Charlotte Ann, and Isabel, a niece Emma, and an adopted daughter, Mary Fehrle. John died in 1886 after which his son Franklin took over the ninety-nine acre farm. His household included his mother Alma, his wife Minnie, and their son George. After Franklin's death in 1914, Minnie and George ran the farm for several more years.

The Seymour Ketchum 120 acre farm was located in the vicinity of today's Fisher's Road. Seymour moved to Perinton in 1835 with his wife, Elizabeth Ann Lee, and children Cynthia, Mary, Jared, Angeline, and Edward. Their first house was a log cabin which was replaced in 1860 by a one and one-half story frame house. The farm's primary crops were potatoes and apples, including Peach Blow potatoes and Red Spy apples. Following a common practice of the times, Seymour sold the farm to his son Edward in 1884 and moved into Victor with his daughters Mary and Angeline. After Edward's untimely death, the three moved back to the family property and continued to run the farm. Later their nephew George and his daughter Helen lived in the family homestead.

A look at the old maps helps locate the various farms. The 1852 map shows the J. (Joseph) Ketchum property and the J.V.N. Ketchum properties on the north side of Ketchum Road and the Seymour Ketchum property near today's Park Road. By 1858, the J. Ketchum property had become the C. (Cornelius) Ketchum property, as Joseph died in 1856 and Cornelius (his son) inherited the property. The J.V.N. and Seymour Ketchum properties are still shown. By 1900 the Seymour Ketchum property had become the Mary & Angeline Ketchum property, the Cornelius Ketchum property had been sold to the Matthews family, and the final piece of property is shown as the Frank J. Ketchum Valley View Farm.

Today that land along Route 96 has been developed primarily for commercial use, but the Ketchum/Matthews farmhouse at 1433 Pittsford-Victor Road still survives as a Perinton designated landmark.

The Knapp Family

There are many Perinton families who have farmed the land and served the community for several generations. The Knapps are one of those families. The first Knapp to own land in Perinton was probably Jonah who had land in lots 12 and 23 in the south central part of Perinton as early as 1820, since he appears on both the 1820 and 1830 census lists. The first Knapp about whom there is significant information is Jonah's son Lauren who settled in Perinton in the 1830's. In addition to owning land in Lots 13, 14, 21, and 23, also in the south central area of Perinton, he ran a general store/grocery on the south side of the canal on Lyndon Road, which was known for its fresh spring water. Appropriately, the bridge over the canal there was known as Knapp's Bridge and the 1852 and 1858 maps of Perinton clearly show "L. Knapp's grocery" at that site.

Lauren and his wife, Mary Wood, had two sons, William and Albert, both of whom followed the family farming tradition. While William and his son Ralph farmed up to eighty-four acres on Ayrault Road just east of Lyndon, as shown on the 1902 Plat map, son Albert and his wife Elizabeth ran a farm just east of the county line road in Wayne County. Albert's son Bruce and his wife Lucy White (also lovingly known as Lucy Victoria) moved to their own forty-eight acre farm on Watson Road, as shown on the 1924 Plat map, after their marriage in 1899. Father Albert lived with them until his death in 1910, Elizabeth having died in 1895. Bruce, Lucy, and their two children, Uretta and Albert, raised cabbage, wheat, oats, corn, hay, and vegetables and also had a small dairy herd.

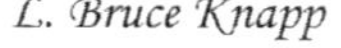

L. Bruce Knapp

Lucy Victoria Knapp

The family had a history of community involvement. Jonah was listed as an Overseer of Highways for a number of years through the 1820's. He was also on the town juror list for 1814 and 1819. Lauren also served as an overseer of highways in 1845, '57, '61, and '62 and was on several juror lists. The family was active in Raymond Memorial Baptist Church (now Fairport Community Baptist). Apparently, William's son Charles hauled stone from the family farm to East Church Street for the church's façade. Later, Albert's son Bruce served as deacon and trustee. As farmers, Bruce and his wife Lucy were both active members of the Fairport Grange. In addition, Bruce was a Mason and Lucy a member of Eastern Star. A family burial plot containing the graves of Lauren, Mary, Albert, and Elizabeth can be found in Mt. Pleasant Cemetery.

Bruce and Lucy eventually retired from farming, but remained in their Watson Road house and leased their land to others. While their son Albert had worked on the farm as a child, he did not choose to return there after high school. At first he worked at the American Can Company, as did many of his generation. For many years he ran the Texaco Station, which was located in the old Rochester, Syracuse, and Eastern trolley station on North Main Street (now Sew Creative). Following in the family tradition of community service, he served as mayor of Fairport village in the 1960's, and was an active member of Rotary and also of Raymond Memorial Baptist (today's Fairport Community Baptist) Church. Albert and wife Harriett served the community and promoted Fairport all their lives.

While no longer a farm family, the Knapp dedication to community continues with the present generation, the sixth. Albert and Harriett's son Warren and his wife Patricia continue to serve Perinton and Fairport in politics, in service and church groups, and in countless other ways, large and small.

Edwin Jordan's Locust Farm

Roads tend to change their names as they progress from one part of town to another. One of those roads is generally known today as Route 250, but it also goes by other names. It is Moseley Road from its southern end at Route 96 to approximately Hulburt Avenue in the village of Fairport. From that point on it becomes South Main Street and then North Main Street. On the 1902 Plat map, the road becomes Howard Road north of Whitney Road. Undoubtedly this portion was named for the Howard family who ran a 185 acre farm that straddled the road. Today, that portion of Route 250 is also known as Nine-Mile Point Road since it is about nine miles from Whitney Road to Lake Ontario.

Between the north boundary of the Howard property and the Penfield town line lies Edwin Jordan's 61 acre Locust Farm. In the early part of the twentieth century, before canned goods became safe and popular, fruits were dried in order to preserve them. Commercial drying houses were common and often individual farms would have their own small drying house Locust Farm was a large drying facility employing a number of workers. In addition to running a large evaporator or drying house, the Jordans also grew potatoes, grain, and other general farm products.

Mr. Jordan is in the foreground of the first photo, while the second photo on the following page gives a good picture of the drying house.

Locust Farm

Locust Farm – drying house

The Talman Family

Darius and Isaac Talman and their children were large landowners and significant contributors to the life of the Perinton community during the middle decades of the nineteenth century. The first members of the family, three brothers, arrived in the United States in 1750 from either Belgium or Holland. Two of the brothers, Isaac and Peter, fought in the Revolutionary War. John, the third brother, who was lame, was not a veteran, but he was the ancestor of the Perinton Talmans. He married Emeline Spraker and they had five sons: Stephen, Darius, William, John, and Isaac. John's grandson, Deacon Isaac, born in 1778, was the first of the family to come to Western New York. A tanner, currier, and shoemaker, he settled in Orleans County and opened a tannery in Medina. Deacon Isaac and Sarah Wilcox were the parents of Darius, who came to Perinton around 1820 to visit relatives and their friends, the Budlongs, who owned land in the town.

Darius saw the possibilities for farming in Perinton, decided to settle in the town, and also urged his parents to do the same. As a result, within ten years both father and son had purchased land on East Whitney Road and had built houses. In 1824, Isaac and Sarah, Isaac's mother Phebe, and children Darius, Rebecca, Eliza, Emeline, John, and Ezra came to live in the new house at 2396 Whitney Road. Two years later, Isaac had also built 2187 Whitney Road. Subsequently, in 1831, Darius purchased 113 acres on Whitney Road for $1,740 and built 2381, where he lived with his wife Cynthia and their six children. The house remained in the family until 1882. Eventually, by the middle of the century, the Talman family owned five houses, three on Whitney Road, one on Budlong Road, and one on Wakeman Road, and farmed upwards of 350 acres. The Budlong and Wakeman Road farms belonged to Darius's sons Luther and Isaac.

The farms were prosperous and innovative. The Talmans, during their sojourn in Dutchess County, had developed the Talman Sweet, an apple that came in either a yellow or green variety. It also grew very well in Perinton. In addition to the apples and peaches, data from 1855 noted that the farms produced 1000 pounds of butter and 200 pounds of cheese, had 180 sheep, and harvested 886 bushels of oats, 418 bushels of barley, 900 bushels of corn, and 600 bushels of potatoes.

The Talmans were active in the community and also in the Abolitionist Movement. Darius held a number of public offices including Highway Commissioner, school trustee, election inspector, and

Supervisor. He was also a Mason and an active member and trustee of Raymond Memorial Baptist Church. In fact, some of the wood used in the congregation's original building on East Church Street came from his farm. Although both Darius' and Isaac's homes on Whitney Road were purportedly stations on the Underground Railroad, the use of Isaac's home at 2187 as a station is documented. In 1859, a man and woman and several children were sheltered there to await transit to Canada. Isaac's son John hid them under goods in his wagon and delivered them safely to Charlotte where they embarked for Canada and freedom. Isaac and his family helped at least twenty slaves escape. In addition, Frederick Douglass printed his newspaper, *The Northstar,* in the Talman building in Rochester, which apparently was built by a relative.

Nakoma Farms

2381 East Whitney Road

Darius Talman died in 1878. In 1882 the property was sold to Frederick Warner who farmed the property until 1902 when 188 acres were sold to the Steffen family who called the property Nakoma Farms, and worked the land until 1928.

Elmwood Cemetery at the corner of Carter and Furman Roads contains many Talman graves including those of Phebe, daughter-in-law Sarah, grandson Darius and wife Cynthia, and a number of children.

Clearly this is a family whose legacy lives on with those in Perinton who serve their community and who love the land and its history.

A Turk Hill Road Farm

Turk Hill Road was originally laid out in 1811, and by 1829 it extended straight through Perinton from the north to the south line. For many years it was known as Baker Road, after Jeremiah Baker, a prominent citizen who lived at the road's intersection with East Church Street. The name "Turk Hill" may have come from the flocks of turkeys that liked the beech trees along the road or it may have come from the fact that the area south of Ayrault, which was originally considered of little value, was occupied by groups of rowdy squatters commonly referred to as "turks." As more settlers moved to the area, however, Turk Hill Road, as a main north-south thoroughfare in Perinton, became a prime location for farms.

One of several farmhouses on the road is located on the west side of the road between Garnsey and Steele Roads. The house at 2429 Turk Hill Road has significant architectural characteristics and is associated with some of Perinton's early settlers. At least one part of the house dates to the 1850's. While the rear portion is at a different level than the front, it was most likely added later, probably in the 1880's or 1890's. Queen Anne style characteristics include the porch with its decorative spindles

Turk Hill Road scene near site of Perinton Town Hall

and knobs, and scalloped gable clapboards. Interior features include hand-hewn beams that support the floor joists, wood trim, and a concrete-block cistern. A number of outbuildings give this property the sense of being an intact farmstead. A privy, an ice house, a pump house, and a barn all remain today.

The property was first owned by one of Perinton's early settlers, Anson Howard. Although the 1852 map shows Howard as the owner, he had probably settled there earlier than that date. Family letters of 1850 and 1851 refer to his farm and to his having been in the area at least since the previous decade. Another source mentioned his purchase of the Turk Hill Road farm as early as 1833. In addition, he served as treasurer of the local Society for the Detection and Apprehension of Horse Thieves as early as 1847. Howard's wife was a Baldwin, the sister of neighbor Giles Wood's wife. Other members of the Howard family also settled in Perinton on Macedon Center Road.

By 1857, the property had been sold to Alex and Lucy Bumpus, and by 1876, it had passed to Thomas and Pernelia Foley, who named it Far View Farm. Foley Road, which used to connect Turk Hill and Moseley Roads, was located on the northern edge of the farm property, which totaled 172 acres by 1902. Ruby Foley, Thomas and Pernelia's daughter, married Elijah Shilling and took over the running of the farm early in the twentieth century, responding to a call from Ruby's parents for help when her father had a stroke. The couple left their cottage on Valentown Road so quickly that they never finished clearing the dinner table. They never returned to that cottage, the work on the Foley farm taking all their time. According to a friend, even at the age of eighty-one, Elijah voiced his sorrow that he and Ruby had not been able to live out their lives there. In 1948, forty years after the couple had hastily left the cottage, it was opened for auction and the dinner plates were still on the table and the old telephone was still on the wall with the 1908 directory.

The major crop at Far View Farm was potatoes, an important crop in the area, and several local farmers, Shillings, Butlers, and Bakers among them, were referred to as "potato kings." At one point it was claimed that Perinton grew more potatoes than any other community in the country. In 1895, for example, Perinton shipped out over nine million bushels. Most of the potatoes were grown on high ground areas such as Turk Hill Road until the 1920's when the muck potato became popular.

It was probably during the Shilling ownership that the house was remodeled in the Queen Anne style. A Shilling niece, Emma Foley Birch, inherited the farm, which remained in the family until 1957. This significant and intact example of Perinton's agricultural heritage continues to be well cared for by its owners.

A farm lane off Turk Hill Road

2429 Turk Hill Road

A Wilkinson Road Farm Family

Wilkinson Road in southeast Perinton was laid out in 1802. Roads in that area of town, including Daley and Ryan Roads, were probably used to travel back and forth from Canandaigua, the Ontario County seat, for any legal business, and at first had no particular name until they became identified with a resident family.

Wilkinson Farm

One of the first residents on the property that would eventually be purchased by the Wilkinson family was Hugh Pound, who shows up on the 1843 tax list. By 1848 ownership had passed to Asher Pound, who lived there with his wife Mary and three children, Clarkson, Mary and Albert. They farmed the land for a number of years until it was purchased by Joseph Wilkinson, Jr. in the 1880's.

The original farm house on the property was certainly built prior to 1852 and possibly as early as 1811, which is what the Wilkinson family tradition maintains. Unhewn and handhewn timbers in the house are consistent with that early date, although there is no confirmation. However, this part of Perinton was the earliest to be settled by people of European descent, and the town itself was incorporated in 1812.

The Wilkinson family moved to Perinton sometime between 1828 and 1831, and by 1843 owned eighty acres of land near the intersection of Wilkinson and Pannell Roads. Joseph was born in Dutchess County in 1783. He married Mary Smith of Poughkeepsie and the couple moved west. Several of their children were born (and at least one died) in Cohocton. The last birth in Cohocton was in 1828 and the next child was born in Perinton in 1831. Three of their twelve children were born on their farm at 340 Wilkinson Road (just east of Pannell Road), including Joseph Jr., Robert, and Phoebe.

Joseph Jr. married Elizabeth Lapham in 1855 and had four children: Gilbert, William, John, and Minnie. Joseph Jr. added to the family land by purchasing the Pound farm at 270 Wilkinson Road. He presented the farm to his son Gilbert on the occasion of his marriage to Alice Jumph in 1886. According to the deed, the couple eventually bought the land from Joseph in 1905 for ten dollars. By that time, Joseph Jr., his brother Robert, and his sons Gilbert and William were farming about 250 acres in the south Perinton area. They raised wheat, beans, and potatoes as cash crops, and vegetables and chickens for their own use. In addition they harvested silage for their dairy herd. Gilbert extensively remodeled the original house in 1917. His diary notes that on June 22, 1917, he "commenced to dig the cellar." In the original floor plan, the front door opened onto a large kitchen-living room, which was flanked by a parlor and a bedroom on the west side. The second floor had three bedrooms with an attic above. Wilkinson family tradition states that it was the first house in (then) Ontario County to have two stories and a full attic. It also had a full basement. In the back was a one-story summer kitchen, under which were a cistern and a woodshed. Gilbert's extensive remodeling included a two story addition on the east side, a generator to pump water from the cistern and the well and to power lights, new larger windows, a large front dormer and dining room in front of the east end of the house, a yellow brick fireplace, and new floors of cherry wood cut from the farm. The summer kitchen was moved nearer the barn and used as a workshop. Gilbert and Alice raised two daughters, Lulu and Ruth, and lived their entire lives there.

270 Wilkinson Road

After her parents' deaths, daughter Ruth Wilkinson Lent continued to live in the house with her two children, Floris and Duane. Ruth recalled that prior to World War II the property, which was about fifty acres at that time, was a "general farm," growing beans, wheat, and potatoes as cash crops. The family also had cows and other stock. At that time, in addition to the smokehouse and privy, there was also a large barn, wagon house, and chicken house to the west of the main house. In the 1940's, these three structures burned to the ground in a fire that probably started from a spark thrown by a threshing machine. Currently the remaining thirty acres are leased for farming.

Ever since their arrival in Perinton, the Wilkinson family was actively involved in the community. The children attended White Brook School (District School #11), and Joseph Sr. was among the founders of the South Perinton United Methodist Church. In 1837 he contributed $1,000, a huge sum at the time, to retire the church's mortgage. Over the years family members have been trustees, Sunday school teachers, choir members, and loyal parishioners of the church. A number are buried in the adjacent cemetery.

Since 1917 when Gilbert remodeled the house, running water has been installed, the former kitchen has become part of an apartment, and a new kitchen was built in the old downstairs bedroom. Large shade trees still surround this excellent example of the evolution of a structure from timber frame to early twentieth century Colonial Revival farmhouse. The surrounding acreage, the outbuildings, the long drive, and the church across the street all contribute to the wonderful setting of this Perinton landmark.

Today Floris Lent owns the house, which has been in the family for well over 100 years. To Ms. Lent, living in her family home is a "joy and a pleasure." It is her fervent wish and hope that the house and land be preserved and maintained as an integral and irreplaceable part of the history and culture of the area.

From Farmland to Suburbs – Perinton's Century Farms

After the end of World War II, the American landscape began to change. The era of suburban growth was beginning. Responding to the pent-up demand for housing, entrepreneurs like William Levitt created subdivisions of affordable housing. Farmland was sold at a significant profit and housing subdivisions began to replace fields and orchards and a way of life. Perinton was no different.

Farmland in northeast Perinton

In the late 1930's, the New York State Department of Agriculture had begun recognizing farm families that had been working the same land for over 100 years in its "Century Farms" program (still in existence). In the 1950's a list was compiled by local historian Marjorie Snow Merriman that identified eleven such farms in Perinton. Unfortunately, the names were never registered with the State Department of Agriculture and today the majority have been sold for development.

As of the 1950's, Perinton's so-called "Century Farms" were located primarily in the eastern section of town. The dates of their founding range from 1811 to 1854.

The Hannan family farm dated from 1811 when James Hannan together with David Cady bought 160 acres of forest land from Joseph Goodwin on the southwest corner of Moseley and Pittsford-Palmyra Roads in the area then known as Antioch. Work on clearing the land lapsed for a time, however, as James went off to fight in the War of 1812. At the end of the war, he returned to his wife Lucretia Packard of Egypt and their log cabin. By 1827, James and Lucretia had added 100 acres to their holdings and had built a more substantial house. Their one surviving son, Jesse B. Hannan, took charge of the farm in 1871 and added another 200 acres, primarily raising grain. Eventually his son Jesse, Jr. took over the operation of the farm, which by this time had become a dairy operation. He also added land, purchasing an additional 100 acres. Jesse's son, Parce, ran the dairy farm for many years until it was sold for development.

At the east end of Furman Road facing on the Wayne-Monroe County Line Road, was a farm that had been owned by the Jones family since 1826. Joshua Ferris Jones bought fifty acres of what would become known as Chestnut Ridge Farm after the abundant chestnut trees that were on the site. In the 1830's, the Jones family added another twenty-five acres. Joshua's youngest son Thomas and his grandson Charles both ran the farm, which grew primarily grain and potatoes, although at times there was sheep-raising. The area is currently under development.

The Ellsworth farm is still located at the corner of Ayrault and Turk Hill Roads. At twenty-one, William Ellsworth found his way to Perinton where he heard there was plenty of work and opportunity. He met the Hannan and Cady families and soon married Irena Cady and set to work on the Hannan farm. In 1832, William and Irena purchased the land that now constitutes the "Ellsworth

Homestead." Here they grew wheat, ran a cheese factory and a cider mill, made and sold fence caps and sections, ran a tannery, and established a loan association. Today sheep, cows, and llamas graze the land, and produce is sold at the family roadside stand.

The Carney farm on the east side of Aldrich Road near Ayrault was established in 1833 by Leander Carney, a Quaker from Maryland. He was a trustee of the District School #4 in Egypt, Overseer of Highways in his area, and a contributor to the building of the Methodist Church in Egypt. George Carney still lived on the farm in 1953, but the area has since been developed.

Seymour Ketchum farmed 120 acres on Fishers Road just south of Pittsford-Victor Road (which used to be called Ketchum Road). The land had many acres of woodland, swamps, and two apple orchards. The main crop was potatoes. The original house was a log cabin, which was replaced in 1860 by a fourteen room house. Ketchum's Stop on the Rochester & Eastern Trolley line was also located on the property. The land has subsequently been developed for housing and offices.

The Furman farm was located on the south side of Furman Road. It comprised about fifty acres that Benjamin Furman purchased from Jonathan Soule in 1847. The farm was always primarily a grain farm. In the early days, the wheat was cut with a sickle, drawn out by oxen, threshed with a flail, cleaned with a hand fan, and taken to Rochester where it sold for thirty cents a bushel. A Civil War era story recounts the departure of a Mark Furman waving goodbye to his parents and heading off through the woods to war never to return. While Furman family descendants still live in the area, the land is no longer farmed.

The Case/Bown farm was located on the southeast corner of Pittsford-Palmyra and Victor-Egypt Roads. The farm was purchased in 1851 by Nathan Case, who came to this area by packet boat from Hoosick Falls. The land was worked by Nathan and his son George before it passed on to George's daughter Marjorie and her husband Bruner Bown. The Bowns ran a dairy farm on the site. The old farmhouse, known as a "marriage house" because it has two sections built at two different times (1820's and 1890's), still stands and is one of Perinton's historic landmarks. The farm land has been developed as Egypt Park Estates and boasts a Bown's Hill Lane in honor of the family's contributions to the community.

Thayer Road is the location of the Noah Baker/Pickering Farm. On December 11, 1837, the land was deeded by Jasper Gardner to Noah Baker. In 1872, the land was deeded to George Pickering, who had married Jane Baker (his brother Willis married her sister Mary). Over time, ownership passed from the Baker to the Pickering family. By the 1950's, five generations of Pickerings had farmed the land. Potatoes were their most significant crop and were considered "mortgage lifters" for two generations. The Pickering family still own and work the land.

The Giles Wood Farm is located on Turk Hill Road about four miles south of Fairport. Letters between Giles and Louisa Baldwin, who often visited her older sister, Mrs. Anson Howard, on her Turk Hill Road farm, were found in the attic of the old farmhouse on the site. Giles' last letter to Louisa stated that "Once you said that you will marry the man who buys the Case Farm, and I am going to hold you to it. My father is buying that farm for me." John Wood, who worked a prosperous farm in Henrietta, indeed purchased Nathan Case's Turk Hill Road farm in 1851 for his son. Giles and Louisa were married five days after that purchase. They built a farmhouse, two barns, a blacksmith shop, an ice house, a tool house, and a small steam mill which powered a feed mill and a turning lathe. Apple and peach orchards flourished. They also grew potatoes and ginseng, the latter crop being quite lucrative at the time. Today part of the land is the Holmes Christmas Tree Farm.

The cobblestone house that stands at 438 Macedon Center Road, overlooking the canal and railroad that run through the valley, belonged to the Howard family who farmed 100 acres from the railroad tracks toward High Street Extension. Lorenzo and Daniel Howard purchased the property from Lorenzo Hunt in 1853. Another brother, Ansel, had a business in the village of Fairport near the future site of the Osburn Hotel, which probably served as an outlet for some of the farm produce. The cobblestone house itself was built with stones hauled from Lake Ontario and set in lime cement. The eighteen inch walls were plastered with mud and trimmed on the inside with ash and pine. The structure, one of three cobblestones houses in Perinton, still stands surrounded by housing tracts.

The ninety-six acre Fair View Farm was purchased in 1851 by John Watson, who worked the land with his sons William, Winfield, George, Rufus, and Charles. At one point George, Rufus, and

Winfield all owned farms along the aptly named Watson Road. Clarence, Rufus' son, was the last Watson to live at the homestead and was a fifty year member of the Grange. He also served several years as Highway Superintendent, retiring in 1956. The farm has since been developed.

Since Perinton was virtually all farmland 100 years ago, there are many, many farms that have been sold for development. Not all available land has been sold for development, however; the town has purchased property for open space and parks, and there are still working farms as evidenced by a drive through the northeast and southeast portions of the town.

It is a goal of the Town of Perinton to preserve a portion of its agricultural heritage. As such, the town has a preservation ordinance and several ways to protect open land from future development. In addition, the Town of Perinton's master plan promises to maintain the area's agricultural heritage by retaining "appropriate rural areas" and protecting the "viability of agricultural activities in the Town."

Ayrault and Turk Hill Roads

- III -
Getting There: Water, Rail, and Roads

The very first white European settlers in Western New York came by wagon or stagecoach and sometimes on foot. With the opening of the Erie Canal in 1825, settlers came west by canal boat and barge. The Erie Canal was soon followed by the railroad, which pushed through the Perinton-Fairport area in the 1850's, offering yet another way to travel west. In the early decades of the twentieth century, the electric trolley provided an easy way to go from city to city, and by mid-century, the automobile had become the preferred way to travel. Inns and taverns opened on all the routes to provide necessary refreshment and lodging.

THE ERIE CANAL

"Low bridge, everybody down..." It took nearly a generation from the time that the idea of building a canal was first considered until people, in fact, had to watch their heads as they traveled the canal.

Where there is water there is opportunity for trade, for people to settle and farm, for communities to prosper. Although Europe had used relatively short canals for centuries, primarily to widen a stream or bypass a waterfall, in eighteenth century New York there was no way to connect the many lakes and rivers or the eastern and western parts of the state. In 1790, however, the Western Inland Lock Navigation Company was founded to look into the building of a canal in New York that would connect the eastern and western parts of the state from the Hudson River to Seneca Lake and Lake Ontario. In 1807 Jesse Hawley, a flour merchant from the Finger Lakes area, wrote a series of essays about the possibility of building an overland canal connecting low-lying areas between Albany and Buffalo. In 1808 the New York State legislature funded a survey of Hawley's proposed route.

In 1817, despite the fact that the Federal government declined any aid, and many thought him crazy, Gov. DeWitt Clinton secured passage of a bill to fund a canal that would extend from Albany to Buffalo, a distance of more than 300 miles.

Ground was broken on July 4, 1817, in Rome, New York. For the next five years work continued across the state, through marsh and farmland, and across streams and rivers. Sometimes the streams and rivers were used as part of the canal itself, and sometimes they were spanned with aqueducts or embankments. Within three years, the first ninety-mile section of the canal was completed and opened. Locally, Bushnell's Basin was the terminus of the canal between 1821 and 1823 during the building of the Great Embankment, which was the approximately one mile portion of the canal running west of the Basin to Pittsford that was built up to seventy feet above the Irondequoit valley. It included a culvert, constructed of wood pilings, allowing Irondequoit Creek to pass beneath the canal. This "Great Embankment" was one of the engineering marvels of the canal project. By the time the canal was fully complete in 1825, it was 363 miles long, four feet deep, forty feet wide, and had more than seventy-five locks. The opening was symbolized by the "Wedding of the Waters," as Gov. DeWitt Clinton carried Lake Erie water from Buffalo down the canal and the Hudson River to the Port of New York.

Canal work required brute labor under harsh and difficult conditions. Winters were frigid, summers steamed, and there was the ever-present threat of cholera or malaria. Epidemics of malaria did wipe out entire work gangs during the digging across the Montezuma Marshes. Workers were also subject to collapsing canal beds, and the occasional gunpowder explosion. Drowning was common. One worker drowned when he fell into the canal and got his leg caught in a lock gate. The pay, however, was not bad. In fact it had to be relatively good to get men to go into the wilderness to dig ditches, work that most were not particularly proud of doing.

Great Embankment

Contrary to popular belief, not all canal workers were Irish. Although a disproportionate number of workers were foreign-born, the Irish got the press because they tended to be young and single and consequently more rowdy. (They were also Catholic, which was a source of suspicion in itself). Permanent residents were not overly happy with this "new element" that had come to the area, and tended to house them in shanty towns apart from the general community.

The opening of the canal meant a revolution in business as well as settlement. Locally, the new waterway from Fairport to Bushnell's Basin precipitated a boom in the village of Fairport, which truly became a "fair port" on the canal. People could now safely settle in the drained lowlands near the canal in the village. According to census records, Perinton's population nearly tripled in the ten years between 1815 and 1825. Canal-related businesses thrived. Goods were shipped for a fraction of the cost of overland travel. One could now travel to Buffalo in less than seven days. The interior, not only of New York, but also of the growing nation, was opening up.

It was now possible to enjoy oysters and other coastal delicacies in Fairport, and to ship goods cheaply and quickly to coastal markets. In 1825 (or 1827), Cyrus Mallett built his tavern on the Northwest corner of North Main Street facing the canal. Henry Amsden and J. Eldredge opened blacksmith shops near the canal. Goodell and Aiken opened a grocery store. The DeLand Chemical Company, a prime reason for the prosperity and growth of Fairport, was located on the canal as well as Cobb's Preserving Company, an early canning company. Bridges were built in the areas of largest settlement: Main Street in Fairport, Fullamtown, and Bushnell's Basin. Other bridges spanned the canal at Lyndon Road (Knapp's Bridge), Ayrault (Wapping) Road, Turk Hill Road, and Parker Street.

Travel was revolutionized by the Erie Canal. Now a traveler could enjoy the natural beauty of Western New York on a packet boat. Such a boat measured about 78 feet long and 14 feet wide. It could accommodate up to forty passengers for the night and approximately three times that number by day. Central cabins were furnished as sitting rooms with carpets and stuffed chairs. Newspapers and books were available and sometimes musicians provided entertainment. Elegant meals were often served, featuring roast beef, ham, and liqueurs. At night, the sitting room became a sleeping room. Curtains divided the men's and women's areas. Tiered berths pulled down from the walls, and linens and blankets were provided. A Scottish farmer, traveling in the 1830's, was quoted as saying, "Few things seem more extraordinary than the sleeping accommodation of the packets."

Packet Boat Drawing

However, some saw canal trips quite differently. The packets were too crowded. Some of those who paid for a berth had to sleep on the floor, suffering snoring, crying babies, mosquitoes, people falling out of bed, and the "stench and effluvia from such a collection of human beings." The famous "low bridge" caught unwary passengers and smashed them to death. Locks malfunctioned and slowed the trip. The truth probably lay somewhere between the two versions.

Canal construction

The canal meant many new jobs. There was a great demand for workers to take care of the horses and mules that were used on the towpath. Many were young boys, often orphans, and men on quests for adventure or seeking work out of desperation. Working conditions were less than ideal. The men and boys often went shoeless and coatless no matter what the weather. Arriving at the barns at perhaps 11:15 at night, they would take care of the horses or mules, eat a meager supper of crackers, catch several hours of sleep with the animals, and start out again at 5:00 a.m. Rest times were usually no more than three or 4four hours between the six to seven hour shifts on the tow path. Fatigue and accidents were constant companions. Furthermore, since most captains assumed no responsibility for their younger workers in the winter when the canal was frozen, many were on their own in the off-season.

Men were hired to man the lift bridges and manage the locks and to oversee the canal itself. Some canal workers intentionally cultivated images of themselves as morally and physically dangerous. They have been described as "a terror to the smiling innocence of the villages through which they float . . . drinking, swearing, and fighting were part of their culture. They hurled curses at ladies, tore down fences and generally flouted middle-class propriety & respect for property."

Others operated taverns and inns and grocery stores for the travelers. Needless to say, alcohol was very plentiful. More than 1500 grog shops lined the canal in 1835, which meant approximately one tavern (or grocery store) every quarter mile. While waiting to go through the locks, workers would drink, and not usually in moderation. As a consequence, snared towropes pulled drivers and workers into the canal and in an era when few could swim, lives were lost. The typical canal worker might hope to survive twelve years.

New developments brought new concerns and worries. Many were unhappy with the new "rowdy element" that had come to build the canal and then had stayed. Schools regularly hired men for the winter term to deal with the new tougher element. People worried about the child labor, used primarily to tend the animals, and there were concerns over the seven-day work week of the "canawlers." Bushnell's Basin church was begun out of concern for the "rising tide of immorality," and a canal boat called the *Good News* attempted to bring the Gospel to the canal itself. A lot of energy was spent in trying to stop Sunday traffic on the canal, while others feared that the canal workers would only spend the extra time in the taverns, certainly not in church.

Erie Canal, c 1921

Because of the growth and prosperity that occurred along the Erie Canal after its 1825 completion, the waterway had to be enlarged almost immediately. Between 1836 and 1840, the canal was widened and straightened. In Fairport, these changes gave it essentially the form that it has today, with a loop north, then south to Fullamtown (Fairport Road at Perinton Park) and Bushnell's Basin. The wide waters south of Fullamtown became what is known today as the Oxbow and was a place for canal boats to winter over. In the early days of the canal, Fullamtown, Bushnell's Basin and Fairport were all active stops. However, Fairport eventually took precedence, as it had a major north-south road as well as the canal to facilitate travel and commerce.

Another widening took place during the 1850's and 1860's and the chronology notes a number of bridges being built during the latter decades of the nineteenth century. In 1903, the voters of the state approved the incredible sum of $101,000,000 for the improvement of the Erie, Champlain, and Oswego canals to accommodate barges. The widening took place over the next fifteen years and included the rerouting of the canal south of the city of Rochester and the closing of the aqueduct. Fairport's famous lift bridge was built during that same time period. The changes ensured the continued use of the canal as a major commercial highway.

Because this was an artificial river, which in places ran above the surrounding countryside, there were bound to be problems in those areas, such as the Oxbow embankment and the Great Embankment. There were major breaks at the Oxbow in 1864 and 1871. The first one was possibly caused by a burrowing muskrat that didn't realize the bank was manmade. The 1871 break may have been caused by some disgruntled unemployed workers, but more than likely also by a burrowing muskrat. The 1864 break closed seventeen miles of canal and required 61,000 yards of earth to repair. The 1871 break carried a barge for a mile and landed it nineteen feet up in an elm tree, and also required the calling up of the 54th regiment to quell a workers' riot over pay. Major breaks occurred in Bushnell's Basin in 1908, 1911, and 1912. In 1912 a two-story house, 150 feet of canal, and 500 feet of the Rochester, Syracuse, and Eastern trolley track were swept away when a culvert collapsed. The most recent break at Bushnell's Basin happened in 1974. This break was of manmade origin, probably resulting from the Pure Waters Agency work on a sewer interceptor tunnel under the canal. More than 100 million gallons of water poured through a horseshoe-shaped break thirty feet deep. An eight-foot wall of water swept into the valley and roared away toward Irondequoit Bay. Warnings by workers and engineers, and the closing of nearby guard gates prevented any fatalities, but residents had learned the hard way "the ugly truth of the old balladeer's lament about '... the raging canal.' "

Bushnell's Basin canal break May 19, 1911

The canal was not without competition. The railroad, which came through Fairport in the 1850's, was always a challenge, especially in the area of commercial traffic. In the early twentieth century, the Rochester, Syracuse, and Eastern trolley provided cheap, regular, and convenient travel. By the 1950's, trains and trucks had just about eclipsed the canal. In the early 1960's, the state considered selling the canal or filling it in.

Nevertheless, the canal today is still the focal point of the Fairport community, albeit in a different capacity. Fairport, like some other villages along the canal, has developed its waterfront to accommodate the proliferation of pleasure boats, and village merchants cater to canal traffic once again. The towpath is now used for walking and biking. Parks have replaced the "grog shops" along the canal. Prime home sites are located along the canal route. Boat launches and moorings have

Canal Dockage in Fairport

replaced the industries. The *Colonial Belle,* a canal tour boat, is moored where the DeLand Chemical Company was once located.

In the twenty-first century, the canal continues to be very much a part of our lives. Congress's designation of the Erie Canal as the twenty-third National Heritage Corridor, and the work of both local and state groups should guarantee that the Erie Canal continues to be, as Philip Freneau wrote in 1822,
"A work that may remain secure
While sun exists and moons endure."

Bushnell's Basin: The Canal Creates a Communty

Ketchum Road (Pittsford-Victor Road) was opened in 1812, providing a link between Canandaigua, Victor, and Rochester. It became a major stage route, and commercial activity centered around the need to provide taverns and shops for travelers. While the Bushnell's Basin area was a significant community on that stage route, it owes its major development to the Erie Canal.

By 1820 canal construction was approaching southwest Perinton and the area that would eventually be known as the hamlet of Bushnell's Basin. Because the topography was right, a "basin" or widewaters had been constructed which allowed canal traffic to turn around. John Hartwell and his son Oliver purchased a large section of land in the area which abutted the widewaters and constructed a store, warehouse and boatyard.

In addition, John contracted to build the embankment over which the canal would pass. Needless to say, both prospered and the area became known as Hartwell's Basin. As headquarters for the construction of the Great Embankment that would extend the canal over Irondequoit Creek to Pittsford and the terminus of the Erie Canal between 1821 and 1823, the Basin became a boom town. The embankment itself raised the canal as much as seventy feet above the surrounding area in order to cross the Irondequoit Creek and valley.

Canal between Fairport and Bushnell's Basin

During the building of the Erie Canal engineers laborers and canallers lived, worked, and played in the Basin. Taverns and businesses thrived. William Bushnell, an entrepreneur, bought out Oliver Hartwell, built a complex of boatyards, warehouses, stores and stables along the canal widewaters, and ultimately gave his name to the growing hamlet. Commercial enterprises took advantage of the safe and efficient transportation offered by the canal. The Rand Powder Company established itself in the area of today's Powder Mills Park. Area farmers also made use of the canal to ship their goods east and west. The community prospered.

Richardson's Tavern, perhaps having the largest bar in the East, was certainly among the most well-known of the canal taverns in the area. Horses and mules were quartered under the porches and regular travelers could find a spot in the straw on the third floor. The more well-to-do might stay with the tavern keeper. By the 1960's, however, the tavern was in such a state of disrepair that it was scheduled for demolition. Happily for Bushnell's Basin and Perinton, however, it was saved and is now listed on the National Register of Historic Places. It stands as a centerpiece for the Bushnell's Basin Historic District along with several other restored nineteenth century buildings.

Charles Dickinson and Cyrus Leonard, however, were fearful that the wild "canawlers" were endangering their children's morals, and gathered neighbors together to sing hymns and read scripture. In 1831 they built a small white clapboard church in the center of town. It served as a Congregational Church, a Methodist Church, an Episcopal mission, and a community church. Susan B. Anthony is said to have lectured there. It was rebuilt in 1873 and has had several additions since. More recently, it has been used for commercial purposes.

Along Ketchum Road (Pittsford-Victor Road/Route 96) and Kreag Road, small Greek revival houses and workmen's cottages fill the spaces between commercial buildings and farms. Bushnell's Basin Cemetery, founded in 1827, is located at the east end of the hamlet as was the Bushnell's Basin District School. Four or five smaller buildings make up what is known as the Canal Walk at the west end of the hamlet and complete the make-up of this nineteenth and twentieth century canal town.

Bushnell's Basin gas station

As other methods of transportation began to overtake the canal, Bushnell's Basin became more and more a suburban community. In the early twentieth century the Rochester and Eastern Rapid Railway came through the hamlet, connecting Rochester with Geneva and also making possible easy access to and from the city for workers. The station was on Pittsford-Victor Road just to the west of today's Exxon-Mobil Station and the line passed over the canal just to the east of Richardson's Inn (the abutments are still visible). After World War II, Bushnell's Basin, like many other rural areas, attracted suburban development. By the 1960's the decline of the canal as a commercial entity, the building of Route 490, and the growth of the strip mall and suburban subdivisions threatened what had been a quiet canal-side hamlet. Many of the small early twentieth century homes had been demolished, were in a state of disrepair, or were in danger of being replaced by malls or office buildings, and farmland was fast disappearing. Some decisions had to be made.

In 1983 a Bushnell's Basin Community Plan was jointly drawn up by the Perinton Town Board, the Bushnell's Basin Merchants' Association, and the Bushnell's Basin Planning Committee. The plan encouraged rehabilitation of buildings and an organized approach to future development while recognizing the unique nature of this canal hamlet and farming community.

In 1986 an organization calling itself "Historic Bushnell's Basin" was formed, "dedicated to the promotion and preservation of the cultural and architectural heritage of Bushnell's Basin...." This group was strongly supportive of Perinton's Historic Preservation Ordinance and was instrumental in getting Bushnell's Basin's 1989 designation as an historic district in order to maintain its historical integrity as a canal hamlet and early agricultural community and to prevent further deterioration. The Town works closely with property owners in the district to maintain that small scale personality and charm that makes Bushnell's Basin attractive. The Historic Architecture Commission continues to work with property owners to guarantee that future changes to the area will be in keeping with the unique charm and vitality of this historic hamlet.

William Bushnell of Bushnell's Basin

Why "Bushnell's Basin?" Towns and hamlets, as well as streets, are often named after significant people who have lived and worked and owned property there. Bushnell's Basin is no exception. William Bushnell ran several businesses and owned a large amount of land in the hamlet. However, he did not live there, and he was not the first person for whom the area was named.

William Bushnell

Land in the Basin changed hands several times before coming to William Bushnell. As plans for the canal developed, a farmer by the name of Pardee decided that he did not want to have property through which the canal would run, so he sold his land in the southwest corner of Perinton to John Hartwell. John and his son Oliver built and ran a grocery, warehouse, and boatyard in what became known as "Hartwell's Basin" and also contracted to build what has become known as the Great Embankment, the mile-long raised portion of the Erie Canal between the Basin and Pittsford village. Even before the building of the embankment, the Basin, located at the terminus of the canal, was a boom town with numerous taverns, stores, and warehouses.

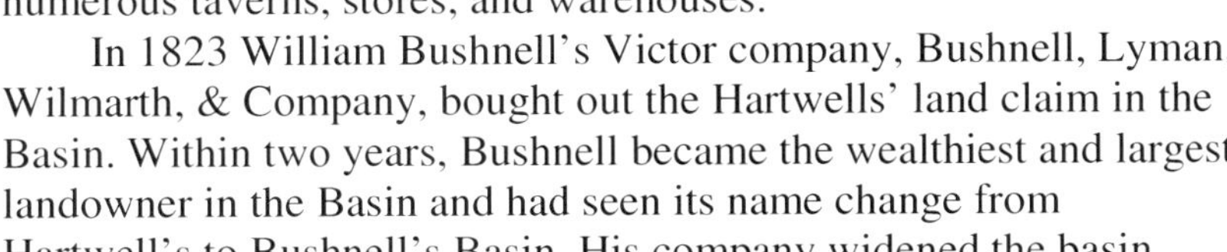

In 1823 William Bushnell's Victor company, Bushnell, Lyman, Wilmarth, & Company, bought out the Hartwells' land claim in the Basin. Within two years, Bushnell became the wealthiest and largest landowner in the Basin and had seen its name change from Hartwell's to Bushnell's Basin. His company widened the basin itself, added a fleet of canal boats and built more warehouses, a general store that supplied the canal packet boats and a distillery. (It was cheaper to ship grain in its liquid form, alcohol, than in its solid form). According to an oft-told Bushnell family story, during the 1830's period of religious revival in the northeast, when the consumption of alcohol was seen to be a significant evil if consumed for other than "medicinal purposes," William "got religion," rushed to his Bushnell's Basin distillery, smashed the kegs and threw them into the canal, swearing never to touch another drop. Apparently he kept his promise.

William Bushnell was born in Sheffield, Massachusetts on June 30, 1775 to Samuel and Hester Bushnell, farmers. One of William's younger brothers, Frederick, moved west to New York and settled in Charlotte, opening a general store with Samuel Latta that sold clothing, horse feed, and farm machinery, among other things. William kept in touch with his brother and in 1816, with no money due to a failed harvest and no interest in continuing farm life in the face of such natural calamities, he purchased a horse and saddle on credit and rode west from Sheffield, Massachusetts, to Bloomfield, New York, where he got work installing carding machinery in a textile mill. When he had earned enough money to repay his debt, he rode back to Sheffield and did just that. Upon his return to New York, he settled in Victor, believing that the location between Canandaigua and Rochester near the proposed canal would be better for business. People in Bloomfield, however, warned him against moving to that "rough" town.

Despite owning land in the Basin, Bushnell remained a resident of Victor, at 146 Maple Street, for the rest of his life, marrying and raising a family there. William died in 1846 just short of his seventy-first birthday. The Bushnell family legacy lives on in the area through his daughter's family, the Osbornes, who remained, for a number of years, part of Victor's history. Although never a Perinton resident, William's legacy lives on in the hamlet named "Bushnell's Basin."

Elisha Fullam & Fullam's Basin

In the early nineteenth century the area around the Fairport Road bridge and Perinton Park was known as Fullam's Basin. Elisha Fullam was born in 1789, probably in Harvard, Massachusetts, to Elisha and Mary Willard Fullam. The family eventually moved to Walpole, New Hampshire, and then Cooperstown, New York, before settling in the area of Northfield that would become Penfield. There Elisha purchased fifty-six acres of land from Daniel Penfield.

Elisha, Jr. married Elizabeth Butler, daughter of Stephen Butler and granddaughter of Zebulon Butler, Revolutionary War veteran in 1811. In 1812, father Elisha deeded twenty-eight acres of his Penfield property to his son for $310. Elisha and Betsy must have lived in Penfield for a time because they don't appear in Perinton until 1822. In 1821 they sold part of the land to Henry Wood and by 1829 they had sold all their Penfield holdings.

Fullamtown Bridge

In 1825 Elisha and Betsy built a hotel and warehouse just west of the Erie Canal on the Fairport-Rochester Road; hence the name "Fullam's Basin." Apparently there was already a structure in the area since the first Perinton post office opened in Fullam's Basin in 1822 with John Hartwell, soon followed by Elisha Fullam, as postmasters. It was an excellent site for business. Before the final completion of the canal, travelers often found it more convenient and faster to disembark from canal boats at "Fullam's Basin" and take the stagecoach into the city of Rochester.

Business in Fullam's Basin prospered only for a short time as the village of Fairport gradually won out as the center of commercial activity. The village had a north-south road which allowed farmers to bring in wagon loads of goods to ship out on the canal and the railroad was looking at routes through the village of Fairport. In addition, after the completion of the Great Embankment between Bushnell's Basin and Pittsford, which then opened the entire canal, passengers no longer disembarked in Fullam's Basin to travel into Rochester. And in 1829 the post office moved into the village of Fairport. Consequently, by the 1830's Fullam began selling off pieces of his land.

Elisha and his family are listed in the 1830 Perinton census and are on the 1836 tax list as having 162 acres of land worth $2788 in lots 52 and 53, in the vicinity of the Canal and Fairport Road. Elisha is listed as an Overseer of Highways in 1824, and as a parent of four children in school district #2 in 1831.

The Fullams had ten children, eight of whom reached adulthood and two of whom remained in Perinton. Otis and Lemuel are both listed in the 1850 census; Lemuel also appears in the 1855 and 1865 census lists. Elisha Fullam died at the age of 52 in 1841. Betsy, Elisha's widow, is listed in the 1850 census as living with son Lemuel. Betsy died in 1861 and both are buried in Oakwood Cemetery in Penfield.

By 1850 the house/store by the canal had been moved to 10 East Church Street in the village of Fairport and was home to a number of families and a series of renters until being bought and refurbished by the present owners. A state historic marker commemorates the history of the building. Another marker just to the east of the Fairport Road Bridge remembers Elisha Fullam. It reads:

Fullam's Basin
Early rival of Fairport
Named for Elisha Fullam
From this settlement Erie Canal Passengers often
took the stage to Rochester

Perinton's Canal Bridges

Irondequoit and Thomas Creeks, the Erie Canal, the railroad, the trolley, the canal, and most recently the expressway have all created the need for bridges in Perinton. The earliest bridges were built across mill ponds and the creeks that wound their way through town, and they were crude wooden or stone affairs needing constant upkeep. Early town meeting minutes noted that a vote allocated $200 to $300 for that purpose. Because bridges were often built by farmers and named for them, town minutes (from the 1860's for example), note repairs for King's, Rap's, Brownell's, Whitney's, Bosworth's, and Sawyer's bridges, among others.

The building of the Erie Canal in the 1820's necessitated the construction of a number of new bridges. All eight main roads in Perinton had a bridge. In addition, farmers whose land had been bisected often built smaller bridges. It was not possible to travel in this area without using at least one bridge, and so their viability was a major concern.

Nineteenth century highway department reports are full of references to bridges. Notations such as "bridge ordered repaired," "repair planking," "planks and spikes bought for bridge repair," "money allocated for bridge repair" occur with regularity. In 1835 the department "worked with Superintendent of Canals about bridge at Fairport." In 1857 the "Lincoln bridge, [and the] bridge at Ackley district were repaired by town men." In 1858 "bridges [were] repaired near Lincoln's, Dutch church, swamp east of Egypt, Fairport, Aaron Newkirk's, Thomas Creek, and Daniel Brown's." Twenty years later in 1878, "Wapping and Lincoln bridge and [a] bridge near Basket Street and Sine's Mill were repaired and one near Jacob Baumer's farm was inspected." Because bridges were often named after an adjacent landowner, it is often difficult to clearly identify today exactly where they were.

Where a bridge crossed the canal was a perfect location for a store, a horsebarn, or a warehouse, and small hamlets tended to grow in those places. The most successful settlements in Perinton were in

Fairport village, Fullam's Basin on Faiport Road, and Bushnell's Basin. For about twenty years they grew at approximately the same rate. However, Fairport's growth soon outpaced the others. In addition to the canal, a north-south road through Fairport village provided access to farmers who in turn patronized the village merchants. The bridge over the canal in Fairport village, then, was of prime importance.

Lift Bridge

For the first eighty or so years of the canal, Main Street was carried over the canal by a fixed bridge, the last one being an eighty foot span. When it was decided in 1903 to widen the canal to 75 feet on the bottom, 125 feet on top with a depth of 12 feet, it was obvious that the 80 foot span would not suffice.

The proposed new bridge presented some significant engineering problems. The old fixed bridge had a ten degree elevation when approached from the north, which had to be lowered. The new bridge would narrow the east end of West Avenue, but could not limit access. Because of the proximity to businesses, the south elevation of the bridge could not be changed. The change in grade had to be built into the bridge itself.

Hence, the only lift-bridge in the world built on an incline (according to *Ripley's Believe It or Not*) was constructed. The bridge is an irregular decagon, having no two angles that are the same and no square corners. It crosses the canal at a thirty-two degree angle, running from southwest to northeast. Although the bridge floor has a 5.54 foot grade, it is raised straight up. The ten degree elevation on the north side was lowered to one degree and the access to West Avenue was solved when a part of the road was built into the bridge.

This engineering marvel bow-string truss bridge was built in 1912 and 1913 by the firm of H.S. Kerbaugh Inc. of Philadelphia at a cost of $75,000. It clears the water by six feet in the down position and by fifteen feet when it is up. The steel deck of the bridge is flanked by sidewalks which are also accessible when the bridge is up. Originally the bridge was raised by two thirty-seven horsepower electric motors. In case of a power failure, it was possible for four men to raise the 375 ton bridge manually using a system of counterweights and pulleys. However, they were not able to lower it. This is no longer a problem as the bridge controls have been computer-operated since 1987 when the bridge was refurbished at a cost of $2.2 million.

At one point in the 1970's it was proposed to replace the lift bridge with a highway that would pass over both the canal and the railroad crossing. While this might have been good for traffic, it would have been a disaster for a village that has since worked to enhance its canal-town ambiance with its docking facilities, restaurants, and shops. The lift bridge is central part of what makes Fairport a canal village.

Old Turk Hill Road bridge

While the Main Street lift bridge may be the most well-known of the town's bridges, there are seven other canal bridges in Perinton that make travel possible, and over the years small hamlets have tended to arise around many of them. Originally there were even more bridges, but when the canal became part of the larger barge canal system and was widened in 1912, only eight major bridges, including the Main Street bridge in Fairport, were rebuilt.

It is claimed that the bridge at Lyndon Road was the first to be built when the canal came through in 1823. The bridge came to be known as Knapp's Bridge, because Lauren Knapp, his wife, and two sons, Albert H. and William F., settled near there in the 1840's. Knappville boasted a canal store, a livery stable, a warehouse, and a boat barn. Canal boat owners would tie up, take their mules to the barn for rest and feed, purchase food for themselves in the store, restock their water supply from a nearby stream, and continue on their journey. The three mile stretch of canal from Knapp's Bridge into Fairport was known as the "Perinton Straight" because it was one of the longest straight places on the entire Erie Canal. In 1911, along with the widening of the canal, the bridge was rebuilt, but this time it spanned not only the canal but also two sets of railroad tracks and White Brook with a length of 455 feet. It was a one-lane wooden decked bridge designed primarily to carry horse-drawn carriages and wagons. Understandably as population and traffic increased during the course of the twentieth century, the bridge deteriorated and was closed to traffic in 1992. After ten years, a new bridge was opened in the fall of 2002.

The next bridge to the west in Perinton is at Turk Hill Road. It was known at various times as Peters' Bridge and Cobb's Bridge, after the owners of adjacent properties. Col. John Peters owned about 300 acres of land across from the canal and ran a tavern near the bridge. After losing a large amount of money in a shipping deal in 1839, he jumped (or fell) into his well and drowned. The Cobb family subsequently owned land near the canal and built the Cobb Preserving Company, whose buildings still stand on the southeast side of the bridge. Like many of the others, this too was a one-lane bridge until its replacement was built in 1984. At the same time, the angle of the bridge and the grade of the road approaches were improved.

A small community also developed where the Ayrault or Wapping Road bridge crossed the canal. E.D. Lewis Pottery flourished for a few years on the north side of the bridge. Two canal barns or warehouses possibly owned by a gentleman named Wilmarth, a grocery store possibly owned by English Ann Hallett, and several houses and farms completed the settlement. New approaches to the bridge were built in 1883, partly due to the need to restructure the height of the canal's earthen banks to accommodate barge and boat traffic. In 1895, canal walls to the west of the bridge were replaced and the culvert bottom was regrouted. Despite constant maintenance, in 1908 one hundred feet of canal embankment between Fullamtown and Ayrault Road gave way, emptying fourteen miles of canal. Five hours after the break, the Ayrault Road bridge collapsed. A new bridge was constructed the next year. It was a single-lane double warren-trussed bridge which crossed the canal at an angle and had a curved and hilly approach on both sides. The bridge was deemed unsafe in 1987 by the Department of Transportation and closed. It was replaced and opened with straightened approaches in 1989.

An important Perinton bridge was built at Fullamtown, where Fairport Road crosses the canal. Before the canal was fully completed, travelers would leave the canal at Fullamtown and take the stagecoach into Rochester. For a while, Fullamtown rivaled Fairport village in terms of growth and was the location of the community's first post office, which opened in 1822 in a store near the bridge. Records note the wooden bridge needed frequent repair or replacement, which occurred in 1833, 1849, and 1884. In 1886 an iron bridge was constructed, which was replaced, together with new abutments and approaches, in 1902, with Perinton's first lift bridge. Construction caused all kinds of disruption since teams and drivers would mistakenly go up the bridge approach and then have to back their animals down in order to return to the towpath. The road surface of the new bridge was quite close to the water and was elevated by pulleys controlled from a small house on the superstructure. A local paper worried about a "new danger for Fairport residents" after a Brighton woman, out walking at night, nearly drowned when she failed to notice that the lift bridge in that town was up. There were, however, no reports of accidents in Perinton. As with the other bridges, it had to be replaced in 1913 when the canal was widened. That bridge continued to be used until 1974, when the current bridge was built.

The Parker Street bridge remains the smallest of the town bridges. It delighted generations of children as a swinging footbridge before it was rebuilt in 1867 as a one-lane bridge. The bridge and street were named for Al Parker, who had a horse barn next to the bridge. Also in the vicinity were a blacksmith shop, a paint shop, a cigar shop and warehouses. This bridge too was replaced in 1913 when the canal was widened, and remains today as a one-lane bridge.

Like most of the other bridges, the Route 31 bridge or the Wiltsie Bridge, as it was once known, was reconstructed in 1913 to accommodate the widened canal. It was replaced by an iron trussed bridge in 1930, which was the same style as the Ayrault Road bridge. Documentation notes that the bill for building that bridge came to $828. The 1930 bridge came down in 2001 and has been replaced by an aesthetically similar bridge accommodating four lanes of traffic.

The last major canal bridge in Perinton is in Bushnell's Basin, another settlement that vied with Fairport village for prominence. The Basin was a booming community during the time when the original canal was being completed between there and Pittsford. It continued to be an active canal community, but was eventually overtaken by Fairport. There have been several bridges in the Basin, the previous one being to the west of the current structure. The current bridge is also a one-lane trussed bridge with a curved and hilly approach.

Other bridges in Perinton span Irondequoit and Thomas Creeks, and remains of the bridges that were built to carry the interurban trolleys across the canal and the creeks still exist. One of the more significant of those bridges crosses Irondequoit Creek on Linden Road. It was originally called the Lincoln Mills Bridge as the mill was located nearby. The bridge was rebuilt in 1990. Old trolley bridge abutments can be seen near both the Turk Hill Road and the Bushnell's Basin bridges.

Perinton's many bridges remind us of how important water transportation has been to the development of western New York.

Mallett's Tavern or the Fairport Hotel

"It was Fairport's first tavern. "It was built in three days." "The name 'Fairport' was coined here." These are only several of the many stories and legends that are associated with the building known first as Mallett's Tavern and then for many years as the Fairport Hotel. It was the first Fairport tavern built on the newly completed Erie Canal, probably completed in 1827, although some sources say 1825.

The tavern was indeed built in three days. The owner of the property on the north bank of the canal, Cyrenus Mallett, offered his friends sufficient food and drink to complete the task. Of course no one had to worry about heating, plumbing, or wiring; so, in fact, it was like a barn raising. Apparently, despite the fact that a liquor license was not issued to the tavern until 1828, Mallett had enough alcohol to keep his volunteers happy, and, as one story has it, to stand upon the framework, swing a bottle of whiskey above his head, break it, and name the building the "Fair Lady of Fairport."

Cyrenus Mallett, the son of Solomon Mallett, one of Fairport's early settlers who lived in the first house built in the village and who laid out Greenvale Cemetery, built his tavern in response to the great need for places to stay on the newly opened canal and to get food and drink, (a response that resulted in a tavern or grog shop every quarter mile the entire length of the canal). Mallett's tavern, however, was the only hotel in town for a number of years, until the Osburn House was built in the 1860's. The front doors of Mallett's establishment opened on the canal path to welcome the canal travelers who either would spend the night or perhaps take the stagecoach into Rochester. The first floor of the hotel featured a dining room, a parlor, one bedroom, and a bar. One story claims that it was in the bar that travelers talked about the "fair port" where they had arrived. The kitchen was located in the rather gloomy basement. The second floor provided two bedrooms and a ballroom. The bedrooms, with their rope beds and cornhusk mattresses, offered a bit more privacy than the usual dormitories which separated men and women with a mere curtain. The ballroom was mentioned in an 1832 article which notes that a dance was held there starting at 4 p.m. Heating was by fireplaces and the assumption was made that the cracks between the floorboards on the second floor were for the purpose of allowing the heat to rise. Candles provided lighting and sufficient privy facilities were available. Walter Edmonds, in his novel *Chad Hanna*, had the hero and his bride stay at the hotel on their honeymoon, where they got "a room for fifty cents, [and] a fine feather bed." They ate breakfast in the "small dining room" where the "windows opened on the towpath." They were served "sausage and fried eggs, and fried potatoes, and bacon cut thin and cooked crisp, and cuts from a peach pie."

In 1862 Theron "Rudd" Pritchard purchased the tavern. He came from Egypt where he had run the "Egypt Halfway House," so named because it was halfway between Palmyra and Rochester on the stage route. He came to Fairport because of the growing railroad traffic, and by this time, the tavern had a second entrance on North Main Street for the railroad clientele. Theron Pritchard and his tavern were very popular. Not only was the tavern a busy canal and railroad stop, but several sources describe the tavern as a place for wedding receptions. One source describes guests walking to the tavern from the bride's home where the wedding took place and being greeting by Pritchard himself. Tubs of lilacs served as decoration and a "sumptuous repast" was provided for the guests. Another source noted that "Old Father Butts" had officiated, and that the abundant food had been prepared by the bride's family.

Tradition says that the phrase "watch your P's and Q's" originated in this tavern. A black-painted board was used to keep track of the "pints" and "quarts" that were ordered by the patrons, and it behooved one to watch his "P's" and "Q's" to make sure he was correctly charged.

During Pritchard's ownership there was extensive remodeling. Steam heat was added, as was a lobby. Pictures from the time show the rooms furnished with lace curtains, heavy Victorian furniture, carpets, and wallpaper. He also prominently displayed a photo of his favorite politician, Democrat Stephen A.Douglas, over the bar. An active member of the community, "Rudd" Pritchard served as a village trustee and overseer of the poor.

Playing Cards

In the early 1900's, under the ownership of E. J. Cary, the tavern was again remodeled. A third story, balconies, and a flat roof with bracketing in the Italianate style replaced the gabled roof, giving the building an entirely new look for the new century.

Evidently, the building remained as a hotel at least through 1913, because the Fairport Directory of that year contains an ad that reads "When in Fairport, stop at Hotel Fairport, W.J. Cary, proprietor, Both Phones." By 1923, however, the property, then owned by Mark Millstone, had become apartments and retail shops. That year, the building suffered a fire which drove ten families out of their apartments and damaged several retail businesses.

The Millstone Block still stands at 9 North Main Street. Much of its architectural significance has been obscured; only a small segment of the east side balcony and the Italianate roofline and bracketing are still visible. The south facade is hidden by a new concrete block building between the hotel and the canal, but when walking along the towpath it is still possible to imagine the welcoming sight of a canal side tavern.

Early Mallet's tavern

The tavern and hotel in 1908

Richardson's Canal House

One of Perinton's most venerable buildings stands by the canal in Bushnell's Basin. Known today as Richardson's Canal House, the structure was built somewhere around 1818 as a stagecoach stop on one of the main stage routes between Canandaigua and Rochester. It was known as the "best inn between Buffalo and Albany on the stagecoach line," and for most of its long life has served as an inn and tavern.

The original inn was small, only one and one-half stories, but a second and third story, wing, and porches were subsequently added. The first floor kitchen featured a stone fireplace that went almost across the entire end of the building. Of course there was also a tap room and bar frequented by canal laborers, boatmen, and area farmers, while a more elegant dining room was provided for the gentry and women. A portion of the first floor might also have been used to occasionally house livestock. The second floor had a hall, a spring dance floor, a meeting room, the innkeeper's quarters, and four tiny chambers, one in each corner, probably used for sleeping. The third floor provided lodgings for common travelers. Wealthy travelers shared the innkeeper's quarters. The architecture is in the Greek Revival style, with Doric columns that support the porch, a wide entablature on the gable ends, and pilasters and side lights at each entry. The canal side has a cobblestone wall. Architects have called it an excellent example of an Erie Canal inn.

Gould and Elias Richardson probably were the inn's builders. Available records indicate that Gould "obtained a license to keep a tavern" in 1827 and that Elias kept the tavern between 1832 and 1837. Between 1821 and 1823, while the Great Embankment over Irondequoit Creek was built, Bushnell's Basin was the western terminus of the Erie Canal and both the Basin and Richardson's flourished. The canal was so close to the inn that packet boat runners found great sport in running their horses or mules on the tow path, making waves that sent water into the bar room, which according to some was the only time the bar was cleansed of patrons. Needless to say it also irked the tavern keeper. It should also be noted that the original canal passed in front of the inn whereas today the canal flows at the rear of the structure.

Old Richardson's

A number of different people ran the tavern between 1837 and the 1890's, and it probably served as a private residence as well for some of those years until John Kossow purchased the property in 1893, renamed it the Exchange Hotel, and ran it until Prohibition forced him to close. Two of John Kossow's daughters recalled that the inn was a home as well as a business. Their father ran the tavern and their mother took in boarders. A Kossow granddaughter remembered the Christmas tree that used to be in the upstairs hall and she recalled her father coming down from the third floor dressed as Santa. After the closing of the tavern, one of Kossow's daughters and her husband purchased the property to use as a private home.

The inn suffered through some hard times in the ensuing fifty years. It served very briefly as a nudist colony but an aroused neighborhood "bred in strict New England tradition, drove the nudists out." The structure served as apartments until the mid 1950's when the county health department ordered it closed because of faulty plumbing. Empty and dilapidated, by the 1970's the old inn was slated for demolition.

Reprieve appeared in the person of Andrew Wolfe of Wolfe Publications who took possession of the inn. It was his intention to restore both buildings and to open the old inn as a restaurant, which he began to do as soon as he took over ownership.

The process of restoration uncovered a treasure trove of items that reflected life in an 1820's canal village. Diggers have found many fragments of tableware, including redware and Wedgwood, a whiskey bottle, clay pipe bowls dating from the 1790's, and a Coke bottle dating to about 1900. Also found was a "commercial token" bearing the date 1820, which was used as a substitute for money. Fragments of wood painted a bright, buttery yellow, which matches the current exterior color of the building, were also found. In addition about ninety percent of the trim survived as well as a beehive oven and an early cooking fireplace. Many of the artifacts are currently viewable at the Fairport Museum on Perrin Street in Fairport.

Richardson's Canal House in 2010

The restorers worked hard to establish the ambiance of a country inn, which was to be run by Andrew Wolfe's wife, Vivienne Tellier Wolfe, who shared her husband's interest in old buildings and architecture. Ms. Wolfe oversaw much of the restoration which was completed in an amazing nine months. The paint colors, supervised by Elizabeth Holahan, were authentic, featuring intense earthy colors, most of which were found during the restoration process. Tinsmith Ralph Rubenstein, who also operated the tinshop at Genesee Country Village, created authentic-looking accessories for the inn while artist Edith Lunt Small did some painting in the cobblestone bar.

The newly restored Richardson's Canal House Inn opened on Valentine's Day in 1979 and soon was receiving rave reviews. The restaurant's five course meal featured American regional and French country cuisine and was designed to get people to relax and enjoy the food without rushing. To the extent possible, ingredients would be fresh and local. Richardson's was featured in the December 1983 issue of *Country Living*, a 1984 issue of *Bon Appetit* called it "probably the finest restaurant in central New York," and in 1990, the inn was featured in the *New York Times*. Ms. Wolfe continued to run this fine popular restaurant until 2002 when ownership was turned over to Johannes Mueller.

Despite its nearly two hundred years of existence and the many changes that have taken place, Richardson's Canal House Inn, which is listed on the National Register of Historic Places, is aptly described as the oldest original fine food tavern still on the Erie Canal.

The Osburn House

An imposing three-storied building with a mansard roof, a wrap-around porch, and a second floor balcony was a welcoming sight to travelers arriving in Fairport for over seventy years. It was the Osburn House, located between the two sets of railroad tracks on North Main Street. The need for hotels and restaurants had been growing since the coming of the canal in 1825, and the laying of the first railroad tracks through Fairport in the 1850's only increased that need. Mallett's Tavern on the bank of the canal was the only hotel in town until the Osburn House was built.

The hotel was built in 1860, 1868, or 1870 by either Patrick Doyle or Robert Mars, depending on the source. What is clear, however, is that it was an imposing building and a well-equipped hotel. It had floor to ceiling windows and double doors that led into a wide hall on the first floor, which had an office, parlor, bar, and dining room that could accommodate up to fifty people. The second and third floors provided eight to ten bedrooms for guests, and living quarters for the hotel owner. The kitchen wing was in the back as was an ice house and a livery stable. Ice came either from the adjacent mill pond or from the Oxbow. It was certainly more elegant than the earlier canal inns where a dormitory was the most common accommodation.

During the first decade of its existence, the hotel had several owners. Lanson Osburn purchased the hotel in 1872 and ran it for five years. He sold it to Robert Conant who owned it for three years before selling out. Several others, including Joseph Smith, owned the hotel before A.J. Cornwell and W.B. Burris, experienced hoteliers, purchased the establishment in 1886. They refurbished the hotel and added modern conveniences such as central heating, plumbing, and electricity. Their livery stable offered eight to ten horses and wagons and carriages by the day or week. Undertaker Henry Relyea's hearse was also housed there.

By the early 1900's, the hotel was owned by Edward J. Cary, whose letterhead advertised the Osburn House as heated by steam, having electric lights, and also having a first-class livery. During this time, the hotel became a popular eating place, offering an "old-fashioned chicken dinner" on Sunday for thirty-five cents. Regular items on the weekly menu included roast beef, pork, and corned beef and cabbage. Mr. Cary and his family lived in the hotel and his son Arthur was born there. A photograph taken in one of the rooms in the hotel shows both Edward Cary and his son Arthur.

The twentieth century brought changes to American life in general, and the Osburn House was no exception. Although the Sunday dinners and the livery were still mentioned, by 1915 advertisements talk about catering to "automobile and special parties." The proprietor changed as well; Nicholas Kelly purchased the hotel in 1907and owned it until 1922. Sometime during this period, the second floor was converted to a meeting hall for the Fairport Grange. They created two large rooms, one with an attached kitchen. One room was used for dining and the other for meetings. A variety of social events including dances, weddings, and, apparently, even the occasional basketball game were held there. Jack Ryan's bar on the first floor, however, was still a popular destination.

W. Lines Baker purchased the building in 1922. He completely renovated and rebuilt, converting the hotel, according to one source, into "one of the most complete gas and auto service stations in the state." His father, Frank J. Baker, joined him in the business that they named the Fairport Oil Company. The Bakers operated a Chevrolet sales agency there as well. They also had service stations in the village of Fairport, East Rochester, and Pittsford. After the untimely death of W. Lines, who was hit by a car and killed in front of his Pittsford facility, and Frank's death several years later, Lois Baker leased the building to Max Humphrey, who had worked there for a number of years. He used the facility to store auto parts and tires and sold American Gas from the gas pump that stood where the front porch canopy had been. The old gas tanks were above the ground and kept filled so that when customers came, the fuel would run down and into their tanks.

Osburn House

In 1938, the elegant old Osburn Hotel was demolished and a rather ordinary, but functional, concrete building was constructed on the site which Max Humphrey continued to lease and to run as an Amoco gas station until his retirement. The building was subsequently leased and then sold to Sidney Spafford and then to the Conking and Calabrese building supply company. It has housed several businesses in the past ten years. As of 2010, the structure is the home of the "Higher Ground" coffee shop. The H.P. Neun Box Company buildings were constructed on another portion of the old hotel property.

Fairport Oil & Gas

The Cottage Hotel

When the canal and the railroad regularly carried passengers, one of the characteristics of any town on those routes was the existence of numerous hotels, inns, and taverns (of which there were so many north of the canal in Fairport that the area was given the nickname "Whiskey Flats"). The Cottage Hotel, located at the corner of North Main and State Street (formerly John Street, currently Lift Bridge Lane East), was one of several hotels located in the village. Turn of the century advertising touted it as having unexcelled cuisine and as being "hotel headquarters" in Fairport.

The structure was built in 1886 on the site of a former blacksmith shop and wagon business. Peter Daily, the owner, built the brick building in the Queen Anne style with a four-story hexagonal tower, bay windows, and recessed porches, one facing on North Main Street and the other on John (State) Street. It included guest rooms, dining facilities, a bar, and a livery stable with horse barns in the back. Its location, in Fairport's commercial north side, was close to the canal, the railroad, and what would later become the trolley line, and as such was convenient for both business travelers and tourists.

Joseph Smith, a hotel entrepreneur, purchased the building in 1889. He had run hotels in Macedon and Ontario, and the Osburn House in Fairport. He added a two story sixty foot long annex to the structure which included a barber shop, a popular reading and writing room with large bay windows, and a third floor with distinctive arched windows. The rooms were heated with steam and there was running water and electricity. All this could be enjoyed for $1.50 to $2.00 per night. By 1915, owner T.J. "Yank" McCarthy was advertising thirty-five rooms and unexcelled cuisine. By the mid 1920's, the structure was billed as a "hotel and restaurant," and the livery and horse barns had been replaced by cars and garages.

Apparently, during the late twenties and early thirties, the Cottage Hotel served primarily as a residential hotel for those who were doing business in Fairport or who were employed in construction jobs on the canal or railroad.

In the mid-1930's, the hotel was purchased by Peter and Lucy Prinzivalli, who made extensive improvements and modernized the building during their several years of ownership. Concrete block sections were added to the front facade and to the annex. The old billiard room on the first floor was transformed into a dining room with an orchestra platform and a floor show area. Fraser's orchestra from Rochester and other groups were engaged to play. The music was enjoyed not only in the dining-show area, but was also carried to the other dining area and the second floor dance floor by a newly installed amplification system. It was a popular night club which hosted many parties and was considered a "nice place to go" by area residents. In the 1940's in particular, the bar area, which was located in the front, became a regular spot, especially for some second shift American Can workers who would stop for a drink on the way home.

From the 1930's to the 1960's, the building continued to serve patrons as a hotel, restaurant, and bar, even as the shift to interstate highways and their adjacent motels was making establishments like the Cottage Hotel increasingly difficult to sustain. In 1968, however, the question of the future of the Cottage Hotel was decided: the old hotel was gutted by fire. Flames were first noticed about 3:30 a.m., and it took 125 volunteers and six fire companies to bring the blaze under control. There were injuries; one, Estile Hampton, an employee of the Stappenbeck Co. of Penfield, died, and several fire fighters were treated for smoke inhalation and cuts. The owner of "Hawk's Restaurant" across the street, Albert DiRisio, opened up in order to serve fire fighters and hotel residents and to be the headquarters for Red Cross aid. Unfortunately, the owners of the hotel, Ben, David, and Gordon Abbott, were unable to salvage the severely damaged building and it was razed the next year.

Although there are a number of restaurants and taverns in Fairport Village, there are no longer any hotels.

The Railroad in Perinton & Fairport

In 1831, the Mohawk & Hudson railroad provided the first rail service in New York State with its sixteen mile run between Albany and Schenectady. It was, like many of the early railroads, a short run prone to accidents and with an erratic schedule. Most of this nation's early railroads ran over short distances, were of different gauges, and tended to connect with bodies of water rather than other rail lines. In the 1850's, however, especially in the north, the shorter lines began to combine and standardize their gauges. Principally because they were highly subsidized by federal and local governments who provided loans and land grants, railroads expanded rapidly in the growing nation throughout the latter half of the nineteenth century. By 1860, for example, the federal government had given grants for over thirty million acres to aid in the expansion of rail lines, and in 1869 the nation was united when the Central and Union Pacific lines met at Promontory Point in Utah.

In 1853, an act of the New York State Legislature authorized the consolidation of nine small railroads into the New York Central and Hudson River Railroad, boasting that "a person could ride from salt water to fresh water, at Lake Erie, along the 'water-level route', without changing cars." In that same year tracks were built through Perinton and the village of Fairport. The first train through Fairport had three cars, was probably pulled by a four-ton engine, and traveled at a speed of twenty to thirty miles per hour as it carried dignitaries from Albany to Buffalo. The tracks, which were built at a cost of about $40,000 per mile, not only changed the landscape and opened up new opportunities, but also accelerated the shift from agriculture to industry. In addition, because the Irish and other immigrants worked on the railroad, and settled in western New York, the population continued to diversify.

Early engines burned wood and threw sparks, constantly endangering buildings and any other dry materials that were close to the tracks. Many stories survive about the effects of those early spark-throwing, noisy engines: horses were spooked, people fainted, and others celebrated with fireworks. Because the engines devoured so much wood, landowners were quick to seize on this new source of income, and forests became long lines of cord wood stacked beside the tracks. By the 1870's, however, most rail companies had switched to coal power, considerably lessening the danger of fire and the total loss of woodland.

After the Civil War railroading boomed. The first mail service on the Fairport run began in 1875. Although the service was faster than previously, some of the mail was never delivered because bags were thrown out of the moving train and occasionally would be caught under the train or would split on impact. Records show that between 1875 and 1917 there were over 9,000 wrecks of postal cars with loss of mail. In 1882, the West Shore tracks, turning southward from Fairport and using the overpass on Fairport Road, were laid (this time by Italian immigrants) increasing service to more areas of western New York.

NYCRR Passenger Station

Steam engine and workers

Fairport, like many others, was a railroad town from the turn of the twentieth century through World War II. Railroads were the prime movers of both people and goods across the landscape. During peak years, 3,000 passenger tickets a month were sold at the Fairport station. An 1899 daily timetable shows nine trains going east, three on the West Shore line, six on the New York Central line; and eight trains going west, four on the West Shore, and the remainder on the New York Central. Because of the demand for service, Fairport village boasted two stations: one for passengers, on Railroad Street, east of North Main, and one for freight, on the west side of North Main Street. In addition, a fifty foot shed to protect the wood from the elements and a brick water tower were constructed near the freight station, thus providing both food and drink for the "iron horse." After the conversion to coal, the New York Central Railroad constructed a coaling station between Lyndon Road and today's Perinton Parkway. This station was capable of refueling 4,100 locomotives a month, using 3,000 tons of coal in twenty-four hours. Coal was mechanically elevated to the trestle before being dumped into the coal cars. In 1950, a diesel refueling station was built at the site, as was an ice station. One of the largest icing stations in the country, the facility could ice eighty cars at one time with ice brought in from Buffalo. It was a noisy operation. Lifelong Perinton resident Don Hull remembers that "the engines started up as hard as they could, and there would be this grinding sound of metal on metal from the train's wheels skidding on the tracks. As the train started up, it would jerk the cars, causing the couplings to bang, and the banging would go right on down the line … [and] would last for four or five minutes." Despite its size, by the mid 1950's, due to the growing decline in rail usage, the operation was shut down.

Train with Osburn Hotel in background

Among the many peripheral benefits stemming from the development of the railroad was the institution of standard time zones. Because it was not possible to have an efficient rail schedule when communities ran on their own time, in 1873 both the United States and Canada adopted standard time zones. In addition, because each rail station had a telegraph office, up-to-date news was always readily available.

For years the railroad provided lifelong employment for both men and women and was a significant element in everyday life in Fairport village. The clanging of bells, the smoke and puffing of the engine, the whistles, the hustling to turn switches and work crossing gates, and the rising of steam as the locomotive took on water and fuel made the arrival of any freight or passenger train an event that did not go unnoticed by anyone who lived in the vicinity of the tracks. Behind the Water Street home of Albert "Hawk" DiRisio there were "dead tracks" where empty boxcars were parked. DiRisio recalled, "As soon as the stub engine took off with its crew, all the neighbors would converge on the box cars manned with crowbars, hammers, and brooms. They would strip the cars of wheat or corn or whatever was left over on the floors from the original load. There was, as the result of cleaning up the cars, plenty of feed for our chickens...." In those days as well, the "milk train" trip from Rochester to Syracuse took five times longer than driving because the train stopped at every little town and even at crossroads, often waiting for the farmer to arrive with his milk cans.

It was not unusual for someone to work for the railroad for over forty years, and even in retirement to continue to watch the trains and hang around the gate tender's shanty. From the beginning both switches and gates had been manually operated and it was with some trepidation about safety that the switch to automated signals began in the early 1950's. One longtime gatekeeper didn't think very highly of the new gates: "So many things can happen, ...Now you take kids – they'll do some foolish things and an automatic gate can't tell them it's dangerous." Nevertheless, automation won out.

Railroads had made it possible to span a continent and to unite a diverse nation. Railroads had helped launch the world's strongest and wealthiest industrial power, had made travel faster and easier, and had made consumer goods available to anyone who lived anywhere near a station. Railroads, however, were not destined to maintain their superiority.

After World War II, with air travel, the coming of the interstate highway system, and the availability of autos and cheap gasoline, the railroad gradually went into decline. Passenger service ended in Fairport in the late 1950's and the freight offices were closed by 1960. Today, the most obvious reminder of the former heyday of railroading in Fairport is the village grade crossing on Main Street.

Rochester, Syracuse, & Eastern Electric Trolley

An efficient, comfortable, affordable way to travel from the city to the towns to the rural areas was the interurban electric railway, a popular answer to mass transit needs, especially in the northeast, in the early decades of the twentieth century. A number of lines were built in the Rochester area: the Rochester & Sodus Bay; Auburn & Northern; Syracuse, Lakeshore, & North; Rochester, Lockport, & Buffalo; Rochester & Eastern, and the Rochester, Syracuse, & Eastern, which had ten stops in Perinton.

The R.S. & E., also known as the "on time line," or "rolling thunder," was one of the most expensive and grand of the area interurbans, covering eighty-seven miles with its double tracks. It was built between 1906 and 1909 for $7,000,000, a large sum at the time for such a project. Each section opened as it was finished, with the Newark to Palmyra section opening first, followed by the Fairport to Macedon section. In 1907 the line was completed into Rochester, passing through East Rochester and ending at Court Street. By 1909 the line was finally complete from Rochester to Syracuse. When the first segment of the line opened on July 2, 1906, passengers traveling from Newark to Palmyra refused to get off the car in Palmyra, fearing that they would not be able to get back on. Palmyra passengers were disappointed.

In Fairport several plans for a trolley line had been presented before the R.S. &E. was finally built. In 1903, tracks were laid on State Street and South Main Street, but were never used. In 1905 a proposal was made to run tracks on South Main Street to East Church Street and then behind the houses on the south side of that street to connect with the main R.S. &E. trolley tracks south of the Turk Hill Road bridge. This proposal failed as well.

Trolley in Egypt

The final route of the R.S. and E. in Fairport came from East Rochester, ran north of the canal, crossed Main Street at State Street, continued north of the canal until just east of Turk Hill Road, then crossed the canal and headed south toward Ayrault Road. In the places where the trolley passed close to the canal, it was necessary to build a fence that separated the two, as the noisy trolley spooked the horses and mules pulling canal barges. The trolley continued south and east, crossing Mason Road and then turning due east just south of Pittsford-Palmyra Road after the Egypt trolley stop, which was at the current site of the Egypt Fire Department. From there the trolley went east, finally exiting Perinton in the vicinity of today's Trolley Bed Nursery, having passed ten stops since entering the town.

Accommodations were quite luxurious and were often referred to as "club cars for the masses." The large dark green cars, which could carry sixty-two passengers, were furnished with two rows of front-facing leather seats separated by an aisle. A single wooden bench in the rear of the car was for workmen, and a small section up front, separated by a sliding door, was set aside for smokers. Leather straps were available for standees. The motorman was in the front and the platform and steps for getting on and off were in the rear. Regulations noted that no one under fifteen was allowed in the smoker unless accompanied by an adult, and that all dogs had to be leashed and muzzled.

Fairport Village trolley station

The line ran both "limiteds" and "locals." The limiteds, traveling up to seventy miles per hour, only stopped at large towns and cities. The locals, however, called at all ninety-nine stops between Rochester and Syracuse. These trains, especially the locals, made it possible for formerly isolated rural communities and farms to have contact with the larger towns and cities relatively easily and for a modest fare. A round trip ticket from Fairport to Rochester, for example, cost thirty-five cents (twenty-five cents on the weekends) and the trip took about twenty minutes. Children under five, with an adult, traveled free, although an adult was limited to three children under five. Those between five and twelve years of age paid half fare. On busy days, or during rush hour, a second car could be added. The line carried an average of 150 passengers per day in the best years. In addition, the line carried freight, including milk, produce, newspapers, and mail.

Financial troubles seemed to have plagued the electric trolleys from the beginning. The trolley lines often paralleled the railroad lines, thus failing to offer any expanded access or a viable alternative for either passenger or freight service. In addition to their failure to compete with the railroads, they had been quite expensive to build and maintain in the first place. Further, in the early decades of the twentieth century, people turned more and more to the automobile for travel, and by the 1930's bus travel and the Great Depression spelled the end for most interurban trolley systems. The last trip of the Rochester, Syracuse, and Eastern through Fairport was on June 30, 1931. One of the last passengers on that run was Vincent E. Kennelley, former freight agent, dispatcher, and conductor on the line.

The former Fairport trolley stop in the village has continued to serve the public in a variety of ways. It was a gas station for a number of years, then was nicely restored as an office, and as of 2010 is the home of a fabric store. One of the few remaining small trolley stops has been moved and renovated and is now serving as the dockmaster's office for the Fairport docks. The old trolley bed has a new life as part of Perinton's system of hiking trails. The legacy of the R.S. & E. remains.

Perinton/Fairport Street Names

Years ago, property lines were described in terms of "links" and "chains" and landmarks such as streams and large trees. Roads and streets were often named after the people who had settled there and the first roads were merely paths between neighbors. Perinton's first road (path) was between Glover Perrin's house on Ayrault Road and his brother Jesse's house on South Main Street. Just a brief look at the 1902 Plat maps of Perinton and Fairport shows that a number of roads were named after families whose farms abutted that road. Not only have streets been named after important (and not so important) personages, but they have also been named for businesses that flourished in the area and for settlements connected by those roads.

In the village of Fairport, DeLand Park A and B, Parce Avenue, and Perrin Street are all named for important families in the history of the town and village. The DeLand family founded the DeLand Chemical Company in the late nineteenth century, virtually putting Fairport on the industrial map during that time. The two streets were originally part of the DeLand property at the corner of North Main and Whitney Roads. Parce Avenue was named for Joseph Parce and his family. Joseph was not only involved with the DeLand Chemical Company, but was a DeLand brother-in-law and the father of Walter Parce, the founder of East Rochester. The large house at 137 North Main Street just north of Parce Avenue was the family home. Perrin Street was named specifically for James Perrin, a nephew of Glover Perrin, who with his wife Johanna and several brothers and a sister, were the first white settlers in the town of Perinton. Filkins and George Streets are in the vicinity of the George Filkins farm. Potter Place flanks the Potter House and property at 53 West Church Street. The Lewis Brooks farm, which occupied the current site of Johanna Perrin School and the aptly named Brooks Hill School, also gave its name to the south end of Potter Place, which on the 1902 map is labeled Brooks Avenue, as well as nearby Lewis Street. Hulburt Avenue runs through what was the Thomas Hulburt farm, which extended nearly all the way north to Fairport Road. Woodlawn Avenue (formerly Woodland Avenue) was part of property owned by Martin Wood. Nelson Lewis owned the area through which Nelson Street runs. A.R. Cole and L. Beardsley owned property on what became known as Cole and Beardsley Streets respectively. Church Street is aptly named for its churches, which have numbered as many as seven. Several streets, among them Clinton Place, Dewey Avenue, Jackson Place, and Monroe Street, were named for presidents and notable heroes.

Sometimes, streets and roads, especially ones that connected settlements, were appropriately named for those areas. Fairport Road was originally called the Rochester Road as it was the main link between the village of Fairport and the city of Rochester. The Victor-Egypt Road and Fisher's Station Road, both in the southern part of town, are named in the same way. One of the town's earliest roads, so designated in 1805, is today's Route 31, which is more often than not referred to as Pittsford-Palmyra Road, indicating the two communities that it connects. (Early on it was also known as Mud Creek Road, probably a descriptive term.) Likewise, today's Route 96 is also known as Pittsford-Victor Road after the two areas it connects. That road was earlier known, however, as Ketchum Road, after the Ketchum family whose Valley View Farm incorporated several hundred acres in the area.

In the Town of Perinton, from Baird Road in the western part of town to Pannell Road in the east, many, many roads were named for local farm families.

The Baird family owned extensive property on both sides of Baird Road, some of which extended as far east as the Howard farm on Howard Road, which was an earlier name of the portion of Route 250 between the village of Fairport and the Penfield town line. That portion of Route 250 is known today as Nine Mile Point Road, so called because at the end of the road at Lake Ontario there was once a large elm tree visible to sailors who knew it was about nine miles from the port of Charlotte. South of the village that same Route 250 is known as Moseley Road, for the Leander Moseley family who owned property there. The intersection of Routes 250 and 31 was once referred to as Hannan's Corners, after the Hannan family, whose extensive land holdings were located on the site of today's Perinton Hills shopping center. James Hannan and his wife Lucretia Packard (daughter of Perinton's first supervisor) settled on that land in the early 1800's. The family owned the property until it was sold for development in the late 1960's. Garnsey Road is in the same vicinity, named for

Mark Garnsey whose Willow Valley Farm flanked that road. Turk Hill Road north of the Erie Canal was, and still is, known as Watson Road after the Watsons who farmed there. Turk Hill Road south of the Erie Canal was once called Baker Road after the Nathan Baker family of that area. Eventually, the name Baker gave way to Turk Hill, perhaps either after the flocks of wild turkeys in the area, or after the gangs of "young turks" that squatted on land there.

Silas Pannell's 100 acres and Warren Pannell's Fruit and Berry Farm flanked Pannell Road. James Daley and Thomas Ryan farmed land in the vicinity of today's Daley and Ryan Roads, two of Perinton's oldest, dating to 1800 and 1802 respectively. Solomon Aldrich, who came from Massachusetts, purchased over 300 acres in the eastern portion of the town in 1806 in the area of Aldrich Road. J.G. Aldrich was still farming there in 1902. Loud Road is named for Oliver Loud, who ran a popular tavern and stagecoach stop in the hamlet of Egypt. The Wilkinson family, settling on Wilkinson Road in the 1830's, were also founding members of the South Perinton United Methodist Church. Their farmhouse is a Perinton landmark and is owned today by Floris Wilkinson Lent. Rufus Watson, owner of the hundred-acre Far View Farm, gave his name to Watson Road, which is the northern extension of Turk Hill Road. Adam Kreag, the creator of Shinola Shoe Polish, had an extensive farm on the road that was named for him. He was also known as the "Potato King," a nickname obviously related to his farm produce. The Jesse Whitney house and farm are shown on the corner of Whitney Road and North Main Street as early as 1852. By 1902 the DeLand family had purchased the land and moved the Whitney homestead to the east. In 1847 Benjamin Furman purchased land along what would become Furman Road and raised wheat, which he sold in Rochester for thirty cents a bushel. The farm was designated as a New York State Century Farm in the 1950's because it had been in the same family for over 100 years. Michael Hogan, Samuel Mason, and Frank Howell, among others, all had farms on roads that now bear their names. Budlong Road, which is now known as Perinton Parkway, was named for Milton Budlong, whose farm straddled the road.

Besides being named for farm families and area communities, old roads and new ones often reflected a business or activity that took place in the area. In the earliest days, a portion of Ayrault Road was known as the Mill Road since it connected Perinton with a mill on Irondequoit Creek. In later years, the eastern portion of the road became known as Ayrault Road for the Ayrault family that farmed over 300 acres between the road and the canal in the vicinity of today's Fairport High School. The western portion of the road was once called Wapping Bridge Road, a name that doesn't seem to have any local connection at all. Jefferson Avenue was formerly known as Basket Road because it was said that the Native Americans collected willow reeds there for basket making. The eastern portion of the road known today as Whitney Road was labeled Cheese Factory Road due to the presence of cheese factories. Salt Road, in the same section of Perinton, was named for its salt wells.

Today's developers do not always use names that relate to families or area activities when they create new subdivisions; however there are some new streets and subdivisions whose names either use a former farm family's name or in some way reflect a former use of the property. The Case/Bown farm was located on the southeast corner of Pittsford-Palmyra and Victor-Egypt Roads. That farm was purchased in 1851 by Nathan Case, and was subsequently passed on to his granddaughter Marjorie and her husband Bruner Bown. The Bowns ran a dairy farm on the site and Bown's Hill Lane now runs through the property. The Lapham family purchased land along Mason Road sometime during the second decade of the nineteenth century and it remained in that family until the 1860's when it was sold to Van Rensselaer Conover. At least three generations of Conovers farmed the land. A portion of the land has been recently developed and the road has been named Conover Crossing. And Schoolmaster Circle is in the vicinity of Fritz Schoolmaster's seventy-seven acre farm between Howell and Wakeman Roads. Kitty Hawk Drive is so named because the development was a former air strip. Streets in the area of Eagle Vale, such as St. Andrews, have been named after famous golf courses. The Colaruotulo family, owners of Casa Larga Vineyards and Anco Builders, have named a number of streets in one of their subdivisions after grape varieties or wines -- for example Chenin Run and Chardonnay Drive. Several subdivision names reflect the area's history. Mason Valley occupies a portion of what used to be Samuel Mason's 150 acre farm. Crystal Springs subdivision is near the old Peddie Springs where Walter Parce operated the Crystal Rock Water Company that bottled and sold mineral water in the early twentieth century. Whitney Farms is named for Jesse Whitney whose farm was in that area.

Conover Crossing

By no means have all of the farming families and family businesses been memorialized with road names, nor does this article cover every road and street that has a connection. Clearly, many more families have contributed to the life of Perinton and Fairport than there are roads to commemorate them. However, in meandering around the roads and streets of the town and village, residents can be reminded of Perinton's and Fairport's history, not only in the old road names but also in the new.

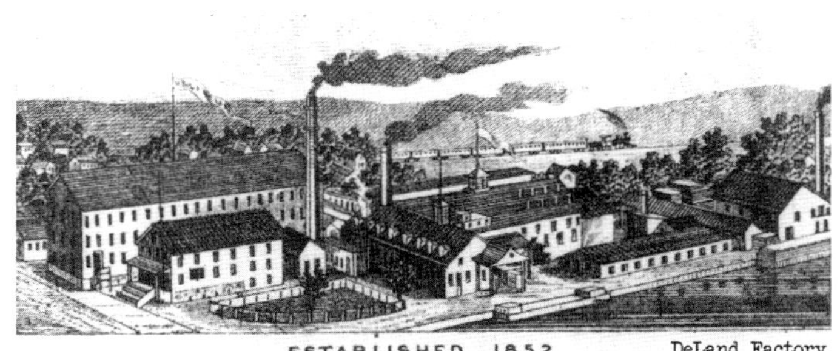

DeLand Factory

- IV -
Business, Industry and Fairport Village

For over one hundred years, until suburban subdivisions and shopping malls changed the landscape, the center of population and business activity in the Town of Perinton was in the Village of Fairport. Industry thrived on the banks of the Erie Canal. Main Street provided nearly all of the goods and services demanded by the population of both the town and the village.

The Mill Industry

The mill industry is one of the oldest in history and probably began when our prehistoric ancestors started to grind grain between two stones instead of pounding it. The Bible refers to the grinding of grain. The Greeks used two stones with the upper one turned by a handle; the Romans used animals to turn the millstones and introduced the first use of water for milling.

After clearing land and constructing a log shelter, settlers in Western New York looked to the construction of a mill for grinding that first harvest of grain. One of the earliest mills was built in Honeoye Falls by Zebulon Norton in 1791. It was in fact to that mill that Jesse Perrin of Perinton went to have his grain milled. Unfortunately, the story says that he was told to go on to another mill as he had both a horse and some money and Norton was only grinding grain for those who walked to his mill. It can be assumed, however, that Perrin was ultimately successful in having his grain processed.

The early mills were usually grist mills for grinding grain; however, as time went on, the mill industry included flour mills for finer processing of grain, saw mills for wood, and fulling mills for wool. These early mills were powered by water, of which there was an abundance in western New York. Irondequoit Creek, the site of many area mills, was quite different 150 years ago. The creek was significantly larger and had several dams along its path for mill ponds. Stories mention canoe clubs coming to Bushnell's Basin on the canal, joining the creek down to Linden Road, portaging around the dam and continuing on to the bay. Another story tells of James Wadsworth being served "delicious trout" from the creek by Daniel Penfield.

The first mill in Perinton was built in 1810 by Joseph Richardson on Irondequoit Creek approximately where it is crossed by Fairport Road. It was followed in 1813 by Isaiah Northrup's mill on Thomas Creek west of Baird Road and in 1818 by Packard and Wilson's mill in Egypt near the intersection of Loud and Pittsford-Palmyra Roads. A number of both grist and saw mills were constructed in Perinton and Fairport in the early decades of the nineteenth century. In 1821, New York State had 2132 grist mills in operation powered by water, wind, horse or oxen.

One of the larger mill complexes on Irondequoit Creek was started In 1821 by Samuel Rich of Penfield and Andrew Lincoln, a Perinton builder, who joined forces to build a grist mill on the south side of Linden Avenue along the west bank of the creek. Their large mill had three sets of

Lincoln Mills

mill stones: two for processing grain into flour and the third for custom grinding. Power for the mill was derived from damming the creek to create a twenty-six acre mill pond.

In 1836 Lincoln bought out his partner and within a dozen years had enlarged the complex, adding another set of mill stones and two overshot wheels, increasing the size of the pond to over fifty acres, and building a larger stone mill to replace the old wooden one. He employed four millers and had agents selling his "Monroe County Flour," which he shipped out on his own boats, in all major eastern cities. Lincoln continued to expand his business, adding a saw mill and manufacturing furniture, partnering with Benjamin Arey in a tannery business, adding 350 acres of land to his holdings, and eventually giving his name to Lincoln Mills Road. Needless to say, Andrew Lincoln was considered one of the most prosperous millers of the county when he died in 1866.

The Lincoln mill was run for a time by Andrew, Jr. and then sold to W.H. Woodhull, who was still operating it in 1877. By 1908 the site was being used by the East Rochester electric light plant to generate electricity, and local ice houses made use of the pond ice. The pond was a favorite recreation spot, drawing picnickers, fishermen and boaters. At one point, there was also a popular speak-easy on the shore called the "Lily-Pad."

By 1920 the mill was no more. The dam was destroyed by a combination of high water and an ice dam causing the pond to drain within hours in 1916. The stone building was gutted by fire in 1920 and its stones were apparently reused in another structure. Sometime after 1920 the property was purchased by Rochester Gas and Electric who in turn donated fifty-five acres to the town of Perinton in 1961. The town opened Spring Lake Park, much of which is the site of the old mill pond, in 1964.

The Evolution of Main Street, Fairport

Fairport's Main Street has been a center of activity since the first settlers arrived at the beginning of the nineteenth century, but its real growth began when the Erie Canal came through in the 1820's and the swampy land that had tended to make the village area unhealthy was drained. Prior to 1820, Oliver Tomlinson, John and Martin Sperbeck, and Isaac Beers all owned property on the future South Main Street and Peter Ripley had built a log cabin on what became North Main Street.

By 1822 Henry Amsden and J. Eldredge were running a blacksmith shop near the canal on North Main Street. Abishah Goodell and Mr. Aiken opened a grocery store on Main Street. These establishments were followed in 1827 by Cyrenus Mallett's tavern on North Main Street near the canal. In the next several decades Main Street added, among other new businesses, a wagon making shop and a hardware store. The railroad came through the village in the 1850's, adding warehouses and both a passenger and a freight station. By the early 1880's the DeLand Chemical Company had located its factory just north of the canal on the east side of Main Street. During the 1890's Main Street was flanked by a number of two-story stone and frame buildings, among them the Bown Block and the Clark Block, named for their owners and builders, as well as by private homes. Fairport was becoming a thriving canal crossroads.

South Main Street, 1932

The streetscape as well as the function of the village remained essentially the same until the early 1970's. For approximately 150 years, from the coming of the Erie Canal to the urban renewal of the 1960's and 1970's, the village of Fairport provided most of the goods and services required by its citizens. Main Street itself was divided by the Erie Canal into South Main Street and North Main Street. South Main Street had a mix of stores and services as well as government buildings and private homes. (Since it would be impossible to list all the merchants and individuals involved in commercial activities on South Main Street, the following are but examples.) Becker's Bank, the Fairport National Bank, and Fairport Savings and Loan provided banking services. Grocery stores included Terpening's, Hart's Food Stores, the Red & White Grocery, the Market Basket, Messerino's Market, and Filkins Meat Market. Irving Bramer and Robert Wagor, among others, ran drug stores. Hardick and Fellows and Wignall and Murphy offered hardware and other necessities. Dobbin and Moore sold lumber as did the Dudley family, who further equipped both professionals and do-it-yourselfers. At various times Drs. Briggs, White, Tubbs, Kraai, Buholtz, and McEachren practiced medicine from their residences on South Main Street. Claude Emery (later Curtis and then Doser) and Howard Root (later Keenan) ran funeral businesses. Drs. Kohler and Reeves, and later Drs. Foster and Pittinaro, provided dental care. Hupp Motors and Church Motors offered new autos and repair for the old ones. Clothing could be bought at Rudin's, the Mayfair Department Store, Smith-Morey's, Saxton's, and the Village Store. The Candy Kitchen offered a place to satisfy both one's sweet tooth and need for camaraderie and could be followed by a movie at Schine's Temple Theater. Shoes could be repaired at Tony's Shoe Store; Quality Cleaners took care of dry cleaning and laundering; Peggy, one of several beauticians, did hair from her shop above Bramer's Drugs, and everything from bedding to televisions could be acquired at C. A. French's. Other businesses and services included lawyers, dressmakers, opticians, barbers, and insurance agencies. Government offices were in the Municipal Building, as were the police offices, the fire department, and the jail. All in all, it was not necessary to go outside the village center to take care of everyday needs.

South Main St., East Side

By the 1960's, the demographics of Fairport and Perinton began to change. Much of the farmland of Perinton was being converted to suburban subdivisions, increasing the population outside the village. The era of the shopping mall was beginning with growth in such areas as the corner of Moseley Road and Pittsford-Palmyra Road. As the 1960's progressed and the country as a whole saw "urban renewal" as the wave of the future, Fairport began to consider removing many of its old buildings and replacing them with new ones.

In the mid 1960's many felt that Fairport's South Main Street was deteriorating and that urban renewal, which would clear out the old and build new, was the answer. Hence the Fairport Urban Renewal Agency was created in 1965. Sometime between then and 1970, a $10 million proposal featuring an elevated highway that would have eliminated the lift bridge and the railroad grade crossing was offered. Shopping areas, or malls, on either side of the highway would have been accessed by means of underground garages or from Perrin Street. Essentially the proposal would have ignored Main Street and the canal. (At the same time, people were proposing that the Erie Canal, which had ceased to be used for commercial traffic, be either sold or filled in). Needless to say, the proposal was controversial and the mayoral election of 1970 turned on the issue. Peter McDonough, a relative newcomer to the village of Fairport and one who opposed the proposal, challenged long time Fairport resident and mayor, Gordon Murphy, and won. The "skyway" proposal was dead, but the issue of urban renewal remained.

West Ave. and South Main St.

In 1972 and shortly thereafter, several significant events occurred. Donald Aures was hired as executive director of the village Urban Renewal Agency and federal funds became available for urban renewal. Grants totaling about $3.1 million were applied for and received. In addition, $500,000 was acquired from the state. The next step was to determine what was going to replace the old Main Street.

The Urban Renewal Agency knew that it did not want a large mall, that it preferred a collection of shops with frontage on Main Street and hidden parking lots. Unfortunately, none of the old buildings were to be saved (a result that probably would not have happened by the 1990's). In 1974, the Agency solicited plans for the area, which the village was in the process of acquiring. The submitted plans, for the most part, were sympathetic to the character of the village, provided for a mix of small shops, a supermarket, parking, and some sort of congregating area. Ultimately, a design submitted by the firm of Barkstrom and LaCroix that incorporated a canal village ambiance won out, and the Village Landing was underway. The developer was Erie Development Associates.

When the Landing opened in 1978, it was fully leased. Tops Friendly Market was an anchor as was the Fairport Public Library. Because of the success of the Village Landing, two years later the development of Packett's Landing commenced and it opened in 1982.

In the years since the opening of the Village Landing, there have been numerous changes. Most of the original stores and store owners have changed; the library, however, has prospered and grown, taking over the space that originally opened as Rose Cali's Restaurant. Tops was replaced by Vix. As of 2010, part of that space is occupied by the Dollar Store and part awaits a new tenant. Kennelley Park, named after former Village mayor and life-long resident of Fairport Vincent Kennelley, is a small area and gazebo by the canal that has been the location of a very popular summer concert series. Fairport's June festival, Canal Days, brings thousands to this canal village. Enhancements to the canal frontage with docking facilities and amenities for boaters have further added to the canal village ambiance.

South Main Street combines old and new. Certainly many of the buildings are new, as are their uses. Gone are many of the goods and services that used to be available. They have moved to Wegmans, Home Depot, Walmart and Eastview Mall. Shops are now directed more to the tourist and the casual shopper looking for that unique gift or antique rather than to the family looking for milk and a new pair of socks. On the other hand, Main Street has preserved some of the old village services like the library and village offices. The famous lift bridge and the railroad grade crossing remain. Visitors can still walk the towpath or enjoy a cruise on the Erie Canal, which continues to be the central element of the village just as it has been since the 1820's.

Traditionally, North Main Street has had a different focus and personality than South Main Street. In addition to the usual mix of groceries and dry goods stores, North Main has been the industrial center of the village as well as the area that catered to travelers with inns, hotels, and bars. It was also the street where Fairport's first industrialists, the DeLand family, built their homes.

The Erie Canal and the New York Central Railroad, joined at the turn of the twentieth century by the R.S. & E. Interurban Electric Trolley, spurred the demand for hotels and taverns. Fairport's first tavern was supposedly built by Cyrenus Mallett and his friends in three days. The hotel was run by Theron Pritchard during the second half of the nineteenth century and by E. J. Cary until its conversion to apartments and storefront shops some time around 1920. Clyde Kelsey's newsstand and Hawk's Restaurant were fixtures for many years in two of the storefront locations, which, as of 2010, still house a series of small businesses. The Cottage Hotel, which stood on the corner on North Main and State Street, was the second of North Main's major hotels. Built in 1886, it served as a hotel even into the 1960's. It was also a popular night spot with a live orchestra and two dance floors. Unfortunately, a fire destroyed the structure in 1968 and the remains were razed.

Ryan's Bar in the Osburn House

A line of bars and small hotels ran between 25 and 49 North Main Street. Today that area features Riki's, Short's Bar and Tanglefoot's. In former days, Riki's was known as the Fairport Lunch Hotel. Scribner's Store, where area farmers could purchase liquor by the gallon and, rumor had it, have a massage courtesy of Mrs. Scribner, subsequently became Blum's Bar and then Short's Bar. The old

Kirkwood Hotel, located at 39 North Main Street, featured Fogarty's Bar in addition to lodging. That building served many years as Mueller's and then as Prinzivalli's Market and was an antique store before burning down in the 1960's. The Lucas Hotel and Sam Saporito's restaurant were next door, located in the vicinity of today's Tanglefoot's.

Across the railroad tracks was the elegant Osburn House, a three story hotel. At one time the home of the Fairport Grange, the hotel was closed and the space converted to the offices of the Fairport Oil Company, a full-service facility complete with gas pumps in the 1920's. In 1938 that building was razed and replaced by a concrete block building housing an Amoco station. As of 2010, the Higher Ground Café occupies the site.

The DeLand Chemical Company, manufacturers of baking soda and related products, put Fairport on the industrial map in the 1880's. The factory was located on Main Street just north of the lift bridge on the site of today's Box Factory complex, and occupied much of the space between the Main Street and the Parker Street bridges. The New York State Fruit Company, then Douglass Packing, manufacturers of Certo, followed the DeLand Chemical Company on the site. The Trescott Company, fruit and vegetable dryers and graders, located just north of the railroad tracks, and the Taylor Company, producers of Taylor's "Oil of Life" patent medicine, located on the southeast corner of North Main and High Streets, were two other early industries located on North Main Street. The Sanitary Can Company, which became the American Can Company and was the major employer in town from the early twentieth century through the 1950's, was located on Parce Avenue, just off North Main. These concerns relied first on the canal and then strongly on the railroad to transport their goods.

Both the Rochester, Syracuse, and Eastern Interurban Trolley and the New York Central Railroad had stations on or near North Main Street. After the demise of the trolley, the station served as a gas station for a number of years, for a time run by Albert Knapp, than as an office, and currently as the home of Sew Creative. The railroad had a passenger station just east of North Main Street on Railroad Street and a freight depot on the west side of North Main. Neither of these buildings exists today.

Even though North Main Street was the industrial and transportation side of town, small commercial concerns included Barranco's clothing; John Beard's shaving parlor, advertising shampoo, fine hair cuts and massage; Pomponio's Barber Shop; the Welkley dairy; Philips chicken hatchery; and an early office of the *Fairport Herald* located along the east side of North Main. (Since it would not be possible to mention every business or resident of North Main Street, these are but examples). Barranco's is still there, as is today's version of a barber shop, Strand's Hair Studio. The dairy and the *Fairport Herald* are gone, and the chicken hatchery is now Recreational Vehicles. Dewey Jackson, who supplied coal to many village and town residents, had his office and tall coal storage facility next to the Cottage Hotel in a building that had originally housed George Fellows' carriage business. The Jackson building now houses a dry cleaning business, but the coal tower and the Cottage Hotel are gone.

Several car dealerships and repair shops were also located on North Main Street. The Fairport Gas and Oil Company repaired and sold autos. The Wheeler Chevrolet Corporation worked out of what is now J & P Upholstery. Lombardi's is a converted garage.

Grocery stores on North Main Street included Mueller's and then Prinzivalli's in the former Kirkwood Hotel. McBride's and Messerino's were located in the Chase block, which burned in 1977 and was replaced by the Fairport Animal Hospital. Biancucci's Meat Market occupied space at 114 North Main.

The Sugar Bowl, located next to the old trolley station (Sew Creative) was a spot for teens to congregate from the 1930's through the mid 1960's. The Oasis (the present Village Inn), and the Soda Bar, located at 112 North Main (Wind Sensations flag store) were two other popular places to get a simple meal and listen to the jukebox. Dessert was just across the street at Fiandack's ice cream and confectionary.

Village Inn 1931

The upper portion of North Main Street was, and still is, primarily residential. Daniel B. DeLand and his wife Minerva, founders of the DeLand Chemical Company, lived at 185 North Main, a house they built in 1856. The property included a large area devoted to rare trees, shrubs, and flowers. After Minerva DeLand's death in 1902, a portion of the land was offered to the village of Fairport as a park. However, the offer was declined and the area was subsequently developed as the residential streets of DeLand Park A and B. Minerva's brother Joseph Parce, who was also involved with the DeLand business, lived in a large house on the corner of Parce Avenue and North Main Street. The house sat on a large plot which was used for gardens and a nursery. The property was long ago developed for homes and the house is now used for apartments and small businesses. The professional/office building at 149 North Main was once the site of another DeLand home that belonged to Daniel and Minerva's daughter Leora and her family. It burned in 1968. Across the street at 176 North Main is Levi DeLand's first house, which his mother, Minerva, sold to him for $1.00. Levi, his wife and five children eventually moved to a large mansion on the corner of North Main Street and Whitney Road, which became the first Fairport Baptist Home. It was replaced by a large double-wing addition to the Home in the early 1970's. An imposing brick Italianate house belonging to the Higbie family was situated on the corner of Main and East, a location now occupied by a gas station. Several homes on North Main were designed to emulate the homes of the elite, sporting mansard roofs and turrets; others were the more standard front-gabled, side ell style prevalent in early residential areas of the village.

Both South and North Main Streets reflect the history of the village from the early days of Erie Canal travel to the heyday of industry, with the DeLand Chemical Company and American Can Company, to the tourism and recreational emphasis of the twenty-first century. They reflect the change in village business from grocery store to specialty gourmet shop, from coal and oil providers to antique sellers and trendy eating places. Main Street from north to south continues to be a vital and thriving part of the village.

An Overview of West Avenue

For over a century, Fairport's West Avenue was a mixture of commercial and residential properties. Commercial enterprises covered a wide spectrum of needs, and due to the street's proximity to the center of the village and the nineteenth century practice of living over or near one's business, area merchants, professionals and other workers lived either where their businesses were located or in the adjacent residential parts of streets like West Avenue. The street originally went from its intersection with South Main Street to West Street. Later it was extended to just beyond Cole Street. Finally it went all the way to Nelson Street. Because of the extensive cherry orchards on the Chadwick property, the site of today's Packett's Glen, it was formerly known as Cherry Street.

Clockwise from top left: Murdoff's store, South side of West Ave., Pool Hall, Hardware store looking east.

The east end of Cherry Street/West Avenue bustled with commercial activity well into the mid twentieth century. Hardick and Fellows' general merchandise store was on the north corner with Bramer's Drug Store opposite. The Hardick and Fellows store was dismantled and moved when the canal was widened in 1912 and part of the building was moved to Roselawn Avenue where it still stands. Bramer's Drug Store was razed when the Village Landing was built in the 1970's and West Avenue was closed off from South Main Street.

A hardware store occupied a series of three buildings on the north side of the street. It was first opened by Fred Schummers in 1890, sold to John Bahler in 1919, and lastly was run by Lin Bruening before being razed in 1975. The One Horse Grocery and the Hollender and Scoville Grocery served patrons' food needs as did Lieb's Bakery and George Peters' Meat Market. There were a harness shop, a dress shop, a hat shop, a tailor shop, a barber shop, a dentist's office, and a laundry. The *Fairport Herald* had an office at number 30. A pool hall, Shaw's Hall, which provided a venue for speakers and eventually for movies, and Oakland Pontiac (Tabberah Motors), which became Carlton Clifford's Fairport Motors, found homes on West Avenue. The library found a temporary home there before moving to the Perrin Street location. The telephone company had a building at number 56 in a building that still stands, and in 1924, the new Fairport High School opened just down the street. Clearly those who lived in the vicinity did not have far to go for necessities or even recreation. Unfortunately all the commercial buildings on the south side of the street were lost to urban renewal and only two remain on the north side, including part of the Schummers block, the former home of the Clifford auto business, and the telephone company building.

150 West Ave.

Beyond Perrin Street, West Avenue became primarily residential. Chauncey King built 62 West Avenue as a one-story house sometime between 1845 and 1851. Jeremiah Chadwick's large Greek revival brick house stood at number 71. The site was subsequently sold to the Schummers family and then to the Fairport Union School, which used the house as a grammar school until it was razed in 1924 for the building of the new Fairport High School. Built by Jacob Hardick between 1849 and 1854, the house at 79 West Avenue has lovely Greek Revival detailing. Originally 94 West Avenue was at the end of Cherry Street, but it was turned ninety degrees and moved back when the street was lengthened. Most likely the old foundation still exists under West Avenue. One of few brick houses in Fairport village, the Italianate-style house at #83 was built by G.L.C. Seeley, a pioneer in the area's hardware business. It still features a mounting block and hitching posts in the front.

Looking down the street from the West Avenue School building, one sees a number of vernacular Greek-Revival inspired houses, each with a front gable and a side wing that is often a porch, sometimes enclosed, and sometimes with an added second story. Residents of West Avenue included the Hupps of Hupp Motors (and Hupp Drugs), Mr. Swift who had a gravestone business, Dr. Briggs and Dr. Whitney, Dewey Jackson of the coal company, the Wignalls, who ran a hardware store, Gordon Kellogg who was a manager at the Sanitary Can Company, and many others who were salesmen, bookkeepers, carpenters, can makers, and teachers, all of whom added to the vibrant mix of people in the village of Fairport on West Avenue.

Today, while no longer a commercial center, West Avenue remains one of Fairport's historic residential areas.

Deland Chemical Company

"DeLand's Chemical Baking powder is a strictly pure *powder,* and as we manufacture our Soda expressly for it, and as it is put together on chemical principles, we claim it has no equal on the market. Try It! Test It! and you will use no other." This ad from the 1870's touts a product that, according to a local Rochester paper, was responsible for the prosperity, if not the existence, of the village of Fairport.

DeLand Factory

As a young man, Daniel DeLand, one of Levi DeLand's fifteen children, left his Budlong Road home to seek his fortune at sea. In 1848, having returned to New York as a canal boat captain, he met and married Minerva Parce, who had been a passenger on his boat. After several years on the frontier in Wisconsin, the couple moved back to Norwich, New York, where Justus Parce, Minerva's father, ran an ashery. It was at this point that the events that would lead to the DeLand fortune and the industrial development of Fairport began. Daniel became an apprentice at the Parce ashery where he learned the process of leaching out potash to manufacture saleratus, or baking soda, as it is known today.

Deland Workmen

The manufacture of saleratus and other soda products made use of an abundant commodity, hardwood ash, which was left as farmers burned trees and shrubs after clearing their land. The ashes were purchased by potash makers for between six and eight dollars per acre, put in wooden barrels, and mixed with lime. Water was slowly poured over the mixture, which leached out a yellowish liquid, lye. After the liquid was boiled away in an iron pot, sediment, literally "pot ash," remained. The potash was refined in a furnace until it turned into white "pearl ash." This ash was mixed with carbonic acid, creating saleratus or baking soda, a powder indispensable not only to bakers, but also to most homemakers.

In 1852 Daniel and Minerva moved to Fairport and started their own "Mom and Pop" saleratus operation. Daniel collected hardwood ashes from area farms, and with help from Minerva and several others he undertook the production of saleratus in his home. The final product was wrapped and packaged in the family pantry. The first year's sales were about $1,000. At that time, only one other American company was producing saleratus. John Dwight of Massachusetts had started producing Cow Brand Soda in 1846.

In 1853, Henry DeLand, Daniel's brother, joined the company as a salesman. Due in part to his vigorous advertising and strong salesmanship, as well as a strong demand, the company sales soon expanded to $9,000 a year. The soda was marketed as "Cap Sheaf Soda." Two logos were used, either a sheaf of wheat or a lion rolling a barrel. By 1854, the company had outgrown the house and moved into a factory of several large buildings on North Main and State Streets next to the canal. Business continued to boom.

The 1870's was a peak period for the company and also a time of change. By 1872 the business was worth about $250,000 and was providing goods to most of the states and territories. Like much of American industry, the DeLand Chemical Company continued to expand and refine production. Elevators were installed in the plant, as was electricity when it became available. Minerva's brother, Joseph Y. Parce, developed a joined arm or double crane that was used to move goods and equipment. Steam engines were used. Boys and girls were hired to do some of the more menial work. Boys could earn two to three dollars a week preparing trays to dry the chemicals. Girls were hired to pack the soda in one pound packages that were packed sixty to a box. By 1876 the company was selling approximately 80,000 boxes per year. In 1874, 100 workers were employed at the chemical plant and sales were over $500,000. After Daniel's untimely death in 1872 as a result of falling down an elevator shaft, his brother Henry took over the job of president. Later in that decade, Levi Justice, Daniel's son, joined the firm and the name was changed to the H.A. and L.J. DeLand and Company.

DeLand Fire, 1893

The 1890's was a difficult economic decade for many Americans and the DeLands were no exception. In 1893 a disastrous fire destroyed the DeLand Company plant. Not even the DeLand Hose Company, which Daniel's son Levi had started, could check the damage. Although the plant was rebuilt, the economic depression of the early 1890's, continuing competition from companies like Arm & Hammer and Cow Brand, and rising costs, prevented the DeLand Chemical Company from achieving its former glory. The company closed its doors in 1903. The buildings were sold in 1904 to the New York State Fruit Company, which manufactured vinegar and cider. The company subsequently was absorbed by the Douglass Packing Co., which by the 1920's was producing pectin, called Certo, for use in jelly and jam making. The pectin business was sold to General Foods in 1928. Operations continued in Fairport until 1948 when the complex of buildings was sold to the Neun Box Company. When the box company moved further up North Main Street in the 1980's, the entire complex of buildings along the canal that had been the source of much of Fairport's industrial development, was renovated to house a variety of businesses and services. Today, the area is the center of a revitalized canal front and downtown area.

Banking In Perinton & Fairport

In an age of bank cards, ATMs, electronic funds transfer, and on-line banking, it is hard to imagine an age when not only were there no credit cards or banks, but paper money was rare and often worthless. In the late 1700's and during most of the antebellum period, each state had its own currency and banking system, and transactions were often based on the barter system. "Banks" might be mere storefronts where one or more people with currency would lend it out and collect interest. There were few rules and certainly no protection for the consumer. The National Banking Act of 1863 and the Federal Reserve Act of 1913 dealt with the problems of multiple state bank notes, over-expanded credit, an inelastic currency, and inadequate bank reserves in order to control wild swings in the economy. New Deal reforms, such as the Federal Deposit Insurance Corporation, continued to add to the protections and controls that would eventually lead to a stable banking system and currency, and a strong, vibrant, and dominating economy.

The first bank to be chartered in western New York was the Ontario Bank of Canandaigua, which opened in 1813, primarily to handle the many land transactions that were taking place as a result of the Phelps and Gorham Purchase. The log cabin land office in Canandaigua needed somewhere to put the money they were collecting for land sales and the property tax. Rochester chartered its first bank in 1824. Bank loans became more important as the Erie Canal was bringing more business to the area. In addition, most farmers worked on a narrow cash margin, often needing loans after bad years. In 1831 Rochester opened its first savings bank, the first one west of the Hudson River.

In Perinton, as in many early settlements, pioneers had little or no cash, but kept what they had hidden or buried close by. Most transactions used the barter system. It is likely that the first "bankers" in the area were members of the Ellsworth family. They loaned seed corn and farm equipment to fellow settlers in exchange for services or other goods.

Virtually no evidence of an actual bank in Perinton occurs until the 1870's. Two cancelled checks dated 1870 and 1872 that have "Bank of Fairport" printed on them are in the historian's collection. It is also known that a Henry Wolcott was a bank teller at approximately the same time. In 1876, Jeremiah Chadwick and DeWitt Becker advertised "produce and banking" at their Cherry Street store near the canal. (Cherry Street was the former name for West Avenue). After the death of Chadwick in 1886, DeWitt Becker discontinued the produce business and moved "Becker's Private Bank" to 36 South Main Street.

Becker was known as a "sound and reliable financier" and his bank, the only one in town, was the depository for residents as well as for village, town, and school tax money. Expenses were drawn from these accounts; a 1902 receipt shows $6.25 in library money for District School #5 in Perinton. Another notes a refund for a"$2.00 dog tax charged to me for a dog belonging to someone else." Yet another reads "Please pay to bearer, William J. Butler, bridge tender on the new lift bridge over the Erie Canal in the town of Perinton the sum of Forty Dollars on account of services rendered. Signed Charles Butler, Town Clerk." In addition to banking, Becker was involved in other businesses and local politics. He invested in Reed Underwear Company and Dudley & Company, manufacturers of Napoleon Brand Baking Powder. He also served as town Supervisor and in the State Assembly. Unfortunately, DeWitt Becker died unexpectedly in 1916. On March 8, he returned from work, complained of indigestion and was dead before the doctor arrived. Although his obituary noted that he was "interested financially in many of the industries of Fairport and had amassed a considerable fortune," his depositors were not quite so lucky. Until the 1930's, banks were only as dependable as the owner/manager who invested the deposits and otherwise managed the money; there was no insurance or protection for the customers. When Becker died, the bank closed and failed leaving the depositors with only their bank books. Among numerous losses, the Boy Scouts lost $5, a local dentist $50, and the Fairport Board of Education $3,000, earmarked for teachers' salaries.

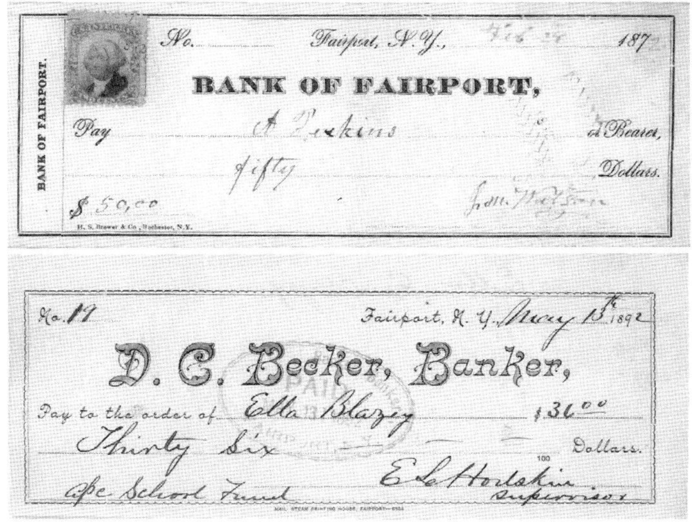

Early checks; 1872 (top), 1892 (bottom)

For the four months after the closing of Becker's Bank, residents had to travel to East Rochester or the city of Rochester to do their commercial banking. Commercial banks handled checking accounts, commercial business and business loans, and usually the town and village accounts.

Savings banks were known as "thrift institutions" and handled savings accounts and home mortgages. It was common for citizens to have accounts at both kinds of banks. Fairport's first "thrift institution" opened in 1888 and was called the Fairport Permanent Loan Company. Martin Gannon, who was the supervisor of the Cox Shoe Factory on North Main Street and would serve as president of the new bank, began by depositing $2 per week. His stated goals were to promote thrift through systematic savings and to help home ownership in town through an amortization mortgage plan. Close to sixty residents soon followed his lead and opened accounts in the new bank. Within a year, the bank was able to issue its first mortgage, to C. W. Rood. In 1938, during the presidency of William Beeton, who served for about fifty years, the bank moved to its present location at 45 South Main Street and changed its name to Fairport Savings and Loan Association. The building, which had been owned by Carlton Clifford's Fairport Motors, was renovated and remodeled. A 1925 article about Beeton notes that "his careful study, good judgment, and wise guidance made the association a leader among loan associations in the state." It seems that continuity has been part of the history of this bank, because the subsequent president, Stanley Peacock, was also with the organization for over fifty years, first serving as secretary-treasurer and then as president. The "Loan", as it has often been familiarly called, changed its name to Fairport Savings Bank, and has added checking accounts, bank cards, an ATM machine, internet access, and a branch office while still maintaining an atmosphere of a friendly, local bank.

The Fairport National Bank, a commercial bank, had its start in 1916 in the Schummer's block on West Avenue, shortly after the demise of Becker's Bank. It opened with $50,000 in capital stock, $5,000 in its reserve fund, a three-ton safe, and four departments. Officers were president Frank Shepard and Vice-President James George; George Mulliner, who had worked for Becker's Bank, was the cashier. Security in the bank, according to one story, consisted of each teller keeping a gun under his desk. Apparently, practice shooting was done out in back over the canal. The institution prospered, making six percent interest on its loans, and was able to move to its new building at 58 South Main Street eight years after opening

The elegant new Fairport National Bank was built in the Italian Renaissance style of brick and granite. The structure radiated security and permanence, important in a time when bank failures were common and uninsured. The bank vault was surrounded by twenty-seven inch thick walls, reinforced with twenty tons of railroad steel rails, and lined with steel. The vault door weighed ten tons, was seventeen and a half inches thick, and was secured by twenty control bolts and two combination locks. The directors met on the mezzanine, the tellers had properly screened cages, and there was a private room for ladies' banking. In addition the bank was protected by a burglar alarm system that relied on a fifty-five pound brass gong.

While still a bank, its name has changed a number of times. The first change came in 1944 when the Fairport National Bank & Trust Company and the Pittsford National Bank merged to become the Security Trust Company of Rochester. After Security Trust there were several more mergers and changes, and as of 2011, the bank is part of the Bank of America conglomerate.

The changes in banking, especially with the advent of computerization and the globalization of the economy, have resulted in a number of other financial institutions opening in the community. Changes in regulations have nearly erased the differences between commercial and savings banks. Not of the least of these changes have been the creation and expansion of credit unions. One, the Fairport Federal Credit Union, is located next door to the Fleet Bank.

Today, banking institutions are concerned with computer problems that cannot be protected by fifty-five pound burglar alarm gongs or twenty-seven inch thick steel walls of a vault. Customers have a variety of ways to access their accounts as well as to spend and pay. In today's world, our funds are numbers on a page or a computer screen more often than they are coins or bills in our wallets, and banking can be done without ever visiting an actual bank or talking to a teller. Nevertheless, here in Perinton and Fairport, despite the convenience of the ATM and online banking, banking institutions continue to provide personal services and a small town atmosphere.

The G.C. Taylor Company

The use of patent medicines grew throughout the nineteenth century as Americans rebelled against doctors and wholeheartedly embraced natural, American-made, often quack, cures. There is evidence that the expansion of the patent medicine business owed at least part of its success to the growing number of daily newspapers which relied on advertising revenue to remain solvent. The sensational claims of these medicines paralleled the sensational bent of the stories that appeared in the papers. "Lydia Pinkham's Vegetable Compound" was the first to use extensive advertising and became the most successful patent medicine of the century. Like many of these remedies, it contained primarily alcohol, vegetable extracts, and sugars. The medicines might also contain such ingredients as cocaine, opium, or morphine. The Sears catalog sold a morphine-based medicine that could be slipped into a wayward husband's coffee in order to keep him home at night. Bored housewives and the homebound elderly were often susceptible to addiction from the cocaine in many of the remedies. Fear, superstition, and the urge to find a miracle cure for everything contributed to the popularity of the drugs.

Ask your Merchant for it. Put up in large, small and medium bottles. If not satisfactory get your money back.

George C. Taylor, taking advantage of that popularity, brought what would become a successful patent medicine business to Fairport in 1866. Soon after, in 1871, he established the *Fairport Herald* that he used to promote not only the village of Fairport, but also his "Oil of Life" patent medicine manufactured by his company, the G.C. Taylor Company.

Published as well were specific instructions as to how to use the oil externally, internally, and on horses and cattle. For burns, one was to "apply at once, and keep from the air..." For rheumatism: "It should be well bathed with it hot, and take a half teaspoonful every twelve hours, and in most all cases relief is certain when all others fail." For coughs and colds: "Take in sugar, or molasses; or sweet milk, from ten drops, to a half-teaspoonful twice or three times a day after eating, and at night before going to bed." The oil was also used to treat horses and cattle. For a horse's bruises and sprains "It should be heated in, or applied hot." For horn distemper in cattle "Rub it between the horns, and put about a teaspoonful in each ear and give internally one ounce." Clearly, this was an all-purpose medicine.

In 1873, due to the growing success of his product, George Taylor built a brick building at the corner of North Main and High Streets in the village of Fairport. His prosperous business required several additions to the original building, including an annex that contained a "commodious, convenient laboratory, operated by steam power." He expanded production to include flavoring extracts, laudanum, paregoric, perfume, cordials, cough syrup, beef iron, breath sweeteners, and wine. His "energetic management" and the "unfailing medicinal properties of (the) products" were the keys to his business success. In 1888, he received a letter of endorsement from William F. (Buffalo Bill) Cody, who wrote, "during our recent ocean trip…it [the Oil of Life] was indispensable." He requested that the company "forward me 18 large bottles immediately" and he promised to "remit upon receipt of invoice."

George Taylor died in 1909, but the business continued to prosper. By the next decade the product line included household ammonia, bluing for the family laundry, and Tayco Soap Powder. During the 1920's, however, the company ran into some trouble with the newly vigilant Food and Drug Administration. In a letter dated April 22, 1929, the FDA noted that Taylor's Oil of Life, which consisted mainly of cod liver oil, turpentine, and oil of thyme, advertised cures which were "beyond the therapeutic limitations of the ingredients." In the view of the FDA, the product was mislabeled "practically in its entirety." In a subsequent letter, the FDA stated that the "reference to 'Life' in the trade name is objectionable" and also wished to call attention to the possibility that the product could cause nephritis due to its turpentine content. Despite these difficulties, Taylor's products continued to be manufactured throughout the 1930's and 40's, and at that time also included such items as shampoo, wave set, facial creams, toothpaste, and the all-purpose Taylor's liniment as well as the previously mentioned products.

A change came in 1942 when Albert Van Wiegen, president of the Gundlach Manufacturing Company on South Main Street in Fairport, purchased the business. Van Wiegen and Emmett Myers, who was the manager of the G.C. Taylor Company, started an expansion program to specifically promote Taylor's Oil of Life and Liniment. Apparently that effort was unsuccessful, because by 1946 the company was listed as selling only drug sundries, and in 1954 the Taylor Company was closed down and the plant space used by Gundlach Manufacturing.

The draw of the cure-all patent medicine, however, is not completely dead. Remnants might seem to linger today, for example, in publications such as *The Old Farmer's Almanac,* in the natural remedies and food supplement aisles in the supermarket and in on-line advertisements.

The Business of Canning

For centuries, people had tried to find ways to preserve food, and up until the nineteenth century the only effective methods had been salting, pickling, or smoking, and then storing the food in wide-mouth glass or ceramic containers. According to one source, Napoleon's army had lost many of its men to malnutrition, and in 1795, the French government offered a reward to anyone who could devise a method for preserving meats, fish, fruits, and vegetables. Nicolas Appert won the prize by packing fresh meats and produce in glass jars, closing them with corks, fastening the corks with wire, and boiling the jars to sterilize the contents. Thus the foundation was laid for a canning industry. In the United States, William (or Peter) Durand applied for a patent for a "sealed vessel of tin plate and metal for preserving food" in 1810. Although the early cans were crude and there was much spoilage, the move toward a safe and efficient method of preserving foods was underway.

The middle of the nineteenth century saw a boom in the cannery business. In 1853, Gail Borden perfected the manufacture of condensed milk packed in cap hole cans. Gilbert Van Camp began to can fruits and vegetables. The first activities that directly led to Fairport's canning industry began in 1851 when Ezra and Ananias Edgett canned the first corn in Camden, New York. Ezra spent some time in New York City learning the canning trade, and then returned to Camden where in 1858 he opened canning operations in the family barn. In 1866, he moved his business to Newark, New York, an area with richer soil and more diversified crops. There he established the very successful Wayne Preserving Company.

Six years later, in 1872, Edgett opened a branch of his canning business in Fairport, hiring his brother Ananias to run the operation. An 1873 news article describes the "First Canning Works," an eight-acre plot located on the south bank of the canal east of the Turk Hill Road bridge. The main two-story building was 118 by 30 feet and had two one-story additions. The ground floor of this structure was a general work area where the fruit was received, sorted, and put into the cans and sealed on several tables that ran the length of the room. The next stop was the steaming room where the cans were placed in vats and processed. If the cans retained their shape after cooling, they went to a third room, and were labeled and boxed for shipment. The local firm of Green, Simmons, & McAuliffe manufactured the boxes. Upstairs in the main building was the tin shop where the cans and also the solder were manufactured. In 1873, the shop used 500 boxes of tin, 3,500 to 4,000 pounds of solder, and manufactured about 150,000 cans.

Cobb's Office

Ezra Edgett was not satisfied with the job that his brother Ananias was doing as plant manager, so he persuaded his cousin Amos Cobb to buy the business and move to Fairport and run it. Cobb was familiar with the food industry, having worked at Kemp and Day Co., food brokers, in New York City, and also having run his own food importing business, Goodwin, Cobb, & Company. Cobb agreed to the deal, and in 1881, Amos, his wife Angeline Hodgeman, his daughter Angie, and his four sons, Frederick, George, Clarence, and Amos, Jr. moved to a house on the corner of East Church Street and Turk Hill Road in Fairport. Ananias Edgett went on to start the Thomas Canning Factory in 1896, located at the corner of Parker and State (Lift Bridge Lane) Streets.

The newly named Cobb's Preserving Company did very well, canning cherries, berries, pears, peaches, quinces, plums, peas, and succotash. Initially, it was all hand labor. Winters were spent crafting the cans from tin plate and soldering the parts together to form sealed cans. A small hole, probably 1½ inches in diameter, was cut in the top of the can where the produce would be inserted – hence the term "cap hole" cans. During the canning season the produce was sorted and prepared by hand. Sometimes a portion of the produce was dropped off at private homes where a whole family would participate in the food preparation. The company then picked up the prepared food the following day and proceeded with the canning process. That process consisted of forcing the fruits and vegetables through the 1 ½ inch hole in the top of the can, sealing up the hole with solder and a small cap, and placing the cans in a hot water bath for a period of time. The cans were stored to see if the process had been successful. If not, the cans that bulged were quietly slipped into the canal, while the good ones were shipped out. The canning process was obviously not yet refined. There was considerable spoilage. Canned goods that were not spoiled still were likely to have bits of solder in them, the fruits and vegetables were often shredded from being forced through the hole, and there was discoloration from the solder as well.

By the late 1890's, the search was on for a more efficient and generally better way to can food than in "cap-hole" cans. George Cobb, Amos Cobb's son, was particularly interested in the possibility of an open top can that could be sealed without solder or acid, and he proceeded to experiment with such a can at the East Church Street plant.

During the same time period, Max Ams and his partner Julius Brenzinger were working to refine a new process of canning, using ideas that had been developed in Europe. Ams had first obtained a patent for the manufacture of hermetically sealed tin-plated cans in which he packed Russian caviar, and he was working with Brenzinger to refine the process. Max Ams' preserving company was not far from the New York City offices of Charles Bogle, a fancy food importer and a man with money to invest, and who was an acquaintance of George Cobb. Eventually, George Cobb was able to interest both Bogle and Ams to join with him in the further development and refinement of the new can. This new can was made of tin plate imported from Wales, and with the use of Brenzinger's double-seaming machine that crimped the end and the can body together in five thicknesses, gave an airtight seal without the use of solder. The era of the open top can was at hand.

American Can Company office circa 1908

George prevailed upon his father Amos to try the new procedure, and in 1898 a line of the new cans was delivered to the Fairport plant. The cans were filled with pears and processed in the usual manner. Despite the explosion of a few of the cans, the experiment was a success. By the following year, a full line of the Ams machinery was at work in the Fairport plant. Nevertheless, the going was not altogether smooth during those experimental years. Workers did not always fully understand the new process and they certainly were not experienced in the use of the new machines and many spoiled cans ended up in the canal as a result. A disastrous pack of Bartlett pears in 1903 nearly led to the end of the new process, but it only resulted in a gentlemanly disagreement over who was at fault, the new can or the Cobb family. As far as consumers were concerned, they noticed with pleasure that black specks and bits of solder had disappeared, along with mashed and lacerated fruit that had been the result of stuffing the produce through the small hole in the top of the old cans.

With the success of the "ABC" team of Ams, Bogle, and Cobb, the experimental stage ended and the age of open top sanitary cans arrived with the organization in 1904 of the Sanitary Can Company. Charles Bogle was installed as President, Frederick Cobb as Vice-President, George Cobb as Secretary-Treasurer, and Max Ams as a director. The new company, with the help of the Fairport Permanent Loan Association, opened in the former Cox Shoe Factory building on Parce Avenue. The canning machinery was moved from the East Church Street plant and Charles Ayers also installed side-seaming machinery. As the process of can making became more and more mechanical, and the open-top or sanitary can became the standard, food would never again be packed in containers that were not airtight and bits of solder would no longer be found among canned fruits and vegetables. With mechanization, the process was constantly being speeded up. The production of twenty-five thousand cans was considered good for a ten-hour day, and in 1904, the company manufactured and shipped six million cans.

Meanwhile, the old factory continued to be used as a canning facility for several more years, and according to a 1904 news article, there were plans for additions to the facility. It was about this time, as well, that the first migrant workers were brought into town to work in the factory. Polish families from Buffalo were transported to Fairport and housed in three or four wooden sheds located along the towpath across from the canning factory. When canning activities eventually ceased at that site, the buildings were used for storage by the American Can Company.

American Can Co. factory at Parce Ave. & Elm Street

The American Can Company, having been organized in 1901 by the amalgamation of a number of can companies, absorbed the Sanitary Can Company in 1908, partly in reaction to the Panic of 1907. Both Charles Bogle and George Cobb continued on with the new company in their New York offices.

The can company, often referred to as Canco, quickly became a major employer in the village, having about 250 workers in 1908. During the first half of the twentieth century, the company continued to expand and innovate. Millions of cans for the World War I American Expeditionary Force in Europe were produced, and soon thereafter, in 1921, the "c-enamel" can that kept high sulfur foods from discoloring was introduced. In the 1930's beer cans were developed, and studies began on the production of sterile paper containers for milk and milk products. Tomato juice and other fruit juices were successfully canned. World War II brought new challenges. Instead of food cans, Canco began producing containers for explosives, signal flares, First Aid utensils, ammunition, and blood plasma. In 1943 alone, the company produced 4,000,000 blood plasma cans and was credited with solving the packaging problem associated with safe transportation of plasma to the front lines.

During the boom period of the 1950's, Canco underwent significant expansion. With an average work force of 560 people and 150 customers, the company produced ninety types of cans, and, at peak capacity, was capable of turning out up to 4,000,000 cans in twenty-four hours. It was estimated that in 1952, thirty percent of the Fairport village population was in some way dependent on Canco money. Continuing the tradition of innovation, Canco introduced efficient methods of lithographing cans, and built a new 300-foot long L-shaped building in the early 1950's for the lithographing and enameling processes. During World War II the company had had to reduce the amount of tin used in cans because the primary sources of tin from Southeast Asia had been cut off. By 1950, the amount of tin had been reduced by one-third and the amount of solder used in the side seams had been reduced by three-quarters. In addition, the new types of enamel used in the cans not only preserved the color but also extended the shelf life of many products.

In the 1950's the can created markets for food and non-food products that had not existed before. For example, beer can sales mounted into the billions as the general public bought beer for the home. Coffee sales boomed when the vacuum can for ground coffee was developed. Petroleum and chemical products for industry became readily available in tin cans or paper containers. In fact, the production of vegetable and fruit cans declined as the demand for beverage cans, cans for oil products, and pressure cans for deodorants increased. A list of "Canco Firsts" is found in a Canco publication of 1951. These include, among others, salt containers with spouts, sliding lid spice cans, oblong asparagus cans, frozen food containers, cans for film, and tennis ball cans. The smallest can produced was a bird biscuit can for R.T. French, which was about two-thirds the size of a box of matches, and the largest a gallon or hotel-sized container for fruits and vegetables. As the 50's progressed, literally the entire can-making process became automated, from cutting to carrying the cans to the freight cars for packing.

American Can Co. (CanCo) assembly line

People who worked at the can company in the 1950's and into the 1960's were often the second or third generation of their family to be employed there. Don Hull, a Canco retiree, recalled a family atmosphere where people worked their way up from stacking cans in the railroad cars to positions of foreman and superintendent, and where over ten percent of the employees had been with the company for at least twenty-five years. Many of the employees during that time were of Italian or Sicilian descent or were people who had grown up on farms, knowing, as Don Hull put it, both how to work and how to use their hands. It was also a time when the sons and daughters of the employees could count on summer jobs that worked them hard, sometimes up to sixty hours per week, but also made it possible for them to earn the necessary money to pursue their education. It was a time when there seemed to be a sense of mutual loyalty between worker and boss. It was a time when employees worked extra hours because that was what everyone did out of a sense of community and responsibility, and there was the feeling that that sense of community loyalty was reciprocal. Frank Fargnoli, who grew up near the Parce Avenue plant, remembered that the kids in the neighborhood would go to the plant nurse for checkups and treatment of minor ailments. Canco, in the words of one retiree, was "...a backbone of Fairport, there was no other major industry."

"Canco" continued to expand and diversify through the 1960's and into the 1970's. In the 1960's a giant coil processing line went into operation. Instead of delivering the raw material for the cans in sheets, it arrived in huge rolls weighing up to 20,000 pounds. The coil unwound at speeds of over 300 feet per minute and was cut into three-by-three foot sheets prior to being printed, cut, and formed into cans. The company now controlled the process from raw material through finished can, which guaranteed greater efficiency and better quality. Further, by the early 1960's, aluminum cans had replaced the traditional tin.

By the mid 1960's, like many corporations in the country, American Can had expanded into six large divisions. The Canco Division, the company's largest, operated sixty manufacturing plants of which the Fairport plant was one, having approximately 600 workers and a $4.7 million payroll. Cans were produced for fruits and vegetables, but also for items such as beer, cocoa, soft drinks, oil, anti-freeze, shaving cream, and shampoo.

With the expansion of the company, its old family atmosphere began to erode. By the mid 1970's, there were no more summer jobs, and the number of workers was declining due to the increased mechanization of the process. According to one account, the only thing that mattered for a plant manager was the last monthly statement. At least once, corporate headquarters replaced nearly the entire management team. Weekly "manning meetings" made sure that there were no unnecessary workers. Union-management relations, which had been good, began to decline.

Canco undertook a major building project in 1976 when the Empire State plant was constructed on Whitney Road. The state-of-the-art plant manufactured the two-piece can, familiar as the typical pop-top beverage can, and was designed to make cans for a Schlitz Brewing Company facility located near Syracuse. Unfortunately, Schlitz closed that brewery in 1979, and Budweiser, which had taken over the Schlitz brewery, contracted with another firm to produce cans at a lower cost. Nevertheless, with some retooling, the plant survived by making over 100 different types of cans for "customers from Boston to Indianapolis." By the mid 1980's the plant was manufacturing over one billion cans per year for such brand names as Quaker State, Comstock, Motts, Ocean Spray, Nestle's, Pepsi, Genesee, Tab, Fresca, Wegmans, and Coca-Cola, from the twenty-two ton steel coils that were delivered to the Fairport facility. Especially important were the Quaker State, Genesee, and Nestle's contracts. Nevertheless, barely five years later, the company was talking about closing the plant.

The number of workers in the newly automated and modernized plant had declined from over 600 workers in 1979 to about 230 in 1988. In 1989, citing lack of local demand, American Can closed the main plant on Whitney Road, but kept the facility on Parce Avenue open. It was no longer profitable for the company to manufacture cans in Fairport and then ship them to the eastern seaboard for filling and processing. According to a former employee, however, the closing was not a complete surprise, for as he said, "...the plant has been on the slide for the last few years...It's not the same American Can as it was years ago..."

The closing of the American Can plant saddened the community, for many had worked at Canco all their lives, as had their fathers and other relatives. Four generations of the Hull family worked for Canco beginning with Chester Hull, then his nephew Ed Hull, and continuing with Ed's sons Don, Duane, and Dave, and then his grandsons. Red Rohr, who in 1984 had been with the company for forty-one years, followed his uncle, grandfather, and father into Canco and worked alongside his wife, sister, and brother-in-law. Longtime employee Frank Marra noted upon the plant closing, "I never thought I'd see the day when American Can would close... It's devastating, an end of an era...It gave me and my family our livelihood. I put my boys through school, bought a house, and now all I can do is watch it close." Mayor Clark King stated that "American Can's closing won't have a major impact on the village economy, but from a nostalgic standpoint, it's the end of an era in Fairport."

Due to Fairport's good business climate, however, which included low electric rates from the municipally-owned Fairport Electric, access to the railroad and the interstate system, and a modern, flexible plant, the area was able to attract a buyer. In 1993, Cantisano Foods purchased the Empire plant on Whitney Road where it currently produced a variety of pasta sauces and salsas for such brands as Francesco Rinaldi, Newman's Own, Hunt-Wesson, Tostitos, and Wegmans. The firm has continued to expand and is known today as LiDestri Foods.

A Trio of Small Businesses

At the turn of the twentieth century the fertile agricultural lands of Perinton and the surrounding areas produced large quantities of fruits and vegetables that provided the raw materials for a growing canning industry. Although the two largest packing and canning firms in the area were Cobb's Preserving Company and the Egypt Canning Company, they weren't the only ones.

Thomas Packing Company, also known as Fairport Packing Company, might well be known as the "other packing company." Ananias Edgett, founder of that company, was the brother of Ezra, who along with George Cobb had founded the larger Cobb's Preserving Company. In 1881 Ananias apparently stopped working with his brother Ezra when the latter decided that Ananias was not a good enough plant manager. He went on to form a smaller canning company on Parker Street just north of the bridge, setting up business in a building that had formerly been a blacksmith shop.

The company changed hands several times in the 1890's, first being sold to the Burlingame brothers, and then to Thomas Roberts, who had worked as a wholesale grocer in Philadelphia. By 1892 Howard Thomas, whose name the company would bear for a time, took over. Thomas had had several years experience in the canning business in New Jersey before resettling in Fairport.

Fairport Packing Company (Parker St.)

Thomas improved the plant, adding new machinery and building a large brick engine and boiler room. He employed between two and three hundred workers who processed large quantities of fruits and vegetables, most of which came from local growers. At times of increased demand, apples, pears, peaches, and other produce were imported from other areas. Brands which were sold nationwide included "Rochester Beauty," "Pride of Rochester," "Park," "New York State," and "Fairport." By 1908 the company had become known as the Fairport Packing Company and was selling Golden Tip, Rochester Beauty, and Oakfield Brand products.

In a similar vein, the Monroe Chemical Company and the E.L. Dudley Company were the "other baking soda" companies, having been overshadowed by the DeLand Chemical Company.

Edward Dudley joined Charles Howe and John Dixon to form Howe, Dixon and Dudley, manufacturers of soda, saleratus, and baking powder. By 1895, it became Dudley and Company, after the departure of Howe and Dixon and the addition of D.C. Becker. They manufactured Napoleon Baking Powder, Napoleon Baking Soda, and Utopia Corn Starch. These three products were also sold in quantity to retailers who marketed them under their own labels. Their business grew rapidly enough to warrant a move from their original location in the Deal block at 34 North Main Street to a larger facility on Railroad Street with better shipping facilities and room to expand.

W. I. Ayers had a spice and baking powder business which he sold to William Newman in 1874. The company was known as Newman and Son and then as Monroe Chemical Company. Ads of the period noted that there was "nothing superior to Golden Shield Soda and Golden Shield Baking Powder," and that the products were "warranted to give perfect satisfaction." The manufacturing facility was located on the east side of North Main Street just north of Railroad Street and the New York Central Railway lines, in buildings now occupied by retail shops.

Willis Trescott & The Trescott Company

There is no doubt that Willis Trescott was a "Renaissance man." He was well-known in Fairport and the surrounding area as a dentist, inventor, businessman, and farmer. Born in Conesus in Livingston County on September 30, 1850, he grew up in Wisconsin. His parents, Solomon and Calesta, had come to New York from New Hampshire with Willis' grandparents in 1812. They had, like many, traveled by oxen and sleigh in the late winter to their new home where they grew corn, planted an orchard, and also cultivated grapevines for the manufacture of medicinal wine. Willis and his family continued west by canal, lake, and trail to settle in Honey Creek, Wisconsin, where Willis grew up and went to school, graduating from high school in Rochester, Wisconsin.

Willis taught in the local rural schools after graduation and also studied dentistry during the summer. Sometime in the early 1870's he married another teacher, E. Lorain Page, daughter of Jesse and Huldah Page, and shortly thereafter moved to Fairport. He opened a dental practice in the city of Rochester and had a part-time practice in Fairport. By 1873 the local paper noted that he had opened a full-time practice in the Chadwick block on South Main Street and that Trescott "was especially skillful in refitting badly fitted plates and proposed perfect satisfaction or no charges would be made." Continuing his dental studies, he received a DDS degree from the University of Pennsylvania in 1875. Eventually he moved his practice to his home at 16-18 West Street.

Dr. Willis Trescott

At the same time, Trescott never lost his interest or involvement in agriculture and horticulture. He always owned and ran a farm in the Rochester area, and he was, for a time, a partner in Trescott Brothers, an apple dry-house in Conesus. Sometime in the early 1880's, he developed and patented a new type of evaporating furnace and a machine for bleaching apples, both of which were used in the apple drying business. By the middle to late 1880's he had opened the Trescott Company in Fairport and was manufacturing machines used in fruit preservation.

Apparently the manufacturing business was very good because by 1905 Trescott had closed his dental practice and was devoting himself full-time to the development and manufacture of machinery used in food processing and preservation. In 1907, while recovering from an illness, he invented an apple grader, which would sort apples according to size. The apples, or potatoes, moved along a metal belt and dropped through holes. The machine, which cost fifty to one hundred, was sold throughout the apple and potato growing states and was quite successful. Subsequent patents included one for a machine that scrubbed pesticides off commercially grown fruits, one that cleaned and waxed apples and similar fruits, and one that defuzzed peaches. The products were sold in the U.S. and Europe.

The Trescott Company was located at North Main and Railroad Streets. A 1924 map shows a complex of three factory buildings, three storage buildings, a woodworking shop, a tin shop, and offices. Incorporated in 1927, the business continued to grow and prosper during the 1930's and 40's.

Willis Trescott controlled the business until his death in 1938 after "a short illness due to the infirmities of age." For the next decade several of his former employees continued to run the business, developing a materials handling line that included conveyor belts, skids, and pallets. They also oversaw the development of a new and revolutionary packaging method using cellophane, which soon spread nation-wide.

In 1950 in order to facilitate the settlement of the Trescott estate, the company stock was sold at public auction. Two Fairport residents, Reginald Kiefer and Elmer Hartman, purchased the majority and continued to run the company successfully, adding the Smith Incubator Company in 1951. Changes, however, were inevitable. In 1954 the grading operation was sold to William Tew. Soon thereafter, Elmer Hartman left and started his own manufacturing business.

Willis Trescott was a true "renaissance man" in the scope of his interests and accomplishments, and, like Daniel DeLand and Amos Cobb, was an entrepreneur who helped put Fairport on the industrial map during the latter decades of the nineteenth century. Trescott's obituary adds, "Dr. Trescott has always been a public-spirited man who has contributed liberally at all times to the social and charitable activities of the community. His benefactions were many and without ostentation."

Trescott's fruit cleaning machine on display

The Pharmacy

The traditional corner drug store or pharmacy has a long history. The ancients of Mesopotamia, China, Greece, and Egypt all worked on compounding various agents that were thought to alleviate suffering or cure disease. The word "pharmacy" in fact comes from the Greek word for "remedy." Seventeenth century British and French doctors worked from documents referred to as the Pharmacopeia of London (1618) and the Pharmacopeia of Paris (1639) respectively and the Americans followed with their pharmacopeia first printed in 1820. Those early publications set the standards for the elixirs and powders common in those days. Today, of course, standards for drugs are set in the U.S. by the Food and Drug Administration under the Pure Food and Drug Act passed in 1906.

In the early days doctors not only treated patients and prescribed drugs, but they also compounded and sold them. It wasn't until the nineteenth century that pharmacy began to develop as a separate profession with the establishment of the Philadelphia School of Pharmacy in 1821. Today there are approximately 72 American colleges that train pharmacists. The pharmacists of the nineteenth and early twentieth centuries, while purchasing some chemicals from an outside manufacturer, compounded many of their own pills and remedies and put up tinctures in five gallon containers. They frequently combined medications into a single dosage and were often called upon to provide first aid. In addition they also dispensed the popular remedies such as herbs and patent medicines like our local Taylor's Oil of Life.

By the mid twentieth century, the role of the pharmacist had drastically changed. No longer was the pharmacist compounding all his own medicines or selling patent remedies. The number of drugs skyrocketed as did the role of the drug companies, which were supplying virtually all of the drugs. Government and health insurance company regulations and the rise of prescription departments in Walmart, Target, and Wegmans have further changed the role of the local pharmacist.

In the early years there were a number of drug stores in Fairport, among them Dr. Weare's, Dr. Pratt's, Robert Estes', Mr. Hoskin's, Mr. Hupp's and Doc Cramer's. Of the drug stores in existence during the first half of the twentieth century, perhaps the two that might be best remembered today are Wagor's and Bramer's Drug Stores. Both were located on South Main Street in the buildings that stood there before the Village Landing was built.

A.B. Hupp had started a drug store in 1909 where he sold drugs and patent medicines, often preparing his own compounds and prescriptions. However, by 1922 he found that he was more interested in autos than drugs and sold his business to Robert Wagor, a graduate of the University of Buffalo School of Pharmacy. Mr. Hupp subsequently opened Hupp Motors on South Main Street and Wagor's Drugs became a fixture in the village.

Robert and Marguerite Wagor were known for their hard work and for creating a friendly and cheerful atmosphere in their store, which became far more than a place to pick up prescriptions, although it was open from nine to nine and delivered. Over the years Wagor's, like many drugstores, became a place to buy not only drugs, but many other "sundries" such as greeting cards, toiletries, film, tobacco products, school supplies, and even tickets for school events. In the 1940's it was considered to be a "modern drugstore" with the expansion of the gifts and sundries section to include kitchen gadgets, magazines, and candy. Growing up, the three Wagor children helped in the family business, and son Bob took over when the elder Wagor died in 1957. Wagor's Drugs remained a fixture on South Main Street until urban renewal changed the face of the village in the late 1970's.

Down the street on the corner of West Avenue and South Main Street was Bramer's Drug Store. Irving "Doc" Bramer, a graduate of the Philadelphia College of Pharmacy, came to Fairport in 1907 after working with his brother in their Norwich, New York drugstore. He purchased Dr. Cramer's drug store, soon changing the name to Bramer's. During the 1930's, he also was in business with Charles French, another South Main Street businessman. Like the Wagor family, Irving's son Louis joined him in the family business. Bramer's was a traditional drugstore that not only filled prescriptions, but also, like Wagor's, stocked other everyday goods. When the old buildings on South Main Street were being razed to build the Landing in 1974, Bramer's too went out of business.

The local drugstore was the place to pick up prescriptions, but it was also a place where one could get advice about medical issues, buy magazines or school supplies or kitchen gadgets or cold remedies. And it was a place where the pharmacist probably knew your name, where you lived, and who the other members of your family were, part of a small town culture that has largely given way to the culture of the shopping mall and the "big box" store.

The One Horse Grocery

At the turn of the twentieth century there were a number of stores in Fairport village, where one could purchase food items. However, it was not possible to purchase everything at one store, nor did shoppers serve themselves. A customer would ask a clerk behind the counter for specific items and the clerk would package the items. Contrary to multitudes of choices, those grocery stores often carried only one brand of each product. While there were chain stores, such as the A&P, they too were all entirely full-service, with clerks serving the customers.

In 1908 Fairport had four bakeries, one shop that sold canned goods (canned goods were very new at that time and not terribly reliable), four groceries, one store selling produce, two meat markets, and two confectionaries. Advertisements from the time period expand somewhat on that list. Stores advertising groceries included H.J. Oram's Grocery Store, B.J. Woolsey & Son, C.W. McBride, and Luther C. Brown. Stores advertising meat included O.C. Adams' Meat Market, the Rainbow Brothers, who offered "the choicest meats," and George Filkins & Sons who touted "fresh, salt, and smoked meats." Several others, among them Lester Heinsheimer's, George Steubing's, W.H. Patterson's and the Fairport Candy Kitchen, sold candy, ice cream, confections, soft drinks, and sometimes cigars and tobacco as well. Quite obviously there was competition among proprietors and choice for the consumer.

Another one of those stores was the "One Horse Grocery" at 21 West Avenue. It was owned and run by Adelbert Hooker who had originally moved to Fairport in 1879 to work at the Green and McAuliffe Lumber Yard. Several years later, Hooker opened his own grocery store. The "one horse" featured prominently in his advertising, which stated that:

> "We are known as the ONE HORSE GROCERY.
> We like to be called the ONE HORSE GROCERY.
> We acknowledge that WE ARE THE ONE HORSE GROCERY.
> Everybody knows WHY we are the ONE HORSE GROCERY.
> Our trademark is "ONE HORSE," and is familiar not only to Fairport people
> but in the surrounding country."

The "one horse" was Bess, who pulled Hooker's delivery wagon.

Hooker carried a complete line of "staple and fancy groceries," which he sold at competitive prices, claiming that people got the benefit of his "one horse prices." Confident of his pricing, he urged his customers to comparison shop. In 1892 he sold 100 pounds of One Horse flour for $1.70; a 2 pound can of Chase & Sanborn Mocha and Java Coffee for $.75; Fairport Vinegar for $.15 a gallon; Saleratus (baking soda) for $.07 a pound; a two pound can of "Roast Beef" for $.20; and creamery butter for $.24 a pound. During the home canning season fruit jars sold for $.67 a dozen for quart jars and $.60 a dozen for pints. Granulated sugar was $.05 per pound.

The store, which was located on the south side of West Avenue, was relatively small, and had a central door flanked by two large display windows. The interior was similar to most stores of its kind at the time, having long counters on both side walls with floor-to-ceiling shelving behind them. Pictures taken in the late 1890's show the counters with glass display cases and shelving filled with goods. The store had a tin ceiling, wainscoted walls, an archway leading to further storage and a doorway which seemed to lead to a small office. Oil lamps hanging from the ceiling provided light. An exterior view shows goods on display in front of the store.

Typical early 20th century grocery store

The grocery was successful, leading Hooker to expand at least once, always maintaining that "we deal in groceries, exclusively, and our aim is to run an up to date store, handle strictly first-class goods and make prices – we lead, others follow." Despite his success, however, Hooker closed his store in 1900. He continued to live in Fairport and worked at the Cobb Canning Company.

Hooker's one horse, Bess, attached to delivery wagon

Perhaps A.C. Hooker saw the handwriting on the wall, for within twenty years the days of the old full-service grocery were numbered. Clarence Saunders, a flamboyant and innovative Tennessean, noticed that the full-service method of dealing with customers resulted in wasted time and man hours, so he came up with an unheard-of solution that would revolutionize the entire grocery industry: he developed a way for shoppers to serve themselves. He opened the first Piggly Wiggly grocery store on September 9, 1916, in Memphis, Tennessee, and offered shopping baskets and open shelves to the customers who now had to help themselves without the aid of clerks. Saunders patented his concept in 1917 and the modern grocery store was born.

The Dudley Family & Their Businesses

Members of the Dudley family have been "businessmen of standing and ability," and active citizens in Perinton for over 100 years. Edward, Richard, and Walter Dudley moved to Perinton from Connecticut in 1873. In those years Fairport was a growing and thriving industrial village, boasting the DeLand Chemical Company, Taylor's Oil of Life, Cobb's Preserving Company, and a number of other concerns. The Dudley brothers opened a general merchandise store selling dry goods and groceries, which they operated for fourteen years before Edward left to join Charles Howe and John Dixon to form Howe, Dixon and Dudley, manufacturers of soda, saleratus, and baking powder.

By 1895, after the departure of Howe and Dixon, D.C. Becker joined Edward to form Dudley and Company, manufacturers of Napoleon Baking Powder, Napoleon Baking Soda, and Utopia Corn Starch. These three products were also sold in quantity to retailers who marketed them under their own labels. Their business grew rapidly enough to warrant a move from their original location in the Deal block at 34 North Main Street to a larger facility on Railroad Street that had better shipping facilities and room to expand.

Edward Dudley traveled a good deal, introducing his product and earning the reputation of being a "hustler," as he put much "vim and energy" into his business. D.C. Becker, a twenty-five year Fairport resident, who managed the home office, had been in the banking business (Becker's Bank) for twenty years before going into partnership with Dudley, and was known as a "sound and reliable financier." Both men were active in the community. Edward Dudley served on the school board and was president of that body. He was also president (mayor) of the village of Fairport in 1894. Becker served five terms as supervisor of the town of Perinton in the 1890's and into the twentieth century.

Dobbin and Moore lumber

Changes, however, were bound to happen. D.C. Becker left the partnership to go into business with his son, forming Reed Manufacturing Company. Raymond Dudley joined his father Edward in running Dudley and Company. Edward died in 1927, and in 1928 Raymond sold the company to Calumet. In 1929, Raymond moved the Dudley family to another Fairport enterprise, joining with Bert Hanby to purchase Fairport Lumber and Coal (formerly Dobbin and Moore Lumber).

The old Dobbin and Moore company was started by William Dobbin and Clarence Moore in the 1870's. Dobbin, a self-taught carpenter, came to Fairport in 1866, and by 1871 had started a sash, blind, and door company. Moore was a Fairport native who, in 1875, formed a partnership with Levi DeLand opening the DeLand-Farmer Lumberyard. That partnership was soon dissolved, leaving Moore free to join forces in 1879 with Dobbin, a relationship that lasted for twenty-four years. Their business was located on the south bank of the canal between Main and Parker Streets, selling a full assortment of lumber, timber, fencing, posts, lath, and sand, as well as manufacturing doors, sashes, and blinds. In 1902 a bundle of shingles cost $5.00 and fifty-four feet of 7/8 pine was $1.89. The yard was described in an 1895 article as being "well-equipped with stock, a large steam mill and extensive woodworking machinery which enables them to turn out fine work." Clarence Moore died in February of 1903 and William Dobbin closed the business soon afterwards.

Dudley and Hanby resurrected the old lumber company in 1929. They stopped selling coal and concentrated on lumber. By 1932 they were advertising lumber, building materials, roofing, and paint. Dudley bought out his partner in 1940 and the business became Dudley Lumber. Raymond Dudley's two sons, Richard and Robert, joined the business after serving in World War II in the Navy and the 209th Anti-aircraft Artillery respectively.

After Raymond's death in 1948, Robert and Richard continued the business selling lumber, paint, insulation, roofing, masonry supplies, and providing millwork. The complex included an office, a lumber shed, a mill, and two storage sheds. They concentrated on the individual do-it-yourselfer and were, for example, willing to cut a piece of plywood to whatever size was needed.

According to Richard Dudley, Saturdays were especially busy. By 1976 the site on the south bank of the canal was nearing 100 years of continuous existence as a lumberyard and business was good. However, the village was undergoing urban renewal, which necessitated the clearing of the site. After the Urban Renewal Agency purchased the property in 1976, the Dudley Lumber Company closed. As Dick Dudley notes, villages are different today. Small family-owned businesses have been replaced by malls and their huge retail chains, forcing village downtowns to reinvent themselves or become ghost towns.

Dudley Lumber 1960's

Raymond Dudley and his two sons, Robert and Richard, continued the family tradition of active participation in the Fairport community. All were active in their churches, and Raymond and Robert were the second and third generation of Dudleys to serve on the school board. As a further honor to the family, one of the elementary schools on Hamilton Road was named the Dudley School. Father and sons were also members of the Rotary Club. Robert Dudley died in 1992. As of 2010, Dick and Dorothy Dudley continue to live in Fairport.

Peddie Springs and The Crystal Rock Water Company

". . . [A] crystal stream which flowed up form earth's mysterious depths showed a pent-up power and its sparkling purity invited the thirsty wayfarer's indulgence. . . . The beasts of the forest [and] the inhabitants of the surrounding country drank of its waters, but the fame of its wonderful properties lay confined to the few who participated in its ample and wondrous benefits."

It would be up to Dr. John Peddie, a Baptist minister from Philadelphia, and Walter Parce, a local businessman, to bring this "health-giving fountain of Nature" and "King of Table Waters" to the general public.

"Taking the waters" was not a new idea. The Romans and Greeks had used hydrotherapy, and during the course of the nineteenth century visits to places like Saratoga Springs, Clifton Springs, and Avon, as well as European spas, were commonplace. Dr. Peddie was a regular visitor to the Perinton-Fairport area in the 1880's, and in 1885, while hiking, he came across a bubbling spring in the area just south of Fairport Road and half way between Marsh Road and Jefferson Avenue near Irondequoit Creek. According to long time residents, the area had been a deer lick and had been frequented by Native Americans who had drunk of the waters for medicinal purposes. Dr. Peddie also drank of the waters and soon became utterly convinced of their curative powers, having experienced a "decided enhancement of his physical powers." He resolved to bring the benefits of the waters to the public.

Walter Parce and other area entrepreneurs, including Levi DeLand and J.H. Snow, became interested in Dr. Peddie's proposals. Land was cleared in the area, and a pavilion, a picnic grove, and a pond for canoeing were built. Having bought out Dr. Peddie, Walter Parce incorporated the Crystal Rock Water Company in 1890, with stock valued at $100 a share. The water, which according to Prof. L.A. Lattimore of the University of Rochester contained "very large" amounts of sulphate of lime and of magnesia, as well as chloride of magnesium and of sodium, was bottled and sold for $7 for a 45 gallon barrel or $10 for 100 pint bottles.

Crystal Rock wagon

Believers in the curative properties of water rushed to buy the new product. A typical treatment might include drinking two to three glasses before breakfast, or "small potations repeatedly through the day" or in such "quantities and with such repetition as to insure a copious diuretic effect" or "one glass an hour after meals." Exercise and plenty of rest completed the regimen. It was, of course, impossible to determine whether the water or the lifestyle changes were of greater significance. This "wonderful product of Nature's great laboratory, its ingredients being so delicately admixed that it reaches, often, diseases not ordinarily amenable to physicians' prescriptions" promised to remedy "chronic inflammation…of the bladder, diabetes, Bright's disease, liver complaint, constipation and dropsy, indigestion and dyspepsia." It would "prove a boon to women....in female complaints and diseases. . . [It would] do more for the complexion by clearing it and removing unsightly blotches and disfiguring skin humors..." Its beneficial effects "are especially apparent in the treatment of all Blood and Skin diseases, Rheumatism, Sciatica and other diseases."

Glowing testimonials flowed in from area residents and doctors. Dr. Briggs wrote that it was a wonderful laxative. Dr. Tubbs prescribed it for severe acne with great success. He also recommended it for constipation. Dr. Cramer served it at his soda fountain. Henry DeLand finally found a cure for his headaches and stomach disorders in the new tonic as did the pastor of the First Baptist Church, the Rev. Horace Hunt. Mrs. Robinson wrote that she "suffered much from Nervous Weakness and some Kidney Trouble, and by its use have been restored to health."

The ballyhoo was short-lived. By the end of the 1890's, the craze for mineral water was fading and the owners of the Crystal Rock Water Company went on to other ventures. Although the 1902 map identifies the company along the banks of Irondequoit Creek, by the 1920's all traces of the company were gone.

Eventually the land was sold for development and became the "Orchards" and "Crystal Springs." The land where the pavilion and bottling plant were located is now an abandoned and marshy site adjacent to White Haven Memorial Park. It is said, however, that one can still detect a faint sulphuric odor coming from the swamp, a small remnant of the area's former popularity.

The Automobile Industry in Fairport

In the last decade of the nineteenth century innovators like Frank Duryea, Alexander Winton, Elwood Haynes, and Ransom Olds were experimenting with steam-driven and internal combustion engines to power a "horseless-carriage." Those early automobiles were manufactured for the rich who could afford these custom-made playthings. In 1896, however, a man by the name of Henry Ford test built a machine that would literally change the face of America. He sold his first car in 1903 and in 1908 introduced the Model T, which sold for $850 and was designed to fulfill Ford's dream of building autos for the general public using mass production and interchangeable parts. Between 1908 and 1927, their last year of production, fifteen million "Tin Lizzies" were sold for as little as $265 (the 1923 price). America was on the road.

The village of Fairport was not only the center of population in the town of Perinton, but also the center of business and commerce into the 1960's. It was possible to purchase virtually anything that was needed within the village itself, and this included the ever-popular automobile. Each of the three major auto companies had dealerships in the village.

Charles Schnepp and Lawrence Hall opened Church Motors on the southeast corner of South Main and Church Streets in 1946. They sold Dodge, Plymouth, and Dodge "job-related" trucks and also marketed Texaco products. Their service department promised mechanical work by experts and even offered to pick up and deliver your car at "no extra cost." The business prospered, leading to the construction of a larger facility, with large showroom windows, at 65 South Main Street. The first autos featured there included the 1953 "Fluid-Drive" Dodge and the 1953 Plymouth, "the first motor car with a Truly Balanced Ride." However, success there was relatively short-lived. As with many American auto dealerships, the 1960's brought unwelcome change with the advent of foreign competition and concerns about safety. Church Motors went out of business in 1965 and the building is currently occupied by Nothnagle Realtors.

Albert Hupp opened his Ford dealership nearby at 92 South Main Street. Originally he had run a drug store, but in 1920 he sold his drug store to Robert Wagor and opened Hupp Motors, fulfilling a life-long dream. The business offered "top to tire" service in addition to both new and used Fords and Lincolns. A 1923 ad offered car washing and simonizing, painting, engine honing, and careful car greasing, among other services. Texaco, Kendall, Tydol, and Sunoco gas were available from the pumps. Included in a 1937 used car ad was a 1935 Ford V-8 Deluxe Touring Tudor for $179 down and $23 per month, and a 1931 Ford Coupe with a rumble seat for $55 down and $12.85 per month. A new

1937 Ford V-8 was advertised as getting nineteen miles per gallon and sold for $627 (bumpers and a spare tire were extra.). During World War II, with relatively few available autos for sale, the dealership, like many others, survived by selling used equipment, providing service, and recycling tires and engine parts. Hupp Motors prospered during the heyday of the American auto in the 1950's, selling autos and providing related services such as custom-made seat covers, rust-proofing, and engine rebuilding. However, with the changes in the auto industry in the 1960's and the growth of the suburbs and malls, Hupp Motors too closed in 1965, and the property was sold to the First Baptist Church. The DeLand Christian Center now stands on the site.

Above: Church Motors
Right: Hupp Motors

General Motors products were sold by two dealers in Fairport. The 1913 directory indicates that Carlton Clifford sold Buicks from his home at 11 West Church Street. He subsequently operated his business, known then as Fairport Motors, at 45 South Main Street, the current home of Fairport Savings Bank. In 1938 he moved to 38 West Avenue, taking over the business formerly known as Tabberrah Motors and added Pontiac to his inventory. Fairport Motors was still in existence in 1962, but like the other local dealerships, would soon close. Chevrolet autos were sold by the Wheeler Chevrolet Corporation at 120 North Main Street. A late 1930's ad touts the value and economy of the six-cylinder 80 horsepower engine in a relatively low-priced auto. Wheeler apparently went out of business before the other dealerships, as 120 North Main Street is listed as vacant in the 1942 directory.

The auto industry spawned a number of other business possibilities, which were eagerly embraced by a number of Fairport village entrepreneurs. By the time the 1932 directory was published, in addition to the auto dealerships, there were nearly a dozen businesses advertising gas, tires, and/or service. The typical garage sold gasoline, oil, probably tires, and serviced the sometimes temperamental new machines. Fairport's Osburn Hotel on North Main Street became the Fairport Oil Company and added gas pumps which operated by gravity, sending the gas down into the tank. The Gulf Oil Company, having leased (and subsequently bought) a portion of the Green Lantern property on the corner of South Main and Church Streets, put in gas pumps and erected a small white service station, which was later run by William Peters. That building eventually became an insurance office. The old Rochester, Syracuse, and Eastern trolley station became a service station, selling gas, refurbished tires, and servicing autos. It was run for a number of years by the late Albert Knapp. "Sew Creative" now occupies the building. Max Humphrey's stood on the southwest corner of Main and Church Streets; Clarence Greene's Underpass Garage and Service Station, selling only "advertised brands," was on the corner of Baird and Rochester (Fairport) Roads; and Clifford Ellis advertised his "general auto repairing" at 7 Parce Avenue. Lee Clouser sold "Dunlop Tires, Tubes, & Batteries" from his 51 South Main Street establishment, and Jesse and Morrison, "specializing in Chrysler Products" worked out of the North Side Garage at 150 North Main Street. T.F. Enter advertised general auto repairing at his Dewey Avenue Garage at number 52 on that street, Corso's Garage was apparently located across from the Fairport National Bank (today's Bank of America), while Russell's Service Station was up the street on the southeast corner of Church and Main Streets.

The insurance industry also benefited from the auto boom. There were eight insurance agencies listed in Fairport's 1932 directory. Irving Warner promised that "every dollar you spend for insurance protects all your other dollars…." while reminding customers that "my rates are lower." George Wilson, who sold Lumberman's Insurance, advertised a twenty-five percent dividend that would not be lost even in case of an accident. He promised to save owners of Ford, Chevrolet, and Essex $14.25 and owners of Cadillac and Packard $17.25.

The advent of a mass-produced auto radically changed the American lifestyle and the landscape of America itself. Not only were new collateral businesses created such as service stations and motels, but the auto accelerated the creation of "bedroom" communities or suburban subdivisions, and most certainly the shopping mall. Demand was created for highways and then fast-food franchises, while the bus, the train, and eventually the small town Main Street suffered decline. Today as the American auto industry competes with Asian and European interests, copes with the increasing globalization of business, and deals with the unstable and finite supply of oil, a new generation of innovative minds will be called upon for creative solutions.

The Jackson Coal Company

Dewey Jackson has been a well-known name in Fairport for nearly 100 years. Dewey Jackson Sr. moved to Fairport from the family home in Penfield early in 1904 at the age of twenty-five. His parents, Thomas and Henrietta Stevenson Jackson were farmers who lived on Jackson Road in Penfield. Of their five children, two came to Fairport. Daughter Mary married Warren Clark and they purchased the DeLand mansion on the corner of South Main and Church Streets. Son Dewey and his wife Augusta Campbell settled at 120 West Avenue. By 1925 the Jacksons had two children, Dewey Jr. and Alice.

The name Dewey Jackson was, for many years, synonymous with coal and then with fuel oil. Because Warren Clark, Dewey Jackson's brother-in-law had had difficulty heating his large house, he had convinced a Syracuse friend, who was a wholesale coal dealer, to sell him a carload so he could get through the winter. This connection, along with the fact that Fairport was a rapidly growing community with new homes that might well use coal instead of wood for heat, inspired Clark and Jackson to start their own coal business in 1904. It was a business that would endure for seventy-five years.

They purchased George Fellows' old carriage shop at 24 North Main Street and converted it into a coal yard. The enterprise was named Dewey Jackson Coal, with Jackson handling the bulk of the day-to-day operations. Warren Clark left the operation in 1905 to pursue other business interests. From

1904 until 1912, the coal was delivered by the New York Central Railroad and stored in a large shed from which it was shoveled by hand into delivery vehicles.

Obviously business was good because in 1912 Jackson opened a 1,000-ton coal trestle. Coal was then unloaded from the gondola cars into a pit from which it traveled by conveyor to the top of the trestle where it was sorted into different bins according to size. Whether the order was for pea coal, chestnut coal, stove coal, egg coal, buckwheat coal, rice coal or coke, the truck or wagon could be driven under the appropriate chute and loaded up. There are different grades of coal, two being anthracite or hard coal and bituminous or soft coal. Jackson carried only anthracite, otherwise known as "blue coal." Although it was more expensive, it burned cleaner. While churches, private residences and small businesses used anthracite, the larger businesses like Certo, the American Can Co. and the Salter Greenhouses used the bituminous coal.

Coal was delivered during those early years by horse and wagon, or horse and sleigh. Most of the deliveries were in or near the village with the Fairport Baptist Home, the municipal building, and village churches being among the largest customers. Rural customers received a discount if they picked up their own coal. In 1927 Jackson purchased a Model T truck from Hupp Motors to facilitate deliveries. However, in exceptionally busy times, the horses and wagons of some area farmers were still put to use delivering some of the coal orders.

Dewey Jackson

The Depression and the Second World War were difficult years for all. A number of Jackson's customers were unable to pay, having lost their jobs or having seen their crops fail. Jackson was known as a man who would not let others suffer and he carried many of his customers during this time, allowing them to pay what they could or barter, but never letting them or their families suffer from the cold. The same was true for any who ran into hard luck.

In the age before credit cards or even checks were common and most everyone dealt in cash, Dewey used his vest as his cash register. He used the different pockets for different denominations of bills. Credit checks were uncommon as well, but knowing who was in real need and who was not, Jackson helped the new businessman across the street, Albert Knapp, by rattling his mail box and then shaking his head to indicate that a particular customer was a bad risk.

In the same vein, George Rafoth, one of Jackson's employees who delivered coal, generally carried \$500-\$600 with him in order to make change for the customers. No one could get away with not paying because they didn't have the right change. It was both a sign of the times and a testament to his size and strength that George did not have to worry about carrying that amount of money in his pockets. Rafoth was a prodigious worker, being able to shovel off a ton of coal in five minutes. In fact George literally died with a coal shovel in his hands, dropping of a heart attack near the coal scales, which were next to the office, after supervising the unloading of a fifty ton gondola.

The post World War II years brought significant changes to the Jackson Coal Co. Dewey Jr. and his brother in law Roger Lund joined the company after the war. Responding to post war growth and demand, they added fuel oil to their product line and built three storage silos that held 12,500 gallons each. They also converted furnaces from coal to oil, and sold furnaces, water heaters, humidifiers, and air conditioners. Walt Pappert, Mike Kemp, and Bob Brown worked installing the new equipment and converting the old. In 1951 the business was incorporated. By 1960, the company was primarily an oil business, running four oil trucks, two service trucks, but only one coal truck. Dewey Jackson Sr. died in 1960, having been in the coal business for fifty-six years. Dewey Jr. ran the operation until 1979 when he sold to Hub Oil. At that time he had 1650 oil accounts in town.

The building at 24 North Main Street, having served as a carriage shop and then as Jackson Coal and Oil and Hub-Langie Fuel Oil, has continued to house a variety of local businesses. A reminder of its days as a fuel provider, the old coal scale remains in the parking lot just to the right of the building.

Dewey Jackson, Jr., a life-long resident of the village, was, like his father, well known and well loved in the Fairport community. He was the sort of person who knew and greeted everyone. An active member of the Congregational Church, Dewey was there for any and all events. He and his wife Charlotte raised four children, Kathy, Dewey, William, and Thomas in their house on Fifth Avenue. When Dewey Jr. died in January 2002, the community lost a great citizen and friend. However, Charlotte, all four children, and seven grandchildren continue to carry on the Jackson family traditions in Fairport and Perinton.

The Rochester Fireworks Company

On the afternoon of November 6, 1942, the Fairport, East Rochester, and Penfield fire departments, along with Red Cross and Rochester emergency units, responded to an alarm originating near the corner of Baird and West Whitney Roads. According to Mrs. John Hanson who lived on West Whitney, there had been "just a puff" from the Rochester Fireworks Company across the street, but then fire had engulfed one of the fourteen buildings on the site. Samuel Kirkpatrick and Arthur Salmon, who were driving along Whitney Road, at first heard a muffled explosion and saw black smoke. Calling in the alarm, they subsequently saw fire and people, mostly women, running and screaming. Anna Morreale, who had just that week started work at the factory, managed to escape with minor burns on her hands, and helped others smother their flaming clothing. She remembered seeing one boy coming out terribly burned. "He just rolled on the ground screaming," she recalled.

Fairport Fireworks workers, 1941

An explosion had caused the fire. The fire developed so fast that the women who were working inside the building had no chance to get out. Eight people died instantly in the explosion, three more would die in the ensuing days, and many were treated in area hospitals for burns. All but one of the victims were women who had gone to work in the factory feeling that they were contributing to the war effort. The victims, all residents of Fairport and East Rochester, had been so severely burned that survivors had to rely on jewelry, dental fillings, and miscellaneous items of clothing for identification. The dead included Evelyn Ellis, Mary Ann Parsons, Bertha Archambo, Evelyn Bigelow, Angeline Mandell, Rose Costanza, Angela Morabito, Minnie Brotsch, Viola Close, Yolanda Covino, and Frederick Seeley. Evelyn Ellis had begun her new job just that day and had been at work a mere thirty minutes before the explosion. Minnie Brotsch had been at work only since the previous October 27th. Evelyn Bigelow had just cashed her first pay check.

Due to the fact that it was wartime, the explosion was thoroughly investigated by the FBI who determined that the blast had been accidental. It was determined that as Frederick Seeley put down a tray of powder which he had brought into the building for the women to work with, it ignited, apparently from a friction spark or static electricity. Seeley along with the eight women, died instantly.

New safety regulations were implemented almost immediately after the investigations. Workers were prohibited from wearing jewelry or carrying objects that could cause sparks. Fabrics that could create static electricity like silk, wool, or rayon were also prohibited. Trays used for carrying the powder were required to be made of non-ferrous metal. Lawsuits over the deaths and injuries, however, were dismissed.

The Rochester Fireworks Company had been started before 1836 by Peter Palmer and was first located on the site currently occupied by the Blue Cross Arena. The company grew and expanded for almost 100 years, moving several times. In 1927, the George H. Robinson Importing Company bought out the Palmers' interests and merged with the company. The new firm imported many types of fireworks displays and "other sundries" from the Far East. As their location in Rochester became more populated and the fire regulations increased, the company began to look for space in the suburbs and chose what was at the time a rather isolated area of Perinton at the corner of Baird and West Whitney Roads. The land had previously belonged to the Lincoln Mills estate and had been occupied by a silk factory and a mulberry grove. In 1930 the company applied for a permit to build a number of small buildings on the site.

The fireworks factory subsequently built about forty buildings, well spaced to avoid fire, and employed about forty men and fifteen women, all local. Until 1939 and the rising need for munitions, the factory produced Roman candles, rockets, wheels and many other types of fireworks displays. Once World War II was underway, the factory expanded its work force and ran three shifts per day producing ammunition for the Army and Navy, work they continued until the end of the war. After the war the company turned to making metal toy tools which they continued to do until the 1960's when they switched to making real tools, doing metal fabricating and manufacturing industrial tools and level gauges. Today the G.A. Robinson Company, part of East Coast Performance Marketing, Inc., is located on the site.

The legacy of the explosion, however, still resonates today. In 1992 the families of the victims marked the fiftieth anniversary of the tragedy and in 2003 the families again met to honor the victims of one of the most disastrous nonresidential fires in area history and the area's only major disaster during World War II. A state resolution, sponsored by Assemblyman David Koon, was passed that entered the tragedy and the names of the victims into the official state history records. In 2003, a plaque with the names of the victims was put on display in the East Rochester Village Hall, remembering those who gave their lives for the war effort on the home front.

Hart & Vick Greenhouse Business

"Acres of glass houses and roses" graced the corner of Hulbert and Moseley Roads for nearly 100 years, from 1885 through 1970.

Al and Dick Saulter, Rochester nurserymen, needed more room for their rapidly expanding business on Conkey Avenue in Rochester and, in 1885, purchased land on Moseley Road just south of the Fairport village line, moving five of their greenhouses to the location and subsequently building four more structures for carnations and a smaller one for violets. The brothers ran another suburban outlet in Webster as well as stores on Park Avenue, in the Powers Building, and on East Main Street in Rochester.

Two foremen, George Norton and George Blake, oversaw the operation of the business in Perinton. Cut flowers were kept cold in buckets of water surrounded by chunks of ice before being shipped by rail to Rochester where they were delivered by horse and wagon to the florist shops.

Meanwhile, in 1905, George Hart, who had started work as an errand boy for the Saulter Brothers at the age of ten, finally started his own floral business in Rochester. He and his wife Mary, investing their savings of $500, rented a room in an old building on Stone Street and delivered cut flowers in a pushcart. By 1912, having successfully grown his business, he was able to construct a building at the corner of Ely and Stone Streets in Rochester and to add florist supplies to his inventory.

In 1917 George Hart came to Perinton, purchasing the business where he had begun his career. The first year was a difficult one as a disastrous fire destroyed all the greenhouses and Hart was forced to rebuild from scratch. However, he was able to plant 15,000 roses that first year and increase the amount to 25,000 in his second year, using 30,000 square feet of glass in the greenhouses. In that second year, Hart joined forces with James Vick of the well-established James Vick Seed Company, forming the Hart and Vick Seed Company and setting the stage for a significant expansion over the next thirty years.

Hart and Vick Greenhouses

Many were skeptical about growing roses commercially in Western New York because of the cold weather and lack of sunshine. A survey had shown that Perinton was said to be the second darkest place in the country in terms of hours of sunlight. Obviously the naysayers were wrong, because by the 1930's, Hart and Vick had twelve acres "under glass" with 145,000 rose plants providing about 30,000 blooms per day which were marketed in cities within a radius of 1,000 miles. In addition they grew 5,000 gardenia plants.

Hybrid roses need plenty of tender loving care, particularly with regard to temperature, soil preparation, and fertilizer. According to an article written by George Hart in 1927, temperatures were maintained between sixty and seventy degrees in the greenhouses by three boilers, fifty-five to sixty cars of coal per year, and three firemen employed around the clock on eight-hour shifts. In that same article, he noted that the soil had to be prepared three years in advance to be ready for the roses, which were replanted in new soil every four years. Until the company began to sterilize and reuse their soil in the early 1930's, the company owned or rented about 400 acres of land, one parcel being across Moseley Road. In terms of fertilizer, roses have, as Hart states, "an enormous appetite." In 1927 he was ordering twenty freight cars a year of cattle manure and spending about $125 per month on water. In addition, insecticides, "principally tobacco and nicotine products," were used "in large quantities."

Preparation for market also involved a specific process that Hart outlined in his article. Four months after planting, the roses were ready for cutting. They were cut every morning and sometimes twice a day depending on the time of year. The blooms were put in water and placed in a forty degree refrigerator for twelve to fifteen hours to "harden;" otherwise they would not hold. Upon removal from refrigeration, they were sorted and graded by quality of bloom and length of stem, arranged in layers of twenty-five, and packed in boxes with chopped ice, similar to fish, and then shipped to retail florists.

In the early 1930's the Hart and Vick Company packed enough of these boxes to equal an annual production of about 3,000,000 blooms, making it one of the nation's largest commercial suppliers of roses. Not only was the company a nationally known producer of roses, but it was also a beautifier of its home community, making plans in 1933 to open some of its gardens to the public. On a tract of land approximately 500 feet by 250 feet just south of the greenhouses, the company built a conservatory and two sets of four "trial gardens" connected with winding paths for walking.

The main conservatory building had a high arched glass dome and was flanked on both sides by service buildings. A columned portico fronted the building and a curved road starting just south of the greenhouses passed under the portico and exited at the south end of the plot. Ample parking was also provided and winding footpaths led visitors to the conservatory and through the gardens. The entire area was beautifully landscaped with lawns, shrubs, and hedges. The Second World War, however, brought an end to the display gardens and the land was offered to town residents for Victory Gardens. George Hart died in 1941 and his son Richard and daughter Mary took over the business.

Hart & Vick adapted to changing floral needs, producing a number of different rose varieties as tastes changed. In fact, seventy-five of all roses produced were some variety of red and for a time, seventy-five of those roses went into spectacular funeral arrangements. Responding to the gardenia rage, the greenhouses at one point produced up to a million and one-half corsages per year using five of their greenhouses. When Alf Landon ran for president, the company had acres of sunflowers, his state's flower, growing along Moseley Road. At another time orchids filled the conservatory and the company grew and exported these exotic flowers. Chrysanthemums and dish gardens were also big sellers. Eight greenhouses were filled with mums, and two women were kept busy all day making dish gardens. By 1955 the company was selling 3.5 million roses, thousands of gardenias, and 15,000 different kinds of florists' supplies. The company had its own delivery trucks and employed forty full-time employees in twenty-six greenhouses. Problems were on the horizon, however. The cost of growing was going up, but the retail price of flowers was declining, mainly due to increased competition from the south and west. Hart & Vick continued to operate successfully, however, by increasing production, but the death of Richard Hart in 1964 brought an abrupt end to a long-standing Fairport institution.

The thirty-six acre parcel of land owned by George B. Hart, Inc. was sold for development in 1967. The sale created fervor among environmentalists since the property included an ecologically significant remnant of a beech-maple forest, which used to cover most of this part of New York State. The Perinton Greenlands Association, whose motivating force was Louise Slaughter, worked to have the land purchased by the town of Perinton and proclaimed "forever wild." Unfortunately, the referendum to allow purchase of the land failed, but fourteen acres of the woods were named to the National Register of Natural Landmarks. The greenhouses were razed and construction took place on two-thirds of the property, but the town of Perinton did acquire 11.4 acres of the woods which remain untouched today – except for a walking path which can be enjoyed by anyone lucky enough to come across this small remnant of pristine woodland, and the last remaining parcel that belonged to George Hart's business.

Casa Larga Vineyards

The story of Casa Larga Vineyards is also the story of Andrew Colaruotolo and his family. Andrew, born in Gaeta, Italy, of an American father and an Italian mother, came to the United States in 1950. Settling in the Rochester area, he worked as a laborer for LeChase Construction while studying English at night. By 1956 he had become a mason contractor and in 1959 started his own business, Anco Builders with Cosmo Viola. Over the next fifteen years, taking advantage of the boom in suburban developments, the company constructed, among others, Crystal Springs subdivision. Moving to Perinton from Greece, Andrew and his family built a home on property they owned off Garnsey Road between Moseley and Turk Hill Roads. Anco Builders completed development of that area which they called Emerald Hills.

As a child in Italy, Andrew had enjoyed his grandmother's vineyard, and as an adult he dreamed of having a small vineyard as a hobby. Fearing that she would never see her husband if he started a vineyard in the Finger Lakes, his wife Ann persuaded him to use their land on Turk Hill Road. Prior to actually planting, Coloruotolo met with Dr. Konstantin Frank, founder of Dr. Frank's Vinifera Wine Cellars in Hammondsport. The two men grafted native, non-fruit-bearing vines with European vinifera vines. In 1974, Andrew Colaruotolo planted his first vines at what would become Casa Larga, named after his grandmother's vineyard in Gaeta. It is also Monroe County's first winery. This very successful enterprise, despite the untimely 2004 death of its founder, continues to be family owned and run by Andrew's wife Ann and their children John, Mary Jo, and Andrea.

From the beginning, the vineyard was a family operation. Coloruotolo and his son John put in about 4,000 posts for the first grape vines, which were of the common Concord and Delaware variety and covered approximately three acres. They subsequently added more acreage and the vinifera vines from Dr. Frank. Soon the plantings included Riesling, Pinot Chardonnay, Pinot Noir, Cabernet Sauvignon and Gewurztraminer varieties. Since it takes three years for a vine to produce grapes, the first vintage, of 2,000 gallons, was not bottled until 1978. The family gave away all but three bottles, which incidentally won three State Fair prizes that year.

Entrance to Casa Larga Vineyards

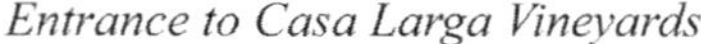

Casa Larga wines have been winning state and national honors ever since. The 1980's saw recognition from the International Wine Center in New York City and awards at the New York State Wine Classic. The 2000's saw numerous awards for their Fiori Delle Stelle Vidal Ice Wine, which was named Best U.S. Unfortified Dessert Wine by the Atlanta Wine Summit International Competition in 2001, an award which followed several years of gold medals and other honors for that wine. In 2005, the winery won the state's most prestigious wine award, the New York State's Governor's Cup, for the best wine in the state, their 2004 vintage Fiori Delle Stelle Vidal Ice Wine. More recent awards include six competition medals in 2010 at the Beverage Tasting Institute in Chicago, a world renowned resource for wine buyers, and seven medals, including a gold, at the New York State Fair. Over the years, Casa Larga has experimented and expanded its varieties. Champagne was added in the mid 1980's, winning a bronze at the 1987 International Wine and Spirits Competition in London, England. The merlot and cabernet sauvignon grapes that had been difficult to cultivate in New York, were successfully harvested in the 1990's. That same decade saw the bottling of ice wine, at first little known in the area, but well suited to a colder climate. The wine is a very sweet dessert wine and is made from vidal grapes that are allowed to freeze on the vine, thereby concentrating the sugar content. It is traditionally served in 375 ml bottles, half the size of a regular bottle, probably because it takes nearly twice as many grapes to make a bottle of ice wine. In 2005 the vineyard introduced a small experimental product, red ice wine, made from the cabernet franc grape. Red ice wine is relatively rare and Casa Larga is one of only a handful of wineries that bottle it.

Casa Larga Vineyards

Caring for a vineyard is very labor intensive. The vines are tied by hand and are cultivated and tilled approximately nine times before the harvesting. Tilling stops two weeks before the harvest to allow the undergrowth to stop the vine growth at its peak. At first, all the grapes were hand picked in the old world way – by family and friends. As the vineyard grew, however, more machinery, much of which comes from Italy, was used. Today all of the grapes except for the pinot noir grapes and the grapes used for the winery's reserve wines are picked by a mechanical harvester. The grapes are pressed, the juice put into stainless steel tanks where yeast is added, and the six to eight week fermentation process begins. After that, the wine is "racked" several times into new tanks as the lees (the yeast residue) is removed. Subsequently the wine is aged, either in steel tanks or oak casks anywhere from eight months to three years, depending on the variety and the type of cask or tank. Finally the wine is bottled and stored at the vineyard in a basement area holding approximately 20,000 cases.

The vineyard grew rapidly. By 1981 there were eleven acres devoted to the vines, which had expanded to seventeen acres by 1985. Currently there are about forty-five acres under cultivation. Buildings have grown as well. According to son John, in the first eleven years of the business there was an expansion project every year. In 1994 the new 5,000 square foot addition won praise from *Vineyard & Winery Management* magazine and also from a publication of *CM Architecture*, an architectural planning and consulting firm. The present facility can accommodate about 400 people in banquet rooms and includes a well-stocked retail shop. The latest building addition is a new "crushing pad" to house two new wine presses. The large building to the north of the main facility is essentially a storage barn. It has three sections: the largest for the grape harvester, a second for cases of wine, and a third for whatever else needs to be stored. The exterior features brick, cultured stones and a tile roof.

Casa Larga caters to the community and the tourist with a number of special and on-going events. In addition to the shop and banquet halls, there are tours and facilities for wine tasting. Since 1995, the fall "Purple Foot Festival" has been a draw for area residents and for tourists. Among such activities such as wine-tasting and tours, "grape-stomping" is probably the event that draws the most attention. (Those grapes are not used to make wine!) A mid-winter "Fire and Ice Festival" featuring Casa Larga's award-winning ice wine is usually held in February.

Begun by Andrew Colaruotolo in the 1970's more or less as a hobby and as a way to recreate his memories of Italy, Casa Larga, under the leadership of his wife and children, has grown into an award-winning winery. From its prominent hilltop location in Perinton, this winery is a destination for visitors and locals alike.

- V -
People and Places

While it is not possible to include every family, person, or place that has contributed to the growth and development of the Town of Perinton, this chapter provides a sampling of the people and places that have shaped our community.

A Sextet of Fairport Nineteenth Century Entrepreneurs

The nineteenth century Fairport village was home to a number of enterprising businessmen. Six of them are featured here. George Seeley owned a hardware business, among other ventures; and William Newman was a builder who also worked in the lumber and baking powder businesses. John Zollman, George Holman, and A.M. Loomis all came to Fairport as young men, and all three were merchants. Holman and Loomis sold coal and produce; Zollman sold a variety of farm implements and fertilizer. F.B. Clench was a photographer whose work includes many local portraits and scenes.

George Seeley came to Fairport in 1847 and worked in the tin and hardware business in the Dickinson block on South Main Street. Within ten years he had built a brick structure of his own on the corner of West Avenue and South Main Street where he did business until his retirement. His residence, a brick Italianate style house, stood on the corner of West Avenue and West Street. In addition, he was active in public affairs, representing the First Assembly District of Monroe County in the State Assembly, and also serving as Town of Perinton Supervisor for six years and clerk for five years. In the village of Fairport he served terms as village president, assessor, and treasurer. Seeley saw many changes in Fairport during his fifty plus years in the village. By the time of his death in 1911 the population had doubled and the village had become a bustling industrial town with canal, railroad, and trolley traffic.

William Newman was a businessman and a builder who came to Fairport from Pawling, New York in 1856. He started out as bookkeeper for the DeLand Chemical Company and then moved on to the lumber business with Lewis Jones. In 1874 he purchased W.I. Ayers' spice and baking powder business, which first became Newman and Son and then the Monroe County Chemical Company. He was said to be "one of Fairport's most substantial and active businessmen, and is a man of sound judgment and strong character." Active in the First Baptist Church, he also served as Town Clerk and as President of the Board of Education. William Newman built a number of residences including a house on the corner of Main and Church Streets, a house on West Avenue, the large house subsequently owned by Walter Parce at 137 North Main Street, and the house at 11 West Church Street which was occupied for many years by Dr. Dean. He also built a planing mill later owned by Green & McAuliffe's lumber company, located between West Avenue and the Erie Canal, and the building used by the Monroe County Chemical Company on North Main Street just north of the railroad tracks.

GEO. S. HOLMAN

Opportunity

Opporchunity knocks at ivery man's dure wonst. On some men's dures it hammers till it breaks down the dure, an' then it goes in and wakes him if he's asleep and afterwards it woirrks for him as night watchman.—Dooley.

Your opportunity to get good COAL (the Lehigh Kind) is NOW

GEORGE S. HOLMAN
The Retail "Hot Stuff" Man
Office, Yards and Trestle, High Street
BOTH 'PHONES

John Zollman was born in Germany and emigrated to the United States with his parents in 1851, settling on a farm in Allegheny County. The land was unimproved and the family worked hard and endured hardships, but even without much money, they managed to clear the land and build a house. Zollman was able to attend school, albeit after a three mile walk. The family came to Fairport in 1868 and purchased the John Swinerton farm on Marsh Road just west of Fairport. John married Amelia Westerman of Perinton in 1873 and moved to a farm east of the village where they lived until moving to 150 West Avenue in 1890. He and his wife had three daughters, Bertha, Ellen, and Alice. Zollman's business was handling agricultural implements and fertilizer and for a time before starting his own firm, he worked as an agent for the Milsom Fertilizer Company of Buffalo. In 1894 he opened his own store in the Chase Block (site of today's Village Landing), occupying one-half of the ground floor. He sold, in addition to farm implements, flour, seed, hay, and straw, and is said to have run a "prosperous business." Active in the Fairport community as a Mason, a member of the Grange, a founding member of the Fairport Protectives (a company of the Fairport Fire Department), and a member of the school board, he also served terms as assessor for the town and village.

George Holman came to Fairport in 1893 from Pittsford, Pennsylvania to work at Efner and Company in the produce business. By 1898 he had bought out Mr. Efner's interest in the company and had expanded the business to be one of the largest produce firms in Fairport. He purchased the best quality farm produce and paid the highest market price according to an 1898 advertisement records from the 1890's indicated that he shipped over 150 train car loads of apples, potatoes, onions, and cabbage in at least one year. Not only did Holman sell produce and a variety of other goods such as Akron cement, Empire Portland cement, Crocker fertilizers, drain tile and brick, barrel salt and bulk salt, but he also sold Flint lumber wagons and advertised "buggies at $50 each." Just as importantly, Holmes was the local agent for the "celebrated Lehigh Valley coal," which was said to be superior in quality. George and his wife Emily lived for many years on High Street near his place of business, but by 1925, the census record shows that they had moved to Fourth Avenue.

Loomis warehouse

Arthur M. Loomis was another well-known produce and coal dealer in Fairport. He arrived in Fairport in 1878 from Coventry, Connecticut. He built his warehouse between the New York Central Railroad tracks and Parce Avenue in 1882. Like Mr. Holman, he dealt in a variety of products including phosphates, cement, and sewer pipe. Loomis, however, was the agent for Plymouth Mine coal from the Pennsylvania Coal Company. It too was touted as a high quality coal and was exceptionally hard and "free-burning." Loomis, his wife Zaida and daughter Adelaide lived next to his business in a house that he built in 1887. Like his fellow purveyor of coal, George Holman, Arthur and Zaida are listed as living on Fourth Avenue in the 1925 census.

F.B. Clench came to Fairport after having run a gallery for over thirty-five years in Lockport. When visiting friends in Fairport in 1889, he decided that the village would be a good place to do business and secured space in the Deal block on North Main Street. He built up a flourishing business in the community and had his work published in an issue of *Wilson's Photographic Magazine* of New York, which said of him: "Mr. Clench is one of the most painstaking and progressive artists....It is seldom we have seen more of feeling and sentiment put into so many different attitudes of the same subject.... All the minor points, which play so important a part in the make-up of the whole, show that a trained mind has directed the execution of the work." He not only did photos, but he also did crayon drawings and enlargements and was known for taking photos of children. Many of the extant photos of late nineteenth century school classes, sports teams, street scenes, homes and individuals that are in the local archives were done by Mr. Clench.

While there are no local burial records for either the Holman or Zollman families, William Newman, George Seeley, and Arthur Loomis are buried in Mt. Pleasant Cemetery, and F.B. Clench is interred in Greenvale Cemetery.

These gentlemen served as leaders who added significantly to the growth of Fairport village, while Mr. Clench, with his photographs, added to the historical record.

Four Generations of Perinton Benedicts

The Erie Canal opened up western New York to trade and travel, settlement and jobs. The Benedicts were one of the many families that took advantage of the new opportunities. Enoch Benedict and his two sons, Gilbert and Jacob, made the trek to western New York from Nassau County in 1824 via the Erie Canal and settled on forty-five acres of land along the Rochester (Fairport) Road on land just west of Schummer's Cemetery.

Gilbert and his elder brother Jacob were both active in the Perinton community. Jacob served as Commissioner of Highways, Overseer of Highways, and Fence Viewer; Gilbert also served as a highway overseer and appears on several juror lists. Both men appear on the 1852 map as having land on the Rochester Road.

Jacob Benedict and his wife Rhoda Beebe, whom he married in 1811, had nine children. The 1836 and 1843 tax records indicate that Jacob was farming eighty-two acres in the vicinity of the Rochester Road and he appears in the Federal census records of 1830, 1840, and 1850. Rhoda died in 1832 several weeks after the birth of Lewis, her ninth child. Jacob died in 1855 and is buried in Greenvale Cemetery with his wife. While his will lists the children, it indicates that most of them had moved west, settling in Illinois and Wisconsin.

Gilbert Benedict, a veteran of the War of 1812, and his wife Cornelia had five children, Nellie, Hannah, Gould, Jane, and Jacob. The 1836 and 1843 tax records indicate that he farmed forty-five acres in the Rochester Road area near his brother Jacob. Cornelia died in 1831, the same year as the birth of her last child, and by 1833 Gilbert had married Lydia Smith of Walworth. They had three children: Elmer, Cornelia, and George. By 1865, Gould, Elmer, and Jacob and their families were still living in Perinton. Lydia had died in 1862 and Gilbert was living with his son Jacob, Jacob's wife Elizabeth, and their daughter Rosanna on the Rochester Road farm. Gilbert's daughter Nellie was also part of that household.

Gilbert died on April 11, 1869, at the age of eighty, after having lived in Perinton for forty-four years. His obituary noted that he "has always been a stable member of society and of the Church of God. He is buried in Greenvale Cemetery as are his two wives, Cornelia and Lydia.

Elmer Benedict, Gilbert's son, was educated at the Red Schoolhouse west of the village of Fairport in East Rochester and later attended Macedon Academy. After teaching at the Red Schoolhouse, he married Rachel Bancroft of Macedon and bought a fifty-two acre farm on Benedict Road, a section that is called Mill Road today, where they raised their two children Adrian and Nellie. Elmer was known as a "radical Republican" and served Perinton as Assessor, Justice of the Peace, and Poormaster. He was also a member of the Grange. He lived on Benedict Road until Rachel's death in

1903, after which he moved to the Cottage Hotel in Fairport village where he remained until his death in 1909. Both Rachel and Elmer are interred in Mt. Pleasant Cemetery.

Elmer's son Adrian was also a lifelong resident of Perinton, having been born in his grandfather Gilbert's house on the Rochester Road. As a child he lived on Benedict Road with his family, and then for over forty years in his home on the southeast corner of Kreag and Pittsford-Palmyra Roads. Like his father he was active in the town, serving as assessor from 1923-43. He lived the last years of his life with his daughter in the village of Fairport, where he died in 1944 at the age of eighty-five. His grave can be found in Mt. Pleasant Cemetery.

The Bown Family

Several houses on South Main Street, a dominant red brick building in Fairport's business section on South Main Street (before urban renewal), a designated Perinton landmark in Egypt, and a subdivision off the Victor-Egypt Road are all associated with the Bown family.

In the early decades of the 1800's the Bowns resided in Ancaster, Ontario, Canada. Edwin Bown was a blacksmith who taught his son George the trade. In 1848 at the age of thirteen, George came to Penfield, New York to live with his uncle, the Rev. Charles Bown. Before long, he had established a blacksmithing business in Walworth, where he married Mary Jane Foreman and started a family. Eventually the couple would have nine children.

Bown Block on South Main Street

In 1856 the family moved to Fairport and George opened a blacksmith shop. By 1861 he had purchased land on South Main near the four corners and built his first house (number 131). In time the Bown family would build and own 126, 127, 131, and 135 South Main Street. Within ten years, he had moved several smaller buildings to the back of the property at 131 South Main and had opened a carriage factory. The George Bown Wagon and Carriage Manufactory included a construction building, a paint shop, a sales room, and an office. The enterprise prospered until 1887 when a disastrous fire destroyed most of the outbuildings. The newly formed DeLand Hose Company was able to use its hoses to save portions of the surrounding property, however.

After the fire, George Bown purchased property from C. J. DeLand nearer the Erie Canal on the west side of South Main Street in the vicinity of today's Village Landing. He soon rebuilt his factory in the new location and also rebuilt his houses on South Main Street. George and his three sons, Frank, Gardner, and William, employed about twenty workers who built, stenciled, and sold wagons and carriages. Besides the carriage shop, George G. Bown and Sons included a blacksmith shop, a salesroom for bicycles, and a woodlot. Bown continued to expand his presence on South Main Street's business district by constructing a large brick structure in 1890, known at the Bown Block. It housed a number of concerns including his son-in-law Robert Estes' drug store, insurance and real estate businesses, as well as the local post office. George Bown in fact served as postmaster between 1897 and 1902. He also served the community as a village trustee, a school commissioner, and Overseer of the Poor. After George's death in 1904, his three sons continued the family business and by 1919 were slowly converting it to an auto dealership and a garage. Frank and Laurence Bown are listed in Fairport's 1932 directory as auto dealers.

7725 Pittsford-Palmyra Road

Seven of George and Mary Jane Bown's nine children lived to adulthood. Of those that remained in the Perinton-Fairport area, Frank married Ella Ellsworth and lived in the house at 126 South Main Street; Gardner married Bertha Bruner with whom he had three children, one of whom, Bruner, married Margaret Case, whose grandfather Nathan Case had first farmed the land on the east side of Victor-Egypt road starting in 1851. Bruner and Margaret ran a dairy farm there and lived in the old farmhouse at 7725 Pittsford-Palmyra Road, known as a "marriage house" because it has two sections built at two different times (1820's and 1890's). In addition, Bruner served his community as Town Justice from 1920-1963. Since then the farm land has been developed as Egypt Park Estates and boasts a Bown's Hill Lane in honor of the family's contributions to the community. The house is a designated Perinton landmark.

The DeLand Family

Minerva DeLand School, DeLand Acres, the DeLand Center, the DeLand Hose Company, DeLand Park A and B. . . Clearly the DeLand family has had a major impact on the village of Fairport.

Early DeLands were most likely Huguenots who fled persecution in the early 1600's, going to England, Holland, and areas in eastern Europe. Claude Charles DeLand, born in France, was probably the first DeLand to come to America, settling in Massachusetts in the mid 1600's with his family, including sons Benjamin, John, and Philip. Within three generations, the DeLand family had turned up in Candor, New York, where Joseph and Mary (Mercy) Lamb settled with their thirteen children. Four of those children, Charles, Joel, Joseph, and Levi came to live, for varying periods of time, in the Perinton area. Charles served as the third pastor of Fairport's First Baptist Church before moving to Michigan. Joel moved to Fairport in 1829 and lived in a house on South Main Street. He owned property in town and worked as a carriage-maker and inventor. Joseph probably married his wife Sally Baker in Fairport, but he too soon moved on to Michigan. Levi moved near Fairport around 1851. He was married twice, first to Hannah Brown with whom he had six children and secondly to Electa Tracy Wilmarth with whom he had nine children.

Levi's children and their descendants would make significant contributions to the community. Sons Charles and William were involved with canal-related businesses, both at one time owning packet boats. Son Joel, following the family tradition of involvement in the Baptist Church, served as a missionary in the Black Hills, and subsequently settled in Michigan, joining a number of other relatives.

D. B. DeLand

Levi DeLand

Minerva P. DeLand

Daniel, Levi's third son, went to sea on a whaling ship and then served as a packet boat captain on the Erie Canal. While plying the canal, he met Minerva Parce, of Norwich, New York. After marriage and a short sojourn in Wisconsin, Daniel and Minerva returned to Norwich where Minerva's parents, Justus and Betsey Parce, had a small ashery business manufacturing saleratus, or baking soda, using wood ashes in the process, hence the name "ashery." Early settlers were happy to sell ashes, of which they usually had an overabundance, often making more profit from them than from their crops. In 1852, after their apprenticeship at Norwich and two trips to Europe to study methods of saleratus production, Daniel and Minerva moved to Fairport. At first they manufactured saleratus or baking soda in their kitchen from the ashes that Daniel collected from area farmers and brought home in his wagon. By 1854, the business had outgrown the house and moved to a group of buildings on Main Street just north of the canal on the east side. In 1856, the DeLands moved to a house at 185 North Main Street, which they surrounded with gardens and trees, a windmill, a gazebo, and summerhouses. In addition to running a very successful business, Daniel, known as Judge DeLand after his appointment to the bench of the local judiciary in Rochester, was also active in the Democratic party and the Baptist Church. He suffered an untimely death in 1872 after falling down an elevator shaft at the factory. His brother Henry and his son Levi took over the business.

The DeLand Chemical Company put Fairport on the industrial map. Daniel's brother Henry proved to be a highly successful salesman for the business, traveling all over the country. Under his leadership after the death of his brother, the company became the largest manufacturer of saleratus and soda in the nation. Between 1853 and 1874, sales went from $9,000 to $500,000 and the company's "Cap Sheaf Soda" brand became a common household item. Unfortunately, the 1890's did not bring continued growth. A disastrous fire in 1893 leveled the factory, and although the company rebuilt, due to increased competition and rising costs, it was not able to sustain itself and it closed in 1903.

Levi Deland's children

The influence of the DeLand family in Fairport continued despite the demise of the DeLand Chemical Company and the death of Daniel DeLand in 1872. Minerva Parce DeLand, Daniel's widow, raised their five children in the house on North Main Street. Levi DeLand, the eldest son, who served as company head, can also be credited with starting the DeLand Hose Company, Fairport's first fire department, and adding to the community's pleasure by underwriting the L.J. DeLand band. He also inaugurated the village's first electric street light system by lighting North Main Street from the factory to his Whitney Road home. Like his father, he was active in Democratic politics, and served as State Assemblyman in the 1880's. Levi and his wife, Mary Lewis, raised their eight children, first in a house at 176 North Main Street that Minerva Parce DeLand had had built and then sold to them for $1.00 and "love and affection," and then in a large shingled mansion on the northeast corner of Whitney and Nine Mile Point Roads, which was surrounded by 600 acres of fruit trees. Eventually that house would become the first Baptist Home.

Daniel and Minerva's three daughters were all educated at Vassar. Leora married Walter Hubbell and moved to a house at 149 North Main Street that is, as of 2010, the site of Bright Start Pediatric Services. Minerva married Dr. J.J. Bennett in 1891, but died in 1892. Stella married the Rev. Dr. James Taylor Dickenson, a Baptist minister, and was called "an ideal minister's wife, devoted and loving, leaving behind her memories like a rich perfume." Son Wayland also made his home in Fairport and worked as an engineer on the Great Lakes.

Daniel and Minerva DeLand's grandchildren continued the DeLand family involvement in the village of Fairport. Minerva Lewis DeLand, daughter of Levi and Mary Lewis, was an educator in Fairport for nearly forty years. A graduate of the Fairport Union School and Vassar College, she prepared for teaching at Albany Normal School and in 1900 returned to teach Classical Languages and Ancient History in Fairport. By 1908 she had been named preceptress or head teacher at Fairport High School, which at that time was on West Church Street. In 1924, when the new high school on West Avenue was opened, she was named principal. In addition to her administrative duties, she also continued to teach Latin because "there was no one else." Miss DeLand, described by Superintendent Thomas Coffee, as a "brilliant teacher, noble guide, and faithful friend," retired in 1935 after thirty years of teaching. Her name, of course, lives on at the Minerva DeLand School on Hulburt Avenue, which was built in 1958-9. Miss DeLand was present at the laying of the cornerstone and at the dedication in 1959. She died at the age of 89 in 1965.

185 N. Main Street - DeLand homestead

Two of Minerva's sisters were also educators. Mary, also educated at Vassar and the Albany Normal School, taught in Auburn and Rochester. Onetah was Supervisor of the Rochester School for the Deaf.

Two more of the Levi DeLand children were involved with the canning business in Fairport. Leora Lewis DeLand married George Cobb of Cobb's Preserving Company, who was instrumental in developing the sanitary can, making it possible to have safe canned food, and also who was one of the founders of the Sanitary Can Company. Daniel Brown DeLand, who worked for both Cobb's Preserving, the Sanitary Can Company, and then the American Can Company, eventually becoming vice president in charge of manufacturing. The American Can Company was a major Fairport employer for many decades in the mid twentieth century.

From the beginning Henry DeLand, Daniel's brother, was the DeLand Chemical Company's premier salesman. He traveled the nation, at first in a horse and buggy and then by rail, touting the company's "Cap Sheaf Soda." He established a network of agents who collected orders that were rushed to the factory. By 1864, under Henry's guidance, sales had expanded to the point that warehouses were built in Chicago and St. Louis. It was reported that they spent $12,000 in one year for advertising, an enormous sum in those days. Upon Daniel's death in 1872, Henry took over as head of the company along with Daniel's son Levi. During the period of time that he was running the business, he built the mansion that is known today as the Green Lantern Inn. He lived there with his second wife, Sarah Parce (Minerva's sister) and their two children Harlan and Helen. At different times Betsey Parce, his mother-in-law, and Eliza Marring, Henry and Daniel's widowed sister, lived there with them. The thirty-two room French chateau-style mansion, built in 1876, continues to be a Fairport landmark. About the same time that he built his house, Henry traveled to Florida and, seeing opportunities in the citrus business, purchased land there. For the next five years, the family divided its time between Fairport and the wilds of central Florida, building a community with John Stetson that would become DeLand, Florida. In 1881, Henry sold his shares in the DeLand Chemical Company to move to Florida full time. The 1890's were an economically difficult time, and the DeLand family was no exception. The winter of 1894-5 brought freezes to Florida that destroyed most of the orange groves in DeLand. After honoring his financial guarantees, Henry was nearly destitute. He returned to Fairport and, at age sixty, began selling saleratus or baking soda for the Monroe Chemical Company. He died in 1908.

Henry's daughter Helen devoted her life to serving first her father and then her community. After graduating from Smith College and teaching for a time at Stetson University in DeLand, Florida, she returned to Fairport with her father to work with him as secretary-treasurer at the Monroe Chemical Company. Those early years of the twentieth century were difficult ones for Helen. She lost her father, mother and brother Harlan in the space of ten years between 1903 and 1913. Within several years, she returned to education, teaching at Fairport High School. Eventually she became the librarian for both the village and the high school, serving in those positions until 1933. She also contributed to the story of Fairport by recording memories of her childhood and writing articles for the local paper about Fairport history and also by belonging to the Fairport Historical Club, a group of women concerned with preserving the story of the community. In addition, she wrote and published *The Story of DeLand and Lake Helen, Florida.* Helen DeLand died in 1956 and is buried along with many other members of the DeLand family in the Mt. Pleasant Cemetery family plot.

Although there are no longer any DeLand family members living in Fairport and the companies they created are gone, the legacy of this family lives on in the institutions they championed, the homes they built, and the tradition of community service they practiced.

George Filkins – Fairport Developer

George Southworth Filkins was born in 1838 in Penfield, New York, to Isaac and Catherine Southworth Filkins. The Filkins family had come from England in 1697 to settle in Dutchess County. By the early 1800's they had relocated to Penfield in western New York. Isaac was a cooper and his products filled a large demand created by the newly opened Erie Canal. He could fashion at least three barrels a day out of the area's abundant hickory and oak.

Isaac and Catherine had at least five children: Thomas, Isaac O., Mary Elizabeth, Jacob, and George Southworth. Relocating in Michigan, Thomas was a cooper by trade and also had a freight business. Isaac and his family settled in Texas, Mary Elizabeth married and moved to Wayne County, and the youngest two sons remained in Fairport. Like most young men his age, George enlisted upon the outbreak of the Civil War. He served two years with the 113th New York Volunteers, Company B, seeing active duty in a number of battles. Mustered out in 1865, by 1869 he had settled in Fairport at 43 West Church Street and had married Adah Benedict. George and Adah had two children, Allen G. and Ernest. Blessed with prodigious energy and personal integrity, George "hewed his way to success and to an honored place among his fellow men." He began development of a large tract of land south of Church Street now known, appropriately enough, as Filkins and George Streets. He liked working in brick, and between 1874 and 1876 had built two houses, 166 South Main, where he lived until 1881, and 164 South Main Street. He most likely built number 160 as well. He also built commercial structures further to the north on South Main Street.

Filkins Street house

Meanwhile, his father and mother had moved to Fairport, and when his father Isaac died in 1874, his mother Catherine and a granddaughter Annabel moved in with George and his family. George himself suffered a loss several years later in 1879 when Adah died at the age of thirty-eight, leaving behind her husband and two children aged eight and eleven. Catherine stayed to care for her two grandchildren.

In 1881 George and his family moved to Filkins Street and in 1883 he married Mary E. White. They had three children, Anna May, Clarence, and Howard. Grandmother Catherine lived with them until her death in 1886, after which granddaughter Annabel took over the task of housekeeper. By the 1890's Allen and Ernest were running a grocery and market in the Filkins building at 45 South Main Street. George continued to buy land and build houses. The 1902 map shows much of Filkins and George Street developed with the empty parcels owned by Filkins.

At the turn of the twentieth century the Filkins family was farming a large parcel of land on Hulburt Road in the vicinity of today's Minerva DeLand School. When the Fairport School District purchased the property, their farmhouse was moved to 110 Hulburt Road where George lived with his sons Clarence and Howard, his daughter Anna May, and his niece Annabel, who kept house.

George Filkins died in 1917 at the age of seventy-eight. Remembered as a successful entrepreneur, he was also a village trustee for many years and a member of the Raymond Baptist Church (Fairport Community Baptist). His legacy lives on in the several brick houses, the elegant farmhouse at 110 Hulburt Road that still stands, and in the two streets he named for himself.

Filkins farmhouse - 110 Hulburt Ave.

Three Generations of Charles Howes

Charles Howe was a Perinton name for three generations. The first Charles Howe was born in 1777 in Florida, New York, where he grew up. Ordained as a Baptist minister, he married Sarah Overbaugh and they raised a large brood of ten children (or eleven, depending on the source). In 1834 the family moved to Perinton, purchasing a farm several miles south of the village of Fairport at the corner of Pittsford-Palmyra and Turk Hill Roads. The Rev. Howe preached in Amsterdam as well as his home town and was a regular preacher at Pittsford, Mendon and Fairport Baptist churches after moving to Perinton.

The second Charles Howe was the fifth child in the family and was born in 1806 in Florida, New York. Because of his father's limited income and the necessity of working on the family farm, Charles II had a limited education, but a seemingly unlimited ability to seek out opportunities. As a teenager he was earning wages as a farm hand, threshing grain for eighteen cents per day and then moving up to a salary of $100 for a year's work. Married to Jane Pettengill in 1829, they had three children and soon thereafter followed the elder Howes to Perinton, a trip by sleigh that took five days. According to information from the 1877 McIntosh history of Monroe County, Charles and his family purchased sixty acres of farmland in the western part of Perinton and proceeded to build a house. Shortly before the house was complete, Jane died, leaving Charles and the three children. By 1835, Charles had married Ailse Slocum, daughter of Perinton pioneer Amasa Slocum and his wife Anna. Together they added five children to the Howe family, one of whom was named Charles.

Apparently the family moved to the Pittsford-Palmyra Road homestead in the 1840's, probably to care for aging parents – the Reverend Charles died in 1849. Charles II lost his second wife, Ailse, in 1853, but then married Mrs. Lucy Butts of Albion in 1854. They were parents of two sons. Charles II lived until 1879, devoting time to his community, his family, and his church. He was a founding member of the First Baptist Church of Fairport, serving for a time as deacon.

The third Charles was born in 1846 on the family homestead, where he lived for his first twenty years. He did not continue the family farming tradition, but moved to the village of Fairport and worked for a time in the furniture manufacturing business. His next venture was as a traveling salesman for the DeLand Chemical Company. He worked in sales for twenty-seven years, the last seven of which were with the J.Hungerford Smith Company of Rochester. He traveled the country, visiting every state, becoming well known and respected. At the same time, Charles was part of the firm of Todd & Howe, who operated a general store in Fairport. He also had an interest in the manufacture of window screens, baking powder, and spices. Not content with those business ventures, he also served as Vice-President of the John F. Bauer Company of Mount Morris, manufacturers of Mo-Ko, a cereal coffee, and a line of patent medicines. Charles Howe was a busy man.

26 Perrin Street

He and his wife Ella and their two children, Mabel and Burton, lived in a fine house which he built at 26 Perrin Street. The house still stands and retains much of its original detailing. Not content with only one property, Howe also owned a large brick building in the center of Fairport village and a productive farm in Nebraska. He believed that because of the many opportunities for enterprising individuals in Fairport, that western New York was the best place in the country to live. Charles died in 1903 and Ella in 1932. Both are buried in Greenvale Cemetery.

The Hulburts of Hulburt Road

Thomas Hulburt was born near the Erie Canal just over the Perinton line in Pittsford on July 21, 1836. His parents were Lewis Hulburt of Monroe County and Roxanna Roberts, a native of Allegheny County.

Thomas attended local district schools and then trained as a teacher at Macedon Academy, where he met and then married Phoebe Hoag. After he left his teaching post in Bloomfield, Ontario County, the couple moved to LaGrange, Indiana, where Thomas became principal of LaGrange Academy and Phoebe, preceptress. Apparently he also taught mathematics and began to study law, since he was eventually admitted to the Indiana bar, following his brother Charles who was a lawyer in Wolcottville, LaGrange County, Indiana.

While in Indiana, the Hulburts befriended Richard Reed, a Fairport banker, and his wife Lucy Ann. Phoebe and Thomas returned to Fairport in 1865 and purchased a house and twenty-five acres of land from the Reeds on what would eventually be called Hulburt Road. Phoebe and their two children moved into the house while Thomas went to Albany Law College. After passing the New York bar, he returned to Fairport to practice law.

In order to reach Fairport village from the Hulburt house, it was necessary to follow the road west to the canal, then follow the canal north to West Church Street and finally turn east into the village. It was not a very efficient route. Consequently, in 1872, Thomas Hulburt and his uncle Raphael Roberts laid out a new road which went due north from the house to West Church Street, making the trip into the village a great deal easier. The two then planted trees along the road and laid out building lots, thereby opening up that section of Fairport for development. The new road was then appropriately named Hulburt Avenue, while the older east-west section was called Hulburt Road.

106 Hulburt Avenue

The Hulburt property of approximately ninety-five acres extended from the Brooks farm, which was located between South Main Street and Brooks Avenue (today's lower Potter Place), west to the canal and then along the canal north to West Church Street. Most of it was farmed. Their house was built sometime between 1852 and 1858 by the aforementioned Richard Reed from whom Thomas and Phoebe purchased it. Originally there were five rooms downstairs and four bedrooms upstairs. There was also a wood shed, summer kitchen, and utility/laundry room. The older photos of the house show a front porch, which no longer exists. Orchards in back of the house overlooked the canal and were a favorite place for Fairport families to picnic. There were, in addition, three barns on the property which at one time housed pigs, cows, and horses.

Phoebe and Thomas Hulburt had five children; however, Phoebe died shortly after the birth of their fifth child. Thomas soon remarried, but only for a short time. The 1880 census lists him as a 41-year-old widower with five children. By 1905 he had married his third wife, Adele. They lived in the house until Thomas' death in 1919 at age 83. Before his death he sold fifty-seven acres of his farmland to the Fairport Development Corporation. Thirty of those acres would become the Fair Acres subdivision at the south ends of Dewey and Miles Avenues, including James Street. After Adele's death the remainder of the property was sold off. As of 2010, the house, owned by Douglas and Susan Angevine, still stands at 106 Hulburt Road and has been designated as a Fairport landmark.

The Potters and their House at 53 West Church Street

In 1858 Spencer Philbrick constructed a large Italianate house and carriage barn at 53 West Church Street. The property, which comprised either five acres or nine depending on the source, included what is today Potter Place from Church Street to Lewis Street, and was surrounded by a picket fence. It was probably the largest and most elegant residence on Church Street.

To Fairporters, the house is associated with the Potter family who moved there in 1872. The family included Alfred, his wife Hulda Thayer and three children: Fred, Alice and Bertha. The Potter family fortune had been made by Alfred's father, Henry, who co-founded the Western Union Telegraph Company with Hiram Sibley, Henry O'Reilly, Samuel Sheldon, and Ezra Cornell. Henry and his family lived for a number of years in the Hoyt-Potter house on Fitzhugh Street in Rochester. After Henry's death, Alfred and his family invested a portion of their inheritance in the Church Street house, a perfect location for raising a family.

53 W. Church St. circa 1908

Hulda Potter oversaw significant renovations in the mansion, removing the Italianate tower and trim and adding a shingle-style third story with balconies and space for a ballroom. She also added a front porch and a port-cochere, which allowed guests to alight from their carriages unscathed by the weather. The house was furnished with antiques and collectibles which the family gathered on their travels.

The family were active members of the First Methodist Church and of the community. The children grew up and although Alice and Bertha married and moved away, Fred did not. Alfred Potter died in 1896 and was remembered as a "liberal and public-spirited man" whose "sweet, unostentatious, gentle manner" won him many friends. Fred, a rather solitary figure, continued to live in the house with his mother, who apparently dominated his life, restricting his activities and his friends until 1925 when Hulda died at age 82, leaving the house in the care of her son.

Although Fred remained a more or less solitary figure, he enjoyed talking with the children of the village and traveling, frequently to Florida. He loved antiques and was an avid collector. A partial inventory from the auction held after his death lists a Chippendale library set; a variety of mahogany furniture including bookcases, a bedroom set, a chest of drawers, and a table with matching chairs; a banjo clock; Oriental rugs; a silver tea service; and sterling silver flatware.

Fred Potter

Cars were another of Fred's pleasures. Even though he could not drive, he owned one of Fairport's first cars, a 1905 Ford, and was driven around town by his chauffeur every day. He was also a member of the Fairport Fire Department.

Fred Potter died in 1943 at the age of 72, leaving an estate worth $574,969 (or $250,000 according to another source) and what was called a "nicely drawn, well-balanced will." He left specific instructions as to what was to be done with the estate. Fairport Library received $5,000, his personal library and his mahogany bookcases. Money was left to several churches, Mt. Pleasant cemetery, and selected friends. $1,000 was left to the Fairport Fire Department for its second floor club room. The largest bequest, $50,000, the house and the carriage barn and five acres of land (or nine, again depending on the source) was left to the village of

Fairport. The village could use $5,000 to alter or landscape the premises, and the remainder of the money was to be held in trust for the maintenance of the property. Up to one-fourth of the land could be sold for residential purposes, the income to be added to the trust. The village had six months to accept the offer and three years to implement it. If no suitable use was found for the house within three years, it could be sold. A citizens' committee recommended that the gift be accepted. Mayor Neiss and the village board subsequently voted unanimously to accept the bequest and a planning committee comprised of Wayne Baumer, Claude Emery, Gordon Ross, Vincent Lawler, and Neal Beach was formed to study the property and make recommendations for its use.

Henry Martin, a local architect, was consulted about renovations to the house, which was to be remodeled as a community center. The grounds were to be attractively landscaped and developed to provide citizens with a place for various outdoor activities such as tennis, softball, and skating. Swings and a sandbox were also included in the plan. The barn was to be renovated to provide a space where "young folks may meet and enjoy wholesome recreation." There would be a manager or director hired to oversee the property and the activities, someone who "likes and can get along with young people." Compensation would include living quarters (in the Potter house), "light, heat, and hot water."

The first part of the project, to convert the house into a "community center" was started in March of 1944 and was projected to cost $2425. Recreation and meeting rooms were created on the first floor and were available to the public by appointment with the resident manager. While initially postponed, work on the park took place during the summer months and the playground officially opened on July 5, 1944, under the direction of Miss Ellen Hawver.

By August 31, 1944, Mr. and Mrs. Hugh Stevely had been hired as managers of the center and subsequently moved to the newly renovated house where they oversaw the property and handled registrations. The Center itself opened on September 1, 1944, and was soon busy with various community group meetings, which could be scheduled from noon to midnight every day except Sunday. Rotary met on Monday evenings and the Red Cross on Friday afternoons and evenings. Scout groups, seniors, garden clubs, and other social groups followed.

The opening of the community center and the playground/park was followed in April of 1945 by the opening of the "Nook" in the carriage house, a youth recreation center to be open from 7 to 11:45 p.m. every Saturday. Entertainment for that first evening was planned to "appeal to all age groups" and consisted of "games, special vaudeville acts and dancing." Refreshments were served and rules of conduct were enforced. Initial applications for membership totaled over 250 young people from the ages of thirteen to nineteen. Despite its popularity, the maintenance costs were high, and in 1957, Mayor Charles Stauber proposed having it razed, stating that the building had outlived its usefulness and that "we would be remiss in our obligations if we continued to buy feed for a dead horse."

Potter carriage house

Obviously the structure was not destroyed, but by the 1980's the entire property was in need of some changes. The former "Nook" had become the "Tiger and Toe" teen center and although it was open more often than once a week, the facilities and the space had become inadequate. In addition, fewer groups were using the main house for meetings.

Several proposals were put forth to deal with the new circumstances. Once again, in 1987, a plan to raze the carriage house and build a new teen center was presented. The old carriage house had no insulation, and in addition to the lack of space, the plumbing often froze in the winter. The Lions Club offer to finance a new building on the site of the carriage house was considered briefly, but the prospect of losing such an important part of the Potter property caused a change in plans. Ultimately the Lions Club funded a new structure behind the old carriage house that incorporated some of the architectural elements of the carriage house, and the new "Lion's Den," opened in 1990, is an appropriate fit with the old Potter house and carriage barn. While attendance has had its ups and downs, the center continues to attract a wide cross-section of the community's young people.

Over the years and with the construction of the Perinton Community Center, the use of the main house for community groups declined, but in 1988 a proposal to convert the structure to senior housing made by the Perinton Senior Living Council was rejected. The house would remain as a community resource. Shortly thereafter, the kitchen was renovated and general maintenance work was done on the interior. In 2000 a major renovation project was undertaken to replace the water-damaged front porch and port-cochere. Old photographs of the house provided the template for the reconstruction and original paint colors were used. The newly refurbished house continues to be a village landmark, and as Fairport resident Matson Ewell stated in a *Perinton-Fairport Post* article, "It's a showpiece."

African Americans in Early Perinton

Slaves arrived in New York as early as 1626, imported by the Dutch to solve a labor shortage both in farming and in commerce. The slave population was concentrated downstate and was quite widely diffused, with the average slave master owning just one or two slaves. By the 1770's the black minority totaled about eleven percent of the population of New York. In the beginning slavery was not formally defined and the laws did not clearly distinguish between indentured servitude and slavery; however, by the mid to late eighteenth century the combination of fear and economic necessity had hardened attitudes, resulting in restrictive slave codes. At the same time, the invention of the cotton gin had reinvigorated slavery in the southern cotton growing states, and slavery became a crucial component of the American economic system. A healthy slave could be worth as much as $2,500.

In 1790 there were about 21,000 slaves in New York, including twelve slaves in Perinton. During the early years of the nineteenth century, New York moved to end slavery in the state, and in 1801 an act was passed banning the importation or exportation of slaves. By 1817 the state had declared that anyone born a slave after July 4, 1799, would be free as of July 4, 1827. After 1827 slavery was banned in the state.

The Ellsworth family, who moved to Perinton in 1832, purportedly brought with them former slaves. According to former Perinton historian Helen Butler, there was a cemetery on the southwest corner of Ayrault and Turk Hill Roads, on the Slocum property, where some of the former slaves were buried along with five Slocum children. Today there is no evidence of those burials. It is said that Julie Rose, who worked as a cook for the Walter Hubbell family and spent her final years in the Fairport Baptist Home, was the daughter of one of the former slaves buried in that plot.

Nineteenth century pre-Civil War Perinton had several African-American families. The John Jackson family owned land along the canal and lived in Perinton probably between 1835 and the late 1840's. "Doc" Sharpe probably lived here around the same time. Said to have been well versed in the use of herbs for healing, he often treated his neighbors. The 1850 census notes a Nancy Armstrong living with the John Knickerbocker family and a William Clency from Georgia living with the Gideon Ramsdell family. The 1855 census showed a "colored" population of ten in the town: five men, three women, and two children.

John Parker, his wife Charlotte, and their children William and Marietta, came to Perinton in the 1870's, John having been born in Maryland in 1827, and Charlotte in Virginia in 1849. William apparently died in childhood, since he is not listed on any subsequent census records. Another son, John, was born in 1880. John owned a barber shop in the village, and his wife, a nurse, was active in church and community affairs, introducing Sojourner Truth when she spoke in Fairport, possibly at Shaw's Hall on West Avenue. She is also said to have been quite outspoken against a commonly used derogatory racial epithet, stating that there was no such word. John died in 1900, their son John, Jr. in 1919, and Charlotte in 1921. All are buried in Greenvale cemetery.

The Abe Taylor family arrived after the Civil War, appearing in the local census for the first time in 1875. He, too, worked as a barber for a time, but then went to work in Albany as a porter for the State Senate. His wife Rebecca and daughter Mary lived on Main Street. Mary attended school here and went on to work at the Sanitary Can Company and then Forman's Department Store in Rochester.

Former Perinton historian Helen Butler wrote about two brothers, Don and Charlie Hull, who lived for a time on Budlong Road where they operated a still. After it blew up and burned the house down, Don left town and Charlie moved to Filkins Street and opened a barber shop. He and his wife Carrie are in both the 1915 and 1925 census records. Charlie was very popular with his customers, making them feel "like kings." Also known as a good boxer and card player, he was a common sight riding his bicycle along Main Street to work. After his bicycle riding days were over, he was always given a spot riding on a fire truck in parades.

As the twentieth century progressed, African Americans continued to move north, leaving the land to work in the growing industrial centers of the north and diversifying the population of the nation as a whole. African-Americans have fought in all of our nation's wars and have in all ways been an integral part of American life, even after years of lynchings, Jim Crow, and the KKK. While the Civil Rights movement of the 1960's ended legal segregation and protected voting rights, it did not end economic segregation or institutional racism. Those issues continue to challenge citizens of a nation whose values state that all persons are created equal.

The Underground Railroad in Perinton

Western New York was strongly involved with two mid nineteenth Century progressive reforms, women's rights and the abolition of slavery. Susan B. Anthony and Frederick Douglass were residents of Rochester; Elizabeth Cady Stanton lived in Seneca Falls, and Harriet Tubman in Auburn. Because of its proximity to Lake Ontario and thus to Canada, Rochester was a terminus for the eastern branch of the Underground Railroad, which ran from Baltimore and Wilmington north to Philadelphia and New York City and then to Syracuse and Rochester and finally to St. Catherine's, Ontario. While northern states were ostensibly "free," the Fugitive Slave Acts of 1793 and 1850, by allowing slave catchers to work in all states, for all intents and purposes extended slavery everywhere, making passage to Canada necessary to guarantee freedom.

The Underground Railroad, a term that really refers to a secret mode of travel, had its beginnings in the late eighteenth century with the Quakers, who did not believe that any human being could be enslaved. According to some sources, the first organized escape took place in 1804 and, by 1830, the organization of "stations" and "conductors" was developed and active with western, central, and eastern branches. It was in this decade as well that various anti-slavery societies began to agitate for change.

Frederick Douglass settled in Rochester in 1847, became active in the Underground Railroad and began to publish his paper *The North Star* in a building owned by the Talman family of Perinton. Despite the fact that aiding slaves was an offense punishable by jail and/or a $1,000 fine, the railroad kept on operating. Stations were spaced approximately one day's walk apart and could be secret rooms, barns, caves, church belfries, root cellars, hollow trees and the like. Lighted lamps or candles often served as signals.

2187 E. Whitney Road, Talman house used for Underground Railroad

Because the railroad was by necessity secret, it has always been difficult to verify the existence of specific stations, but there are four confirmed sites in Perinton. The Talman house at 2187 East Whitney Road and the Ramsdell house on Mason Road still stand; however, a wood-frame house on Fishers Road and a large hollow tree at Steele and Turk Hill Roads are gone.

John Talman, whose grandfather, Isaac Talman, had built 2187 East Whitney Road in the 1820's, writes that the farmhouse . . . was "owned by my father, John Talman, Sr., one of the 'black Republicans' of his day, as implacable and intolerant an enemy of human slavery as the North could boast, and as sturdy, fearless, and unfailing a defender of what he deemed as right as I ever knew." He goes on to recount an event typical of activities on the Underground Railroad:

> "I have a distinct recollection of the time when in the winter of 1859-60 a runaway slave from Georgia, his wife and half dozen little children were concealed in our house for a week or more on their way to Canada. They were quartered in the kitchen and provided with food, not only for present needs, but sufficient for several days after leaving us. I had never seen a negro [sic] child before, and no sooner had the dusky family found refuge with us than my childish curiosity aroused, my fingers were exploring the thick crop of wool that thatched the wide-eyed pickaninnies. The family remained with us until the time agreed upon by the liberators, when my father, in the dead of night, packed them in a large lumber wagon under quilts and blankets and drove them to the next station."

A newspaper clipping signed by Elizabeth N. Shilling, who was born in Fairport in 1858, recounts several stories told to her by her brother. In one, her mother places sandwiches on a gatepost near the intersection of Steele and Turk Hill Roads, declaring that she would feed the fugitives, officials or no. The sandwiches were always gone the next day. Perhaps that gatepost was near the hollow tree. Another story tells of Samuel Williams, a conductor, arriving at their back door saying, "We have to help this man. We can't GIVE him any money, but we can LEND him some." Twenty years later that same brother heard a black man describe help he had received when he was fleeing and was sure it was the same man.

Although there are no extant stories of escaped slaves staying in the Ramsdell house on Mason Road, the Ramsdell family were Quakers, ardent abolitionists, and are known to have used their home as a station.

Despite the support for fugitive slaves in the area, there are examples of resistance to the movement. When Frederick Douglass came to speak in Egypt, he found the church doors locked, forcing him to address the crowd outdoors. The same John Talman describes Douglass:

> "[he]...wore a long blue broadcloth coat with brass buttons. He was tall, erect, a massive figure, his noble bronze countenance surmounted by an enormous halo of thick crinkly hair. In speaking he had a habit of accentuating each decisive utterance by slightly bending his head, shutting his jaws like steel traps, and widening his mouth in a smile of sardonic grimness."

A lecture in a Penfield church was ended when smoke from the stoves filled the room, driving the audience out. The stovepipe had been stuffed with rags.

In the end the forces for justice and dignity and conscience won. Although there is no way to definitively number those who used the Underground Railroad, this loosely organized and of necessity secret group of brave and dedicated individuals, a number of them Perinton citizens, clearly were a force in ending the scourge of slavery.

Carrie Williams Buss: Newspaper Woman

"Loyal, informed," "nigh on indispensable," "a mechanical genius," the "answer girl" are all adjectives used to describe Carrie Williams Buss on the occasion of her retirement after thirty-five years with the *Herald-Mail* and its predecessors. For those thirty-five years, Carrie worked tirelessly and without much fanfare to keep the presses running and the copy accurate in order to inform the people of the Fairport-Perinton community.

The local newspaper underwent many changes over those years. The first paper in Fairport, the *Fairport Herald,* had been founded in 1871 by George Taylor primarily to tout his "Taylor's Oil of Life" patent medicine. It was joined ten years later by the *Monroe County Mail* whose main purpose was to inform the public about issues of temperance, political scandal, and law and order.

Carrie and Alfred Buss

Carrie Williams, a Fairport native, was hired in 1914 as a reporter for the *Fairport Herald* by Floyd Miner, the newspaper's editor. She soon added printing duties. As a printer, she operated the Unitype machine and its successor the intertype press. Both machines required a certain amount of mechanical knowledge to run and maintain. Co-workers referred to Carrie as the "mechanical genius" because of her ability to solve problems and keep the presses running. As a reporter, she grew to know "the story" of hundreds of families, both the good and the not so good. She knew who was married to whom and how many children they had; her knowledge of the community was as extensive as any historian's. Accuracy and precision in writing were equally important to her. "Ask Carrie" was often heard in the newsroom, as much for information about people and issues as about grammar and spelling.

In the years between 1914 and 1950, the local paper underwent a number of changes. Floyd Miner sold the paper to F.M. Elliot in 1925 and in the same year the *Herald* merged with the *Mail* to form the *Fairport Herald-Mail.* Carrie Buss continued to work for the new paper. Twenty years later, in 1945, Curt Gerling purchased the paper, making it part of *Empire State Weeklies*, and Carrie Buss became editor. She once said she felt like a baseball player because she'd been sold so many times.

Carrie Williams Buss did have a private life. She married Alfred Buss in 1937. They lived in East Rochester before moving to a house at 129 Jefferson Avenue in Perinton. Active in the community, they were members of Fairport's First Methodist Church where Carrie served as treasurer of the Sunday school. She was also a member of the American Legion Auxiliary in East Rochester.

Carrie retired in 1950. In the course of her career she had gone from a reporter for a small country publication to an editor of one of the papers in the Empire State Weeklies chain, and had in the process become vital to the success of the paper. She had seen the community survive two World Wars and a Depression, and begin to evidence suburban growth. In recognition of her many years of dedicated service, her name remained on the masthead as editor emeritus. She was fondly remembered as a team player, a dedicated worker, and "nigh on indispensable."

Carrie Williams Buss died in 1960 after a protracted illness.

Helen Tooke Butler: Historian and Genealogist

Genealogist, story teller, and community activist, Helen Butler served the town of Perinton as historian from 1966 to 1983 when at the age of seventy-eight she was forced to retire by the retirement rules of the State of New York. She stated in no uncertain terms that she was resigning "under protest" and that it would take any replacement "10 to 15 years to get to know all I know."

Helen Tooke was born in Syracuse, New York, and spent summers at her family's Madison County farm learning about nineteenth century farm life. As a young person, she was always interested in history and genealogy, researching the Tooke family tree in her teens, tracing the family back to England and Ireland of the 1700's. Professing a dislike for both sewing and cooking, she nonetheless entered the School of Home Economics at Syracuse University because her aunt's sister was the dean of that school. She received her bachelor's degree from Syracuse and subsequently earned her master's at Columbia University.

Returning to Syracuse, Helen taught home economics and special education classes in the city's schools. At one time she also supervised the cafeteria programs in five different schools. She spent much of her free time traveling the world, visiting Europe and Russia, touring nursery schools and hospitals and doing genealogical research. In 1937 she moved to Pittsford and soon thereafter married Charles Butler. He was a wholesale rose grower who, for a time, helped operate George Hart's greenhouses. The Butlers lived for a time in Pittsford before moving to a large farmhouse, formerly belonging to Darius Talman, on East Whitney Road in Perinton.

Continuing her interest in genealogy, Helen established the Tri-Town Genealogical Society, members of which sought to compile genealogy records for the towns of Perinton, Pittsford, and Penfield. In 1966, she found another outlet for her interest in history and genealogy when she was asked by Perinton Supervisor Ken Courtney to fill in as town historian after the death of Alta Fisher, who had served in that post since 1955. The following year she was formally appointed Perinton Town Historian by then Supervisor Lake Edwards, moving into a small office in the Clark Block on South Main Street. However, for most of her years as historian, Helen worked out of her house on East Whitney Road. "I work all over the house....I spread all over the dining room table," she noted.

Helen Tooke Butler

Commenting on her job, Helen noted that one of her biggest tasks was correcting mistakes. Two of the more common misconceptions had Johnny Appleseed, rather than Glover Perrin, planting Perinton's first apple orchard at the corner of Turk Hill and Ayrault Roads; another tale falsely told of an underground tunnel linking the Green Lantern Inn and the First Baptist Church. Most of her time, however, was taken up answering questions about family and house histories and contributing articles to the local paper on a wide range of topics relating to Perinton history. Helen was also primarily responsible for bringing Peter Wiles and his canal boat the *Emita II* to Fairport. It started as a program for school children who would tour the canal between Fairport and Pittsford's lock 32 while listening to a taped history of the waterway, but it soon expanded to include social and professional organizations and eventually tourists. Today the Erie Canal is a major recreational resource for the communities that line its banks and many tour boats, as well as private ones, ply the canal from May to November.

Helen Butler was not content just to be the historian. She was also active in AAUW, the Red Cross, and the local Republican Party. In addition she taught adult education courses in genealogy. For all her many activities she was named Perinton Chamber of Commerce Citizen of the Year in 1979, the first woman so selected. On the occasion of Butler's retirement in 1983, Shirley Husted, former Monroe County historian, called her the most active town historian in the county.

Helen was honored in her retirement by the Monroe County Legislature, who made February 16, 1984, "Helen Butler Day," as well as by County Executive Lucien Morin, who praised her work and presented her with a commendation and a medallion. Perinton Supervisor Jim Smith also presented her with a medallion and noted her appointment as Historian Emeritus. Louise Slaughter, who was serving in the New York State Assembly at the time, presented her with a state resolution recognizing her as an "outstanding citizen" and for her service as town historian.

However, perhaps the most lasting memorial to Helen Butler are the notebooks of Perinton historical and genealogical information, a good deal of which she was responsible for compiling, that line the office of the current historian and that continue to provide answers for those who visit.

Helen Butler died of a heart attack in December of 1984, less than a year and one-half after her retirement. She was seventy-nine years old.

Charlotte Clapp: Clerk and Historian

Historian, town clerk, amateur photographer, active Republican, Charlotte Clapp was a professional woman who served the town of Perinton for over thirty years. Born to Dr. Wesley and Roxa Hodges Clapp in 1884, Charlotte was a lifelong resident of Fairport, never moving from the family home at 15 Perrin Street. Their Greek Revival house had three parts: an apartment for Dr. Clapp's mother Almira, Dr. Clapp's offices, and living quarters for the family, which included Charlotte and her siblings, George, Lewis, Marion, and Robert.

Charlotte graduated from the Fairport Union School on West Church Street in 1904 and attended Mt. Holyoke College, graduating with majors in biology and Latin. Returning to Fairport and the house on Perrin Street, she assisted her father, helped care for her mother, and began to get involved in community affairs, serving on several World War I service committees.

Charlotte Clapp

In 1921 Charlotte Clapp was appointed Perinton's first historian, with the initial task of compiling the records of those Perinton residents who had fought in World War I. This was in line with a bill that had passed the New York legislature in 1919, which called for the designation of local historians, whose first task would be to assist the State Historian in preparing a study of New York's role in the war. The resulting compilation, entitled *Perinton in World War,* includes a detailed list of those who served overseas as well as those who contributed on the home front. Some of the information was subsequently included in the *Monroe County History of the War.*

Shortly thereafter, Miss Clapp was named deputy town

clerk. At that time the job of clerk also included being Receiver of Taxes and Assessments, Registrar of Vital Statistics, and Secretary to the Planning Board, the Board of Appeals, and Zoning Commission. In 1924, despite caring for her invalid mother, Charlotte accepted Supervisor Jesse Hannan's appointment to the full-time position of Town Clerk upon the death of A. Worth Palmer. Her description of the job reveals its breadth. "My office is where you pay town and school taxes, buy your hunting and fishing licenses, get a marriage or a dog license, pay your water bill…You can ask how to get a building permit, inquire as to election laws, ...and complain about ...the fact that John Jones' dog barks all night long." She also noted that "Everyone knows what I do in my office...probably to their sorrow, for this office is where they leave their money. It has all the privacy of Grand Central Station."

When Charlotte Clapp took over the office of clerk, "There was a table used as a work table and around which members of the board sat for meetings. There was a rocking chair and other chairs for visitors and numerous cuspidors strategically placed for their convenience." There was a "roll top desk….a wooden cabinet in which contracts and legal forms were filed and one pasteboard box for town correspondence. Down in the basement, on the floor, all earlier documents, including highway records, were packed in wooden boxes – at the mercy of mice and water in the Spring." The salary was $100 per month. It wasn't long before the rocker and cuspidors were gone, replaced by an office desk, a filing cabinet, an adding machine, and a typewriter. The highway records were transcribed to make them legible, and many of the records were retrieved from the basement and filed by year. The clerk's office in the growing town of Perinton now had a professional aura.

In addition to her numerous duties in the clerk's office and her ongoing work of maintaining the historic files and scrapbooks as historian, Charlotte Clapp also found time to serve as assistant secretary to the Board of Health and as treasurer of the Republican Finance Committee of Perinton. In addition, she was a founding member of the Perinton Historical Society and the Perinton Business and Professional Women's Club. At the same time, she continued to care for her invalid mother, Roxa, who died in 1935.

The 1930's and 1940's brought new growth and new challenges to the community and to the office of clerk. During this time the services provided by the towns increased. New building, with the resulting new water districts, highway construction, and maintenance, coupled with an increasing assessed valuation, added to the duties of the town clerk. The years of the depression brought a rapid rise in relief, or welfare. Money was raised through bank notes and loans from the county to a total of $79,000, all of which was repaid. World War II required the towns to maintain a mobilization board that cost approximately $1,500 per month. As historian, Miss Clapp kept extensive records of Perinton's involvement in the war, compiling an eight- volume record of all Perinton service personnel in the *Town of Perinton War Service Record.* In the late 1940's she wrote a history of Perinton and World War II.

In 1955, when Supervisor Raymond J. Lee, under whom she had worked for twenty years, announced his retirement, Miss Clapp retired as well. She had served as clerk for thirty-one years and as historian for thrity-four. During her tenure, the population of Perinton had doubled from 7,799 to 14,117 and town government had become big business.

In her retirement years Charlotte Clapp traveled extensively and pursued her hobby of amateur photography. She continued her activity in the Perinton Historical Society and the Business and Professional Women's Club, and was active in the 1962 Perinton Sesquicentennial celebration, contributing photographs of old houses and opening her home on Perrin Street to the Sesquicentennial house tour.

On December 11, 1964, just eighteen days short of her eightieth birthday, Charlotte Clapp died. This professional woman, this lifelong resident of Perinton, to whom anyone who values the history of this community is indebted, is buried in Greenvale Cemetery, and has been honored with a place on the Wall of Fame in Fairport High School.

Julia and Emma Dickinson: Missionaries and Librarians

Charles and Mary Parks Dickinson resided in Bushnell's Basin, where Charles was a junior partner with his brother Thomas in a mercantile firm. Seeing opportunity, in 1828 he and Thomas took over the Goodell and Aiken store in the village of Fairport and in 1837 Charles moved to Fullam's Basin (near the present site of Perinton Park), to run an inn and the local post office. While living there, he and his wife had three daughters, two of whom, Julia and Emma, lived to adulthood.

After twenty years at the Fullam's Basin site Charles saw that the future lay in the village of Fairport and he moved his house up the road to 10 East Church Street (where it still stands). He converted the former inn into a private residence and proceeded to become very involved in the business of the village. Over the years Charles served as Town Clerk, Overseer of Highways, and a school trustee and librarian. Brother Thomas built a house for himself around the corner on the present site of Shaheen's paint store. The brothers shared a huge yard which extended all the way from East Church to Orchard Street

The Dickinson women, Julia and Emma, grew up to be very active in the Congregational Church, where they taught Sunday school. Emma was a founding member of both the Women's Foreign Missionary Society and the Home Missionary Society and also was leader of the "Pine Needles," a youth missionary society. Julia herself spent a good portion of her twenties as a missionary in Japan and provided her father with oriental art for his store and exotic plants for his gardens.

In 1874 the Dickinson women embarked on a new venture. Julia, having returned from her missionary travels, and Emma, together with their good friend Elizabeth Dowd, started a subscription library in the wide second floor hall of the 10 East Church Street house. The fees for borrowing were nominal: \$1.00 per year, \$.50 for six months, and \$.25 for three months, with no late charges. While the public had access to school libraries, there had not been, to that date, any free (or relatively free) access to popular literature, and the new library was a huge success. Titles included *Two Years before the Mast, A Civil War Tale* and *Life of Horace Greeley*, for the adults, and *Lucy at School* and *Lucy at Play* for the younger reader. When books went missing, there was often a notice in the paper urging readers to "look over your books and see if you accidentally kept any of them. If you find a tenant, please return at once and oblige the librarian."

Julia Dickinson

The new library soon outgrew its upstairs hall location and moved around the corner into two rooms on the first floor of the Thomas Dickinson house at 123 South Main Street. The day-to-day operations of the library were overseen first by Mr. and Mrs. Buckland, and subsequently by Mr. and Mrs. Charles Chase. Despite the move to larger quarters and the apparent popularity of the books, according to some sources there was a general indifference and even hostility toward the Dickinson library, leading to its abrupt closing in 1894. A small notice in the local paper read, "It having been decided to close the Public Library permanently, subscribers who have books will confer a favor by returning them promptly, and any amounts due on unexpired subscriptions will be refunded at the library on application." The first Fairport public library had operated for twenty years. Fortunately, the creation of free public libraries was underway and Fairport received its charter in November of 1895.

Julia Dickinson had been forced to give up her church and library work because of ill health and for that reason she spent a portion of each year in the Bahamas where she continued to be active in such organizations as the Women's Christian Temperance Union. She died there in 1892 at the age of fifty-three much praised for her generosity, thoughtfulness and self-sacrifice.

After her sister's death and the closing of the subscription library, Emma continued her church work and became involved in mission work in Japan as her sister had before her. There she ran a small business printing leaflets, religious tracts, and Bibles. She returned to the United States in 1923 after a disastrous earthquake in Japan and died in 1926 at the age of eighty-one.

Julia and Emma Dickinson, who clearly can be credited with starting Fairport's first public library, are buried in Greenvale Cemetery.

Deva Ellsworth: Musician

Deva Ellsworth was born in 1894 on the Maple Grove Stock Farm, located across Ayrault Road from Perinton Center Cemetery. She was one of Purdy and Eva Ellsworth's four children, the other three being Elwood, Ruby and Lilly. The children attended District School #6 on the corner of Ayrault and Pittsford-Palmyra Roads. Deva, a talented musician, then went to East Rochester High School, graduating in 1916.

In addition to being a musician, Deva was also somewhat of a free spirit. Not interested in returning to the farm and a conventional life, she joined Madame Meyers Ladies' Band as the cornet soloist and played at Atlantic City during the 1916 summer season. During the following two years she toured New England and the West while playing for several different bands. At the time, the professional concert band was the most popular form of public entertainment. The most well-known of American band leaders of that era was, of course, John Philip Sousa. Women, however, were not allowed to join the professional bands except perhaps as vocal or harp soloists and, as a result, formed their own bands.

With the entrance of the United States into World War I, Elwood Ellsworth enlisted and a month later was followed by two of his sisters, Deva and Ruby, who joined America's Ladies' Military Band. The band was directed by Helen May Butler, a noted cornetist and composer who was often referred to as the "female Sousa." The group of about fifty women came from all over the country and included many who had held jobs as teachers and office workers before enlistment. All were musicians, volunteers, and had brothers in the service. The band was to tour military training camps in the U.S. before going to Europe to entertain the troops there.

Deva Ellsworth

The Ladies' Band played for the Fourth Liberty Loan Drive in Michigan, Pennsylvania, Ohio, Maryland, and West Virginia. They visited a number of cities each day with a parade and a concert in each. Army camps in Pennsylvania, Michigan, Illinois, Missouri and Indiana were treated to visits of one to two days which included a two and one-half hour concert, a memorial concert at sunset when the flags were lowered, and time at the base hospital and officers' tent. Since 1918 was the year of the Spanish Flu, which struck a number of military facilities, the band would often go to camps that were under quarantine. Deva recalled that "we went inside and stood only about a foot from the bedside of some who were dying of the flu. They were dying at a rate of seventy-five a day when we were there. One fellow died and his last words were 'Please play that last selection over again.' The selection we played was 'My Belgian Rose.'" Deva had a mild case of the flu, her sister Ruby a more severe one, and one of the saxophonists from the band caught the flu and died. Although both Deva and Ruby were anxious to be sent overseas, the war ended before that happened, and the ensemble was disbanded.

Ruby returned home to the farm and married life; Deva, however, chose to continue her musical career and joined the New England Chautauqua circuit, playing with the Boston Fadette Military Band. She also toured with both B.A. Rolfe's musical company and with Lapham's Band, playing at exclusive resorts like Savin Rock Park in West Haven, Connecticut. Her last engagement was with the Ladies' Eleven Piece Jazz Orchestra.

Deva Ellsworth became ill in 1924 and died at the age of thirty in 1925. In her obituary she is described as "possessing a loveable character and [was] always striving for pleasure and comfort of those with whom she came in contact." In an age when most women settled down, married, and had children, she earned a living doing what she loved and in the process gave joy to many people. Her love of music was evident at her funeral at Fairport's First Baptist Church. Edith Street sang "Dream Vision of You" accompanied on the piano by Cora Dunn; Lucille Fitzgerald played the "Violin Requiem," and Stanley Ellsworth, a cousin, sang "Softly Now the Light of Day." Members of Lapham's Band played at the graveside and mourners included members of the Musicians' Protective Association.

Deva is buried along with many members of the Ellsworth family in Perinton Center Cemetery on Ayrault Road.

Elma Nau Gaffney: Librarian

Elma Nau Gaffney was well known to several generations of Fairport library goers. She served as head librarian from 1938 until 1969, overseeing many changes and much growth.

Elma Nau was born to Mr. and Mrs. Fred Nau in Honeyoe Falls. She graduated from the local high school and went on to earn a degree from Syracuse University in library science. In 1922, after working as a librarian in Buffalo, she married Mason Gaffney, a teacher at East High School, and moved to Rochester where she worked part-time in the East High School library. Tragically, their only daughter, Patsy, lived only nine years, dying in 1933.

Elma Gaffney

Gaffney's career in Fairport started in 1924 when she joined the library Board of Trustees. When the West Avenue School opened that same year, head librarian Helen DeLand also took on the job of head school librarian. The two jobs soon became too big for one person to handle and Elma Gaffney moved from volunteer library work to regular part-time employment in 1933. By 1935 she was serving as temporary library director and was appointed director in 1938.

During Gaffney's tenure as temporary director, the library building at 18 Perrin Street, described at the time as "an old frame house with bulging walls, mice running under the desks, cracks in the floor, tilting stairs, and a chimney that intermittently dropped bricks," had to be replaced. Robert Douglas of the Douglas Packing Company had left shares of stock in his company to the library for rebuilding, but the depression had severely decreased their value. By 1931, they were only worth $22,652, not enough for a new library building costing $44,000. Plans that had been drawn up by local architect Henry Martin were shelved until 1936 when the WPA took on the library as one of its projects.

Elma Gaffney found a temporary home for the library in the Schummer's Block on West Avenue. She supervised the demolition of the old building, the preparation of the site, and the construction of the new building. Under her leadership, a fund drive was held to raise money for new books. 105 volunteers raised $5,000 and purchased 2,500 books that brought the library collection up to 22,000 books. The move back to the new building on Perrin Street took place in March 1938.

The war years were difficult for the Gaffneys and ultimately tragic. Mason had enlisted in the army in 1942 and was stationed in California. In 1944, he died of a heart attack and Elma took a year's leave to work in the hospital library at the Treasure Island Naval Base in San Francisco. However, she returned to Fairport in 1946 and would remain as library director until her retirement in 1969.

It was said that Elma Gaffney *was* the library. She knew all the patrons and their reading preferences and was always ready with new suggestions. She took care of the children while guiding their reading habits. Her welcoming presence made the library a place everyone wanted to visit. Her vision of a library shows in the following description she wrote in 1938:

> There is a warm corner where old pensioners
> Catch up on their afternoon naps.
> There are tables at which Bobby-soxers may sit
> While waiting for eligible date material to appear.
> There is a snug vestibule for waiting.
> There is a children's room where harried mothers
> Deposit their scamps for the afternoon.
> There is an alcove where parcels are left
> While house wives are bill-paying.
> There is a telephone over which dates are made – or broken.
> There are obscure sections of the stacks
> Apparently well suited for clandestine kisses….
> The Public Library also has books to lend.

In addition to making the library a welcoming place, Gaffney expanded the collection, established the Library Guild, a group of volunteers that helped with filing, shelving, and book repair, and was instrumental in forming the Monroe County Library System. The system made it possible for individual libraries to benefit from mass purchasing, inter-library loans, and rotating collections. She was part of "the missionary team that spread the gospel of library systems throughout New York State, speaking to all interested groups and the New York Library Association about the benefits to be derived when a group of libraries banded together to share resources." Fairport joined the system in 1953.

Elma Gaffney retired in 1969 and immediately returned to the library as a volunteer. She also presented popular travel talks and book reviews at the library and continued to be an inspiration to those who knew her until her death in 1980. The large meeting room at the library is named in her honor.

Anne Burns Hartigan: Serving the Community

Anne Elizabeth Burns was born to Michael J. and Mary Esther Caffery Burns on July 16, 1898, in a house located on the southeast corner of Whitney Road and North Main Street. Anne was the third generation of her family to live in Fairport. Her grandparents, Thomas and Mary Kelly Burns, had emigrated to this country from County Wexford, Ireland, probably in the 1840's or 1850's, and settled in Fairport, most likely to work on the Erie Canal or on the railroad.

Anne attended the East Avenue Elementary School, also known as District School # 9 or Northside Elementary, and then the Fairport Classical Union School on West Church Street. She graduated in 1916, one of twenty-seven students, and attended the Rochester Normal School, intending to become a kindergarten teacher. Those plans did not come to fruition, however. A kindergarten teacher needed to be able to sing and play the piano, neither of which Anne was able to do. She subsequently attended the Mechanics Institute (today's RIT) from which she graduated with a degree in Engineering Drafting, at the time a quite unusual degree for a woman.

Stromberg-Carlson hired Anne and another one of her female classmates to work in the Rochester office. Needless to say, the two women were resented. Any mistake resulted in the necessity of redoing the project, usually without being told what the specific error had been. Their male counterparts, however, benefited from having their mistakes clearly pointed out. Anne worked there for about five years. (Ironically, her boss contacted her in 1941 as World War II was beginning and asked her to return to work.)

In 1924 Anne married a co-worker, Frank Hartigan, and the couple settled on DeLand Park B in a house that they would occupy all of their married life. Two sons were born there, Francis Michael and William Thomas.

Anne B. Hartigan

After the birth of her two children, Anne had the opportunity to become involved with local village affairs, an interest which would occupy her for the rest of her life. During the early 1930's Dr. George Price, the town's public health officer, gathered a group of women, including Anne, his daughter Ruth Price Bowlby, Julia Anderson, and Helen Martin to form the Public Health Nursing Committee to deal with issues of public health. Anne had no nursing background, but she learned what was necessary from Dr. Price, who was also a long-time friend. As members of the committee, they helped to raise money for the Child Health Fund by collecting nickels, dimes, quarters – whatever people would give. The fund aided children who needed eye glasses or procedures such as tonsillectomies. In addition, they assisted Dr. Price with immunization clinics by canvassing the village and town, and providing clerical help and nurses to inoculate and vaccinate pre-school and school-aged children. Anne also worked at the Loan Cupboard, a Community Chest organization which provided wheel-chairs, hospital beds, and other sick-room supplies to Perinton residents.

During World War II when there was a great need for child care while women were working, Anne worked with the Perinton Youth Commission to create after-school and summer activities for children. She hired Ellen Hawver to oversee a summer playground program and in 1946 was instrumental in the hiring of Joe Cummings as recreational director. When the Potter carriage barn opened as a teen center in 1945 (the Nook), Hartigan coordinated the volunteer chaperones and the programs.

Anne Hartigan began a long period of involvement with the Fairport School District when her young sons were in elementary school. As a member of the PTA she worked with teachers on a number of projects, even knitting mittens for each member of one class who was putting on the play "The Three Little Kittens." When centralization became an issue in 1949 and 1950, Hartigan served on the Perinton-Fairport Centralization Committee. As a member of that committee, she visited the various district schools to answer questions about centralization. In 1951 she was elected to the newly created Fairport Central School District school board. She served for thirteen very busy years when the district opened Johanna Perrin Elementary School, Minerva DeLand High School, and Martha Brown Junior High School, closed Midvale School and Northside (East Avenue) School, and razed the West Church Street School. When the new Northside Elementary School was opened on Hamilton Road in 1970, it was dedicated to this active and tireless worker for education.

The Perinton Historical Society counted Anne Hartigan among its members. She worked with other members on a WPA project which recorded cemetery data and she helped research land titles and family genealogies. Because her family had known the DeLand family very well, she was able to help the members of the Society document the history of the DeLand family and the DeLand Chemical Company.

Anne Burns Hartigan died in 1965. She was the quintessential volunteer who dedicated countless hours to her community in a variety of ways. The Perinton Historical Society summed up her generous and giving nature in their recognition of her as someone who "gave herself generously for the health, safety, and education of the children of our tow ...and contributed her time and talent faithfully and steadfastly toward the … fostering of a sense of historical continuity in this town…."

Mary Laird: Nurse

"Many had her spirit, but not her capacity…" Mary Laird was a woman of many talents, enormous energy, and gritty determination. She was born in Bristol, Quebec in 1884, the youngest of three children, but really grew up in Rochester, moving to the city in 1887 with her family. As a young child caring for her brothers' stubbed toes and skinned knees, mothering neighborhood sick animals, and bandaging the fat legs of the family's grand piano legs with strips from discarded sheets, she already showed interests and talents that would in later years lead her into the nursing profession. Mary fulfilled her dream of becoming a nurse, but not without some opposition. Her application to Rochester General School of Nursing was initially rejected because the directress thought she was too small to handle the physical labor involved. She persisted, was finally accepted in 1907, and graduated in 1909. After several years overseeing probationers at Rochester General, she moved to New York City to continue her education at Columbia University and to teach nursing at Bellevue Hospital.

Mary Laird

World War I changed Mary Laird's focus. In 1918 she volunteered for active duty with a Rochester medical team known as Base 19, headed by Dr. (Colonel) Swan. They were sent to Vichy, France to set up a field hospital. Mary was one of three team members, joining a doctor and a corpsman. During the battle of the Argonne Forest, the team cared for all the "shock" cases. About the experience she said "….no one knew where we were for sure, we just got as close to where the fighting was as we could, and did what had to be done." After the signing of the Armistice, Mary requested to be sent "wherever I could best serve." She was transferred to a medical group from St. Louis, Missouri, and put in charge of a 500-bed hospital there. Her assistants consisted of one nurse for each floor of 100 beds and some corpsmen.
Rochester was still in the grip of the Spanish flu pandemic when Mary Laird returned home in 1919. At that time, patients who had no regular physician went to the out-patient clinics for treatment and, in the process of doing that, both weakened themselves and spread the contagion. Along with social workers and other charitable groups, Laird studied the possibility of establishing a traveling nursing service to treat the sick in their own homes, thereby controlling the spread of the disease. She then went about setting up a visiting nurse service with the assistance of Ella P. Crandal, a director of a national organization for public health nurses.

The Visiting Nurse Service started with Laird, a staff nurse, and a secretary. Their job involved walking many miles, sometimes down alleyways and over fences, to reach the people they needed to treat. Early on there was hostility both from physicians, who didn't understand the concept of nursing outside the hospital, and also from many of the immigrant poor patients, who feared "modern" methods. Nevertheless, Mary Laird's determination won out and it was not long before the service employed eight nurses, each of whom covered a section of Rochester. In addition, the Community Chest (now the United Way) began to help with financing during the group's second year.

Visiting Nurse Service - 1920's

In the decade following the flu epidemic, the service began to concentrate on maternal/child health, nutrition, and education. Nurses taught child care to mothers, held pre-natal classes, (an alien idea to poor women who could not afford the luxury of a hospital delivery and who relied on often unqualified midwives), ran well-baby clinics in the attempt to counter the belief that high infant mortality was inevitable, and set up milk stations where mothers could get fresh milk before refrigeration was common. Despite the resistance to these "modern ways," the work was successful and the organization developed a solid footing.

After seven years it was time to move on. Although Laird stayed active with the Nurse Service, in 1926 she went to work for the Council of Social Agencies in Rochester to establish their health division. While there, she promoted the idea of preventive medical care, especially for children, and the care of the chronically ill at home. She also worked with the poor at the Lewis Street Settlement House, beginning each day with a trip to the public market to purchase fresh fruits and vegetables for the children.

Meanwhile, in the 1920's, Laird had purchased several acres of land in Bushnell's Basin, finding relief from the stresses of her job in its rural atmosphere. She cleared the land, planted trees and a garden, and in the 1930's, after retiring from full-time work, built a small house where she cared for her invalid mother and aunt. Her house, a charming cottage on Laird Lane, was constructed by local men who needed work. Although retired and caring for ill family members, Mary Laird continued to support the development and growth of the Visiting Nurse Service, which by the 1950's provided physical therapy and home health aides, as well as general nursing care. In addition, the service pioneered the country's first medically sound Meals on Wheels program.

After the death of her mother and aunt, Laird returned to work in a doctor's office, remaining there until she was seventy-three years old. During this time she learned how to weave and became quite active in the Rochester Weavers' Guild. Her cloth was beautifully woven and her wall hangings were especially prized. She incorporated flowers, leaves, and grasses into each unique piece. Many of her creations appeared in craft shows and local gift shops. Even after full retirement, Mary remained active. Her small car was a familiar sight as she ran errands for those in need. As she grew older, her eyesight began to fail, and during the last years that she was able to stay in her house, she benefited from visits by the nursing service that she had started.

The last nine years of Mary Laird's life were spent in the Fairport Baptist Home where she went after surviving several heart attacks and a broken hip. Despite her failing eyesight and fragile health, she continued her weaving, using a small table loom.

Mary Laird died in 1985 at the age of 101. Marjorie Storey, a former nursing service colleague, described her as "a small, enthusiastic, vibrant person." Friends described her as "enthusiastic, lively and . . . someone who took a keen interest in helping people." Her friend Marion Finlay said, "She was the kind fairy of Bushnell's Basin. She was always available to families in need." The chaplain of the Fairport Baptist Homes at the time, the Rev. Elizabeth Stroop, said in her tribute, "We thank God for Mary – for her great gifts to her community, her profession, her family, her neighbors. We thank God for her humor, for her grit, for her love. . . Mary Laird is indeed an inspiring model of a life well lived, a race well run."

Marjorie Snow Merriman: Historian

Having been born into one of Fairport's important families and in one of its most well-known houses, Marjorie Snow was probably destined to become an historian.

Marjorie was born in 1886 in her great-uncle Henry DeLand's house on the corner of South Main and Church Streets (better known today as the Green Lantern Inn). Her grandmother Eliza was Henry's sister. Eliza and her only daughter Leila had returned to Fairport from Michigan upon the death of Eliza's husband, Delos Marring. Leila was one of five students who graduated from the Fairport Union School in 1877. She taught school until her marriage to Edward Snow in 1883. Members of the Snow family followed Edward to Fairport and the family opened Fairport's first department store. E.C. Snow & Company carried men's, boy's, and children's clothing, shoes, furniture, art goods, and picture framing.

Marjorie Snow Merriman

Edward, his wife Leila, and their daughters, Marjorie, Helen, Alice, and Evelyn made their home at 88 West Church Street. Edward worked in the family store and Marjorie and her sisters attended Fairport schools. Marjorie graduated in 1904 and attended Cornell University for two years before she met and married Paul Merriman, a fellow student. After Paul's graduation, the couple moved to Richmond, Virginia where Paul taught biology at the University and Marjorie looked after their daughter Elizabeth.

In 1925 the Merrimans returned to Fairport and moved into a brown-shingled saltbox house that they had built on Ayrault Road. It was from this time that Marjorie began to focus on Perinton and Fairport history. She was a meticulous recorder of information. One of her first projects was to trace the ownership of as many of the original sixty-six lots into which Perinton had been surveyed as possible. (The information is contained in two large looseleaf binders in the historian's office.) Marjorie spent countless hours researching the histories of early Perinton families and compiling summaries, and her "Book of Reminiscences" contains nuggets of information about many of Perinton's families and places. Following are just a few examples:

> Jacob Hardick's brickyard was where the bungalows on Midvale Drive are.
>
> Mr. Bortle also said that Ayrault's Woods along the canal north of Egypt were full of Indians who were directed by the US Government to go to the Tonowanda Reservation, but they refused to go. They used to steal canned goods from the Edgett Canning Factory, but would never steal from their neighbors, the Ayraults.
>
> Ann Hallett's canal grocery was at the south end of the Oxbow and on the west side of the canal.
>
> There was a swing bridge made of rope across the Erie Canal at the end of Beardsley Street.

Besides the clay pipe factory at Bushnell's Basin, there was one in back of Kelsey's at the corner of Summit and South Main Streets.

The first millinery store in Fairport was owned by Caroline Ford, sister of Joseph Ford and Ruth Delano, probably after 1838.

Merriman's *Early Days in Perinton* (1964) and her newspaper articles contain information about the Erie Canal, local businesses, geology, early settlers, Native Americans, Italian and Irish immigrants, the village of Fairport, and significant local individuals, among many others. In addition, the material that the historian's office and the Historical Museum have on the history of local roads, gravestone inscriptions, and historic structures is due to the tireless work of Marjorie Merriman. Again, her devotion to local history led to her being a charter member and the first president of the Perinton Historical Society, founded in 1935.

Marjorie Snow Merriman died in 1966, leaving a wonderful legacy in her contributions to the community's knowledge of its history.

Perinton Supervisors

Perinton Democrats 1892; (l.to r.) Patrick McAuliffe, Levi DeLand, Fletcher Defendorf

Forty-one men have held the position of supervisor since Perinton's incorporation in 1812. In the early years, the supervisor was assisted by an elected clerk, tax collector, constable, fence viewers or pathmasters, Overseers of Highways, and Poormasters. The clerk kept the record, the fence viewers made sure that land owners maintained their fences in order to keep livestorck contained, the highway overseers oversaw work done (by local landowners) to keep roads passable, poormasters administered public money to aid the indigent, the constable kept order, and the tax collector took care of the finances. All were overseen by the supervisor. Town meetings were held once a year, often in private homes or the local tavern. Then as now, the essential job of town government was to oversee land usage and development.

Perinton's first supervisor was Cyrus Packard, who was elected at the first town meeting in April, 1813. Packard ran a tavern in Egypt on Pittsford-Palmyra Road where that first meeting was held. He ran a farm and a grist mill in addition to his other pursuits. Apparently public service ran in the family. Grandson Jesse B. Hannan held the office from 1867 to 1868 and from 1881 to 1886. Great-grandson Jesse Hannan was supervisor for eleven years from 1924 to 1935. The Hannan family ran a farm on the corner of Moseley and Pittsford-Palmyra Roads, the site of Perinton Hills Mall.

Perinton politics has been dominated by Republicans and has had only two supervisors who were Democrats. Patrick McAuliffe served in 1887, but Fletcher Defendorf was Supervisor three separate times: in 1890, 1904-1905, and 1916-1918. Defendorf, who lived in the house on the east side of Parker Street at East Church Street, also served a term as president of Fairport Village, was elected to the New York State Assembly from 1886-1890, and was chosen as a delegate to the 1892 Democratic National Convention.

Most of Perinton's 41 supervisors have served relatively short terms; however, Raymond Lee, Lake Edwards, and Kenneth Courtney served for twenty, seventeen, and ten respectively, covering the years from 1936 to 1983. It was during those years that the Town of Perinton was transformed from a sparsely populated rural town to a thriving suburban community with an extensive park system, its own town hall complex, and active recreational programs.

Over the years, as the population and complexity of the community as well as the franchise has grown and changed, the organization of town government has changed. Town meetings are held twice a month instead of once or twice a year, an elected four-member Town Board assists the Supervisor, whose job like the job of assessor has remained essentially the same. The Department of Public Works does the twenty-first century version of the jobs that were done 200 years ago by the fence viewers and the pathmasters. There is still an elected clerk, but the town no longer has a constable or a poormaster; the jobs of keeping order and government assistance to the poor are now done at the county level.

Raymond Lee

Kenneth Courtney

Lake Edwards

Raymond Lee, who was supervisor from 1936 to 1955, was elected in the midst of the Great Depression when twenty-five percent of the population was on relief. During his time in office, the town population increased fifty percent, suburban subdivisions were beginning to replace farms, a system of parks and recreational programs was inaugurated, and new zoning and assessment regulations were put in place. Progress continued under his successor, Kenneth Courtney. During Lake Edwards' tenure, the population continued to increase, doubling during his 17 years, and the park system continued to expand. Suburban growth led to the development of long-range plans for growth. The building of Eastview Mall, just outside the Town of Perinton, and the opening of the High Acres Landfill, two significant developments for both the town and the area, happened during Edwards's time in office.

As of 2010, James E. Smith is the longest serving supervisor. He has served in that capacity for twenty-six years, since 1984. During his tenure, Perinton has had well-planned growth, has maintained solid property values, and has a superb parks and recreation program including a community and aquatic center that is the only one of its kind in the area.

Carl Peters – Local Artist

From a small house and studio at 208 Jefferson Avenue in Perinton, where he spent much of his life, Carl Peters gave the world a body of paintings that depict the upstate New York landscape. His work also includes a large collection of paintings from his many summers in Rockport, Maine. It has been said of him that he "captured the New England summers as loyally as he captured upstate New York winters." Peters did note, however, that Monroe County was not "as painterly" as the Maine shoreline.

Carl Peters came to Fairport with his parents when he was about twelve years old, probably around 1909. He and his five brothers and sisters and his parents farmed a nine acre plot where Carl eventually built his own home. Always interested in sketching as a child, later in his teens he attended the Mechanics Institute (Rochester Institute of Technology), taking courses in drawing and illustration.

His artistic studies were interrupted by World War I, when he served in France with Troop B of the 15th Cavalry from March 1918 to April 1919.

Returning to his art studies, Peters attended the National Academy Summer School in Woodstock, New York, where he studied with John Carlson, Charles Rosen, Walter Galtz, and Harry Leith Rose. He gradually developed his own style, showing influences from American impressionism as well as realism, and primarily painting landscapes and seascapes.

Although Carl Peters did not seek or like publicity, during the 1920's he was honored with a series of awards including the prestigious National Academy of Design's Hallgarten Prize, which he won three times, in 1926, 1928, and 1932. In 1929 he had a rare solo show at Rochester's Memorial Art Gallery. In the 1950's his paintings were on exhibit at the Rochester Public Library. In addition he won a number of prizes both in Rochester and in Rockport; however, as a man who cherished his privacy, he generally failed to attend award ceremonies where he was the honoree.

Carl Peters is known for a number of murals that he painted during the 1930's under the WPA's Federal Artist Project. Eight 19 by 9 foot murals remain in the auditorium of the Charlotte Middle School and two more large ones are in Wilson Magnet School in Rochester. Each depicts upstate New York life, from Native Americans to the early industrial age. The Fairport Historical Museum features a twenty-five by six foot mural in the main room that shows aspects of life along the Erie Canal. A reviewer at the dedication of the mural noted that "One must conclude that Peters' mural stands as nothing short of a masterpiece, a work worthy of the indelible American spirit he infused into its making." Other murals by the artist have been lost to rebuilding, remodeling, and reconstruction.

Carl Peters at work

Peters delighted in the beauty that he saw around him and exulted in the opportunity to share it through his painting. He loved painting outside, even in the winter, bundled up in coat, hat, and gloves. He might be found in the snow, up to his knees and in sub-freezing temperatures, painting a delicate and beautiful snow scene. Good friend and student Thomas Miller said of him that "he was consumed with the beauty of nature, the light and the reflections from streams, snow, trees, and hills in Upstate New York. He was also fascinated by the shapes and colors of the houses, boats and fishing shacks around Rockport and Gloucester, Massachusetts . . ." He believed that wonderful painting material was always close at hand, and painted perhaps 100 canvases in his front yard over several decades. Countless sketchbooks were filled with his ideas and preliminary drawings. Painting was his full-time job, which usually provided only a meager living, partly because Peters, who was often reluctant to engage in activities for mere financial gain, did not easily agree to sell his paintings.

Not only did Carl Peters delight in painting, but he also enjoyed teaching. For many years he held classes at Potter Memorial on weekdays for his "ladies" and on the weekends for his "gentlemen." One former student noted that "As a teacher, Carl had some difficulty verbalizing his instructions. But with just three or four strokes of a brush, he could show you how to paint a powerful figure or cluster of them."

As often seems to happen, Carl Peters has received more recognition and popularity since his death than he enjoyed while alive. In 1986, six years after his death, one of his snow scenes was added to the collection of the National Museum of American Art in Washington, D.C. In the early 1990's the R.H.Love Galleries in Chicago showcased his work. The show subsequently made a six-city tour and the value of the paintings tripled. Local galleries have shown his work, and for a number of years after his death, Peters' widow, Blanche, showed his work from the studio on Jefferson Avenue.

Two works by Carl Peters hang in the Fairport Library. A work, "Winter Stream," that had been purchased in the 1960's and had been hanging in Potter Memorial, is now hanging in the library complementing a second painting, "Canal Park, Fairport." The paintings flank the large window in the library's reading area. Fairport is indeed fortunate to have been home to Carl Peters who is remembered by a former student, Thomas Miller, as "quiet, humble, withdrawn, with a wry smile when amused, a gentle man…who responded when asked what was his best painting, replied, 'My last one.'"

Growing Up On West Avenue: A Conversation with Imogene Blum

Imogene Blum grew up on West Avenue in the village of Fairport. She described West Avenue, Roselawn Avenue, Main Street, West Church Street, Woodlawn Avenue, Cole Street, and the Erie Canal as being the boundaries of her world. All her needs and the needs of her family could be met within walking distance of her house at 78 West Avenue.

Her parents, Bert and Lillie Smith Copeland, married in 1903 and moved to the West Avenue house in 1904. The property had originally belonged to Fairport businessman G.L. Seeley and was subsequently deeded to Polly Benedict, whose daughter Hattie owned it when the Copelands moved in. Built in the vernacular style with a front gable and side ell, the house was divided into two residences, the Copelands living on the east side and Hattie Benedict living on the west side. The front yard was fenced with a pear tree in the yard, and the deep back yard had a vegetable garden and more fruit trees. West Avenue itself was unpaved with plank sidewalks.

Bert Copeland (or Berton as he was sometimes called) grew up in East Penfield, but Lillie (or Lillian or Lil) grew up on Roselawn Avenue with her aunt and uncle and cousins. Bert maintained his extensive vegetable garden and his fruit trees in their big back yard. The children enjoyed catching fireflies and swinging on the rope swing. Bert worked in the village at a variety of jobs, as a store clerk in Hollender & Scoville's market, as a custodian in the Fairport National Bank, and in several offices and a laundry. While some women worked in local factories and farm wives labored on the farm, Lillie, like the majority of married women, did not work outside the home. She was there when the children came home from school, took care of the house, and canned all sorts of fruits and vegetables like berries, pears, beans, peaches, and tomatoes, most likely from her husband's garden. Imogene particularly remembered the home made chili sauce. The Copelands had four children: Stuart Ralph, the eldest, was born in 1904, but died at the age of five from appendicitis. Isabelle Louise was born in 1906, Imogene in 1918, and Gerald in 1921.

The West Avenue neighborhood was diverse. In addition to the large cherry orchard across the street on the Schummer's property, which gave the street its original name of Cherry Street, there were many fruit trees on the street. Businesses were located on the eastern end of the street with private homes owned by doctors, business owners, and later by American Can Company workers, filling in the rest of the area. Businesses at the east end of the street included Hollender & Scoville Market, Lieb's Bakery, Bahler's Hardware, the office of the *Fairport Herald*, Clifford's Buick dealership, the One Horse Grocery, Shaw's Hall, Dr. Whitney's dental office, and Ella Bennett's hat shop.

Dr. Briggs, Dewey Jackson, who had operated a coal business, the Hupp family of Hupp Motors, the Wignall family of Wignall & Murphy Hardware, the Cotter family, whose son ran a meat market, the Forster family of the Forster Pulley Works, and the Clark, Seaman, and Burlingame families, among others, were residents of West Avenue.

As a child, Imogene Blum did not go far from her home. She had a number of friends including Barbara Park, Mary Burlingame, Edith Hupp, and Elizabeth and Helen Waterstraw who lived in the neighborhood. The girls roller skated in Barbara Park's barn and on the newly paved roads, used the swing in the Park's lean-to and went sledding on Beardsley Street in the winter. There was no ice skating allowed on the nearby canal, but it was notorious for its several suicide drownings. There were movies to attend in Shaw's Hall (otherwise known as the Bijou Theater) down the street. The early ones, of course, were accompanied by piano. Summer events included weekend concerts by the Firemen's Band at the Village Hall on Main Street. Imogene and her friends did not find it necessary to go the "north side," but they would usually go to the Candy Kitchen, which she describes as having black and white tile, colored glass mosaic, and tables and chairs with bent wire legs. The candy, ice cream, and peanut brittle were all home-made. Riding up and down on the lift bridge while watching the tug boats and the oil barges was another popular activity.

78 West Avenue circa 1900

Imogene and her siblings and friends all attended grammar school on West Church Street and high school on West Avenue. Minerva DeLand was the principal of the high school, Dr. Coffee the superintendent, and Martha Brown was her 8th grade teacher. Martha Hodson was one of Imogene's favorite teachers. She remembered sororities, fraternities, hazing and other rituals. Football and basketball were the most popular sports and of course there were dances and proms and the junior and senior plays. Imogene recalled that she didn't know how to dance and had few dates, but having a good voice for reading and projecting, she joined the drama club and had a part in the senior play. And living on West Avenue, she and her family had "front row seats" from which to follow all the school activities.

Imogene graduated in 1936 from the West Avenue School, which had opened in 1924, and went to work at the Fairport National Bank, which became Security Trust in 1944 and is now the Bank of America. Most people went home for lunch when the whistle blew at noon. The bank, however, had staggered lunch times, probably to accommodate those who wished to do their banking during their lunch hour. Most people she knew from her neighborhood worked locally; others would take the R.S. and E. Trolley to the East Rochester car shops or the city of Rochester for work.

Imogene Blum had a full working life. After leaving the bank in 1944, she worked at a doctor's office in Rochester until 1975. After that she worked at a dental supply company and then for a chiropractor. She did find time to marry Harold Blum in 1963 and they lived in the family home on West Avenue until 1975 when they moved to Pittsford Palmyra Road (still in Perinton, however). When Harold died in 1985, Imogene moved first to High View Manor and eventually to the Fairport Apartments.

In retirement, Imogene volunteered many, many hours as curator of the Fairport Historical Museum and had a wealth of knowledge about the village of Fairport. One could walk West Avenue with Imogene and she would recite the names and histories of all the residents up and down the street. She loved Fairport and was a marvelous resource to anyone curious about its history.

Imogene Copeland Blum ultimately moved into the Fairport Baptist Home where she died at the age of ninety-one on March 7, 2010.

Growing Up on the North Side: A Conversation with Matthew J. DiRisio, Jr.

By the turn of the twentieth century Fairport village had become home to a number of families whose members had emigrated from Italy. Between 1890 and 1910 approximately nine million people, arrived on American shores seeking new opportunities in a new land. Many, if not most of them, came from southern and eastern Europe. The DiRisio family came from the area of Abruzzi in Italy and settled on Railroad Street in the village of Fairport, joining other Italian families already here. Joseph (Matthew's paternal grandfather) came in 1909 and married Jenny Polito shortly after his arrival. Jenny, born in the United States in 1896, was thirteen years old at the time of her arranged marriage.

Joseph and Jenny had ten children, seven boys and three girls. Sadly, Jenny died at age twenty-nine during the birth of her last son, John. Albert (Hawk), Anthony (Dixie), and Charles, salutatorian of the Class of 1935, graduated from Fairport High School. Matthew and Marco finished 8th grade at the age of fourteen and went to work in East Rochester's car shops. Matthew worked for fifty-one years, never missing a day of work. He worked at a time when there were no sick days and no benefits – a missed day resulted in lost pay – and was grateful to have the job. Brother Floyd was an East Rochester policeman and Anthony worked at Kodak. John, the only brother to leave the area, settled in New Mexico and was on the staff of the Manhattan Project. Daughter Virginia did factory work at Rochester Products; Josephine (Pip) and her husband, James Porta, owned the "Par 3 Bar and Grill" on Route 31. Daughter Sarah and her husband Tito Tiberio had five children. Her grandson Bill is known as Fairport High School's "Music Man." Six of the sons (but not Matthew) fought in World War II.

Joseph and Jenny's oldest son, Matthew, and his wife Antoinette Rose had two sons: Matthew Jr. and Larry. The boys grew up on Railroad and Frank Streets where they developed a strong sense of family and community. Known by all the neighbors, they had a sense of belonging wherever they went. While discrimination was very real, it also fostered an intense desire to do well and succeed. Everyone was expected to work hard and to volunteer in the community. The boys had jobs by the time they were ten or eleven, usually paper routes. Young Matthew later worked at Steffen's Greenhouse making $1 per hour (double what full-time African-American workers were making – a stark learning experience.) Antoinette worked at The American Can Company and Qualitrol until she retired.

The Italian community in Fairport took care of its own. Matthew DiRisio Jr. shopped for Christmas gifts and worked out a payment agreement with the village merchants to pay a dime a week. According to him, even though he never fully paid off his debt, the merchants always told him he had. The local kids would go to Messerino's Market (then located on the corner of North Main Street and Parce Avenue) and borrow dimes to play pinball, charging the dimes to their parents' accounts. On a more serious scale, families knew that no matter how hard the times, they would never go without. Before the advent of the shopping mall, most shopping was done within the confines of the village. Besides Messerino's Market, the Rudins and Barrancos sold clothing; both Frenzi Pomponio and Joseph Fiandach had barber shops; "Snuffy" Carlomusto ran a soda shop, the Pomponio family also operated the Green Tavern, and of course there was Hawk's Restaurant, run by Matt's uncle. On the darker side, others were involved in bootlegging, the numbers game, and betting.

Despite the fact that grandparents didn't want their children and grandchildren to hold onto the old ways and the old language, they wanted them to be proud of their heritage and to work hard and do well in school. Furthermore there was to be no whining about unfairness or discrimination even though there was discrimination, which had the insidious effect of making a person ask "what is wrong with me?" Anti-Italian bias tended to come from community parents, rarely from children, and generally not from teachers; there were, however, a few teachers that did make it known that non-Italian girls from the south side were not expected to date Italian boys from the north side. On the other hand, athletics was a great leveler as the teams tended to mix students from all the grade schools. The result was increased tolerance. DiRisio remembers the time he got into a fight, was taken to the jail, and gave his name as "Joseph Smith." When his grandfather arrived to take him home, he smacked young Matthew, asking, "Are you ashamed of your name?" At another time, he notes that after having been kicked out of the Temple Theater (current Masonic Lodge), he and his friends were asked by Policeman Butch Santillo why no blonds had been kicked out, and were told that they were disrespecting their heritage and embarrassing and disappointing their families. No one wanted to disappoint parents or grandparents.

Matthew DiRisio, Jr. credits his maternal grandfather, Frank Marangi, who used to take him to the library every week, for his love of learning. His grandfather taught himself to read and write and would have liked to have been a professor. Instead, he worked as a furniture maker at the Gunlock Company. In general all the children were encouraged to do well academically; expectations were high. If grades went down, parents wanted to know why, telling their kids that they were capable, that poor grades were below them, that they had to do better – and no excuses were accepted. Young Matthew saw school as an opportunity to be made the most of.

Joseph and Jenny DiRisio, 1920

Matt DiRisio, 1944

School, particularly high school, was a good time for Matthew DiRisio, Jr. He was quarterback for the high school football team and consequently a hero in the Italian community. Perhaps even more importantly, he was a good student. And it was expected that he would get good grades. Florence Stolt, French teacher and of the Italian community, was, according to DiRisio, one of his particular favorites. He remembers her giving him money for his senior trip (with the explicit expectation that he repay it) because he had not raised sufficient funds for the trip by selling dish towels and moth cakes. He also remembers Miss Stolt as an elegant and successful professional woman, which was fairly unusual for the time and place in which he grew up. Joe Cummings, his football coach, was also significant in Matt's life, he says. He understood Matt, at one point stepping in to take him to a father-son communion breakfast in the absence of his father. Coach Cummings was always out looking for the boys when the team curfew was in effect. One time Matt and his friends figured that they could safely go to Uncle Hawk's restaurant and not be found. The coach, however, was waiting for them when they arrived at the restaurant past curfew. It was nearly impossible for Matt and his friends to be anonymous in the community. The presence of Coaches Cummings and Paddock, teachers Florence Stolt, John Clarke, and Grace Dubendorf, among others, as well as a large family and tight-knit community, helped a bright but headstrong young man who liked to push the envelope grow up successfully.

Matt DiRisio graduated from Fairport High School and went on to college and graduate school, eventually earning his doctorate. He taught social studies for four years in Henrietta before becoming an assistant principal. His maternal grandfather (who had taken him to the library as a child and who wanted to be a professor) wept with pride when he saw his grandson's vice principal name plate on the door in Rush-Henrietta. Matt went on to become high school principal at Onondaga Central School near Syracuse, and then served as principal at Churchville-Chili High School. Before retiring and returning to Fairport where he served on the school board and as Board President, Matt was Superintendent of Schools in Lyons; Locust Valley, Long Island; and Gananda. Back in his home town, he often spoke to community groups about growing up in Fairport. He noted that he always liked to be in charge. He did it as the older son in the family, as a high school quarterback, as a principal and superintendent, and as President of the Fairport School Board.

Matthew DiRisio looks back at his childhood as a time of struggle, laughter, difficulty, and the need to be resilient. He believes that those hard times along with the people who helped him along the way, gave him the chance to live an honorable life. He certainly has done so.

The Green Lantern Inn

The plot of land on the northeast corner of Main and Church Streets in Fairport probably was owned first by Col. John Peters, one of the major landowners in the area that would become the village of Fairport. In 1817 Isaac Beers built the first house on the site. Abishai Goodell, who owned the property in the 1820's, used some of the rooms in the house as classrooms. Major changes took place on the site in 1874. Henry DeLand, the new owner of the house, had it moved down East Church Street to a plot at number 39 (where it still stands), and commenced the building of what would come to be known as the Green Lantern Inn. The Second Empire French chateau-style mansion was constructed at a cost of about $46,000, and in 1876, Henry, his wife Sarah, his two children, Harlan and Helen, moved in. At various times Sarah's mother Betsey Smith Parce and Henry's widowed sister Eliza Marring and her daughter also lived there.

Green Lantern Inn

The thirty-four room, four story house was surrounded by lawns, trees and formal gardens, and had a kitchen garden and chicken yard in the back. In addition to a large barn/carriage house, there was also a summer house and a reflecting pool on the property.

The interior had extensive black walnut and chestnut woodwork, doors, and trim. Many rooms had interior shutters carved to match the trim. The parlor was graced by a crystal chandelier and decorated in a red and gray color scheme with long lace curtains and a pastel carpet. Sliding glass doors separated the parlor from the sitting room, which had a marble mantel and fireplace, and, with its piano, family portraits, and aquarium, was the gathering place for the family. The dining room had at least five black walnut doors and a massive black walnut sideboard and china closet. A glass door led into the conservatory, which housed exotic plants, and at one time, at least one mocking bird and maybe even an alligator. The remaining part of the first floor included a library, the master bedroom, and mother-in-law Betsey Parce's bedroom. There was also a separate bathroom. The house had a basement cistern from which water was pumped to an attic tank and was then available for use, certainly a novelty for the times.

The second floor, which was quite light and bright compared with the first floor, had bedrooms for the children and for guests. The third floor was a playroom for the children with shelves for toys and access to the roof, from which the children could view the street and the gardens.

The Clark family at the Green Lantern Inn

In 1890, Henry, having suffered losses in a Florida citrus freeze, sold his properties in Fairport and DeLand, Florida, in order to honor his guarantees and to repay those who had invested with him. The house had a number of owners over the next fifty years. In 1903, the Warren Clark family purchased the house. They electrified the structure and added stained glass windows and stained glass lanterns to the four entrances.

Sometime in the first decade of the twentieth century, the house was threatened with demolition as there was a proposal to route an electric trolley line through the property. Obviously that did not happen. Victor and Fanny Holmes purchased the mansion in 1923 and named it "Villa Rosenberg." Under their ownership it became known for its elaborate gardens. In 1928, Geraldine Harridine and her sister and brother-in-law purchased the property, hoping to turn the house into an inn. They hung five green lanterns (one of which still remains) from the porch ceilings giving rise to the name "Green Lantern Inn." There is strong evidence that the third floor was used as a "Black Pig" (a bring your own bottle establishment) during the years of Prohibition. Sometime between 1928 and 1932 the front part of the property was leased to the Gulf Oil Company, (or the Pure Oil Company) for $100 a month. The little white building was then built as a gas station. The structure has since served as a dry cleaners and an insurance office.

Interior of the Green Lantern Inn

In 1954, John O'Neill and Ray Placious opened a dining room and a bar which became quite popular. In 1964 a large banquet facility was added to the rear of the house.

John O'Neill's son Terry O'Neill, ran the popular party house and tended the house that he loved until 2004. Largely through his efforts, the house was placed on the National Register of Historic Places in 1980. Terry

O'Neill also spent countless hours and large amounts of money restoring and maintaining the structure itself. Among other things, he restored the porches, the gutters, a good portion of the roof, the decorative bracketing and frieze moldings, and repainted the exterior. O'Neill opted to use brown and bisque with brick highlights, historic colors, but not original to the house, which had been painted a single taupe color.

In 2004 the house was purchased by Matthew and Stephanie Laurence, who maintain the party house tradition expanding that area to include parts of the main house. There are also plans to reopen a downstairs pub. In 2006 the house was redecorated to serve as the Rochester Philharmonic Orchestra's show house. In 2011, the former basement pub was reopened as *The Cellar Door* restaurant and pub.

This wonderful house is a reminder of Fairport's earlier days, and it is also expressive of the love, dedication, and pride of those who work to preserve elements of those days.

Fairport Baptist Homes

"The finishing touches are this week being put on the Baptist Home of Monroe County, the DeLand mansion at the crest of the hill on North Main Street. The decorators are at work and with other small matters completed, it is expected that the formal opening will occur week after next." Thus did the local newspaper announce the opening of the Fairport Baptist Homes in September, 1905. Within several weeks, the home was dedicated and the first residents were admitted.

The driving force behind the establishment of the home was Dr. Marcena Ricker, a graduate of the Rochester General Hospital nursing school and the Cleveland Homeopathic Medical College. In the course of her practice in the city of Rochester, in addition to serving as Susan B. Anthony's physician, Dr. Ricker had frequent occasion to visit a number of poor and needy elderly who lacked care and were lonely. As a member of the Baptist Church, she talked to many of her friends about the need for a place where elderly Baptists could receive adequate care and share time with people their own age. After hearing Ricker's plan, the Monroe Baptist Association formed a committee to investigate the possibility of establishing a home for the elderly. Within two months the Baptist Home of Monroe County had been created, and negotiations were taking place with Walter Hubbell of Fairport, Levi J. DeLand's brother-in-law, to purchase Levi's home at 4646 Nine Mile Point Road for the Baptist Home. The deal was completed and the house along with twenty acres became the property of the Fairport Baptist Home in December, 1904. The choice was appropriate as the DeLand family were strong supporters and loyal members of the Baptist Church.

The Baptist Home was a success from the start. Financially it was well-supported by area Baptist churches and numerous individual donations. By the second year there were seventeen residents, mostly in their 60's and 70's, with several more awaiting entrance. According to the 1906 Annual Report, the life of the home was brightened by "frequent entertainment" and the farm "yielded beautifully", providing sufficient fruits and vegetables not only for the table, but also for storage for the winter. In addition, the treasurer's report noted that the Home was "free from debt."

Between 1910 and 1912 a new barn had been erected, electricity had been installed, the number of residents had swelled to forty, and it became apparent that the Home needed to be expanded. A new building, to the west of the DeLand mansion, was constructed at a cost of $45,000, $34,000 of which was raised by pledges. It was opened in December of 1913. The new facility was able to accommodate up to fifty residents and had a new dining room and chapel. That year's Christmas dinner was enjoyed in the new dining room, and the chapel was dedicated on January 11, 1914. Within ten years, among other improvements, an elevator was installed.

The Home continued to thrive during the next several decades, accommodating up to fifty-eight residents, with preference being given to members of the Baptist Church. The Home also had a six-bed infirmary. In the 1950's, most of the residents were from the area, thirty-four were between the ages of eighty and ninety, three were over ninety, fifteen were between seventy and eighty and only two were under seventy. According to a booklet from the time, residents were to be members "in good standing in an American Baptist Church" and "at least sixty-five years of age." While all residents could have private rooms, there were also accommodations for married couples. In addition there were three parlors, a small sitting room, wide porches, and several acres with large trees and flower beds. Croquet tournaments were also popular. According to one source, a ninety-three year old gentleman maintained a workshop in the basement where he did fine woodworking. The residents were regularly treated to concerts, book reviews, and movies, and also had books, puzzles and television available in addition to scheduled church services.

First residents of the Baptist home; Mr. & Mrs. William Ordway

From the beginning the Home was funded by contributions, particularly from the area Baptist churches, but from other interested individuals as well. The earliest residents were required to pay an admission fee of $300 and to turn over any personal property to the Home upon entrance. Total disbursements in the first year came to $7,689.32. By 1927 the admission fee was $500 and disbursements totaled $181,493.12. By the 1950's the Home was receiving monies from the Rochester Community Chest in addition to its funds from the New York State Baptist Convention, other private charities, and of course its residents. The residents were expected to provide their "per diem cost of maintenance from personal funds, family funds, or from the provisions of 'Old Age Assistance'" and also to deposit a "sum of at least four hundred dollars with the Capital Fund of the Home."

The Home was considered to be a place for the "well-aged" and had minimal staff: three nurses and three aides in the infirmary, a housekeeper, a maintenance man, and six people in the kitchen.

The second half of the twentieth century would bring significant and even revolutionary changes to the Baptist Home. The institution of Medicare and Medicaid in the mid 1960's significantly changed the way Americans cared for their seniors. Previously, the elderly had often been taken care of by family members if and when they became unable to care for themselves. With the advent of those two Great Society programs in addition to Social Security, seniors were able to remain independent for a longer period of time and also to provide for their own living arrangements in their later years. In addition, with advances in medical care and the introduction of new drugs, people were living longer. Hence there developed an increased demand for nursing home space and for nursing home services, and in the case of the Baptist Home, these demands resulted in a long waiting period for care.

Fairport Baptist Homes responded to this situation with a major addition and renovation project begun in 1964 under the leadership of its administrator, the Rev. Ernest Mount. The new wing, which was opened in 1966, provided for an additional thirty residents, bringing the total served to eighty-five. In addition, the facility added regular nursing service. The cost of the new north wing was $785,000, $400,000 of which was a bequest from the estate of Mrs. Lillian Andrews. The remainder was raised through a capital funds campaign led by John L. Remington. In addition to new rooms for residents, the project provided a new dining hall, improved kitchen facilities, a rooftop solarium, and offices. It was, in fact, just the first phase of a long range plan that would include independent living apartments to the east of the main Baptist Home Campus.

The Rev. Alvin C. Foster came to the Baptist Homes as administrator in 1968 after serving as senior minister of the First Baptist Church in Fairport. In his twenty-two years as president he oversaw many changes. As the elderly population continued to grow, the Home responded by expanding its facilities in two ways. In 1972, on four and one-half acres adjacent to the Home, Perinton Churches Housing build a 104 unit complex of small apartments for middle and low income seniors, called the Fairport Apartments. In 1971 the Levi DeLand house, which had housed the first residents, was razed in preparation for the building of a major new wing. The new double-wing addition, opened in 1973, accommodated up to 196 residents. It also added a dementia unit. Remnants of the old DeLand house still remain, however. The new building was erected over the old foundation, parts of which are still visible in the basement. In addition several mantelpieces were saved, one of which stands in the chapel foyer.

From its beginnings as a home that provided simple care for the aged to one that provided acute and chronic nursing care as well as independent living facilities, the Home did not stop looking to the future and at new and better ways to care for a fast-growing segment of the population. In 1989, with the building of DeLand Acres, a cluster of small "patio homes," the Home expanded its commitment to independent living. In the 1990's and extending into the twenty-first century, the Home would be one of a few pioneering nursing homes to provide a whole new concept of care.

As early as 1996, the Rev. Garth Brokaw, President, and the Board of Directors of the Fairport Baptist Homes began to study plans for expansion and the creation of a new design concept that had been instituted at a few homes around the nation. Confusion and noise in the 42-bed dementia unit dining room was the impetus for a new plan. There the Home created three smaller dining rooms and used the former large dining area to create a living space which included a kitchen, a living room, and an "attic" containing familiar items such as a baby carriage and a typewriter. A cookie jar was available at all times (at the time worrying nurses and food service staff). Residents responded positively to these attempts to create a homelike as opposed to an institutional atmosphere; behavior improved and confusion was lessened.

With major renovations to the buildings looming in the late 1990's, Brokaw and the board of the Home decided to investigate a construction plan that would replace the traditional hospital/institution format with the home and family format that seemed to be working on a small scale in the dementia unit. It would be a revolutionary change, because for decades, nursing homes had been generally organized in the most efficient way possible with long hallways and dormitory-like rooms. Residents had been grouped by their levels of disability, and central kitchens provided meals three times a day at specific times.

After visiting several institutions, most notably the Evergreen Retirement Community in Oshkosh, Wisconsin, the decision was made to proceed with a new design concept. The plan proposed to do away with hallways and individual rooms and replace them with "households" of between nine and twelve residents whose rooms would be clustered around a kitchen, dining area, and living room.

The "From Hallways to Households" project began in 1996 and the first residents moved into their new households in 1998. Gone are long hallways and obvious nurses' stations. They have been replaced by kitchens, where residents may cook a late breakfast for themselves, or provide coffee and a snack for relatives, or even cook a meal for the entire household, as well as a dining area, living room, and adjacent parlor. Surrounding the common area are the residents' rooms. The once-obvious nurses' station has been replaced by some shelves in the kitchen under the cabinets.

The Rev. Garth Brokaw, President of the Homes, has said "This is the beginning of a new age for the Fairport Baptist Homes. We have taken great leaps of faith to get here." And the concept seems to be working. Said one resident: "This morning I made lemon cake for my friends. They were delighted, but it was really my pleasure. I have always loved to bake." From another: "We have a lot of fun…tell tales, reminisce." Aside from the comments and anecdotal evidence, facts show that the quality of life is better under the new system. Between 1997 and 2002, falls were down forty percent, fifty percent fewer residents were inactive, there was a 150 percent increase in social interaction; behavior problems among dementia patients was down forty percent, nursing assistant turnover was down twelve percent, and perhaps most significantly, the mortality rate was down thirty percent and continues to remain below the NY state average. Surely a system based on how most people live their lives, in households, can be nothing else but successful. The astonishing thing is that it has taken so long to apply the obvious to the nursing home setting. The Home continues to respond to changing needs and changing demographics. In 2009, the Home's north wing was converted into assisted living apartments, fulfilling a needed niche between independent living and a skilled nursing facility.

The Fairport Baptist Homes Caring Ministries encompasses not one but a number of facilities. Included are DeLand Acres, Fairport Apartments, ElizAl Court, and the Northfield near the Home itself, Roselawn Shared Living Residence on Roselawn Avenue, and Rose Hollow Apartments on Durant Place. The Home also provides an adult day care center and a transitional care center for those undergoing rehabilitation. SOFI, Senior Options for Independence, helps monitor the community's seniors and connect them with needed services. Seasons Child Care day care center is also part of the Fairport Baptist Homes campus, whose effect is summed up by the following statement from a two-year old: "I like seeing all the grandmas and the grandpas."

What began as a home for the "well-aged" has developed into a complex of residences that helps those "grandmas and grandpas" stay in their community and receive the services they need in an atmosphere that in as many ways as possible mirrors a home and family atmosphere.

Fairport's Municipal Building

Although Fairport was settled as early as the 1820's and was incorporated as a village in 1867, there was no formal location for government business until 1906. Prior to that, both town and village meetings were held in local taverns, public halls or auditoriums. Perinton's earliest town meetings were held in Egypt and Perinton Center, the early centers of the town's population. In addition to schools and taverns, Shaw's Hall, on West Avenue in the village, was a venue for meetings as well as for voting. By 1905, both town and village officials began to talk about the need for a building to serve the needs of the local government. In March of 1906 the local paper quoted Perinton Supervisor Thomas Bridges as saying that both the town and village boards had the authority to arrange details of occupancy and on "what terms a building shall be built and used."

In May a public notice requested that any land owner in Fairport who owned a suitable site for a town hall should send in a sealed description with the price of the property. Three were submitted that warranted consideration. In October, Justice H. A. Walker determined that the Root property on South

Main Street, one of the three, was the best location. The property was purchased for $4,000 and the existing house was sold at public auction and moved. Not everyone was happy with the decision. East Rochester residents felt that the Town Hall should be closer to them as did the residents of the hamlet of Egypt, who thought it should be nearer the center of the town, in the vicinity of Ayrault and Moseley Roads. Plans for a new structure on South Main Street, however, proceeded.

Town officials allotted $20,000 for the construction of the building and the Syracuse firm of Kirkland and Hallenbeck was hired to submit plans. Two sets of plans were drawn up, but only one firm bid on the project, the James Leamey Co. of Syracuse, and that bid was $10,000 more than had been allocated. Ultimately, the plans were redrawn, providing for a sixty by fifty foot building with a twenty by seven foot wing for the fire department, and the final bid was $20, 235. The firm was hired.

The completed Municipal Building opened in 1906 with town offices located on the first floor, the jail in the basement, and an auditorium and balcony on the second and third floors. The village rented office space from the town for $350 per year; the auditorium, while used primarily for movies, was also available for public rental.

Municipal Building circa 1912

By the middle of the 1920's, with the opening of the West Avenue High School, auditorium rentals were down and village offices and the fire department needed more space. Both the fire department and village officials investigated the possibility of building a new structure; however, not only would the cost be prohibitive, but the current location was really ideal. The decision was made to reallocate existing space and transfer the ownership of the building from the town to the village. In 1931, the town sold the structure to the village for one dollar and perpetual use of a town clerk's office, a court room, an elections office, a lock-up, and a storage room. The fire department planned to build a two-story addition providing room for equipment and also meeting rooms on the second floor. The architectural firm of Wiard and Martin submitted plans for the space reorganization. Renovation cost was estimated at $45,000; $10,000 was contributed by the firemen and the remainder raised by issuing municipal bonds. Sale of the building was approved by the voters ninety-two to forty-eight and the deed was transferred from Perinton Supervisor Jesse Hannan to Fairport Village Mayor Glezen Wilcox on October 5, 1931.

When the project was completed and reopened in April 1932, both town and village officials had offices. The second floor auditorium became village offices and the village board room. Town offices were on the first floor along with the Municipal Commission and the Assessor's office. The jail, court room, and jury room were also on the first floor. The old jail in the basement was remodeled for use as public restrooms and the new addition housed the Fairport Fire Department.

Essentially the "new" village hall served both town and village until 1980 when the town of Perinton moved to a new facility on Turk Hill Road. Subsequently in 1981 the fire department moved to its new facility on East Church Street and the Fairport Police Department moved into that space. In the late 1980's the issue of renovation was again raised, noting that space was tight and that the building did not comply with the Americans with Disabilities Act. Renovation was put to a vote in 1991 and soundly defeated; however, a pared-down plan went forward in 1993 and the renovations, including a board room, an elevator, and a new rear entrance, were completed.

The most recent changes include new front doors that replicate the original ones and new stairs and railings. This well-cared- for structure stands as an example of Fairport's concern for preservation as it enters its second century as a municipal building.

Movable History

Houses at 10, 39 and 62-64 East Church; 2677 Baird Road; 11and 62 Filkins Street; 154-156, 205, and 234 South Main Street; 10 Clinton Place; and 94 West Avenue have something in common. Each one was moved all or in part from another location. (There are surely other properties in the community that have been moved; these are merely some examples.) While not a common practice today, it seems that during the mid to late nineteenth century the practice was to move a structure rather than raze it.

Number 10 East Church Street was perhaps moved the furthest. That structure began life as Elisha Fullam's inn/store/post office next to the canal at the appropriately named Fullamtown, a small canal community in the vicinity of today's Perinton Park and Fairport Road Bridge. Before the canal was completed, passengers would disembark there and pick up the stagecoach to complete their trip into Rochester. After the completion of the canal and the growing dominance of the village of Fairport, Charles Dickinson, the owner of the store in the 1850's, decided to move his building into the village, choosing the site at 10 East Church Street. The move took place in 1853 or 1854. Over the years, the house has served as a store, a subscription library, a doctor's office, and an apartment house and has recently been refurbished as a business office.

Number 39 East Church Street is one of Fairport's oldest houses, built in 1817 by Isaac Beers and originally located on the northeast corner of South Main and Church Street. While at that site, the house was owned by Oliver Tomlinson and then by Abishai Goodell, who rented out a room as a classroom for which he was paid $12.30 per term. In 1871 Henry DeLand purchased the property and subsequently moved the house to its present location at 39 East Church so that he could build his thirty-two room French chateau-style mansion on the site. Nearby 62-64 East Church Street was also moved. It was relocated from South Main Street in order to make room for the Bown Block, one of old South Main Street's major structures erected in the 1870's and razed in the 1970's as part of urban renewal.

Fairport Community Baptist Church at 20 East Church Street first met in a Greek Revival style structure that stood on the site of the present stone structure. The church decided to construct a new building in 1892, and on May 20, 1892, a resolution was adapted accepting the offer of Mr. O.C. Adams of $50 for the old building, "the same to be removed by him without delay." He promptly moved it around the corner to 154-156 South Main Street. However, since it was not possible to turn the building around in the moving, it was placed on the lot back to front. Consequently, the rear of the old church, which is now apartments, became and remains the front of the house today. Apparently it was not uncommon for moved structures to end up back to front on the new site because 2677 Baird Road was also placed back to front on its new foundation. Built by E.V. Rowell around 1869, the house was moved from the east to the west side of Baird Road sometime in the first decade of the twentieth century to avoid being demolished in the wake of the new Rochester Syracuse and Eastern Interurban Trolley that would pass over Baird Road. The new reverse placement put the living and dining rooms in the back of house and the kitchen and small front door in the front.

Several other houses on South Main Street have either been moved or combined. Number 234 South Main was most likely built by pioneer Abner Wight (Glover Perrin's brother-in-law) on the east side on the street. It was moved across the street in the 1870's when some renovations were done. Number 205 is a combination of two structures, one built by War of 1812 veteran Larry Wilcox around 1844 just north of the current site, and the second by Hiram Wilbur between 1872 and 1885 on the present site. The two parts were joined in 1885, the overlap being visible from the inside.

Filkins Street boasts two houses that were moved there from other locations. Number 11 was originally the chapel of the old First Baptist Church on the corner of Church and Main Streets. It was built in 1842 and moved in 1876 when the current brick structure was erected. Number 62 was built as a tavern at the north side of Cobb's Bridge (now the Turk Hill Road bridge). It was subsequently moved across the canal, then to Perrin Street, and finally to 62 Filkins Street.

In 1852, West Avenue, formerly known as Cherry Street, ended at West Street. The house that now stands at 94 West Avenue stood at the end of that street perpendicular to its present location facing the village. When West Avenue was extended in the mid to late 1800's, the house was swung around ninety degrees and placed on a new foundation. The old foundation remains under West Avenue. Another old village house was moved from South Main Street around the corner to 10 Clinton Place when that road was cut through around the turn of the twentieth century.

While not a common practice today, houses are still being moved. The Oliver Loud house that is currently located in Bushnell's Basin behind Richardson's Canal House was originally situated in Egypt in the vicinity of today's Towne Centre Plaza, and served as a popular tavern on an important stagecoach route between Canandaigua and Rochester. In 1985, facing demolition, the old tavern was purchased by Vivian Tellier and moved to Bushnell's Basin where it served as a bed and breakfast as part of Richardson's Canal Village complex. It has recently been converted to a private residence. In 1997 the Orlo and Irene Peters house at 1355 Fairport Road was moved to a new location on Pittsford-Palmyra Road to make room for McArdle's Restaurant.

As people continue to celebrate history and seek to preserve the past as well as conserve resources, perhaps moving a structure rather than razing it will once again become more commonplace.

Forest Hills and the Dygert Brothers

Tucked in the northwest corner of Perinton on the border with East Rochester, just off Fairport Road, lies a unique suburban subdivision called "Forest Hills." The area, like much of East Rochester, is a planned development whose homes were custom built by Harold and Lawrence Dygert.

Harold P. Dygert was born on May 23, 1889 in South Hammond, Lawrence County, New York. When he was two years old, his parents moved to Despatch (later to be named East Rochester). Harold graduated from high school in East Rochester and then, according to his grandson, he took an architectural engineering/drawing correspondence course from Columbia University. During his lifetime, beginning in the 1920s and through the 1960s, Harold claimed to have designed and built over 600 homes – mostly in the East Rochester area – but also in Brighton, Pittsford, and the City of Rochester. Harold's brother, Lawrence (Larry), supervised the construction of most of the Dygert homes, acting as a business manager and building superintendent. According to Dygert family members, Lawrence was as able an engineer as Harold was a draftsman, but apparently was a better businessman.

Prior to development of the Forest Hills area, Harold designed and built some individual houses, but Forest Hills became his first major project and apparently remained his favorite, probably due to its variety of architectural styles. His earliest known plans for the area are penciled "overlays" superimposed on a site survey done for him by John Abner Stuart in 1927. Part of the surveyed area, referred to as "Parkcroft," included a section bounded by East Filbert Street, South Lincoln Road, East Ivy Street, Park Drive and Madison Street. The undeveloped area to the south, today's Forest Hills, was designated Parkcroft Heights, and included a street, Buena Vista Drive, of 51 plots, which is known today as Ridgeview Drive. The penciled overlays show an extension of Madison Street and a suggestion of what eventually would become Fair Oaks Drive. Whatever construction was proposed for the late 1920s did not occur, however, presumably because of the Great Depression.

Titles and abstracts of the properties that surround the wooded areas of Westwood Drive and Fair Oaks Drive show that ownership was transferred from Daniel Turrill to Roswell Turrill in 1821. Turrill then purchased adjacent properties from Asahel Lusk, Jr. and Lucy A. Mann. He eventually left the property to his wife, Letty, and the property was known as the Letty Turrill Farm until the late 1890s when it was sold. In 1898, owner Egbert Etts deeded the farm to his daughters, Emma M. Leaman and Sarah Aldrich.

The 1924 Plat map shows that Emma Leaman owned the land to the north, corresponding to Fair Oaks Drive, Regency Drive, and the wooded area of Westwood Drive. Approximately three acres of land to the east of 39 Ridgeview Drive was owned by Elizabeth Waite and is undoubtedly the derivation of Waitefield Drive. The land to the south, which today includes Lake Crescent Circle, was owned by Marjorie H. Cox. Lawrence Dygert purchased this tract of land in 1931.

Despite the Depression, the 1930's was a busy time for Harold Dygert as he designed custom homes for the Forest Hills lots. Title abstracts record plots that were sold to original Forest Hills residents from 1932 to 1939 and include many whom Dygert included in his promotional brochures (Rockwell, Witham, Kerner, Kellogg, Payne, Covert, Hoffman, Gross and Abel). Interestingly, the first of these properties was purchased in 1932 by John Abner Stuart, the gentleman who had done the early site survey in 1927. By 1942, Forest Hills boasted about seventy-five finished Dygert-designed homes. Advertised prices for a house and lot ranged from $5,980 to $8,500.

Apparently construction of houses in Forest Hills did not begin on the street first plotted along "the Ridge" but commenced along Lake Crescent Drive. Photographs show land adjacent to the Lake Crescent pond on Fairport Road being cleared, and the house at 6 Lake Crescent Drive progressing to roof level. In the background, trees on "the Ridge" are evident but the area is devoid of any signs of construction.

Harold Dygert personally did the architectural design work in collaboration with each original resident, which accounts for the one-of-a kind nature of Forest Hills homes. Residents who dealt with Dygert came to know him as an opinionated and determined man with strong stylistic feelings. The fact that individual residents had an influence in the design process may well account for the wide variety of architectural styles in Forest Hills, and the fact that all plans were drawn by a single draftsman may account for the evident harmony of those multiple architectural styles. Dygert also took great care with the details. Members of the family indicate that many trips were made to Pennsylvania to bring back oak timbers for the floors, paneling, doors and woodwork that distinguish the homes. Stone masons were brought from the Adirondacks and camped on-site while completing the impressive brick and masonry highlights.

The seventy-five Dygert designed homes within Forest Hills feature a variety of architectural styles. Approximately a third of these are Tudor Revival in style. There are an equal number, approximately thirty percent, of English Cottage and French Eclectic design, the later characterized by round tower entrances and referred to by Dygert as "Norman style." Approximately twenty percent of the homes fall into the category of Colonial Revival, completed in wood, brick and stone, many featuring second floors, and one having Southern Colonial columns. One of the two built in French Regency style gives its name to Regency Drive. In general, building progressed from Lake Crescent Drive in the early 1930s to Ridgeview Drive and Westwood Drives (in the mid-1930s) to Fair Oaks Drive and Regency Drive in the late 1930s. The Art Deco house at 13 Regency Drive was begun in 1941 and finished in early 1942, the last of the "classic" Dygert homes to have been completed.

With the onset of World War II, all construction ceased. When building resumed after the war, ranch style homes of the 1950s filled the remaining vacant lots. Today Forest Hills remains a distinct and easily recognizable section of the Town of Perinton.

With thanks to Kenneth Dodgson whose research provided much of the information in this article.

- VI -
HEALTH AND SAFETY

Our community owes a significant debt of gratitude to all those who protect our homes and businesses, fight our fires, aid in any and all emergencies, care for our health, and provide us with the essentials of light and water.

Law Enforcement

A constable is defined by *The American Heritage* Dictionary in part as "A peace officer with less authority and smaller jurisdiction than a sheriff...." Both Perinton and Fairport appointed constables from the very beginning. The first constable in the Perinton-Fairport area was Jonas Sawens, who was appointed Constable and Collector for Northfield (early name for the Perinton area) in 1796. In 1812, when Perinton was incorporated, Levi Treadwell, Joseph Beal, and Charles Aldrich were appointed constables. When the Village of Fairport was incorporated in 1867, J.C. VanNess was appointed as constable and the Fairport Police Department was born.

The job of constable was in some ways very different from the job of today's police. They served warrants, took people to jail, and perhaps most importantly, worked as night watchmen on the lookout for fires and other emergencies. In some cases the constable might also have been involved in enforcing the laws regarding the height of and materials used in fences, although Perinton records note that Fence Viewers were appointed for this purpose. Since there were laws regulating when and where one's livestock could wander, it is possible that the constable was involved in enforcing those regulations as well. In addition, constables might have been on the lookout for Canadian thistles, as it was a crime to allow them to grow on one's property.

Apparently it was not always easy to attract people to the job of constable. There is evidence in the Town records of people refusing to serve. In fact, the pay was not good and sometimes non-existent, but constables were allowed to keep any fees that they might collect. Evidently the constables were not very active in 1832, because in that year a group of citizens formed the Society for the Detection and Apprehension of Horse Thieves in order to crack down on rampant stealing of horses and mules. The Society remained active for several years. It seems that the sale of stolen horses and mules to canal boat owners was quite a thriving business.

During the course of the nineteenth century the office of Police Constable became a paid position. The first references to salary indicated that in 1869 a constable could earn fifty cents per day plus fees. In 1874, the night watchman earned $2 for serving as the Saturday night watchman from 7 p.m. to 5 a.m., and by 1879 a constable was earning $30 per month, paid from a tax levy, plus fees. By 1897 that amount had been increased to $40 per month. New responsibilities included additional night duties and the arresting of any person found intoxicated in public. In addition, any dog found to be running at large and not muzzled was to be put down. In 1898 the village of Fairport more clearly defined the duties of the constable. In general he was to see that all ordinances of the village were observed, to arrest anyone willfully violating such ordinances, and to arrest vagrants and any person found intoxicated on the streets.

The first jail or "cooler" or "lock-up" was set up by the Lock-Up Committee on John Street (Lift Bridge Lane). Dr. James Welch, a life-long Fairport resident, remembered that the jail was a "one-story brick building, about 15x18 feet. It contained three cells with steel bars, and a cot in each cell." The small anteroom contained a coal stove for heat. Prisoners were only held overnight and their breakfast was provided by the police chief.

Chief Charles Kenney and Officer Joseph Santillo with two new Ford Police cars (1951)

Dr. Welch provided another anecdote about the jail and the Cottage Hotel, which was located across the street. One time, some of the village youths decided to "help" an intoxicated prisoner. They attached a hose to one end of a beer keg in the hotel, ran the hose through a window, across the alley, and into the jail window to the thirsty captive. Needless to say, the next morning the prisoner was as intoxicated as he had been when he was arrested.

The present Village Hall which was constructed in 1907, included a "modern lock-up" that served the town of Perinton, the villages of Fairport and East Rochester, the railroad police, and the game wardens. The basement jail area was reached by steep wooden stairs and lighted by two small windows high up on the wall. Two portable steel cells with white enameled bars and fold-down steel bunks stood in the center of the room. They were furnished with blankets, waterproof mattresses, and a slop bucket. Two toilets and a sink were in the next room. The area was heated in the winter, but quite damp in the summer.

The lock-up was used not only for prisoners, but as far as space would allow, for what we would refer to today as the homeless population. In times of economic difficulties or on cold winter nights, the lock-up could be quite full with vagrants, hobos, migrants and other people on the margins. In 1908 the record only shows that ten prisoners were incarcerated. In 1916 about fifty prisoners (no women or children) and about fifty "lodgers" used the jail. The records from 1925 note that the number of prisoners per night fluctuated between one and eleven. Many of the arrests were for intoxication. During the first six months of 1926 there were forty-three prisoners in the lock-up and sixty-three lodgers. 1927 showed ninety-three detainees.

The two "cages" in the basement of the town hall that served as the local "lock-up" were the topic of considerable disagreement between the town and the state for about 15 years between 1916 and 1931. A 1916 letter from the state recommended that the lighting be improved and that wash basins and toilets be installed in the cells. The state inspector noted that when these changes were done, the site would be a "credible lock-up." There followed an exchange of letters between then Perinton Supervisor Fletcher Defendorf and the state inspector about possible changes. The supervisor proposed that "slop pails" be put in the cells, but indicated that "closets and lavatories freely accessible to prisoners…would be abused." The state responded with "We don't know where you get your authority for such a statement" and stated that all modern jails had facilities. They recommended "vitreous ware" toilets. The state also questioned the lighting and the proximity of the cells to the walls. The final letter in the series, dated May 17, 1917, stated that the lock-up, due to its being mostly underground, could not be approved and should be closed.

Prohibition raid; cellar in Fairport

By 1921, the town had added a sink and toilet to each of the two cells and had enlarged the windows. A state letter from that year seemed to imply that all was in order. Nevertheless, by 1925 the state was again recommending that a new lock-up be built to deal with dampness and a rough floor, the lack of a good fire escape, the danger of the steep stairs, leaky toilets, inadequate bedding, and a lack of general cleanliness.

State criticism of the Fairport lock-up continued until 1931 when the state Commissioner of Corrections finally closed the facility. Fortunately, after purchasing the municipal building from the town of Perinton in 1930, the village of Fairport was planning extensive renovations, which included the construction of a new jail as well as a fire hall. Architect Henry Martin planned a first-floor jail that would have four cells, three for men and one for women, with three solid walls and a barred front. Each cell would be equipped with a steel bunk, adequate bedding, toilet, sink, and drinking fountain. Windows would provide sufficient light. The construction was completed in 1931 and the lock-up met all the necessary state criteria. The 1931 lock-up remained in use until the 1982 move of the department into the old fire department facility next to the Municipal Building. Today's well-lighted, stainless steel equipped cells would have pleased the inspectors of the 1920's and 1930's.

A police department's job is to keep order, and the decade of the nineteen twenties, the era of Prohibition, was unquestionably a particularly busy time. In addition to arrests for intoxication, there were a number of successful raids and subsequent confiscation of illegal booze: "So carefully had the raid [of May 17, 1922] been planned that everybody was surprised. ... Arrangements were made for raiding, officers to be stationed at each place at 9 o'clock. ... Although the amount of liquor discovered in some cases was not large, it was sufficient to constitute evidence of violation of the law." The proprietors of the establishments reacted in different ways. "In the Fiandach café an Italian gentleman in charge offered resistance (and) he pulled a knife ... In the Casey restaurant the man in charge announced heartily, 'Go to it. I'll go 50-50 on everything you find.'... and the officers found plenty." Another person "was inclined to be argumentative and wanted to be convinced that the officers actually had authority for the raid. He was speedily convinced." In the end, no arrests were made, but the people involved were served with orders to appear in Federal Court, and "all the liquor collected was confiscated by Sheriff Morse and transported to the Monroe County jail."

Earlier in the decade, there was a substantial "riot" in the village of Fairport, which involved about forty or fifty men from Rochester and about 200 villagers. Seventeen Rochesterians were arrested and one man was killed. Apparently the riot was a result of an argument that had taken place during a dance the previous week. Ultimately sixteen youths were convicted, fined and sentenced to jail time. The issue of youth gangs was in the news again in the 1950's when there was a push to double the night force to two officers in order to deal with the youth gangs from Rochester. "Hoodlumism" continued to be a concern every now and then, as groups of youths seemed to congregate in various parts of the village such as the Sugar Bowl restaurant in the 50's and 60's and the Village Landing ever since its construction.

For the most part, however, local policing seems to have been involved mainly with issues of petit larceny, traffic infractions, and personal disagreements. For example, a "young girl reported that a boy had put snow in her face...Boy and his parents were talked to by patrol and parents will handle the matter...;" "... Youngsters playing hockey in the street were sent over to use the skating rink;" "... received a report of a hit and run accident that demolished a tree. Patrol arranged for car owner and tree owner to get together and settle the matter;" "... not one but two trains broke down simultaneously and caused the main crossings to be tied up for 1½ hours...Patrol took care of traffic until the mess was cleaned up;" "...Patrol dispatched an opossum to the great beyond after finding it in a lady's garbage can." Occasionally, the police have dealt with crimes of a more serious nature. In 1979, a gunman armed with a rifle holed up in police headquarters and held off a SWAT team for eight hours. The standoff was resolved peacefully, but the incident dominated the news for several days.

During the 1950's the Fairport Police Department, which was located in a storefront building on South Main Street next to the municipal building, consisted of the chief, a sergeant, two officers, and two part-time officers. During their shifts, officers routinely patrolled the streets, followed school buses to ensure safety and monitored the 170 parking meters and the one and two hour parking zones. The remainder of the shift was taken up with investigating complaints, filling out forms, sending out notices of traffic violations and serving warrants. A 1958 report indicated 1057 parking tickets were issued that year and that the officers had responded to a total of 2919 calls. It was in the 1950's that the first women joined the police force as crossing guards. Their uniforms were powder blue with "gold braid and buttons and matching blue caps, white shirts and gloves, and navy blue ties." The uniform has changed, but the job continues to be of crucial importance to the safety of Fairport's children.

The Fairport Police Department has ten full-time officers, including the chief. All receive extensive training, including monthly in-service requirements and twice-yearly firearms training. Officers come to the force after six months at the Police Academy and about twenty weeks of field training. All officers are rigorously trained in what is known as "continuum of force," the progression from verbal confrontation through the use of mace or the night stick up to the use of weapons. Two officers are on each eight-hour shift where they log approximately thirty to forty miles patrolling the streets. In addition, the night shift checks village business locations. The small size of the department as well as the small area of the village makes it possible to respond quickly to calls, and unlike larger departments, the Fairport police continue to be available to check homes for vacationing owners.

In general officers would say that their job is "routine and often monotonous." They also speak of it as both frustrating and very rewarding. In addition to knowledge of the law, the job entails a good deal of paper work and numerous court appearances, but it also allows a certain amount of freedom that comes from being out on patrol and having to make decisions on one's own. Common complaints include the strain that odd hours and emergency calls can place on family life and the hostility that is often directed toward the police. During all shifts, maintaining rapport with citizens and generally being seen and known are of crucial importance to success.

The last decades of the twentieth century saw significant changes in, and challenges to, policing in Fairport. The many social changes and especially growing drug use continue to be challenging for law enforcement. As has always been the case, law and order outside the village of Fairport are maintained by the Monroe County Sheriff's Department, while the village is covered by the local Fairport Police Department.

Succeeding Thomas Aldrich and Jack Faucher, who served as village police chiefs from the 1960's up to 1975, Joseph Picciotti made major changes in the department. His stated goal was to make the police force more visible and more professional. Soon after becoming chief, he said, "we had to get hold of a community that was wild...There were rowdy taverns and fights in the streets." There was also a drug problem. Picciotti introduced a training program, streamlined procedures, and generally brought the department up to date. He also was responsible for starting the DARE program in the Fairport schools. His changes proved successful as the number of burglaries decreased and the number solved increased. In 1982, also during his tenure, the department offices were moved to the former fire department facilities adjacent to the Municipal Building and the department was staffed by seven full time officers. In 1987, due to budget issues, the village proposed that the third shift of the department be eliminated and replaced by the Monroe County Sheriff's Department. The change was approved to the dismay of Chief Picciotti who felt that the loss of the third shift would mean loss of continuity in the department and would inevitably lead to its demise. In fact the department did decline to a total of six officers in addition to the chief after the shift was eliminated.

Many village residents missed the third shift and by August 1989, after some reports of an increase in crime, the Citizens Organizing for Police Services (COPS) was formed under the leadership of Debra Tandoi. And in April, 1990, after continuing pressure from COPS and an easing of budgetary constraints, the village leadership voted to reinstate the third shift. Chief Picciotti noted that from a personal point of view this was not good news, (meaning that he would have to readjust to his police radio being on twenty-four hours a day), but professionally he was elated, stating that it "will make this village a better place."

Brian Page became chief in 1991 and saw drugs as the root cause of most of the area's crime. Vowing to make the local officers more visible, he introduced foot patrols and made the police department office more accessible to the public. The new style appeared to work, as crime dropped twenty percent during his first year. The department also began work to obtain state accreditation, a three-year process that was successfully completed in 1996, making Fairport one of only sixty departments out of 500 in the state to receive accreditation. His commitment was not only to professional policing, but also to community policing, creating a visible presence in and positive interaction with the citizens of Fairport. All his officers were expected to spend at least one hour of their eight-hour shift on foot. The department also instituted a part-time bike patrol, which continues to be quite popular and consequently effective.

Brian Page retired in 2002 and was succeeded by Kirk Parsons, former night sergeant in the department. Parsons held the post until 2008. During his tenure, the department became part of the Greater Rochester Area Narcotics Enforcement Team, a county-wide group, and also became a community service site.

In 2008, Maureen Chisholm was named chief. In her several years as chief, she has seen the creation of a "Senior Academy" which familiarizes seniors with the workings of the department and also includes safety issues and scam awareness, and has instituted a place for the safe disposal of prescription drugs, which are seen to be the source of abuse among some teens. While continuing to deal with the minor crimes and drug issues inherent in any community, her goal has been to continue the philosophy of community policing, create a partnership with the community, and enhance communication with all.

Fire Protection Comes to Fairport

The date was March 8, 1877. This notice appeared in the *Fairport Herald*, "Some provision should be made for fire protection … A resolution will be offered to levy and raise by tax … the sum of $300 for the purpose of purchasing at least 75 good, durable buckets, and a suitable number of ladders …" One month later, the first fire company in Fairport was established. The group was organized by the workmen of the DeLand Chemical Company to "protect the property of the Chemical Works first, [but] always [to be] ready to aid in other places when not needed there." The DeLand Fire Company No.1, sometimes referred to as the DeLand Hose Company No. 1, was formally incorporated on August 23, 1877 with Levi DeLand as president and with fifty-three charter members. The issue of fire protection apparently was on the minds of many during this time because within the next decade two more fire companies were organized in Fairport. The Fairport Hook and Ladder Company was also organized in 1877 and incorporated in 1881 with twenty-five charter members. The Fairport Protectives, whose job it was to "restrain crowds at fires and to remove property from buildings and protect it after removal" was organized in 1888 and incorporated in 1890. Since 1910, these three companies have comprised the Fairport Fire Department. In 1877 they purchased 300 feet of fire hose and received permission to use the DeLand Chemical Works steam pump. The hose, when used in connection with hose the DeLand Chemical Company already had, would reach most of the central business district.

The real work of any fire company is, of course, fighting fires. During the 1880's there seemed to be few fires of significant proportions, but in 1893 the fire companies of Fairport were severely tested. On the night of February 3, the firemen responded to a fire at Marlow's barn on Summit Street and shortly thereafter to a fire at Chadwick's warehouses in the area of West Avenue near the canal. Three streams of water served to contain that blaze, although the temperature was near zero and there was a strong west wind. The next morning, fire was discovered in the DeLand Chemical works. For the third time within twenty-four hours, the fire fighters were called out. The hose was in poor condition due to the cold and the fires of the previous night. The engine was out of commission and the canal and Thomas Creek, the only sources of water, were frozen. Although help was sent from Rochester, the fire had advanced too far. Before long, not only the chemical works but also the electric plant were in ruins. It was a devastating loss for the village. Within days the community held a public meeting to discuss the need for a water works that would serve the entire village. The first customers were connected to that new water system in December of 1893, too late for the chemical works, but available to prevent another such catastrophe.

Many of the spectacular or significant fires that the Fairport companies responded to over the subsequent half century involved local businesses. The Bown Carriage Works on South Main Street was destroyed in 1919, the Trescott Company on North Main Street endured a fire in 1930, and the Boylands Feed Mill, also on North Main Street, sustained significant damage in 1940. The 1921 fire at the Douglass Packing Company (Vinegar Works) caused between $300,000 and $500,000 damage. The 1942 fire at the Fireworks plant on West Whitney Road claimed several lives. These losses, however, were far outweighed by the preservation of life and property made possible by the dedicated and knowledgeable volunteers of the Fairport Fire Department.

Equipment is vital to any fire company and a source of pride. From the very earliest of hand drawn engines and hand pumpers to the latest hi-tech equipment, fire companies have taken great pride not only in maintaining, but also in demonstrating the abilities of their equipment. In July of 1877 the DeLand Fire Company held the first demonstration of their equipment, stretching their 650 feet of hose down North Main Street and throwing a stream of water up forty feet. A parade led by the Fairport Cornet Band followed, which ended on West Avenue at Shaw's Hall where a grand ball was held as a fund raiser for the purchase of a hose cart. Another Shaw's Hall fundraiser featuring a production of "Ten Nights in a Barroom" by the New York Dramatic Lyceum also raised money for the hose cart. By September of 1877, the company had also raised $600 for the purchase of a hook and ladder wagon "with six ladders ranging from 9 to 40 feet in length, hooks, pike poles, axes, lanterns, ropes, two dozen buckets and two small hand Babcock Extinguishers." The wagon was stored on the floor of the Herald Building (subsequently the Fairport Hatchery and now Recreational Vehicles). The hose cart, which was hauled by twenty men and carried about 100 feet of hose, was also stored in the same building. In 1878, Levi DeLand arranged to purchase a Silsby Steam Fire Engine to add to the DeLand Fire Company's fire-fighting ability.

clockwise from top left: 1877 fire cart, 1920's fire trucks, 1951 fire truck

The first motorized equipment, a Brockway Truck purchased from the American LaFrance Company, was acquired between 1918 and 1919. Within several years, the entire company was motorized, including a Hook and Ladder truck, a three tank chemical truck, a 350 gallon pumper, and 1,000 feet of hose. All of that equipment cost $11,000. By the early 1950's the Fairport fire companies maintained four completely motorized pieces of equipment. A combination truck, consisting of a pumper, booster tank and 1,000 feet of hose was housed on the north side of town in a small fire house on North Main Street. The main fire house, located next to the Municipal Building on South Main Street and erected in 1931, accommodated a second combination truck; a triple combination hook and ladder truck with ladders, poles, a smaller pump, and 900 feet of hose; and an emergency truck or squad car which carried search lights, blankets, an inhalator-resuscitator, first aid equipment, and a Foamite generator. In addition there was also a surplus auxiliary pumper. Each truck was equipped with gas masks and chemical hand extinguishers as well.

In subsequent years the fire companies continued to upgrade their equipment and their facilities. In the early 1970's, a new structure, named Stewart Station in honor of long time fireman and chief Clair Stewart, was built on West Whitney Road to house equipment for that part of the town. In 1981 the main firehouse for Fairport's companies moved to a new building on East Church Street. The Fairport Fire Department maintains a full complement of fire fighting equipment including pumpers, ladder trucks, rescue vehicles and a grass fire or off-road truck. Nearly all of the vehicles carry EMS supplies. One of the newest pieces of equipment is a thermal-imaging camera which allows firefighters to see through dense smoke and identify victims or hidden hot spots.

Prior to 1916, a fire alarm consisted of one general blast of the fire whistle, followed by another series of one, two, three, or four blasts depending on which quadrant of the village the fire was in. District one was to the southwest of the canal, two was to the southeast, three was to the northwest, and four was to the northeast. In 1917 a new alarm system was installed along with fire alarm boxes, and in 1921 a new fire whistle was installed in the Municipal Building. By the 1950's each segment of the village was identified by a signal code and alarm boxes were readily available. The number of calls has been increasing consistently over the years along with the population of the community. In 1962, the Fairport Fire Department responded to 130 alarms; by 2002 the number had risen to 785 and has remained fairly constant since then.

Fairport's fire companies have always been volunteer organizations, depending in large part on donations for their revenue. Consequently, from the beginning they have been concerned with raising money. Today, as they have done at least since the 1950's, the fire department has a yearly fund drive, usually in October, to coincide with fire prevention week. During that week there are often demonstrations of fire equipment, open house at the fire halls, and programs to encourage fire safety.

Fire Department Captain

Nevertheless, all the best equipment, the latest technology, and large donations would serve no purpose without dedicated volunteers. The DeLand Hose Company, the Hook and Ladder Company, and the Protectives, the three companies comprising the current Fairport Fire Department, have over one hundred members. All serve on a volunteer basis. In addition to the numerous hours devoted to answering calls, each member is required to attend training programs in fire suppression and safety, and all receive training on the equipment. The state and county provide training in the fundamentals of fire fighting, and members attend regular training drills, which cover the state and OSHA requirements. Training in CPR and in specialty rescue procedures is also required. Several members are Emergency Medical Technicians (EMTs) and others are trained in high-angle rope rescue and water rescue. As is the case with many all-volunteer entities, there is always a need for new volunteers. Recruitment is mainly by word of mouth and there are many in the department who have followed fathers and brothers.

The training and dedication of the members of any fire company are continually being tested. Fires are always a challenge and firefighters remember the significant ones. In 1968 the historic Cottage Hotel at North Main and State Streets burned, taking six fire companies and 125 volunteers to control the fire. The hotel was destroyed and was demolished soon thereafter. Another historic building on the corner of North Main Street and Parce Avenue, a four-story brick building that had housed McBride's Store early in the century and had also been the early site of Messerino's Market, was destroyed by fire in 1958. In the 1970's Shaw's Hall, an historic building on West Avenue, burned, as did another historic building between Short's Bar and Tanglefoot's that housed, among others, the old Kirkwood Hotel and Prinzivalli's market. A part of Apton's Antique store just north of the railroad tracks on North Main Street was destroyed by fire in 1983. The 1991 and 2003 ice storms, the 1998 windstorm, and the 1999 blizzard also demanded the time and expertise of the local fire companies. In addition to real emergencies, the department must deal with false alarms, the majority of which are caused by home alarm systems and by gas calls that are routinely referred to the fire department by R.G. & E.

Fire Department Logos

ORGANIZED MARCH 8th. 1877. INCORPORATED AUG. 23. 1877.

FIREMAN'S CERTIFICATE.

THIS IS TO CERTIFY

THAT

Isaac K. Quackenbush

Is an Active Member of

DELAND FIRE COMPANY, NO. 1,

OF

FAIRPORT, N. Y.,

And is Entitled to all its Rights and Privileges.

Levi J. DeLand, Chief Engineer. Secretary.

Sec'y. Village Board.

SEAL

Fireman's Certificate

Although quite obviously fighting fires is the primary reason for the existence of fire companies, the groups readily enjoy good food and drink as well as other social activities. Parades and social events have been part of a fire company's life since the very beginning.

The first Fairport fireman's parade was held on October 11, 1877, mere months after the incorporation of the first fire company. The fire department band headed the parade and was followed by the newly purchased Hook and Ladder truck and hose cart, which had its lamps burning. The forty-eight firemen wore uniforms of red flannel shirts, blue trousers with wide black belts, and large rubber hats. Both the DeLand Fire Company and the Fairport Hook and Ladder Company participated in out of town parades as well as local patriotic events. Both marched in the 1881 Decoration Day parade, which was the first time the Hook and Ladder Company had made a public appearance, and according to the *Fairport Herald* they had "new hats, with shirts, belts, and gloves.... They are a fine looking body of young men, and although they may not have quite so much muscle as the old company, we believe they will do just as effective work in case they are called out by a fire." Both companies marched to the "old cemetery" (Mt. Pleasant) and grouped around the soldiers' memorial there for services. In 1882 both companies also marched in the annual fire parade of the village of Newark. In 1885 the Hose Company traveled to Syracuse to march in the state parade. Each member was allotted $2 for lodging and meals and $1.30 for train fare.

The firemen instituted an annual supper almost immediately and, as the paper records, a second annual supper that was held in 1878. The firemen were fed at the Osburn House and they were "filled, they were satisfied, and they were happy." After supper they heard speeches to "revive the mental faculties," and listened to Ed Walsh's humorous verses. The *Fairport Herald* concluded that "....The DeLand Fire Company is now one of the features of our village."

Starting in 1896, the North-Central New York Volunteer Firemen's Association held an annual convention. Although the first day was given over to business meetings, the second day featured "parades and contests." It was noted that all three of Fairport's companies, DeLand Hose, Hook and Ladder, and Protectives, were present along with the "Fairport Military Band." Contests included a hose race, a hook and ladder race, and a prize drill.

The tradition of parades and carnivals continues. The departments are always a major presence in both the Memorial Day and Independence Day parades. In addition, they continue to participate in the annual Firemen's Association Convention, as well as other festivals and firemen's carnivals in the state. In 1995, the 100th convention of the North Central New York Volunteer Firemen's Association was held in Fairport. Further, the Fairport Fire Department Band, which was organized in 1972, has been a regular winner in Firemen's Association competitions.

Members of the fire companies also enjoyed competitive sporting events. The Old Home Week booklet of 1908 shows the undefeated DeLand Hose Company's running team. The Hook and Ladder Company also had a running team, probably at about the same time. At one time, the Fairport Fire Department also had a softball team. The story would not be complete without mention of the Ladies' Auxiliary whose dedicated members over the years have fed firefighters, entertained children, marched in parades, raised money, and contributed to charities.

The Fairport Fire Department, whose district includes the village of Fairport and the areas of Perinton generally bounded by Ayrault Road in the south, Baird Road in the west, and the town lines in the east and north, has an updated firehouse which includes an improved communications and ventilation systems as well as a six-person bunk room. Equipment is constantly upgraded to accommodate the new technology and the increasing demand for services. Despite inevitable changes and significant challenges, there is no doubt that the tradition of exemplary service that marks the Fairport fire companies will endure.

Bushnell's Basin Fire Department

In 1940 a group of men from the Bushnell's Basin area fought a fifteen-acre grass fire in thirty mile per hour winds by throwing sand and water from a two-wheeled cart. The fire consumed two barns, a house, three chicken coops and a hog pen. After having finally doused the fire, the men were sitting behind Jim Behan's store when a customer came in, bought three pounds of beans and commented that the loss due to the fire "was a shame. You should have had a fire truck." Thus was born the idea of a Bushnell's Basin fire department.

Within the week a delegation had visited the Fairport Fire Department to learn about the process of forming a fire company. Not only did they get the necessary information, but they also were given a vintage 1917 fire engine. The group became official on September 12, 1940, when ten men signed the incorporation certificate. Within several months, they had moved the body of the old engine to the chassis of a 1933 Pierce Arrow limousine that they purchased from Alfred Hart of Rochester.

The equipment was stored in an old barn, but the company soon began looking at the possibility of building a real fire hall. They held a carnival and a clambake for fifty-seven fire companies in 1941 and raised a significant amount of money from the two hundred attendees. The next year they hosted a horse show to raise funds. By 1943 they were able not only to build their firehouse, but also to pay for it. Most of the work was done by the men of the Basin who worked nights and weekends under the supervision of Association President Frank White, Chief George Moss, and Assistant Chief William Armstrong. The new firehouse accommodated the twenty-five volunteers, their 1300 feet of hose and their engine, "a truck that looks classy, but will make 65 easy on the level." Jim Behan asserted that they were ready "for anything from incendiary bombs to grass fires…."

The post-war years through the 1960's were a period of growth for Perinton and also for the Bushnell's Basin Fire Department. A Ladies' Auxiliary was formed in the late 1940's. Equipment and facilities were regularly updated with the purchase of additional trucks, the installation of a two-way radio system, and the construction of a new fire hall on Pittsford-Palmyra Road. In addition, with the formation of the Bushnell's Basin Fire District by the town of Perinton, the town began to help support the department financially.

Old Bushnell's Basin fire house

As the need for service continued to grow along with the town, a second fire station, operated with the Egypt Fire Department, was opened on the corner of Garnsey and Moseley Roads in 1972. That decade also saw the addition of an aerial truck and a new pumper. By its 50th anniversary, the sixty-four volunteer members of the department were answering between 200 and 240 service calls per year. By 2007 the number of volunteers numbered over seventy and the number of calls approached 400.

Throughout their history, aside from their primary job of fighting fires, one of the major concerns of the department has been fund raising. The clambake, which raised funds for the first fire hall, continued as a popular annual event through 1960. The last one served 800 people all they could eat of steamed clams, fried shrimp and oysters, ham, corn, tomatoes, rolls, and sherbet for $5. Although the 1960 profit was $1350, the time and the increasing costs proved too much for this well-known fundraiser to continue. Turkey raffles were another long-term fund-raising highlight, having being held between 1943 and 1988. Four-day carnivals were held between 1941 and 1947 that included rides for the children, booths, and food. Other projects included showing movies and providing food at the Powder Mill Park Ski jump. The annual fund drive remains a crucial source of funding.

Among the many memorable challenges for the Bushnell's Basin firefighters were the 1973 Perinton Manor gas explosion, the 1974 Erie Canal break, the 1991 ice storm and the 1998 Labor Day windstorm. Of those, the canal break and the windstorm particularly affected Bushnell's Basin, and called upon the emergency and disaster relief expertise of the department. Longtime firefighter Ed Broderick remembers working non-stop from the Tuesday of the canal break through the following Sunday, nearly 150 continuous hours. "You slept here and there on the hose bed of the fire truck, the back room or in your car somewhere…." In all thirty-nine houses were destroyed or damaged, but there were, miraculously, no injuries. The 1998 wind storm, a vicious, localized event, destroyed hundreds of trees, downed twenty-six of twenty-seven telephone poles, and damaged a number of homes, causing overall losses in the hundreds of thousands of dollars.

Enjoying a new state of the art facility on Kreag Road, the fire company, like the Fairport fire companies, continues to enhance its equipment with hi-tech items like thermal imaging cameras. The volunteers continue to practice their skills with, among other things, live training exercises which allow the firefighters to study the behavior of fire "to see how it swirls around, how it gets into walls and ceilings." Volunteers visit schools to teach fire safety and hold neighborhood drills to demonstrate the essentials of fire fighting and the use of the equipment. One young observer noted that he thought "firemen are cool because they save lives and save people from buildings and fires." Surely that is the goal of the Bushnell's Basin Fire Department and all its dedicated volunteers.

Egypt Fire Department

On December 14, 1945, twenty-six men attended a meeting at the Egypt schoolhouse. Motions were made and seconded to organize a volunteer fire company, to name it the Egypt Volunteer Fire Department, and to collect a "membership initiation fee" of five dollars. Amos Rush was elected President, Raymond Connick, Vice-President, Carvel Martin, Treasurer, and Martin Hoyt, Secretary. Within a month, forty men had paid the membership fee. The formal Certificate of Incorporation was issued March 1, 1946.

The first year was a busy one for the newly formed fire company. Members wrote a constitution, established boundaries, applied for membership in the Monroe County Firemen's Association, created a Ladies' Auxiliary, and planned fundraisers. Funds were needed for equipment and also for a fire hall. Brighton donated a used fire siren and the company purchased a Ford pumper from U.S. government surplus. In addition they acquired 1900 feet of hose and purchased a lot for the fire hall. An August carnival, which included games, food, and a turkey raffle, was quite successful, raising a total of $2,548.09. Plans went ahead for the new fire hall.

The Egypt Fire Hall, located on the corner of Mason and Pittsford-Palmyra Roads, was designed by local architect Henry Martin and completed by September 1948 at a cost of $25,000, about half of which was in the form of volunteer man-hours donated by the members of the fire company. In addition, members loaned the fire association $1500 toward the cost of a heating plant. Minutes of an early 1949 meeting noted that a motion was made and seconded "that toilets be installed immediately."

An open house in the new fire hall, which housed the pumper, the original 1900 feet of hose and an additional 1000 feet of hose, was held for the public in January of 1949. Other significant events of that year included the naming of collie "Laddie" Tolhurst as the official mascot, the holding of square dances every two weeks during the winter, a turkey raffle, a clambake, a ham dinner served by the Ladies' Auxiliary, and of course, a carnival. In addition, the school children of Egypt held their Christmas parties in the fire hall and probably greatly enjoyed the candy and large Christmas tree donated by the fire fighters. The department continues to host an annual open house and turkey dinner fund raiser, among other events.

The 1950's saw the establishment of the Egypt Fire Protection District in the town of Perinton, which meant that the association received financial assistance from the town. Equipment was updated as well. A new 500 gallon-per-minute pump was purchased, as was a 1,500-gallon tank truck chassis and new hoses and ladders. The fire hall received a new siren, new lights, an improved parking lot, an enlarged kitchen, and also a new addition.

Egypt firehouse 1947

There seem to be few records of the number of calls the association received, but between April and December 1951, there were eleven alarms and twenty-one service calls. When the fire alarm sounded, firefighters had to call the telephone operator to find the location of the fire, but the members of community also wanted to know, and as a result the phone lines were often jammed in times of emergency. The problem was solved with the introduction of a code word. Unless a caller used "highball", an early code word, the operator would respond with a "no report." Later in the decade special phones were installed in several locations that only rang in the event of a fire and in 1958 the fire house got its first telephone.

During the next several decades the Egypt Fire Association continued to grow and thrive along with Perinton. Equipment was continually upgraded, including several new pumpers, a grass fire truck, a ladder truck, and a rescue truck. In 1970 the old fire hall was expanded to six bays, the outside was refaced and the interior renovated. In 1979, to cope with the increasing population, the Egypt Fire Association, together with the Bushnell's Basin Fire Association, opened a second hall on the corner of Garnsey and Moseley Roads. By 1995, the Egypt facility was in need of expansion and renovation, a job that was completed in 1996, in time for the 50th anniversary celebration. Continuing to upgrade equipment, the association added five new trucks in the first decade of the new century.

Today the fire association continues to serve the community in a number of ways besides directly fighting fires. The volunteers teach school children and scouts about fire safety, hold annual open houses to familiarize citizens with the workings of a volunteer fire department, and sponsor an active Explorers group and a Little League team. The volunteers themselves undergo rigorous training. For example, once a month, members suit up, blindfold themselves and work in a wooden maze located in the basement of the fire hall. The exercise is designed to simulate what it might be like to enter a burning building on a search and rescue mission.

A volunteer fire-fighter's routine is never typical and often does not involve fighting a fire. A 2008 call involved delivering a baby and one from 2004 saved a pregnant woman who had stopped breathing. Downed wires, basement water, and emergency medical situations make up the bulk of the department's non-fire calls.

Egypt Fire Department has sixty-five volunteers who faithfully continue to serve its twenty square-mile district from its Pittsford-Palmyra Road facility.

Medicine in Fairport

While records indicate that there were doctors who provided care in Perinton and Fairport early in the nineteenth century, most people chose to rely upon themselves and whatever home remedies they could find to cope with illness and accidents. Epidemics of "swamp fever" (a type of malaria), cholera, and typhoid would at times sweep through a population that had no concept of the germ theory of disease. Accidents and fires claimed numerous lives, as did common childhood illnesses and childbirth itself. Doctors did what they could, but they had very little at their disposal besides herbs, patent medicines, purgatives, and bleeding. Sometimes it was safer *not* to see the doctor! People in remote areas often used Native American remedies as cure-alls and collected herbs like slippery elm, wintergreen, and burdock to dry and use in case of illness.

Most of these early doctors were primarily self-taught, serving an apprenticeship with another physician, doing a lot of reading, and perhaps attending a medical society's lectures. Early doctors rode around on horseback visiting the sick, often providing little but a sympathetic ear. Their medical kit contained perhaps a mortar and pestle, a few herbs, assorted knives and saws, bandages, a bottle of leeches, and purgatives. They were poorly paid and, according to old records, were often given things like goose feathers, muskrat pelts, turnips, potatoes, eggs, and woven cloth for their services. In the 1860's there were three types of physicians. The regular doctors or "allopaths" believed in "bleed, blister, and purge." The "homeopaths" believed in letting nature take its course and perhaps giving a few harmless placebos. The "eclectics" combined what they deemed best from the other two. In those days it was not always clear whether one died from the disease or from the treatment.

Dr. Tubbs

Dr. Price

Dr. Fox

Dr. Clapp

Records indicate that Dr. Elijah Northrup started his practice in Perinton in 1821 and was paid by Poormaster Asa Perrin for "visits and medicine" in 1822. Dr. Northrup had moved to Michigan by 1840. By 1850 the town had Dr. John Brown, Dr. Richard Lemon, and Dr. William Devoe, who had been trained in England. In 1858 Dr. Thomas Durand and Dr. Francis Wilcox opened practices.

In the late nineteenth and early twentieth centuries, like many communities, Fairport and Perinton had numerous resident physicians in private practice. Most of them had attended a medical college and most had studied or interned with another physician. The 1880's and 1890's saw at least six physicians open practices in the village of Fairport.

Both Dr. Wesley Clapp and Dr. Charles Briggs opened offices in 1880. Dr. Clapp had his office and home at 15 Perrin Street. The Greek Revival house had three parts: an apartment for Dr. Clapp's mother Almira, Dr. Clapp's offices, and living quarters for the family, which included daughter Charlotte and her siblings, George, Lewis, Marion, and Robert. Two of the Clapp sons became physicians, and Charlotte served as Perinton Town Clerk and also Historian for over thirty years.

Dr. Briggs

Dr. Magill

Dr. Charles Briggs practiced medicine in Fairport for over fifty years. After serving an apprenticeship under Dr. H.D.Vosburg in Lyons for one year with duties that included work at the Wayne County Almshouse and Asylum, and attending Buffalo Medical College, Dr. Briggs settled in Fairport with his bride Louise Meade of Macedon Center. Sadly, "Louie" died in childbirth a mere year later. Dr. Briggs subsequently married Nettie Palmer of Fairport and fathered three children, Edith, Charles, and Irving. After Nettie's death in 1922, he married Lillian Pannell of Fairport.

Specializing in obstetrics, it is estimated that Dr. Briggs delivered approximately 1800 babies over the course of his career. He recalled spending all night at the patient's home during the birth process and having to keep five horses in his barn in order to be ready to go out at a moment's notice. His granddaughter, Betty Briggs Satterwhite Stevenson, remembered his office on South Main Street in the Bown Block as being a bit scary yet intriguing, since upon entering the office one was greeted by a human skeleton and shelves of glass jars containing small fetuses, gallstones, and a tape worm that resembled yards of flat, white noodles.

Dr. Briggs saw many changes in medicine over the years of his practice, concluding that "people have learned more about hygiene, sanitation, proper eating...." He noted that after fifty years the "most important change is along the lines of preventive medicine. I've seen five or six die in one family from diphtheria... Deaths from diphtheria these days [1931] are not common...." That interest in public health and preventive medicine led to his being named the first Health Officer in this area and also led him to encourage the establishment of a Board of Health in 1901.

Active in the Methodist Church and a founder of a Y.M.C.A. branch in Fairport, this committed doctor, husband, father, and lover of his community died at the age of 77 in 1933.

In the late 1880's Dr. J.W. Magill and Dr. J. Franklin Tubbs opened offices in the village. Dr. Magill was born in Canada and after moving to Pittsford studied with Dr. Paul Carpenter. After graduating from the University of Buffalo Medical College, Dr. Magill opened his Fairport practice in 1887. Dr. Tubbs of Lockport studied at Hahnemann Medical College and the Hospital of Chicago, and after practicing in Holley for a short time, he came to Fairport with his wife Sarah and his two daughters Belle and Anna. His home and office were at the corner of South Main and Pleasant Streets where orthodontist Dr. David Huff currently has offices.

The best educated of Fairport's physicians to date began his practice in 1893. Dr. George S. Price was the son of well-to-do Rush farmers. After graduating from Rush schools, he attended the Genesee Wesleyan Seminary in Lima before spending three years as a teacher and another as the principal of Henrietta's Classical Union School. Attracted to the profession of medicine, Dr. Price interned for a year in the Rush office of Dr. Kellogg prior to enrolling in medical school in New York City. Before starting his Fairport practice, he spent time at the Eclectic Medical Institute of Cincinnati and a St. Louis hospital. He first opened offices on South Main Street, but eventually moved his practice and his wife and children to 52 South Main Street. George Price's wife Elizabeth, was the daughter of Fletcher Defendorf, who was active in local politics around the turn of the twentieth century. Elizabeth was a Cornell graduate and worked for a time as a librarian. In 1916 Dr. Price joined the war effort as a captain and served as commanding officer of the Hospital for Communicable Diseases at Camp Wadsworth, South Carolina during the Spanish flu epidemic of 1918-19. After his 1919 discharge he returned to Fairport and his practice. Both Prices were active in community affairs. Among other positions, he was the town health officer and served on the school board and the Fairport Municipal Commission. Mrs. Price also served on the school board and was a long-time member of the library board. Dr. Price, the "dean of Fairport physicians," died in 1947. He was followed by his wife, Elizabeth, in 1953. Both are buried in Greenvale Cemetery.

Dr. James Wilson Fox began his Fairport practice in 1897. Dr. Fox was born in Memphis, New York, and attended school in that community. Lacking the funds to attend college immediately, he worked as a ticket agent and telegraph operator at Palmyra's West Shore Station for three years while he saved money. At the same time he studied with a private tutor. Eventually he was able to attend the University of Buffalo Medical College, graduating in 1896. After spending an additional year in the telegraph office in Palmyra, Dr. Fox moved to 29 South Main Street in Fairport and opened his practice. By 1913, according to a local directory, he was practicing at 41 South Main Street and remained at that address until sometime between 1925 and 1932 when he disappears from the record.

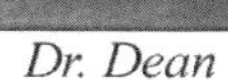
Dr. Dean

Dr. McEachren

Dr. Kraai

Dr. Buholtz

Between 1930 and 1950, a number of physicians established their practices in Fairport: Dr. George Dean, Dr. John McEachren, and Dr. John Kraai came in the 1930's, Dr. Erich Jacobsen in the 1940's, and Dr. Wilbur Buholtz in 1950. All their offices were on either Church Street or South Main Street.

George Dean practiced medicine in Fairport for forty years, first at 61 South Main Street (currently Nothnagle Realtors), and then at 11 West Church Street, only missing several years during World War II when he served in the Navy. Dr. Dean received his undergraduate education at Cornell and earned his M.D. from the University of Buffalo in 1929. To finance his medical education, he worked nights at the American Brass Company in Buffalo, picked peaches with migrants, and served as a deck hand on a Great Lakes steamer.

In addition to his private practice, Dr. Dean was the senior attending physician at Genesee Hospital, clinical assistant professor of medicine at the University of Rochester's School of Medicine and Dentistry, and Associate Physician at Strong Memorial Hospital. He was particularly interested in allergies, taking post-graduate courses at Harvard Medical School. He volunteered to be chief of the allergy clinic at Genesee Hospital and as assistant chief at Strong, and was recognized with the prestigious Award of Merit from the Rochester Academy of Medicine in 1961 for his work on allergies. Although Dr. Dean was involved in medical research, most notably contributing to the discovery of cortisone, he preferred his private practice. According to his daughter, Barbara, not only was he brilliant, but he was also thoughtful and caring, interested in knowing about the lives, not just the illnesses, of his patients. Practicing during the era of house calls, he would often be called out three or four times a night. And his wife, Louise, would always wait up for him.

Dean, like many physicians before and after him, was active in the community, serving both as school doctor and several terms as the town health officer. The local health officer's job included keeping track of and reporting contagious diseases, posting any necessary quarantine signs, and inspecting all restaurants. One story notes that he was able to remove a cook, who was infected with typhoid fever, from the Cottage Hotel before any damage was done. As school physician, he examined each school child every year and also presided over the administration of the first polio vaccines.

George Dean died in June 1970, at the age of 66. He was survived by his wife, Louise, his children Barbara and Andrew, three grandchildren, and scores of grateful patients.

John McEachren was born to a Scottish farming family near London, Ontario. Before entering the University of Toronto Medical College, he worked on bridges and as a punch press operator in Detroit. He served his internship and residency and met his wife, Margaret, who was a supervising nurse in obstetrics, at the Genesee Hospital. In September of 1932, after being told by the chief of medicine at Genesee Hospital to "pick a spot and put out your shingle," he opened his first office at 84 South Main Street, subsequently moving to number 64 and finally to number 70 where he remained until retirement, leaving only for a stint in the Army Medical Corps during World War II. Dr. McEachren remembered being on call twenty-four hours a day, especially for home deliveries, noting that "the fee for prenatal care, the delivery, and postpartum care, altogether was $25." His training had been primarily in the areas of obstetrics and gynecology, but as he recalled, "in those days, you were a mixed bag of a little of everything." He commented that "there were practically no specific medicines for any illnesses except for diabetes, because insulin had been discovered." He also remembered seeing many polio victims in those years before the Salk vaccine. His fondest memories were of the people he served who were, as he said, not only his patients, but his friends. McEachren retired in 1985 after over fifty years in Fairport. As his longtime secretary Helen Spafford said, "He has taken care of my family for four generations." The McEachren house is currently occupied by the Fairport Federal Credit Union.

Dr. Wilbur Buholtz opened his practice at 20 West Church Street in the 1950's. He was a 1941 graduate of Cornell Medical School and interned for three years at the Genesee Hospital. He enlisted in the navy and, as a member of the "Greatest Generation," served aboard landing support craft at Okinawa and Iwo Jima. Like many veterans, he never discussed the horrors of war, nor did he display his Victory Ribbons and his Letter of Commendation for treatment of "casualties under fire." After the war he did post-graduate work at Bellevue Hospital in New York City before beginning his private practice in Fairport. Dr. Buholtz was described by friends as a "very private, shy, marvelous person, who treated any and all who came to him with a gentleness and compassion whether they could pay or not." Like most doctors of that time, he also made house calls. At his quiet funeral in 2000, there was no body because he had donated his remains to the University of Rochester Medical School.

In 1945 Dr. Erich Jacobsen purchased the house at 10 East Church Street and had his home and office there for over thirty years. The doctor was born in Germany and as a child often had accompanied his physician father on his rounds. He studied medicine there, assisted in his first appendectomy when he was eighteen, and practiced as a pediatrician for about twenty years before he was forced to flee the Nazis in 1939. He lived in New York City for several years until a friend persuaded him to move to the Rochester area. Dr. Jacobsen lived and worked in Fairport until his death in 1977 at the age of eighty-two. He and his wife Gabriella are buried in Greenvale Cemetery.

John Kraai was born in the Netherlands in 1909. He and his family came to the US in 1920 and John grew up in Pittsford and Penfield, graduating from East Rochester High School in 1926. He completed his undergraduate work at the University of Rochester, received his MD from the University's School of Medicine and Dentistry, and completed his residency at Rochester General Hospital. He began his practice with Dr. Libby Pulisfer in Rochester, and then opened an office in his family's Penfield home. In 1937 he opened his Fairport practice in his home at 84 South Main Street, where he lived with his wife Elizabeth and eventually his seven children.

Over the course of his nearly fifty years of practice in Fairport, Dr. Kraai became somewhat of a legend. Late night office hours, house calls, and his absolute devotion to his patients have become the sources of many stories.

It was said of John Kraai that his "heart and soul was medicine", that he was "one of the better people on earth", that he found his "ultimate joy and satisfaction in healing, tending, and nurturing life in every way he was able." He was known for telling funny stories and for really being able to swear. He had candy in his office for children and showcases of mementos and gifts. Counselor and friend as well as prescriber of medicine, Dr. Kraai took the time to ask about a patient's family. The Kraai family rarely had a big dinner when a plate wasn't taken to some patient. In his later years, he asked friends who were alone or lonely to drive with him to appointments, thereby giving them a purpose.

The doctor probably delivered over 5,000 babies during the course of his practice. Often bringing gifts of fruit or flowers, he made innumerable house calls at any hour of the day or night – many at no charge.

Although never taking much time for vacations, Kraai was an avid outdoorsman and member of the local Polar Bear Club (those who often remove ice from a swimming area in order to take a winter swim). He hunted raccoon with a group of friends, who fully understood that they might have to ride with him to see a sick patient or a pregnant woman because his patients always came first. He loved his properties, planting seedlings, clearing overgrown areas, pruning trees, and harvesting fruits and nuts from his trees. Eventually he donated seventy acres of his land along Pittsford-Palmyra Road to the Town of Perinton.

At the doctor's funeral in 1985, the Rev. John Cedarleaf said of him: "If a saint is one who lets life shine through, then most certainly, John was that."

Since the 1950's, while there continue to be a number of physicians in the area and in Fairport village, most practice in facilities specifically designed for that purpose. House calls have become a thing of the past, while visits to specialists have become routine. In the field of medicine, the 21st century may well be as different from the twentieth as the twentieth was from the nineteenth.

Perinton Volunteer Ambulance

When doctors made house calls even in the middle of the night, and a public health nurse was readily available, and medicine was relatively low-tech, an ambulance service was probably not necessary. People in the Fairport area could easily obtain hospital equipment from the Perinton Consolidated Health District Loan Cupboard and were transported to the hospital by private car, or in extreme cases, by Rochester ambulances. By the 1960's, however, the population was increasing, fewer doctors were making house calls, and people were making greater use of hospital emergency rooms. As a result, in 1964, with the help of the Lions Club, the Greece and Henrietta Ambulance Corps, and George Heisel of National Ambulance, a part-time volunteer ambulance corps was established in Perinton.

Incorporated on April 30, 1965, the Perinton Volunteer Ambulance Corps began service with fourteen volunteers and one ambulance on September 1, 1965. The ambulance was purchased with $16,000 that Harvey Howe and Dr. Robert Silha borrowed, using their homes as collateral. The corps answered their first call on September 10th. Operations were from 6 p.m. to 6 a.m. on weekends and holidays out of a Perinton Department of Public Works building on State Street (now Lift Bridge Lane). Space was limited, and one early volunteer recalls that "We had one bay for the ambulance and one other room which had the radio and two bunks and a desk. When we had training classes, we had to back the ambulance out to give us room." Nevertheless, the corps was off to a good start with a first-year fund drive that netted enough money to pay off the ambulance debt and leave $8,000 for operating expenses. In addition, the Welcome Wagon and Rotary Club gave money and others donated equipment such as resuscitators and oxygen equipment.

Within about a year the corps had expanded its services from 6 p.m. to 6 a.m. Monday through Friday as well as weekends and holidays. In that same year non-emergency service, with 24 hours' notice and a doctor's request, was instituted. In 1967 the corps moved to its own location at 1169 Ayrault Road and by 1970 had instituted twenty-four hour, seven days a week service. In addition, two ambulances provided stand-by services at sporting and other public events. Classes in first aid and advanced first aid were offered to the public. The corps handled 523 emergency calls and 150 non-emergency calls in 1970. They offered twenty first aid classes where 100 people learned basic and advanced first aid. Including household operating expenses, ambulance operating expenses, administrative, and capital expenses, the corps spent $38,700 in that year. Since the creation of the corps, the number of calls as well as the budget has steadily increased, a result of both advances in emergency medicine and an increasing population. While in 1985 the corps answered roughly 2,000 calls, an average of five or six calls per day, by 2010 the corps volunteers were responding to approximately 3,500 calls.

Early Perinton Volunteer Ambulance station on Ayrault Road

Perinton Ambulance started out in 1964 with fourteen volunteers covering the three categories of medic, dispatcher and driver. As of 2010, the corps has over 100 members. When not on call, volunteers take care of the administrative work that keeps this complicated organization running. A volunteer typically is expected to be available at least ten hours a month or thirty hours a quarter Occasionally, some of the members spend up to fifty hours per week. Shifts range anywhere from four to eight hours depending on the time of day and the volunteer's availability. When there is not an available crew, the time period is covered either by other area volunteer corps or by a professional ambulance service.

Unfortunately, as the number of calls has increased and the equipment has grown more sophisticated and expensive, the number of volunteers and the amount of money donated has not kept pace. As a result, in 1989 the town of Perinton created an ambulance district, which earmarks a portion of the tax levy for the ambulance corps. Organized much like the fire districts, volunteers are able to obtain liability and death-benefit insurance and the corps has a capital reserve fund for the purchase of equipment. Perinton was the first community in the county, and perhaps in the state, to organize such a district.

Dispatch area of the Ambulance Station

A major move took place in 1975 when the facility on Turk Hill Road opened. With three ambulance bays, space for volunteers, classrooms for first aid and CPR training, and a place for the equipment loan cupboard, the ambulance corps' finally had an adequate facility. Even so, the facility expanded in 1991, adding rooms for eight beds, office space, a shower room and a meeting room. In addition, there is a large kitchen with a dining table, a playroom for children, and a laundry room. As one member put it, the corps' headquarters is like "a home with a very large garage."

Since its move to Turk Hill Road, the job of ambulance corps volunteer has become steadily more sophisticated and more expensive. As one corpsman put it, "In the old days, we jokingly called it 'grab and run,' meaning we would show up at an accident and immediately take the person to the hospital. Nowadays, we are literally an extension of the hospital when we're out there." Volunteers have come a long way from the days when they were unable to use even basic equipment like a stethoscope and had little or no training in anything but first aid. 1965 saw the beginning of Emergency Medical Systems and Emergency Medical Technician (EMT) training. Within a decade the initial group of "category 3" medics (early paramedics) was in place, which in turn led to the formation of the Southeast Quadrant Mobil Critical Care Unit, which provides the Advanced Life Support Corps. Training is extensive. A basic EMT, who is able to treat and care for non-life threatening emergencies, receives upwards of 140 hours of classroom training and three to six months of field training. Topics include CPR for professional rescuers, HAZMAT, AED, and blood borne pathogens. Both the medic and the driver are expected to participate in yearly training to remain current in those areas and licenses need to be renewed every three years. They are also encouraged to take part in occasional "training stations" to practice skills such as dealing with severe hemorrhaging or extracting victims from an auto wreck. In addition the driver must complete an emergency vehicle operations course.

Having started with a single ambulance, the corps as of 2010 has access to a shared mobile critical care unit, and three ambulances with the most up to date equipment, the last one purchased in 2002 at a cost of $105,000. An ambulance can put on well over 100,000 miles in a space of five years; consequently, they are usually replaced about every four years. In addition the vehicles are equipped with technology that allows them to communicate directly with the hospital as they are bringing in a patient. Since 1998, the corps has been equipped with the Emergency Medical Dispatch System run from Monroe County, which enables dispatchers to determine the problem, code the call according to its severity, and pass that information along to the ambulance drivers.

Perinton Volunteer Ambulance is an integral part of the community, serving to enhance the community's quality of life. As the demand continues to grow, the corps continues to deal with the issues of financing, advances in technology, and perhaps most important of all, the issue of adequate volunteer staffing, for without the volunteers all the rest is useless. Perinton volunteers have great pride in their organization and want to keep it one of the best, if not the best, ambulance service in the county. Quite obviously, the satisfaction of knowing that a life has been saved or an injury cared for, as well as being part of a close-knit group, is enough to keep corps members spending countless hours either in a rig or at 1400 Turk Hill Road. Perinton residents are lucky to have such a dedicated group of people to care for them.

Fairport Municipal Commission

Just over one hundred years ago, John Stebbins, Charles Kinney, and James Root, among others, were making their daily rounds cleaning, filling, lighting, and extinguishing Fairport's oil lamps. Cleaning and filling the lamps with kerosene required one or two visits, lighting another, and extinguishing a final trip. The village lamplighters were appointed by the village Board of Trustees, but also made a little extra cash by carrying a supply of kerosene that they sold to householders. It was said that both Charles Kinney and James Root had horses that knew the route so well that they would go on to the next lamp if they felt that their masters were taking too long with the cleaning and filling. It was also about one hundred years ago that Levi J. DeLand installed electric lighting in the business district, sounding the death knell for the era of lamplighters and kerosene in Fairport.

From the earliest days of electricity, specifically since 1882 when Thomas Edison pioneered centralized electric service at his Pearl Street Station in New York, there have been both public and privately owned electric utility companies. Private utilities, as profit-making concerns that exist in part to satisfy stockholders, tended to concentrate their efforts around densely populated areas. Rural towns had to produce their own power or go without. The resulting public or municipal utilities that were created are locally owned and operated by the citizens of the community they serve and are not profit making entities. Fairport Electric has, for example, one stockholder, the village of Fairport. As a booklet published by the American Public Power Association puts it, "public ownership of a utility is like owning your own home. Private ownership is like renting it."

The United States is one of only a few industrialized countries to maintain a mix of both public and privately owned utilities; most others consider electric service along with postal, highway, sewer, and water services to be a governmental obligation. As of 2010, there are over 2,000 community owned electric utilities in the nation, of which 51 are in New York, including, in addition to Fairport, Churchville and Spencerport in Monroe County. The benefits of public power include lower rates and more efficient service than is usually provided by private concerns. Local control means that the utility works in concert with the community to achieve long-term goals. These benefits also tend to attract significant business and industrial development.

The State Legislature passed a law in 1875 allowing villages to "furnish pure and wholesome water to the inhabitants thereof," and another law in 1894 that authorized villages to "furnish electric light or gas light" to residents. Fairport taxpayers had authorized a municipal water system in the spring of 1893 and appointed a commission to oversee it. In January of 1901, Fairport officials constructed a municipal electric plant and began to generate electricity under the jurisdiction of a Board of Light Commissioners.

The final demise of the oil street lamp in Fairport was sealed with the formation on March 12, 1901, of the Fairport Municipal Commission, which would henceforth oversee both water and electricity systems in the village. A three-member commission, F.A. Defendorf, C.Clarence Moore, and H.H. Howell, and Superintendent F.E. Pritchard were appointed by the Village Board. They borrowed $28,000 to install a small steam generator at the water plant on what was then known as John Street (then State Street and now Liftbridge Lane), and construct a pole line to furnish power. This early plant, with a capacity of 150 kva produced by three 50 kva transformers, was able to power twenty streetlights and forty homes daily, from one hour after sunset to one hour before sunrise. (A Kilovolt ampere, or kva, indicates the size or capacity of the transformer.) By 1905 there were sixty streetlights and 194 customers. By 1930 Fairport Electric was serving nearly 1400 customers 24 hours a day under a contract with Niagara Mohawk Power Corporation, negotiated in 1925.

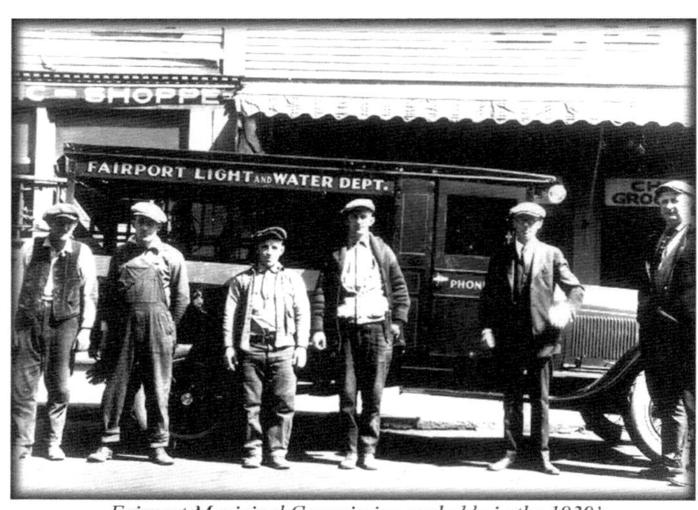

Fairport Municipal Commission probably in the 1930's

Fairport Electric finished converting to a 60-cycle system and retired its 25-cycle equipment by the middle of the 1930's. A new substation was built about 1½ miles from the village distribution center that by 1942 provided an additional 3000 kva. By this time the commission was serving 1451 customers in Fairport village and 449 in the Town of Perinton and had distribution lines that covered thirteen miles of village streets and thirty-five miles of rural highway. Production of kwh increased about six fold between 1922 and 1942. In 1949 another substation was opened in the Egypt area that provided an additional 750 kva of power.

The 1950's and 60's saw a tremendous increase in the Perinton's population as suburban subdivisions replaced farmland. All the new developments needed electricity and Fairport Electric responded. Changes were made in the way that electricity was produced and distributed. The village plant was expanded in 1950. A substation on Turk Hill Road, later to be named for Vincent Lawler, a long-term member of the Municipal Commission, was opened in 1952, providing five new circuits. By 1959 the state Public Service Commission franchise that had been granted to the Fairport Municipal Commission covered an area of approximately twenty-seven square miles, including all of Fairport village and most of Perinton.

Between 1957 and 1961, the Power Authority of the State of New York (PASNY) constructed two major hydroelectric plants, one on the St. Lawrence River and one at Niagara Falls. An agreement between PASNY and municipal utilities like Fairport Electric allotted municipal utilities and rural electrical cooperatives fifty percent of the new hydroelectric power. When the new service came on line in April of 1961, Fairport Electric was able to purchase power from the two new plants at wholesale prices and, because it was a publicly owned utility, it was able to sell power at a lower rate than the for-profit utilities. The new hydropower agreement made it possible to reduce Fairport Electric rates by about ten percent.

During the 1960's and into the 1970's, as the community grew, Fairport Electric continued to ask for and receive additional power from the Power Authority. In the early 1970's, however, requests for more power were suddenly denied as the Power Authority claimed that the power had already been sold elsewhere. Municipal electric companies were facing their first crisis and the first of a series of challenges to their promised allotment of fifty percent of the hydropower output from the Niagara projects. According to Robert Vaisey, who was Fairport's General Manager at the time, "If we don't have preferential power and are put at the mercy of private utilities, we'll go out of business." Fortunately, Fairport Electric and its fellow municipal utilities kept their preferential status. These crises, however, and the publicity that accompanied them served to raise the community's awareness of the value of its municipal electric company.

The 1980's saw allotments and preferential treatment continue to be an issue. Although the courts found that the municipals were not entitled to as much power as they had previously been awarded, they continued to receive significant amounts of power from the hydroelectric generating stations. However, due to the greatly increased demand over and above the hydropower allotment, electricity had to be bought on the open market at substantially higher prices. As a result, there were two rate hikes in the 1980's, a ten percent increase in 1981, and a twelve to thirteen percent increase in 1987. At the time, with the increase, the rates were about forty percent of those paid by customers of Rochester Gas & Electric.

In the wake of the challenges of the 1970's and the greatly increased demand, Fairport and other public power communities in the nation initiated a "Public Power Week" to spotlight the special characteristics and unique benefits of public power in 1987. The celebration helped the community to realize that cheap electricity comes not only because of the availability of hydropower, but also because Fairport Electric has not-for-profit status, and is small and well-managed. The result is good service not only to individual customers, but also to the community as a whole.

"Fairport Electric was a major consideration in our decision to locate a major facility in Perinton..." "...your people demonstrate a true concern for the satisfaction of their customers." "The favorable electric rates help us to maintain savings in a marketplace that continues to be extremely competitive." Testimonials such as these are clear evidence of the impact that Fairport Electric has had on the economic growth of the community. The municipal commission has also received special grants of low-cost electricity for several local businesses, which is in line with New York's policy of encouraging businesses to remain in the state. Furthermore it is not uncommon to read real estate ads that tout the fact that a property is served by Fairport Electric, whose rates are about one-third less than those of the Commission's major competitor.

Not only do customers appreciate the low rates, but they also benefit from excellent service. At no time are people more aware of their service than during storms or other power emergencies. Hurricane Hazel in 1954 only caused a fifteen minute total outage and all power was restored within two days. During the great Northeast blackout of 1966, Fairport was one of very few communities that still had power, despite the fact that the Commission was only receiving half of its usual allotment. Given the area's climate, the Commission regularly dealt with snow and ice storm damage. Notable events were the ice storms of 1991 and 2003, both of which did over one million dollars worth of damage, the Labor Day storm of 1998 which destroyed many, many trees and took down over twenty electric poles, and the blizzard of 1999 which closed down the area for several days. One of the main problems with any storm is that most utility lines in Perinton are above ground and are subject to entanglement with any and all downed trees. In addition, in several subdivisions the poles are behind the houses, causing more difficulty. Crews work around the clock during these times to restore power as quickly as possible.

Mutual aid is a common practice. Many crews came to Fairport's aid after the 1991 ice storm. In 1997 workers came from Bath, Wellsville, Spencerport, Salamanca, and Plattsburg, among others. Fairport crews were in turn sent to Rouse's Point and Plattsburg later in that same season to aid in an ice storm cleanup. Feeding and housing not only the local workers but also the out-of-town ones becomes a job in itself during those times. In 1998 and 2003, many crews were fed at the Town Hall as well as at other local restaurants.

Fairport Electric has around forty employees working under Supervisor Mitch Wilke, who has been with the organization for over thirty years. All workers undergo significant training. The Municipal Electric Utilities Association of New York organizes training for several levels of line worker proficiency, as well as training related to safety. For example, apprentice line workers attend four day training sessions over the course of a year. The training includes lectures, demonstrations, and hands-on experience in such areas as utility pole climbing and the handling of high-voltage repairs.

Perinton has seen significant growth over the last three decades and Fairport Electric has had to keep up with that growth. Not only has the number of customers increased, but the amount of electricity used on the average by each household has quadrupled. Many more homes are completely electric and are equipped with multiple television sets, computers, and other items that constantly draw electric current. The increased demand has created the need for expanded or upgraded facilities. A new receiving station was built on Hogan Road in 1977, which together with a newly expanded Vincent Lawler Receiving Station on Turk Hill Road receives power from the Niagara projects. In 2000 the Lawler plant was expanded again. The power comes in to those two receiving stations and is subsequently stepped down at five substations.

The Commission's agreement that was signed in 1996 with the New York State Power Authority to provide power was renewed in 2003 and will remain in effect until 2025. The Commission receives a fixed amount of electricity from hydropower while the remainder, termed incremental power, comes from other sources like nuclear or coal-fired facilities. The cost of the incremental power is twelve and one-half times the cost of the hydropower.

Despite expansion in customer base and demand, Fairport Electric has had two rate increases since 1988, one in 1993 and another in 2005. In 1993 the Commission inaugurated seasonal rates which charged more in the winter months, but reduced some rates during the summer months. Winter bills tend to reflect higher usage and consequently increased usage of the more expensive incremental power.

Because the challenge to Fairport Electric is to continue to provide adequate low-cost electricity into the future, conservation is encouraged. Just because Fairport Electric rates are low does not mean that the supply is endless or that it will always be cheap. In 1992 the "Watt Buster" program was initiated for those whose homes were 100 percent electric. Energy audits were available and customers could qualify for water heater blankets, pipe insulation and low-flow shower heads, all small but significant ways to conserve. At one point, the commission sponsored a refrigerator buy-back program with the goal of retiring old, inefficient ones. The Commission also began to provide rebates to customers who switch from electric to gas heat. The long-term goal is to limit the increase in usage because once the low-cost hydropower allotment is used, higher cost incremental power must be purchased.

Fairport Electric ran its operations out of several small buildings on Lift Bridge Lane until 2003 when the 100-year-old structures were replaced by a larger, up-to-date facility. The new buildings increased available space from 19,000 square feet to 39,000 square feet, providing room to map electric grids on computers, as well as more space for training and a 25 slot truck bay. The three brick-faced buildings complement the architectural design of the canal corridor. Other developments since the turn of the 21st century include replacing existing residential meters with digital ones and gradually replacing and burying electric lines.

Members of the community are fortunate recipients of the wise decision made over 100 years ago to create a municipally-owned electric utility. Like the other forty-seven municipally-owned utilities in New York, and in an era of increasing population and increasing per household use of electricity, Fairport Electric continues to provide low rates and efficient service. Challenges for the future include keeping up with Perinton's growth and keeping the current facilities, lines, poles, and transformers maintained. According to supervisor Mitch Wilke, however, the most important challenge, as well as the goal of those at Fairport Electric, will be to continue to provide the safest and lowest cost electricity possible.

A letter written in 1928 by Sam Jacobson hailed the benefits of a municipal power commission. In comparing electric bills, he noted that his electric bill was about twenty percent cheaper than those in neighboring towns. The cost of a street lamp in Fairport was less than half of one in Newark, which was served by a private utility. He spoke of the profits that return directly to the village for payment of debts and also for the purchase of such items as ornamental lights. Jacobson's statement that "The people of the village of Fairport should realize that they are shareholders in a paying corporation, a corporation that pays dividends each month, one that they control and serves them well." is as relevant today as it was in 1928.

Fairport Waterworks

Civilizations and communities have always developed near water sources, both for crops, livestock and personal use. While the primary concern was for the quantity and not the quality of water, from the earliest times, taste, odor, and turbidity were concerns. Ancient Greek and Sanskrit writings from 4000 BC recommended remedies including filtering water through charcoal, exposure to sunlight, boiling, and straining. Egyptians used alum as early as 1500 BC to cause suspended particles to settle out. By the 1800's in Europe, slow sand filtration was in regular use. In the mid-1800's the link was established between contaminated water and diseases such as typhoid, cholera, and dysentery. Hence, water systems built in the late 1800's and the early 1900's were designed to reduce turbidity, thereby removing pathogen-containing particles. It wasn't until 1908, however, with the introduction of chlorination, that water-borne diseases were significantly curtailed.

Early settlers in Perinton found a number of streams and creeks that were suitable for farming, but well water tended to have a high lime content making it unpalatable. In addition, many of the streams in low-lying areas created mosquito-infested swamps, leading to the notorious "Genesee Fever," which impeded settlement in a number of areas, including the present village of Fairport (until the Erie Canal effectively drained those areas). The early settlers also crammed as many mills as possible onto the banks of fast-flowing streams, creating pollution with their varieties of wastes.

The people of Perinton and Fairport depended upon streams, wells, and rainwater for their water supply until the 1890's. In 1893, as a result of several factors, residents of Fairport village decided to explore the possibility of establishing a municipal water system. In addition to industrial and population growth, the village had suffered a major fire loss in February of 1893 when the DeLand Chemical Company burned to the ground, partly because the available water supply from Thomas Creek and the Erie Canal was frozen. There was also a public health issue. Several years earlier the village had built a sewer system, but with no municipal water supply there was no way to flush out the sewers, and editorials in the local papers warned against "a pestilence of typhoid and other fevers….if the sewers cannot be washed out."

Fairport watershed in East Bloomfield

In Shaw's Hall on March 21, 1893, Charles Peacock, Fletcher Defendorf, Clarence Moore, Luther Salmon, C.G. DeWitt, and Joseph Duncan were elected as water commissioners. They hired Walter Randell, a Syracuse engineer, to advise them and reported back to the village in June 1893 with a decision to dig four wells on John (State) Street to supply 600,000 to 800,000 gallons a day at a cost of about $40,000, which would be funded by a bond issue. The commissioners stated that "the water will be hard and suitable for fire, drinking, cooking, and sanitary purposes." The proposal was voted on and passed that same month.

During the summer of 1893, the wells were dug and connected to a ten-inch pipe that carried the water south to a 28 foot, 75 foot high standpipe, with a capacity of 300,000 gallons on Summit Street. It was connected to seven miles of pipe laid five feet below ground along the main streets of the village with a shut-off valve at each street corner.

Isaac Peters' house at 146 West Avenue was the first house to be supplied with the new municipal water. The village charged between $7 and $9 to bring the pipe to the curb and the homeowner paid between $15 and $30 to lay the pipe from the curb to the house. Regular fees for an individual homeowner included $5.00 for the first faucet and $.75 for each additional one, $3.00 for a tub, and $3.00 for a water closet. Fees differed for hotels, boarding houses, saloons, and various other businesses. Users were expected to maintain their own pipes, stop cocks, and apparatus, and only to use water for the purposes stated in their applications.

Street washers had rules about the time, place, and duration of their use, and understandably there were strict guidelines with regard to hydrants. Plumbers had their own specific rules to follow, often requiring the written consent of the water commissioners. Business responded to the new opportunities. Local hardware stores began to stock a line of bathtubs and George Gates and two other plumbers from Rochester, Thomas Beveridge and H. H.Bridges, opened for business in the village.

In 1901 it was decided to combine the administration of Fairport's electric and water systems, and a special election abolished the separate boards and established a three man Municipal Commission comprised of F.A. Diefendorf, C. Clarence Moore, and H.H. Howell. F.E. Pritchard was chosen as superintendent.

By 1922 the water system had eleven miles of mains and 800 taps. Unfortunately, the water was very hard and apparently not very popular. The Rochester city health officer, Dr. Goler, wrote that drinking Fairport water was liable to produce "hardness of the arteries and joints." Another city doctor warned of damage to the kidneys. Frank Snyder, a chemist, wrote that he had "undertaken the analysis of a sample of drinking water from a water line at random in your village and found it absolutely unfit for home consumption." On the other hand, Dr. George Price, a Fairport physician, stated that although the water was hard, it was safe, and he noted further that there had been no water-borne epidemics in thirty years.

To mitigate the hard water problem in May of 1923, a proposal to acquire land in East Bloomfield and create two surface water reservoirs was approved. Two forty to fifty foot dams were built on Sucker Brook and Great Brook, creating two large lakes that had a capacity of about 320 million gallons. The cost for the project was $325,000. A twelve inch pipe carried the water (up to 1.3 million gallons per day) by gravity to a filter plant just south of Hannan's Corners (Route 31 and Moseley Road). After filtration, chlorination, and softening, it was delivered to the mains and the standpipes. The Moseley Road standpipe had a capacity of 300,000 gallons and in 1935 an additional standpipe was erected on Summit Street with a capacity of 750,000 gallons. The treatment plant was rebuilt and modernized in 1955 to allow for greater filtration and softening and in 1957 fluoride was added to the water for the first time.

Outside the village of Fairport, Perinton was served by wells until the mid-1930's when the town established three water districts, Egypt, Bushnell's Basin, and Jefferson Road, and reached an agreement with the village to purchase water on a wholesale basis. Pipelines were constructed under Depression work relief programs and residents of the districts paid all the costs of the projects. By the early 1960's, with population increasing in the town, the three water districts were organized into one consolidated district, getting their water from the newly created Monroe County Water Authority.

The 1980's and 1990's would bring changes to the local water supply. The Town of Perinton continued to see growth and expansion of its population and services. In the late 1980's the town proposed the Southeast Perinton Water Distribution Area, which included the building of a water tank as well as the extension of the public water supply to areas that included the Woodcliff subdivision. An expanded project, the Perinton Water Distribution and Improvement Area, was created in 1992 to supply the remaining fourteen miles of roads in the town whose water came from mineral-laden wells. The project was completed before the end of the decade and residents were happy to be rid of orange colored water and dingy laundry.

Higher standards required by the 1986 Safe Drinking Water Act caused the village of Fairport to take a hard look at its municipally owned water system. Looking at large expenditures to update water quality and dispose of waste-water sludge, in 1988 the village decided, after months of consideration, to shut down its water system, sell the ponds in East Bloomfield and purchase its water from the Monroe County Water Authority. The former watershed was sold in the early 1990's to East Bloomfield, Victor, and West Bloomfield to be developed as a park.

Both the village of Fairport and the town of Perinton purchase water for all their residents from the Monroe County Water Authority. The village Municipal Commission continues to maintain control over its distribution system while the town of Perinton leases its infrastructure to the Monroe County Water Authority and maintains a contract with them to provide the community with water.

Often taken for granted and the envy of much of the world, clean water is literally at the fingertips of all Perinton and Fairport residents.

- VII -
Perinton Goes To War

Perinton residents have honorably and unselfishly served their county in every war since the Revolution. While they are not specifically written about here, gratitude and honor is also due to those who served in Korea, Vietnam, Iraq, and Afghanistan and to those who continue to serve.

The American Revolution

From Lexington and Concord in 1775 to the victory at Yorktown in 1781, the American colonists waged an improbable war against one of the world's foremost military powers – and won. The men who fought were villagers and farmers from a loosely knit group of thirteen separate colonies who were often poorly provisioned and trained, but in most cases, cleverly led. At the end of the war, many sought a new beginning in "the west," which at that time meant places like western New York. After the land south of Lake Ontario was opened up to settlement with the Phelps & Gorham Purchase in 1790, Revolutionary War veterans along with many others flocked west, settling in Perinton in the early years of the nineteenth century.

Census, cemetery, and pension records list a number of Perinton residents who were Revolutionary War veterans. Among them were Samuel Bennett, David Cady, Steven Eaton, Elisha Fullam, Ebenezer Still, Jesse Perrin, Thomas Richardson, Benjamin Slocum, William Gregory, Abner Wight, and Enoch Benedict.

Samuel Bennett must have been a tough and colorful character. Serving as a fifer in Captain Elijah Abel's Wadsworth division, he was captured at Fort Washington in 1776 and was interned first on a British prison ship and subsequently in a prison called the "Sugar House" where he suffered frostbite costing him all his toes and severe damage to one leg, leaving him with a limp. Nevertheless, Samuel came to western New York to start a new life as a blacksmith, setting up shop under a tree in the vicinity of Ayrault and Turk Hill Roads under a sign reading "Horses shod unless the weather be rainy." A devout Baptist, Bennett was instrumental in the founding of several churches in the area and was also one of the trustees of the local Perinton Center Cemetery. Samuel and his wife Paulina died in 1819 while on a visit to Cayuga County where they "took the fever." Unfortunately there is no record of their being returned to Perinton for burial.

David Cady, however, is buried in Perinton Center Cemetery on Ayrault Road. His gravestone reads:

> "Here sleeps the dead who once has
> Fought on Brandywine, but not for
> Fame was wounded and for his
> Country sought the blessing of
> Liberty and we revere his name."

Captain Cady was General Washington's only aide at the Battle of Brandywine. Arriving in Perinton sometime between 1790 and 1810, he and his wife, Lurena Pratt, settled in the vicinity of the intersection of Pittsford-Palmyra and Moseley Roads and raised six children, among them Irena, who eventually married William Ellsworth.

Abner Wight, brother-in-law of Perinton pioneer Glover Perrin, served as a corporal in Captain Jesse Holbrook's company and is buried along with his wife Hulda Perrin in Perinton Center Cemetery. Also buried in Center Cemetery is veteran Steven Eaton who purchased 100 acres of land from Glover Perrin upon coming to Perinton.

William Gregory fought with Connecticut troops and after the war came west with his wife Mary. He purchased a large amount of land including the parcel at 5935 Pittsford-Palmyra Road. The house that currently stands on that property is one of Perinton's designated landmarks. Gregory served the town in several capacities in the early decades of the nineteenth century, as Pathmaster, Fence viewer, Overseer of highways, and Poormaster.

Both Enoch Benedict and Thomas Richardson served in their fathers' regiments. Richardson's regiment was from Chester, New Hampshire, and Benedict was part of Col. Joseph Benedict's Westchester County Militia, Fourth Regiment. Richardson is buried in the South Perinton Cemetery and Benedict and his wife, Hannah Boughton, are buried in Schummers' Cemetery, which originally was part of his farm.

Despite his Quaker anti-war beliefs, Benjamin Slocum served in Captain Amos Parker's Berkshire Regiment. Subsequently the Slocum family moved from Adams, Massachusetts, to 320 acres on the west side of Turk Hill Road between Ayrault and Pittsford-Palmyra Roads. Benjamin and his four sons were active for many years in Perinton affairs and the farm remained in the family for over sixty-five years.

For most of the veterans who came west after the war, gravestones and census records are all that is left of their war experiences. Their real stories are told in the lives they carved for themselves out of the wilderness and the communities they helped to build.

The War of 1812

While the Revolutionary War won independence for the thirteen colonies, it did not establish a viable nation in the eyes of Europeans or, in some cases, in the eyes of many colonists. Two events changed that perception. The first was the ratification in 1789 of the Constitution, which established a strong federal government with the power, among others, to create and enforce a unified foreign policy. The second was the War of 1812, which, while militarily a draw, forced the European powers to take the new United States seriously.

Prior to 1812 the former colonies attempted to remain neutral in the conflict between England and France, while trading with both. At sea, United States ships were being boarded and sailors impressed. On the frontier, the British were inciting Native Americans to attack settlers; the Great Lakes had become a battleground and ports were under blockade by both English and French.

The war was not supported by all colonists, most particularly those in the northeast. Those in the west and south, however, looked to the possibility of annexing Canada and perhaps Florida. The "war hawks" won out and the new nation declared war in 1812. Buffalo was attacked and burned in 1813. The British fleet moved on to anchor on Lake Ontario off the mouth of the Genesee River. "Rochesterville" mustered a small force, but being severely outnumbered, had to resort to trickery. By marching in circles in and out of the woods, with files of men passing visibly through a clearing a number of times, the Americans fooled the enemy into thinking their force was quite large. The British, not knowing how many troops they might face, decided the gains were not worth the battle, and on the third day sailed on to the east. Rochester had escaped, thanks to its trees.

While the British took and burned Washington, DC, the United States gained control of the inland lakes, strongly aided by Oliver Hazard Perry's victory on Lake Erie, and held its own on the high seas. The Treaty of Ghent ended the war in 1814, and, most significantly, resulted in the acceptance by the European powers of the new United States of America. (One of the most significant events of the war, the victory of Andrew Jackson in the Battle of New Orleans, took place after the signing of the treaty –

an example of the slowness of communications in that era.) In sum, the new nation was now able to turn westward with pride and confidence and concern itself with expanding the frontier.

Military training was compulsory and a number of Perinton residents fought in the war, not in small part because some of the engagements took place relatively nearby on Lake Erie and in the Buffalo-Niagara Falls area. According to the record there were fifty-eight Perinton men who served in the War of 1812 and many are buried in area cemeteries. While it is not possible to mention them all, several continue to have connections to the community today.

James Hannan, who had married Lucretia Packard of Egypt, the daughter of Perinton's first Supervisor, and who ran a farm at the corner of Pittsford-Palmyra and Moseley Roads, served in the war. Lucretia was left at home to take care of the farm and the children. The Hannan farm was a fixture in Perinton until well into the middle of the twentieth century.

Levi DeLand also served in the war. His son Daniel founded the DeLand Chemical Company which in the last decades of the nineteenth century was one of the primary industries in Fairport. Both Olney Staples and Isaac Arnold were tavern owners as well as war veterans. Staples owned a thriving tavern in the vicinity of today's Quailbush subdivision in Egypt on Pittsford-Palmyra Road. Arnold ran a tavern on the northwest corner of Turk Hill and Ayrault Roads in a building that remains standing today.

A number of Perinton's old cemeteries contain veterans of the War of 1812 and the historian's office has a list of those Perinton residents who served in America's "second War of Independence."

The Civil War

The American Civil War was the bloodiest and most divisive of any of the nation's conflicts. The election of Abraham Lincoln on the Republican platform, which promised to restrict the expansion of slavery into new territory, led directly to the secession of seven southern states (later followed by four more) and the eventual establishment of the Confederate States of America. Lincoln's belief that secession was neither legal nor acceptable led to his decision to provision the Federal garrison at Fort Sumter, South Carolina. The subsequent surrender of the fort to Confederate forces provided the spark for war.

In April 1861 both sides mobilized for war, the north to preserve the union and the primacy of the federal (or central) government, and the south to organize its own form of government, a confederacy, which reserved more power to the states. However, the underlying issue and the one which aroused the most passion was, of course, slavery, an institution that the nation had wrestled with unsuccessfully since its inception. While the Union had the edge in manpower and industrial capacity, the Confederacy clearly had the superior leadership. Expecting an easy win, the Union was shocked by its defeat at the Battle of Bull Run, and the conflict raged for four bitter years, exacting an horrific toll in life and treasure. The end finally came in 1865 at Appomattox Courthouse with the defeat of the Confederacy. Slavery would be abolished with the ratification of the 13th Amendment to the Constitution in the same year. Effects of the conflict would color the political, social, and economic landscape for the remainder of the nineteenth century, all of the twentieth century and even into the twenty-first.

Two hundred sixty-five Perinton residents served in the conflict; forty died on battlefields, in hospitals, and in prisons. The *Complete Record, as Required by Chapter 690 of the Law of 1865, Relating to Officers, Soldiers, and Seamen* detailed the war experience of approximately 150 Perinton veterans. Notes include such entries as "discharge on account of poor health," "health permanently impaired, wounded twice," "wounded 3 times," "eight months in Andersonville Prison," prison 11 months at Libby Prison," "wounded and discharged," "gunshot wound in shoulder," "wounded in knee," and "discharged on account of deafness."

Civil War soldiers (back row left: Joseph Kelsey; front row right: Alanson Pepper; others unknown)

Perinton and Fairport commemorated those who served in the Civil War in several ways. In 1879 the veterans themselves formed the Fairport chapter of the Grand Army of the Republic, E.A. Slocum Post #211. Named after Edmund Slocum, who was killed at Gettysburg, the post worked for veterans' benefits, assisted indigent veterans and their families, and cared for veterans' graves. The GAR was also instrumental in establishing Decoration Day ceremonies in Perinton. In 1865 at the dedication of the Mt. Pleasant Cemetery, the Reverend Mr. Butler called for a monument to be erected in memory of those who had died in the Civil War: "...a fierce and deeper struggle has been passed. Now let us honor these men who have bared their bosoms in this storm for us, and died to save our country. Let their names be fresh in our memory...We appeal to all who have an interest in the future of Perrinton [sic] and in the names and deeds of our departed heroes, to do all in their power in this noble cause." Within the space of about a year, $2,000 had been raised for a monument, which was dedicated on Thanksgiving Day 1866 with an inscription that recognized those "Who so nobly responded to their country's call in its hour of peril and sacrificed their lives in an effort to suppress treason and armed rebellion in the Civil War of 1861."

Among Perinton and Fairport's 265 veterans, Fairporters Jerome Brownell, John Dryer, John Smith, and John Fassett, who served in New York's 108th Regiment of Volunteers, recorded their reminiscences in 1890.

Jerome Brownell was born on a farm in Perinton in 1813. After attending school and working in a flour and feed mill and for a Mr. Ely in Rochester, he enlisted as a private in Company E, 108th Regiment New York State Volunteers under Captain A. K. Cutler in August of 1862. He was present at Antietam, Chancellorsville and Gettysburg where he was wounded twice. The second wound sent him to the hospital and necessitated surgery to remove a minié ball (a type of rifle bullet) and several pieces of loose bone from his shoulder. He returned to active duty only to be sent to the hospital again with inflammation in his lungs. He was discharged in July 1865, and returned to the Fairport area where he married and went to work in his father's mill. Brownell spent the next several decades working in various mills in New York. At one point he moved to Cedar Key, Florida, to take charge of the Fenimore Mills, but was forced to return north after a bout of malaria. In 1886 he was working as foreman of Patterson's Mills at Salamanca, New York.

John Dryer was born in Switzerland in 1829 and emigrated to western New York in 1850. After spending a year in Brighton, he moved to Fairport and worked as a gardener. He, too, enlisted as a private in the 108th Regiment and was part of Captain E. P. Fuller's Company H. Dryer saw action at Antietam where he was wounded in the ankle, which eventually resulted in his discharge in May of 1863. Returning to Fairport, Dryer resumed his former occupation.

John Smith was born in Germany in 1838 and came to a Penfield farm where he worked until August of 1862 when he enlisted in Company C of the 108th Regiment under Captain William H. Andrews. Smith was with his regiment at Antietam, where he was wounded in the foot. He served at Harper's Ferry, Fredericksburg, and Chancellorsville, where he was wounded again. Briefly hospitalized, he rejoined his regiment at Gettysburg, where he was again wounded. Subsequently transferred to the 96th Battalion of the Second Invalid Corps at Baltimore, Smith was finally discharged in 1865 and returned to the Fairport area where he did "such work as my health and wounds would permit."

John Fassett was born in 1840 in Fairport and "worked at my trade" until 1862 when he and his father, Alonzo, enlisted in Captain William H. Andrews' Company C of the 108th Regiment. Alonzo was taken ill and died at Harper's Ferry later than same year. John was also ill and was away from his regiment for nearly a year. He returned in time to take part in "the hot fight" at Morton's Ford in 1864 and saw action in every battle from the Wilderness in May 1864, to Reams' Station in August 1864, where he was taken prisoner. He was held at Belle Island and Salisbury, North Carolina for six months. Returned to Union lines in 1865, Fassett was mustered out in June 1865 and gratefully returned to Fairport and his former occupation.

Civil War monument at Mt. Pleasant cemetery on Orchard Street

It is evident from these stories that surviving veterans, while striving to live a normal life, shared experiences that forever changed them as the war itself changed the nation.

The Indian Wars and the Spanish American War

During the period between 1865 and 1898 the U.S. military concentrated for the most part on subduing the Native American population as the government completed rail lines connecting the two coasts and white settlers flocked west taking land and slaughtering buffalo. The Native Americans had two choices: surrender or fight. The fighting was essentially a guerilla war characterized by "skirmishes, pursuits, massacres, raids, expeditions, battles, and campaigns, of varying size and intensity," and its result was never really in doubt.

Aside from the Civil War and the disruptions in life and community it caused, three government actions during the 1860's encouraged the move westward. In 1862, the Federal government named two companies to build a transcontinental railroad. In the same year, the Homestead Act and the Morrill Act were passed. The former offered 160 acres of land for $10 to anyone who would work it for five years (and former soldiers could deduct their service years). The latter granted land to the states with the expectation that the proceeds from the sales would endow colleges. With easier transportation and available land, ranchers, farmers, and homesteaders flocked west and in order to establish settlements, proceeded to decimate the buffalo herds upon which the Native Americans depended for sustenance.

By 1885 the buffalo were mostly gone and the native population had been forced onto reservations where they were for all intents and purposes dependent on the US government for food and shelter. Names like Red Cloud, Geronimo, Sitting Bull, Chief Joseph, the Little Big Horn, and Wounded Knee, to name but a few, are part of western story and legend and tragedy. The Battle of the Little Big Horn in 1876 was probably the high-water mark of native rebellion and led to more determined efforts to settle the question once and for all. Chief Joseph and the Nez Perce were defeated and resettled in 1877, Geronimo and the Apache were subdued in 1886, and the infamous 1890 "battle" of Wounded Knee sealed the fate of the Sioux nation and Native Americans as a whole. The so-called "Indian Wars" were over.

It was now possible for national attention to turn outward. Interest in developing markets in China and plans for a canal through Central America set the stage for new government activity. By the late 1890's American citizens owned about fifty million dollars' worth of Cuban property, primarily in the sugar, tobacco, and iron industries. Spanish rule in Cuba had become progressively harsh and revolution had broken out in 1895. President William McKinley was under tremendous public pressure to defend U.S. interests on the island and the popular media eagerly highlighted Spanish atrocities. William Randolph Hearst, editor of the *New York Journal*, supposedly telegraphed illustrator Frederick Remington and told him to "Please remain [in Havana]. You furnish the pictures and I'll furnish the war."

Two specific events in 1898 led directly to war with Spain. The DeLome letter, a stolen private letter describing McKinley as a weakling, and the well-know sinking of the battleship *Maine,* led to the passage of a Congressional joint resolution on April 19, 1898, known as the Teller Amendment, declaring Cuba to be "free and independent." When President McKinley signed the resolution, war was inevitable.

While the United States wasn't well prepared for war, the Spanish were even less ready. In Cuba both the Spanish navy and army were defeated within months. In the Pacific, the Spanish fleet was destroyed in Manila Bay by Commodore George Dewey and the army surrendered to the U.S. and Filipino troops. The war was over by August.

The Treaty of Paris gave the U.S. possession of Cuba, Puerto Rico, the Philippines and Guam. This "splendid little war" (in the words of Theodore Roosevelt) had secured for the United States a place as an international imperial power.

However, the Filipinos, who had expected independence after the defeat of the Spanish, found themselves in a nasty conflict with their former American allies whose goal was to control this strategic location. In the end, after three years of fighting, the Filipino hopes for independence were dashed as the US consolidated control, which they retained until 1946. The U.S., however, kept a military presence at Clark Air Base and Subic Bay Naval Base until 1992. Ostensibly Cuba maintained control of its internal affairs, but the Platt Amendment gave the United States control over Cuba's foreign policy, the right to interfere in her internal affairs, and the right to establish a naval base on Cuban soil (Guantanamo Bay). It wasn't until 1934 that the U.S. gave up its rights under the Platt Amendment (but retained Guantanamo Bay). Both Puerto Rico and Guam remain U.S. territories.

George Kelsey, US Navy

Several men from Perinton and Fairport served in the conflicts. Chester Hull served both on the Western Frontier and also in the Spanish-American War where he was joined by four others: William Lauer, George Kelsey, Lee Hazen, and Charles O'Ray. George Kelsey was the only casualty. George joined the Naval Reserves in 1897 and was ordered to Norfolk, Virginia where he served as a surgeon's clerk. He contracted typhoid fever and died at the Portsmouth Naval Hospital on October 9, 1898, at the age of 32. His funeral was held in the First Baptist Church and burial was in Greenvale Cemetery with full military honors. "All Fairport did honor to the deceased sailor."

The Story of Chester Hull, Soldier

Chester Hull, son of Henry and Elizabeth Hutchins Hull, was born in 1865 in Albany, New York. By the time he was 27, he was living in Perinton and working as a laborer.

Chester, however, was looking for something more exciting, and in May of 1886 he enlisted in the U.S. Cavalry. His enlistment papers note that he was 5'9'' tall and had gray eyes and brown hair. He was assigned to Troop G of the 6th Cavalry and was stationed at Fort Niobiara, Nebraska. Hull participated in the 1886 campaign against Geronimo and the 1890 and 1891 campaigns against the Sioux. He was also ranked as a Marksman 1st Class in 1888, 1898, and 1890. In 1891 he reenlisted and was sent to Fort Wingate, New Mexico, as part of Troop G of the 2nd Cavalry, where he reenlisted again in 1896 and in 1899. By 1899 Hull had become First Sergeant and was seen by his superiors as excellent in character and "honest and faithful" in service. During this time he also attended Non-Commissioned Officers School at Fort Reilly, Kansas.

In general, Hull served during times of relative peace with no major wars. During his early years in the service he participated in the on and off "Indian Wars" and then in the Spanish-American War, serving in Cuba from February 1899 to January 1902. While stationed at Mataznas, Cuba, he reenlisted for yet another three year term. By the end of that term (1902) he was back in the United States and stationed at Fort Myer, Virginia, where he again extended his service until 1905.

In 1902, the Captain and Adjutant of the 2nd Cavalry received a letter from the Adjutant General dated March 7, 1902, which in part stated the following:

> *The Lieutenant General commanding the Army directs that a Sergeant of Cavalry, a good horseman, mounted, provided with a reliable well broken horse be temporarialy [sic] detailed for the President of the United States during the illness of Sergeant McDermott, 4th Battery Field Artillery. The Sergeant detailed will report at the Office of Colonel Bingham, room 24, War Department so as to be able to go on duty at 3:30 o'clock this afternoon.*

Sergeant Chester Hull was chosen and served as orderly to President Theodore Roosevelt until March 24th, when Sergeant McDermott returned.

Sergeant Hull's next posting was to the Philippines with Troop C of the 2nd Cavalry. He served there from 1904 to 1906 at Camp Stotsenburg, Pampanga, and San Mateo, Rizal, Philippines.

Returning to the United States, Hull was stationed at Fort Assinniboine, Montana in 1907 and Fort Des Moines, Iowa in 1908. However, he was sent back to Augur Barracks in Jolo, Philippines in 1909. His enlistment was up in 1910 and this time Chester Hull chose retirement. As of November 12, 1910, Sergeant Hull was "placed upon the retired list" and was furnished "the necessary transportation", which meant a 2nd class train ticket and six days travel allowance, to return to his home on South Main Street in Fairport, having served twenty-four years in the 6th and 2nd U.S. Cavalry. While he had not participated in extensive battles, Hull was an exemplary soldier, receiving "excellent" character ratings and "excellent" horsemanship ratings. He maintained either a "sharpshooter" or "marksman" ranking in marksmanship and received Certificates of Proficiency in Security and Information, Firing Regulations, and Small Arms Firing Manual (1909).

Chester Hull settled in at 130 South Main Street, joined the United Spanish War Veterans and then the American Legion, and lived quietly for seven years. He never married.

In June 1917, as the United States entered World War I, Hull was recalled to active duty and ordered to report to a Buffalo recruiting station where he served as recruiting officer until his second retirement on September 9, 1918. He subsequently returned to his residence at 130 South Main Street and, according to the 1932 Fairport directory, worked for the American Can Company. He died on September 24, 1945, and is buried in Macedon Center Cemetery.

Cavalry life was good for Chester Hull. This "most excellent first sergeant" in the course of his service had seen the United States go from a country seeking to subdue and settle its own lands, to a nation with colonies, and finally to a nation that, however reluctantly, had become a world power. Sergeant Hull was one of many that helped that transition take place.

World War I

On June 28, 1914 Archduke Franz Ferdinand, heir to the throne of the Austro-Hungarian Empire, was assassinated in Sarajevo by a Serbian nationalist. This event was the spark that plunged Europe and eventually the world into a new kind of warfare, symbolized by trenches and gas attacks and unbelievable carnage. By August 1914 members of Europe's two major alliances, the Triple Entente (the Central Powers – Germany, Austria-Hungary, and Italy) and the Triple Alliance (France, England, and Russia), were at war. Spurred on by nationalism and new military technology, World War I would continue for four years and engage all of the major nations of Europe and their colonies and eventually the United States. The war would be notorious for its carnage, both of soldiers and of citizens. It was the first war to use tanks as well as gas and air power. It was the first war to use long-range shelling, making the enemy more anonymous and involving more ordinary citizens than ever before. By the end, 10 million soldiers would die, as would 10 million civilians. The war was also significant for the political changes that ensued: four empires came to an end – the Ottoman Empire in the Middle East, the Austro-Hungarian and Russian Empires in eastern Europe, and the German Empire in central Europe.

Joe Palermo

From the beginning, the United States, under the leadership of Woodrow Wilson, proclaimed its neutrality, determined not to get involved in European affairs. That, however, was nearly impossible given that the U.S. was a major supplier to the members of the Triple Alliance, especially Britain, and Germany was patrolling the Atlantic with U-boats, taking aim at any ships possibly supplying their enemies, the *Lusitania* being a prime example. In 1916, despite having won the presidential election with the slogan "he has kept us out of war," Wilson was finding it more and more difficult to maintain neutrality. Attempts to restrict U-boat activity were less than successful and in March 1917 two specific events occurred which made U.S. entrance into the conflict all but inevitable. Firstly, the British intercepted a note from German Foreign Minister Zimmermann to the Mexican government proposing an alliance with the promise of the return to Mexico of former Mexican territory in the southwest United States, and secondly, the Russian Revolution, which resulted in their exit from the conflict and the closing of the eastern front.

In April 1917 President Wilson asked for and received a Declaration of War from Congress. In his speech to the nation he proclaimed that "the world must be made safe for democracy." Not particularly well-prepared for war, the entire nation moved to rise to the challenge of mobilization. In May, the first Selective Service Act was passed and the first 687,000 men were drafted. Eventually about three million men would be chosen, trained, and shipped to Europe as part of the American Expeditionary Force under the leadership of Gen. John J. Pershing. Over the course of approximately one and one-half years, Americans, both soldier and civilian, would become familiar with such names as Belleau Wood, Chateau-Thierry, Meuse-Argonne, and the Marne.

A total of 285 Perinton citizens served in the war, including four women. Most were in their twenties and entered the service as privates or seamen. Under the new Selective Service Act, 719 men from the town of Perinton were initially eligible for the draft. James D. McCartney was Perinton's representative on the county's Draft Board #3 and Dr. George Price represented the town on the examining board for the same district. Draftees and enlistees were sent to several different camps, including Camp Dix and Camp Jackson. They were sent off to the "Great War" with a service at the Town Hall on South Main Street and a crowd of people waving flags and escorting them to the train station to the accompaniment of rousing marching music.

The women who served included Mary DeLand and Vesta Esten, who worked with the YMCA, and Deva and Ruby Ellsworth who played with America's Ladies' Military Band. The men who served from this community fulfilled a variety of roles. Navy men chased U-boats or planted mines or convoyed troops in the North Atlantic; army soldiers served in the Meuse-Argonne and Verdun sectors, at St. Mihiel and the Hindenburg line. Others marched as victors to occupy a defeated Germany and still others served in the Air Service. At least two continued their service in Siberia. A number were wounded, several gassed, and at least one received the "silver button" for being wounded at the Meuse-Argonne. Of the nine from Perinton and Fairport that died, several are noted as dying in camps, perhaps indicating that they died of the Spanish flu, which raged in 1918. Others are recorded as having been killed in action.

Perinton's Brooks-Shepard VFW Post is named after two of those who gave their lives. Private J. Willard Brooks died in the Argonne Forest on October 15, 1918. Sergeant Howard L. Shepard was killed in the first attack on the Hindenburg line, on October 1, 1918.

Local gravestones of those who served are marked with flags and all are remembered every Memorial Day.

On the Home front: World War I

The "war to end all wars," this "crusade for democracy" mobilized not only the military, but all elements of society. Everyone from school children to grandparents was involved in some way in the war effort. Sacrifice was not only expected, but it was almost welcomed. There was no question that everyone would "do his part" to defeat the enemy.

In May 1917 the Fairport Tuesday Musicale met and reorganized as a local branch of the American Red Cross and became one of the most active groups that worked to support the war effort. Using part of the Schummers block on West Avenue as their headquarters, they equipped the space with sewing machines for making needed garments to send overseas and created a distribution center for yarn for the 295 people who knitted sweaters, socks, and scarves. The ladies of the local W.C.T.U. and the Baptist Home did an incredible amount of knitting as did Mr. Hubert Brown who used a knitting machine to complete 900 pairs of socks. The Fairport Red Cross was the largest branch in the area and also held the record for raising money.

In addition to the Schummers building, the Red Cross used the Green Lantern Inn for instruction in the making of surgical dressings. The group also formed a committee to "aid and assist all families or relatives of the soldiers." Under their direction school children collected items to be put into "comfort bags" for the soldiers. Each bag was supplied with thread, needles, scissors, buttons, and darning cotton, and was sent with a sweater, three pair of socks, a scarf, wristlets, and a Bible.

Gordon Kellogg, Bruner Bown, R.R. Sanders, and C. J. Clark formed the Perinton Patriotic League for "the promotion of military training, the protection of property in the community, the conservation of food, and welfare work." They organized the Perinton Military Corps which met once a week for military drill under the direction of Chester B. Hull. When the soldiers left town, the group presented them with New Testaments, escorted them to the train, and provided the band for the send-off. For food conservation they furnished seed for war gardens. In addition they ran the Liberty Loan drives. For each loan (there were five), Perinton more than doubled its quota and once trebled it. A local paper reported that "Fairport led all the towns in Monroe County in its oversubscription of the Fourth Liberty Loan."

The Liberty Loan was just one of many ways used to finance the war. Citizens were also encouraged to purchase up to $1,000 worth of War Saving and Thrift Stamps, which were on sale in every business and factory in Fairport. Even youngsters contributed, investing a weekly penny. The total sale in Fairport was over $14,000. In 1918 an organization called the War Chest was formed to coordinate war contributions for the entire year. Becker's Bank was used as headquarters for the War Chest and was even open two nights a week to accommodate subscribers. One elderly widow pledged $5.00 from her $180 yearly income. When asked how she could afford that amount, she said she was going to give up two things of which she was fond: her weekly orange and piece of candy. 1544 members of the community pledged $14,212.25 to the War Chest.

The government worked hard to rally the home front to support the soldiers and the lofty goal of making the world "safe for democracy." The Committee on Public Information presented appeals to buy Liberty Bonds to finance the war, supplied propaganda material to newspapers, and distributed pamphlets and patriotic posters. They encouraged citizens to buy "liberty cabbage" and "Salisbury steak" (instead of sauerkraut and hamburger) and to refer to German measles as "patriotic measles." The Food Administration under Herbert Hoover encouraged, for example, "wheatless Mondays," "meatless Tuesdays," and "gasless Sundays." An Espionage Act and a Sedition Act insured that anyone who appeared to sympathize with the enemy would be silenced. Groups of men referred to as the "Four-Minute Men" were organized to give four-minute speeches informing citizens of whatever the government wished them to know. Fairport's "Four Minute Men" were J.W. Davies, Daniel B. DeLand, Harry Greenman, and Raymond L. Lee.

The local Food Administrator was C. J. Clark who oversaw the general conservation of food as well as the issuance of permits for the purchase of sugar and other foods for which there was a shortage. In addition to the "meatless" and "wheatless" days, school children and Boy Scouts circulated cards asking each housekeeper to economize in order that there be sufficient food for the troops. In 1918, when potatoes were plentiful, a campaign called "potatoes for patriotism" encouraged the use of potatoes with an exhibit in Bramer's Drug Store that also offered some new recipes.

The conservation of fuel was also enthusiastically embraced. Gasless Sundays were strictly observed and the following excerpts from the local paper attest to the cheerful acceptance of sacrifice by the community:

"The Sanitary Can Company's plant cut down such departments as were possible, but continued the manufacture of containers for perishable food products."

"All grocery stores and markets closed at noon Monday…."

"Drug stores were allowed to remain open all day Monday, but cigars and tobacco were not on sale anywhere…."

"The four Protestant churches of the village have discontinued entirely evening services…."

"In spite of the fact that hundreds of men and many women were idled temporarily by the order, hardly a word of complaint was heard, and many even seemed glad to be in a position where they realized they were actually making a personal sacrifice in helping to win the war."

Local libraries were called upon to raise money and also collect books and magazines for the military. Fairport's library was asked to raise $180; they collected $245.11. The Boy Scouts collected, catalogued, and forwarded a number of books and magazines to the military camps.

Nearly every organization in town was in some way involved in the war effort. The Women's Relief Corps of the E.A. Slocum Post of the G.A R. collected money and sewed for the Red Cross. The Order of the Eastern Star raised money and purchased a Liberty Bond. The Fairport Historical Club donated to the Red Cross and raised money for books. Fairport's Masonic Lodge donated money. Several other involved organizations included the San Sebastian Society, St. Luke's Guild, and the Eddy Class of the Congregational Church Sunday School.

Schools were actively engaged in the war effort as well. Students completed knitting projects and quilts, worked on surgical dressings, and donated money. Seventh grader Viola Jacobs wrote the following on February 26, 1918, which seems to sum up the general attitude of the community:

"Early one bright morning there was a great crowd at the Town Hall waiting to see the soldiers go. Each soldier was given a useful gift and about seven-thirty the soldiers marched down to the station by the music. It seemed like a long time to wait before the train came. Some felt very sorry and sad to see the soldiers start, but the soldiers all seemed to have a smiling face. At last the train came, the soldiers saying good-bye or waving their hands made a pretty picture. The soldiers all seemed to be glad to think they had such a wonderful country to fight for."

Propaganda Posters

The design of World War I propaganda posters appealed to people's emotions, as well as to their better natures. The enemy was depicted as a monster who murders innocents, and allies and friends were often shown in ways that recall patriotic or biblical images. The goal of all the posters was to rally home front support for the war by asking for everyone to sacrifice something. People were asked to enlist, to conserve food, and to contribute money, time, and talent.

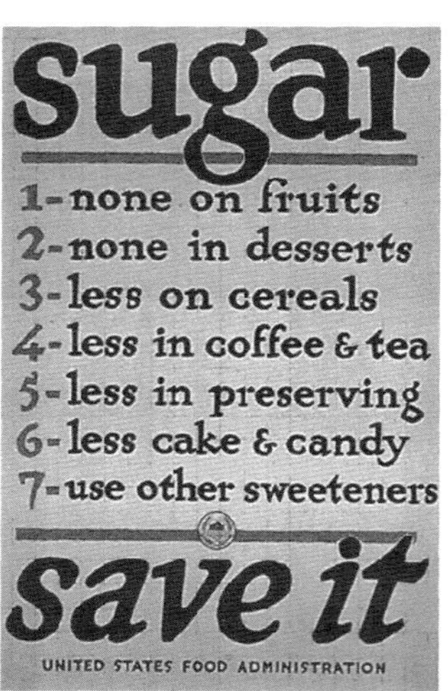

World War II

World War II started for the United States with the Japanese bombing of Pearl Harbor on the "day that will live in infamy," December 7, 1941. However, war had been going on in Europe since 1938 when Hitler trooped into Austria and had fully encompassed the continent as of September 1, 1939, with Hitler's invasion of Poland. By June 1940, after approximately forty days of *blitzkrieg* warfare, all of Europe except Great Britain was under Nazi control. Hitler then proceeded to "soften up" the British with aerial bombardment before invading. The Battle of Britain, about which Winston Churchill uttered those famous words, "never in the field of human conflict was so much owed by so many to so few," referring to the RAF pilots who fought against the German *Luftwaffe*, ensued. The British held fast and in June 1941, Hitler inexplicably turned his back on England and invaded Russia, a former ally. War in Asia had commenced with the Japanese invasion of China in 1937 and rapidly spread throughout Southeast Asia. While the United States did send aid to Great Britain via the "cash and carry" and Lend-Lease programs, the government maintained a policy of neutrality and the overwhelming public attitude was isolationist.

Isolationism and neutrality ceased to be issues with the attack on Pearl Harbor which essentially destroyed much of the US Pacific fleet. President Roosevelt's declaration of war on the Axis Powers (Germany, Italy, and Japan) on December 8, 1941, was the beginning of the greatest mobilization of the twentieth century. The draft had been reinstituted in 1940 and although approximately a million and one-half men were under arms, millions more were going to be needed. Factories would be converted from consumer to military goods (60,000 airplanes in 1942 and 125,000 more in 1943 and 120,000 tanks in the same period) and a plan for prosecuting a two-front war had to be created and implemented.

The war affected every community in the country by calling up its young men, employing its women in war work, and in general mobilizing the home front to support the troops and sacrifice for the duration. In Perinton over 600 men and women served in the armed forces in all the theaters of the war. Four families sent five sons; the DiRisio family sent six. Two families sent a father and one or more sons. Five spent time in POW camps and five were veterans of World War I. There were two Lt. Commanders, three Majors, one Lt. Colonel, and seventeen women. All of them went to places they had never imagined, with buddies from parts of the country they had never been to. It was said that "At no time in history have so many American men and women been compelled to leave their homes and move from place to place within the United States and beyond its shores. Nine young Americans out of ten were sent, if not abroad, at least to hitherto unfamiliar parts of their own country."

Albert DiRisio

Draftees and enlistees served in all branches of the service, from Europe to the Far East, on land, sea, under the sea, and in the air. George Bluhm flew bombing missions over Germany, Jack Dixon was shot down by Japanese anti-aircraft batteries, and Frederick Heil took part in forty-four missions over Japan. Joseph Saporito, stationed in China, delivered fuel for the first B-29's to raid Japan. Paul Hagreen was a top turret gunner on a B-17 and was in the entire North Africa campaign. Vincent Kennelley was a tank gunner in four major campaigns. Melvin Buck fought on Luzon in the Philippines while George Clark did intelligence work in China and Norman Alfe worked with the French underground. Gordon King, an aerial engineer, completed 150 hours flying "the hump," over the mountains from Burma into China, said to be one of the world's toughest air routes. Gerald Earl, a crewman on the *USS Missouri*, was present when the Japanese surrendered, and Paul Chapman served with the forces that occupied Japan. Paul Vineberg was probably the youngest commanding officer in the 2nd Air Force. Harry Bieler served with a supply unit keeping equipment moving to the men in combat in Europe. Oakley Crane served as a paratrooper and a commando. Michael Sperino helped build concrete breakwaters which were floated across the English Channel after D-Day to wall in the harbors of the Normandy beach head. John Burke, John Deal, and Ernest Streppa served under General Patton in Europe. Dr. John McEachren, serving as a surgeon in an army hospital in England, visited Buchenwald concentration camp ten days after its liberation.

Of the over 600 young men that went to war from Perinton, thirty-one were lost. These members of "greatest generation" who gave the ultimate sacrifice include:

Rayfield Ames
Kenneth Bridges
Clifford Brizee
Oakley Crane
Francis Crowley
Charles Frontuto
Mason C. Gaffney
Frank P. Garofano
Lawrence K Hembrock
Paul Humphrey
Carl E. Kishbaugh
Robert Kramer
Henry Lampman
Frederick Leary
Donald LeFrois
Maitland McDonald
Charles Moore
Howard Parkison
William S. Phalen
Mario Pomponio
Raymond Rugenstein
Alfred Rinaldo
Nooney T. Shamon
Horatio Spafford
Arthur H. Teeter
Lloyd Thornell
Edward L. Towner
George Vane
Curtis Vincent
Charles White
Donald Williams

The Perinton Historian's office keeps profiles of each of the men who served.

World War II - The Home front

The attack on Pearl Harbor united the American people unlike any other war has ever done, before or since. Business and industry geared up to produce the necessary war material and the newly formed draft boards and recruiting centers were immediately busy. Families all over the nation prepared to sacrifice for the duration of the conflict.

The Federal Government created boards and commissions to oversee such things as production, rationing, scrap metal drives, and the sale of war bonds. The War Production Board awarded defense contracts and oversaw the conversion of industries from civilian to military. The Office of Price Administration oversaw the domestic economy including stabilizing prices, wages and rents. The Perinton Civilian Mobilization Center coordinated local efforts which also included the Red Cross. Centers were set up to coordinate information about county and local defense work and services. In addition, air raid shelters were set up and blackout guidelines were created. Monroe County had a list of 9,364 homes to be used for evacuees in case of a war emergency. Perinton had 99 homes available.

The war offered unprecedented opportunities for women in the workforce. "Rosie the Riveter" took over the factories, and by 1945, women made up thirty-six percent of the nation's total workforce. Locally women worked "on the line" at Kodak and Bausch and Lomb, among others. Many were paid by the piece at a maximum of 99 cents per hour for a forty-eight hour week. The wartime economy resulted in nearly full employment even causing labor shortages in some industries. In addition, African-Americans migrated in increasing numbers from the fields of the south to the factories of the north where the need for workers overrode racial issues. Many were concerned over the rise in "juvenile delinquency" which appeared to be a result of relocation and disrupted families. In 1943 in Fairport the concern over children resulted in the creation of recreation programs for children behind the West Church Street School under the direction of Ellen Hawver and volunteer director Louise Dean. In 1944 a playground was opened at Potter Park and Joe Cummings joined the staff.

Local businesses were of course directly involved in the war effort. The East Rochester Car Shops shifted from making railroad freight cars to making steel landing mats for airstrips. The Rochester Fireworks Company on Whitney Road produced munitions for the army and navy (and suffered a disastrous fire in 1942).

War Bonds provided a crucial source of revenue for the war effort. By sponsoring public stunts such as celebrity auctions, the Federal Government used War Bonds to sell the war to the American public instead of relying on American involvement in the war to sell bonds. Locally the town and village held bond drives.

As in World War I, everyone was involved in the war effort. The Federal Government encouraged Americans to conserve and recycle materials such as metal, paper, and rubber, which factories could then use for wartime production. Everyday household trash had value: kitchen fats, aluminum foil, old metal shovels, even empty metal lipstick tubes. One publication urged families to cut down on fat use so as not to rob the soldiers in the field or needy European families. The government even turned to making zinc pennies to allow the copper to be used for weaponry. Newspapers were full of ads and articles urging people to save and reuse whatever they could. Farm scrap metal was said to be the best for open hearth furnaces (steel-making). Ladies' groups were urged to give up sewing and begin collecting scrap metal. Old toys, golf clubs, old stoves, radiators and water tanks would all make "hard-hitting weapons." Citizens were encouraged to "get a rivalry going" and to "put a little of the old football spirit into the game, and there'll be plenty of scrappy touchdowns."

Ration cards were required in order to purchase items such as gasoline, coffee, sugar, and meat. Applications for rationed heating oil were required of homeowners. Coffee drinkers lamented the reuse of old grounds to brew the drink and had to endure periodic halts in the sale of the product. While sugar was strictly rationed, households could qualify for an extra twenty pounds during the canning season. In 1942 it was decided that no more sugar permits for "occasional parties or dinners held by clubs, churches, lodges or similar institutions would be issued." On the other hand the manufacturers of Coca-Cola and Wrigley's chewing gum received unlimited supplies of sugar because those items were sent to the soldiers on the front and were good for morale. It was difficult if not impossible to obtain silk stockings (the silk was needed for parachutes) so women would draw lines on their bare legs to simulate stocking seams (yes, stockings used to have seams in the back). People were allowed two pair of shoes per year. Gasoline was, of course, rationed and a speed limit of 35 mph was enforced to further save gas. Tires had to be registered and no one was allowed to have extras. The government in fact discouraged travel: one slogan read "Millions of troops are on the move…is your trip necessary?" Automobiles were simply not produced – the last Ford rolled off the assembly line in 1942 and then the plants converted to bomber production.

Most homeowners had "victory gardens" and those with extra land were encouraged to let neighbors use it. Potter Park was sectioned off for gardening to encourage people from downtown Rochester, who had no land, to come out and plant.

In a sense World War II was unique in that there was little if any opposition to the war. It was easy to identify the "good guys" and the "bad guys." Consequently there was unanimity in the nation with regard to the war effort. Sacrifices were required of everyone; shortages and rationing affected all and people generally felt that they were doing something positive for the war effort.

Rosemary & Frederick Leary

Fairport resident, World War II chronicler, lover of history and the outdoors, painter, member of the Rochester Police Department, Rosemary Leary was a Renaissance woman.

Rosemary and her brother, Frederick Daniel, were the children of Frederick John and Anna Marie Reeb Leary. During the 1920's and 30's they made their home on Jefferson Avenue and subsequently on Moseley Road. Both Rosemary and her brother attended Fairport schools. In her notes, Miss Leary remembered being sent to "the glass office" at West Avenue school, but escaping any punishment other than being sent home early. Although her brother Frederick was a 1940 graduate of Fairport High School, because of a family move, she graduated from Pittsford High School in 1944.

After serving briefly in military intelligence during World War II, Rosemary Leary spent the major portion of her work life as a member of the Rochester Police Department, one of few women the force when she began in 1956. She served with the Vice Squad and with Missing Persons, and also "walked the beat" in Rochester. She was seen as a fair and honest officer, being told by one man "...you have always treated us right. You have always treated us fair. We're watching out for you." She retired in 1977 after more than twenty years with the force.

Fishing trips to the Canadian "Hinterland" to fish for speckled trout and hunt for goose with her father, Frederick nurtured a love of nature in Rosemary. On those trips, Father and daughter dined with their Cree guides on trout, goose, and caribou, the latter, according to Rosemary, being about the finest meat she had ever tasted. Her love of the outdoors extended to gardening and pets. A story about her and her dog is included in *The Dogs of Our Lives*, by Louise G. Murray, a Perinton resident. Painting was also one of Rosemary's hobbies. At one point she took a six-month leave from police work just to spend some time painting. Two of her paintings, "The Wall" and "The Voices of Mystery and Magic" were given to the Rochester Museum and Science Center.

It was World War II, however, that would have the most profound effect on Rosemary Leary. Rosemary's brother, Frederick, enlisted in the Army on August 30, 1940. He served in Puerto Rico before the outbreak of World War II, and then in the European Theater from September 1943 until his death in 1945. Having landed in France three days after the Normandy invasion, Frederick was killed by a land mine on the road to Aachen on February 8, 1945 just months before the end of the war in Europe. He is buried in a U.S. Military Cemetery in Margraten, Holland. His sister Rosemary would spend countless hours and untold energies over the next forty years to see that his memory, as well as the memory of others who had served and died in the war effort, particularly those from Fairport and Perinton, would not be forgotten.

In 1985, Rosemary Leary sought to find the originals of the "Town of Perinton War Service Record", a copy of which she had found among her belongings. She guessed that the original had been given to the wartime historian, Charlotte Clapp, and that perhaps others existed as well. The historian in 1985, Susan Roberts, initiated a successful search, finding ledgers that were buried in a trunk under two layers of books. The ledgers contain profiles, newspaper clippings, other vital information about families, and service records of the 518 Fairport and Perinton residents who fought in World War II.

Thanks to the generosity of Rosemary Leary, the historian's office has papers and items from Frederick Leary that make personal and thus clear both mundane and militarily significant events of the war in Europe. There is a small pressed flower from a German field manual and ribbons commemorating the liberation of Liege, together with the letter from General Eisenhower which was issued on the eve of the Normandy invasion. A letter dated July 7, 1950, from a Catholic priest, writes about the cemetery where Frederick was buried and gives Rosemary the name of the person who had adopted her brother's grave. The invitation that Frederick's father had when he visited his son's grave and attended Memorial Day services in Margraten in 1969 is also among the items. Finally, Rosemary Leary saw to it that her brother was remembered on the fiftieth anniversary of the end of the war. Lt. Leary's name was inscribed on the Wall of Liberty in Caen, France, which remembers those Americans who served in the European Theater during World War II.

Rosemary Leary's lifelong interest in the Fairport/Perinton community led her to give a number of items to the Fairport Historical Museum and to the Perinton historian's office. In addition, she also remembered the historian's office in her will, making possible the framing of a number of World War II posters that she had donated.

This strong woman, who was devoted to her family and to her career, and who was a caring and thoughtful lover of art, nature, and history, died July 19, 1997. Rosemary Leary was a person that it would have been a privilege to know.

Veterans of Foreign Wars

For as long as citizens have gone to war, there have been veterans' organizations of some sort. In 1879 local Civil War veterans formed the Fairport chapter of the Grand Army of the Republic, E.A. Slocum Post #211. Named after Edmund Slocum, who was killed at Gettysburg, the post worked for veterans' benefits, assisted indigent veterans and their families, and cared for veterans' graves. In 1899 veterans of the Spanish-American War formed Veterans of Foreign Wars (VFW) essentially to provide aid to needy or disabled veterans.

The Grand Army of the Republic's national commander, General John Logan, officially proclaimed Memorial Day on May 5, 1868, as a day to honor the war dead. It was first observed on May 30, 1868, when flowers were placed on the graves of Union and Confederate soldiers at Arlington National Cemetery. The first state to officially recognize the holiday was New York in 1873, and Fairport's chapter of the GAR oversaw the establishment of Decoration Day (now known as Memorial Day) ceremonies in Perinton. The E.A. Slocum Post closed in 1937 when Horace Waddell, its last surviving member, died. Aside from one photo taken in 1914, little else is known about the activities of the Post.

Those who fought in the Spanish-American War, the Boxer Rebellion, the Philippine Insurrection and the Cuban Pacification, as well as the numerous wars of the twentieth century, and were honorably discharged, have all been eligible to join the VFW, which was founded in 1899. At first the groups were small and widely scattered and as a result had little clout in trying to obtain government aid for needy or disabled veterans. However, after World War I, where about 4,000,000 Americans saw service, the organization grew to the point where they were able to lobby successfully for adequate pensions and medical care. World War II, in which about 16 million served, added to the size and influence of the VFW. The landmark GI Bill of Rights, passed in 1944 with VFW support, gave returning service men and women stipends, health benefits, and access to higher education and loans for financing the purchase of a home or for starting a business. In effect, the bill contributed significantly to the rise of a strong educated middle class.

E.A. Slocum Post, 1914

Locally, 95 Perinton and Fairport veterans established the Perinton Memorial Post #8495 of the VFW in November of 1946. Official recognition of the Post and installation of officers took place in the Cottage Hotel on North Main Street. Officers were Ted King, Commander; Ken Maine, Adjutant; Richard Hogan, Officer of the Day; Robert Laird and Thomas Streppa, Color Bearers; E. Sipple and Albert LaPietra, Color Guards; and William Zimmer, Guard. The Post first met in various places, including the Green Lantern Inn, the Cottage Hotel, the fire hall, the American Legion hall, and in members' homes, but by 1948 had acquired land on Macedon Center Road where they planned to construct their own building. One of their many fund raising methods was the sale of 7500 "building blocks" at 25 cents apiece, eventually netting $2,321. The concrete blocks were to create the foundation for the building. Combining successful fund raising with the talent of many of their members, the VFW's new home was completed and dedicated in 1952.

VFW 8495

Over the years the VFW has sponsored many community events. A 1948 news article describes the All-Vets celebration, which was to feature a "gigantic military parade," with bands and floats and prizes for the best unit and for those who traveled the farthest; a concert by the VFW band; attractions on the grounds of the VFW facility including a Shetland pony and cart to provide rides, culminating with a "mammoth fireworks display." Carnivals, dances, concerts, and Christmas parties have all been activities sponsored by the Post as have various fund drives for those in need.

Today the VFW sponsors the Memorial Day Parade and the ensuing ceremonies to honor those fallen in war. They have constructed "Freedom Hill," a memorial at the Post's home on Macedon Center Road featuring an M-60 tank, a Huey helicopter, and a walk with bricks that have been engraved with veterans' names. Along with the American Legion, they see that flags adorn the graves of fallen service people and sell poppies to raise money. For over 20 years, Wednesday has been Bingo night at the Post and regularly draws nearly 100 players. Proceeds from the games allow the Post to support veterans' and community causes which include, among others, the Perinton Ambulance Corps and Little League baseball. The plaque at Potter Memorial, honoring all those from the Perinton-Fairport community that served in the nation's wars and memorializing those who died, was co-sponsored by the Post.

The Post has also made an effort to reach out to those veterans of more recent wars like Korea, Vietnam, and Iraq who were not welcomed home with parades and hoopla to help them feel appreciated and valued. In all of its activities the VFW attempts to live up to its motto: "Honor the dead by helping the living."

The American Legion

While the Veterans of Foreign Wars (VFW) was founded in 1899, after World War I, veterans formed the American Legion to promote patriotism and civic pride and to "preserve the memories and incidents of our association in the great war." It was organized in St. Louis in May of 1919 as a patriotic, mutual-help wartime veteran's organization, and held its first meeting in Minneapolis of the same year.

The Preamble to the Constitution of the American Legion states the goals of the organization and reads as follows:

We associate ourselves together for the following purposes:

- To uphold and defend the Constitution of the United States of America
- To maintain law and order
- To foster and perpetuate a one hundred percent Americanism
- To preserve the memories and incidents of our associations in the Great Wars
- To inculcate a sense of individual obligation to the community, state and nation
- To combat the autocracy of both the classes and the masses
- To make right the master of might
- To safeguard and transmit to posterity the principles of justice, freedom and democracy
- To consecrate and sanctify our comradeship by our devotion to mutual helpfulness

In 1920 the Fairport Post was established with Lauren Knapp as its first commander, and was named for James Willard Brooks and Howard Shepard who gave their lives in the conflict. Private Brooks died in the Argonne Forest on October 15, 1918, and his citation for bravery reads in part:

> *"Private Brooks stuck to his post under the most intense artillery fire, and when mortally wounded he refused to leave his post until another runner had been sent to relieve him."*

Brooks is buried in the Argonne American Cemetery. Howard Shepard was a member of the National Guard and was mustered into federal service in April 1917, promoted to Sergeant, and sent overseas in May. On September 30, 1918, his right thigh was shattered in the battle of the Hindenburg Line near St. Quentin. He died of his wounds on October 1, 1918 and was buried in the Somme American Cemetery.

Like the VFW, the American Legion supports a number of community projects, perhaps the best known being their baseball team. The Legion has traditionally supplied the village with flags that usually are flown between Memorial and Veterans Days. They also plant flowers and flags on the graves of veterans. The Legion helps to support a number of local organizations, among them the Dollars for Scholars program. The plaque and World War I guns at Potter Memorial owe their placement primarily to the Legion. In 1933 the Legion secured the cannons for a patriotic area in the new Perinton Park. Together with a flag pole, the symbols remained there until they were moved to the war memorial next to the Potter house in 1948. The original plaque at the site was in memory of those who died in World War II. It was replaced in 1988, by both the Legion and the VFW, to honor all those who had served and died in all of America's wars.

Military Parade

On the national level, the Legion lobbies for veterans in such areas as pension and health benefits. In 1935, concerned about the future of democratic institutions and deciding that the best way to learn democracy was by practicing it, Legionnaires began to gather teenage representatives from high schools for a few days each summer to participate in creating mock governments and holding mock trials. They called it Boys' State and it remains a strong program in forty-nine of the fifty states. The Legion Auxiliary runs Girls' State.

Today the members of the local Brooks-Shepard American Legion Post and the VFW, as well as the smaller Vietnam Veterans and Korean War Veterans groups, continue to remind citizens of the sacrifice that so many have made to preserve our freedoms and they urge others to honor country, flag, and, most importantly, those who continue to serve.

Village War Memorial at Potter Park

- VIII -
EDUCATION & INFORMATION

Schools were among the first institutions to be established in the Town of Perinton, shortly followed by a postal service, and by the turn of the twentieth century, two newspapers and a public library service. All served to open communication and increase knowledge of the rest of the nation and the world.

DISTRICT SCHOOLS

District School #1- Bushnell's Basin

When Perinton was established, District School #1 stood on Ketchum Road, (now Route 96), in Bushnell's Basin. It was a one-room frame building, sparsely furnished like most early schoolhouses, with benches, a wood stove, and a few books and maps. Land records note that the one acre parcel where the school stood was to be "laid out for a school house lot and burying ground." At that time, schools were financed by a general tax assessment, tuition payments, and a small amount of state money, and commissioners and inspectors were appointed by the town government as overseers.

Bushnell's Basin students

During the nineteenth century, Bushnell's Basin, like most schools, had a winter term of twenty weeks and a summer term of twelve weeks. Generally, a man would be hired to teach for the winter term, the better to deal with the larger (and more rowdy) male student population, while a woman would be hired for the summer, when the boys were in the fields. In 1827 the school had 38 students; by 1845 there were 82, and by 1851, 107.

Continued growth led to the need for a new building. In 1866, the district was authorized "to levy and collect any amount not exceeding $2,000 for the purpose of building and furnishing a School House in said district." The resulting brick structure stood in front of the cemetery, across from Garnsey Road.

School meeting minutes provide small glimpses into the year-to-year concerns of the school district. In 1881 a committee was formed to adapt a reading series; they chose the "American Educational Series." There was also a discussion about "arithmetics." In 1884 the tax collector was short $31.00, "for which he can give no satisfactory account." A committee was formed to investigate. In 1885 Henry Scovell was paid $5.00 for building fires at the school during the winter term. No longer would that be the teacher's task. Expenses for 1886 included $16.38 for coal and $238.00 for the teacher's salary: $8 a week for the winter term, and $6.50 a week for the summer term. By 1892, the school year had been lengthened to thirty-eight weeks, and, by 1905, teacher Emma G. Briggs' salary was $38.00 per month.

During the first half of the twentieth century, there was considerable concern about the school building and student safety. New desks were purchased, a new floor was laid, and a cupola was added to the building. In 1914 an addition was built at a cost of $3,006.50, and a second teacher was hired.

During the 1920's a new heating plant, electrification, and an improved water supply were added, and in the 1930's the schoolyard was fenced.

In the early 1940's there were forty-two students at the Basin school, and twelve attending high school in Pittsford. By 1944 the budget of $4,610.00 included money for busing the twelve students to Pittsford High School and for a hot lunch program. The teachers were paid $1,200.00 and the janitor was paid $25.00 per month.

In February of 1947 the community voted to centralize with Pittsford. Over the next thirty years, the old school building was used as a community center and was for a time considered as a possible site for the storage of town records. Unfortunately, in 1978 a heavy snowstorm collapsed the roof and the structure itself was razed later that year.

District School #2 - Midvale School

Organized in 1813, District #2's first schoolhouse was a one-room frame building on the Rochester Road (Fairport Road) just west of Baird Road. The district saw significant growth in the early nineteenth century primarily due to the Erie Canal, which brought growth to the village of Fairport and the surrounding area.

In 1827 allocated funds totaled $30 for 89 pupils. By 1852, with 146 students, the teacher earned $113.88 and the library was allocated $5.99. By 1867 the school year had lengthened into a winter and a summer term.

Midvale school

In 1883, Town Road Commissioner Garrett DeNise proposed purchase of the school property for the widening of the Rochester Road. The sale was agreed to and netted $400 for the building of a new one-room brick structure around the corner on Baird Road, and an additional $350 was raised for the new building and fences for the school yard.

The School Commissioner's reports from 1905 and 1906 noted that the structure was sound and well cared for and that the library had increased its collection from 190 to 250 books. Teacher May Johnson was rated as "fair," receiving a salary of $32 per month in 1905, and teacher Frank Welsher was rated as "OK" with a salary of $40 per month in 1906. The flag was properly displayed and the attendance laws were followed. The only problem in 1906 was that the boys were in need of a "urinal trough." A letter from the Third Assistant Commissioner of Education threatened a cut-off of public money if the problem was not rectified.

Midvale School was enlarged to its present size in the 1920's. The three levels of instruction, elementary, intermediate, and higher, were taught by Bernice Bridges, Rolla Rice, and Bessie Kenney respectively. Each year the school graduated seven to nine students.

In 1927, as in most other years, the entire Midvale School took part in the graduation ceremony. There were songs by the elementary and primary grades, a piano duet, speeches by the graduates and the Superintendent, and, of course, the presentation of diplomas and awards to the nine graduates. By the 40's and 50's the songs had expanded into full-scale operettas and were financed by suppers put on by parent groups. An invitation from the same period advertises a "Community Dinner - Come to eat, sing, and be merry with your neighbors – at the community tureen dinner at 'Midvale School,'...Bring your favorite dish ...." Clearly, Midvale School was a community center as well as a school.

Midvale class of 1928

By the early 1940's Bessie Kenney had become principal, Adelle Goetzman was teaching kindergarten, Jane Bourne, first and second grade; Verna Luke, third and fourth; and Eugene Bouchard, fifth and sixth. Helen Vollbracht taught music and Effie Andrews taught art. Due to two fatal accidents, a bus was purchased to transport students. Because students were bused, kindergarteners had to stay for the full day. As a result, Mrs. Cornelius, who lived across the road from the school, provided hot lunches, using government surplus food and homegrown produce.

In 1955, parents voted to send their children to Johanna Perrin School on Potter Place, the new centralized elementary school. In 1960 the Midvale structure was sold for office space and was briefly a restaurant and disco in the 1970's. Since 1983, it has been used as offices and is an anchor point of the Baird Road Historic District.

District School #3 - Turk Hill Road

District School #3, located on the east side of Turk Hill Road south of Ayrault, was built in 1822 by Aruna Bradford on land donated by John Peters. School records note that Bradford was "exonerated from the residue of his tax ... viz 148 cents" for his efforts.

Familiar Perinton names like Ellsworth, Slocum, Arnold, Hannan, and Ayrault appear frequently in the records of District #3's annual meetings as clerk or trustee. Darius Arnold was paid $7 for building a "backhouse" in 1825. A Franklin stove was purchased in 1827 for $20 and a new chimney was built. In 1828 each student was required to provide 1/2 cord of wood. If the wood was not procured in a timely manner, the family had to pay 67 cents per cord for someone else to supply it. 1845 saw the purchase of an 8-day clock for $6.50 and a bell for 38 cents, and the library was opened to the community from "12 ½ o'clock to 4 ½ o'clock p.m. on Friday of each week for the inhabitants to draw and return books." In 1850 Thomas Slocum was paid $388 to build a new one-room structure, just to the north of the old one, which was "painted on the outside with two good coats of good white lead & linseed oil".

The School Commissioner's Report for 1905 found the school in good condition, with twenty-four students, an excellent teacher in Emma Fisher, who was paid $34 per month, and only in need of a new "closet." The school was enlarged in 1929; electricity was added in 1932, followed by running water, a new roof and flush toilets in 1935.

Sara Casella Smith and Lettie Ellsworth Bortle described the school during the first half of the twentieth century. There were approximately six rows of desks, a long blackboard and a furnace in the one big room. The bench in the front of the room was used if someone was ill or misbehaving. A second room and teacher were added in 1929. School began at 8:15 with the ringing of the bell and the pledge to the flag. Grades one through three had basic reading, writing, spelling, and math. Books included those subjects, plus geography and civil government. Everyone had art, writing, and hygiene on Fridays. All students were required to help with the cleaning, appointed two at a time. The older boys also had the responsibility of adding coal to the furnace and cleaning out the ashes. Homework was rare; students completed work while the others were having lessons. Ten a.m. was recess time when all went outside for the fresh air, a "cold dipper of fresh water," and games like "snap the whip" and "drop the handkerchief." Major school events included an annual spring "Month of May" hike to study and pick flowers, a June picnic with games and prizes, and a Christmas party with plays, recitations, and singing.

In 1950 District #3 voted to close for one year and send all students to the Fairport Village. The change was made permanent in 1951 and the school, having provided a "good basic education" for well over 100 years, closed for good. The building housed the Fairport American Legion Brooks-Shepard Post 765 from 1957 to 1981, and since 1981 has been a private home.

District School #4 – Egypt

As early at 1810, a small wooden building on the north side of Pittsford-Palmyra Road served as Egypt's first schoolhouse. By 1826 another small wooden building near the present site of the Town Centre Plaza housed the school. Sixty-seven students attended in 1827, fifty-six children from twenty-one families in 1832, and seventy-four scholars in 1844. Sometime before 1848, the school location was moved to the south side of Pittsford-Palmyra Road near the corner of Loud Road. It is not clear whether a new school building was constructed or the old one was moved to the new location.

By the 1850's, #4 school had moved to the north side of Pittsford-Palmyra Road opposite Victor-Egypt Road. The first building on the site was a wooden structure. It was replaced in the first decade of the twentieth century by a one and one-half story concrete block building. Cast-block concrete was a relatively inexpensive, durable, and popular mass-produced building material at the time. The 1908 Sears Catalog, in fact, devoted eight pages to concrete block-making machines. The School Commissioner's Report from 1906 commends the good condition of the school – the desks having been varnished and the boards painted. The school served thirty-five pupils, the teacher was paid $36 per month, and there were twenty-seven new and sixty old volumes in the library. The Commissioner stated that "Miss (Agnes) Dwyer is teaching in a good school." In 1907 a list of materials included Peerless maps of the world, Bridgman's School Map of the State (the "only state map approved for rural schools"), Bardeen's county maps, and W. & A. K. Johnston's globes.

As with district schools in general, #4 was the focal point of the community. The library was the community library, community meetings were held there, and, of course, the school itself was run by community members. Reminiscences of former students prove that the school was also where life-long friendships and local loyalties to town and community were formed. In 1936 a school reunion brought together a number of former students and teachers. Charles Butler and ten of his pupils were there. Effie Herendeen, a teacher from the 1890's and twenty-two of her former pupils attended, as did Ella Blazey, another teacher from the 1890's. John Woolsey, who attended the school from 1896 to 1901, wrote how fortunate he felt to have attended the school and that "a country school embracing all grades is one of the basic institutions of America…" He spoke of several classmates and wondered if students "still drink out of the same dipper." Jenny Plumb, who had taught in Egypt in 1870, presented a poem remembering school times and classmates:

"...Take a long look backward,
Scan the register
Read the list of those who
Once were pupils here.

Wouldn't it be joyous
To meet that long line
And with them recall the
Days of Auld Lang Syne?..."

After centralization, the schoolhouse was sold to the Fairport Grange in 1955 for use as their meeting hall. In 1993 it was designated as a Perinton landmark, and most recently has been beautifully restored as offices by its owner, attorney Thomas Klonick. The building continues to be an anchor point for the Egypt community.

Egypt school circa 1900

District School #5 - Carter Road

As early as 1813, classes were being held in a one-room frame building at the corner of Carter and Whitney Roads. District School #5 served forty-two children for six months at a cost of $10.85 in 1819. By 1821 the number had increased to seventy-nine and the money to $18.34. The number of students remained more or less in the seventy to eighty range through 1845.

Reflecting the development in the village of Fairport between the 1850's and 1900, the school population in District #5 declined from earlier highs to an average of about fifty students per year with an average yearly cost of about $70. By 1905 and 1906 the student population had declined to twenty-eight and thirty respectively. The little schoolhouse itself was in good repair with the exception of what seems to have been a common problem, the need for a new and better "closet." Ella Kennedy, the teacher in 1905, was rated as "good" in all respects and earned a salary of $32 per month. Clark Furman, the teacher in 1906, was only rated as "fair," and as "not strong in discipline," but his salary was $36 per month. In 1905 Bessie Newton's report card shows that she studied spelling, reading, writing, grammar, arithmetic, geography, history, and physiology and that she was a well-behaved high 90's student. A student at District #5 from 1899-1905, she eventually became a Fairport teacher herself.

Jennie Plumb, a former #5 student, wrote about her childhood, giving readers a glimpse into a rural child's life both out of school – chasing geese, picking apples, skating on a local pond – and in school. She writes that the teacher would call the students into the building by rapping her ruler on the window sill. Roll was called and lessons began. If it was cold, a fire would be kindled in the stove with the wood brought by the students. The children sat at their wooden desks and studied a list of vowels or consulted the globe or dictionary, both of which were scarred from use "like soldiers from the war." Parsing sentences, doing equations and cube roots, and preparing for the spelling bee from Sander's Spelling Book also occupied their time. If two students were lucky, they were chosen to go for water from the well and "...got away from studying hours..."

Noontime meant lunch pails of sausage, bread, pies and doughnuts. It also meant being outside and throwing snowballs in the winter, and playing baseball or skipping rope with grapevines in the better weather. It meant singing "Daisy Dan" and "The Cabbage Line" and playing "pom-pom pullaway" or "Blind Man's Bluff" or "drop the handkerchief," and walking along the stone fence "with dexterous skill."

Returning inside for the afternoon, the students demonstrated their knowledge of grammar and arithmetic on the blackboard with chunks of chalk that their teacher had broken off with the stove poker or a jack knife. Perhaps they participated in a spelling bee. In the spring the teacher might lead a "science walk," which often took longer than planned, as the students were "very fond of loitering to play."

District School #5 closed for good in May of 1951 and was sold to Merton Bridges. The building no longer exists, but its story lives on in memoirs and records.

District School #6 – Ayrault Road

Perinton established its sixth District School in 1816. The first classes were held in a one-room frame building on Wapping Bridge Road (today's Ayrault Road), near the intersection with Pittsford-Palmyra Road. The first building was replaced in 1857 with another one-room frame structure which, with its several additions, and its moves to accommodate the realignment of the road, still remains in essentially the same location today.

In 1819, the school was in session for eight months and eighteen days and served fifty-two students. The number of students had declined to thirty-eight by 1824, but then stayed relatively stable, usually between forty and fifty students during the 1840's and 50's. The teacher's salary was about $50 per year, and the money allocated for the library varied from about $2 to about $7. As was common with many district schools, the boundaries changed several times during the first half of the nineteenth century, most likely due to the increase and shifting of the population.

District #6 students

School #6 was well maintained. In the 1880's a well was dug and a chain pump was installed. The heating system was converted from wood to coal. The State Commissioner commended the school in his 1905 reports for its good condition and noted that the thirty-three volume library was "well-selected" and used by "about 2/3 of the pupils." First-term teacher Sadie Morse was commended for her scholarship and for her "excellent control." Perhaps that was the reason her monthly salary was increased from $32 in March of 1905 to $40 in October of 1905.

In 1920, with the help of teacher Mildred Girk Palmer, the mothers formed a PTA. There were eight charter members who paid $.05 monthly dues. The group organized suppers and dances, held teas, and pieced quilts to raise money. The funds were spent on new blackboards, a hot lunch program, a new clock, and holiday parties for the children with ice cream, cake, and candy. The PTA further helped the students by working with the 4-H clubs, by taking the children to dental clinics and by introducing them to the parks. The group remained active until 1952 when the school was closed. By then there were forty-two members and their annual dues were $.60.

John Ward, who started at #6 in 1929, remembered his years there. In a letter he mentioned that teacher Myrta Blood had a long black buggy whip on her desk with which she could reach almost any student. There were four rows of desks, all on moveable skids, – row one for the 1st and 2nd graders, row two for grades 3 and 4, row three for grades 5 and 6, and the last row for the 7th and 8th graders. Ward also recalled that the building had been shifted because it was believed that all students should have morning sun on their left. In addition to the classroom, he remembers two cloakrooms and two bathrooms, one set for the boys, and one set for the girls, a library, and a kitchen.

The building served as a reserve building for the central district until it was sold in 1955 for $4,000. It has since been a private residence.

District School #7 and #12 - The Joy School on Macedon Center Road

"...beginning at the Southwest Corner of lot No twenty eight, from thence running north half a mile, thence East to the town line, from thence South on the town line to the Swamp, thence westerly following the swamp to the place of beginning."

In this manner District #7 School was laid out on April 4, 1816, on Macedon Center Road opposite today's Perinton Parkway. The earliest records, dated 1819, note that school was in session for four months, and served sixty-five students. The first classes were probably held in a private home, as a school building wasn't built until 1823. The "Joy School," named after the pioneer Joy family, was built on land that had been purchased by school trustees Warren Joy, Asa Bullock and Constant Wood.

Between the years of 1844 and 1852, the student population grew from fifty-seven to eighty, and the budget from $42.63 to $79.75. In 1866, Luther Curtis, School Commissioner of the First Commission District of Monroe County, ordered that Perinton District #7 be re-designated as District #12, since the proximity of Victor's #7 school to Perinton's #7 had caused confusion. The boundaries of District #12 were modified at least five times between the 1820's and 1840 as the population changed and shifted.

District #7 school building

The school records of the late 1800's show the usual preoccupation with the raising and allocation of money, but also an emphasis on maintenance and improvements to the new building that was constructed in

1876. In 1877 $100 was raised for twenty-two new double seats, a teacher's seat, and four new back seats. A new chain pump was purchased for $10, and the old one sold to Garrett DeNise for $4. New shade trees were bought and the trustees were "empowered to have them set in good shape."

Vandalism is not just a modern phenomenon. School records of 1898 note that after some damage had been done to school property, a "resolution was introduced and carried that the sum of ten dollars be paid to any person furnishing evidence that will lead to the arrest and conviction of any person found mutilating and destroying the school property of the district."

The school commissioner's report for 1906 describes a building in fair condition, except for the heat which was "poor." The "side walls and ceiling need plaster and paper, stove escapes gas very bad, i.e. not very old but the pupils say it alway (sic) escaped gas, something should be done to do away with the gas and a new stove is about the only way out of it." The twenty-five students were taught by Carrie Hurley, who was rated as OK to very good and received a salary of $36 per month. The library contained seventy-seven volumes.

As early as 1916, women were recorded as voters in the district, and in 1917 Mrs. William Diedrich was elected trustee, Mrs. Kate Schoolmaster, collector, and Mrs. A.J. Hull clerk.

A new school building with central heat, indoor plumbing and electricity was opened in 1924 at a cost of $7000 to be paid over seven years. The new school was also used as a community center for "strictly social affairs, dancing being particularly specified...." During the next twenty-five years, school meetings dealt with salaries and upkeep as well as with two stubborn problems: poison ivy and water in the basement. In 1950 it was decided to close the school for a two year trial period and send all students to the Fairport schools. The next year the Fairport schools centralized and the Joy School was permanently closed and sold. The building, now a much modified private residence, still stands on Macedon Center Road.

District School #8 - Whitney Road

On April 24, 1819 Town Clerk Asa Wilmarth recorded that school district #8 had been laid out by school commissioners Ezra G. Jones and Reuben Willey. The 1852 map of Perinton shows a school on the north side of Whitney Road in Lot 42 just east of Watson Road, which, according to a brief history of the school by May Watson Fisher, was an old red building on the John M. Watson farm. Apparently, Winfield Watson, John Watson's son, taught there before a new structure was opened in the fall of 1857 at the southeast corner of Watson and Whitney Roads in Lot 32. That land was purchased from Asa Perkins with the stipulation that a board fence 4.5 feet high be built on the east and south sides of the school and maintained for as long as a school existed on the site.

District #8 was the second largest district in the town behind District #2, reflecting the population growth that was occurring with the opening of the Erie Canal. District #8's boundaries were changed no less than four times as a result of population growth and shift, which saw the school population increase from sixty-two to ninety-two between 1821 and 1824.

The 1844 record shows only forty-one students, with public funds allocated totaling $30.66 including $24.52 for wages and $6.14 for the library. By 1855 the number of students had increased to fifty-nine and the allocated money to $70.28, $67.34 of which went for wages. Although the student population in the district had increased to seventy-two students by 1867 and was costing the taxpayers $78.35, the average daily attendance was only twenty students. Mrs. L.M. Shaw and Jane Plumb were teachers there during the 1870's, and Ruth Vane taught during the summer terms in 1873 and 1874.

Students of the 1870's were, of course, required to obey certain rules and regulations. The following excerpts from an 1872 educational journal are an historical curiosity, but they also show that some things don't change very much.

Scholars are required:

- To be punctual at school.
- To bow on presenting or receiving anything.
- To raise the hand as a request to speak.
- To follow every classmate while reading, and correct all errors discovered.

Scholars are forbidden:

- To meddle with or take out inkstands, or disturb the contents of another's desk.
- To use any profane or indelicate language.
- To nick name any person.
- To indulge in eating in school.
- To waste school hours by talking, laughing, playing, idling.

District #8 School, 1947

The School Commissioner's Report of 1906 provides a glimpse into the life of District #8 at the turn of the last century. The building itself was in adequate shape except for the chimney and the blackboards, which needed repair. As seemed to be the case with many of the school buildings, the "closets" needed to be replaced. The library had sixty-seven volumes and the care, suitability, and use of the books was "O.K." Teacher Ella Kennedy was responsible for thirty-one students with an average daily attendance of twenty-four, earned $30 per month, and was rated as "O.K." in all categories. The school was supplied with a U.S. flag, which was lacking a rope on the staff, maps of the state and county and foreign countries, but not of the United States, a dictionary, and "material for busy work," among other items.

District #8 school continued to serve its students until 1952 when it was closed due to centralization. The building was subsequently sold to Anthony Carlomusto for $2,006 and was razed a short time later.

District School #9 - East Church Street

The earliest record of District School #9 states: "Pursuant to publick notice a meeting of the freeholders inhabitants of School District No. 9 was convened at the house occupied by Cyrenus Mallett in the Town of Perinton....April 12, 1826." At that meeting John Peters, Abishai Goodell, and Larry Wilcox were elected trustees. It was voted "that the trustees fix on a site for the School House at some point between the southeast corner of A. Goodell's land and the Fairport Burying Ground [Greenvale Cemetery on East Church Street] on either side of the road – ," "that a school house be built by the first day of November next," and "that said schoolhouse be twenty four by thirty feet, to be built of stone..." Approval was given to raise "a sufficient sum of money" as well.

Unfortunately, the record does not indicate anything about students or teachers until 1830, when it is noted that the school was in session for ten months with duly appointed and approved teachers. Seventy children attended the school and a total of $94 was spent. The number of students steadily increased during the decades of the 1830's and 1840's, due to the growth of Fairport as a canal village. Probably because of the growing number of students, in 1839 a tax levy of $10 was allocated to start a library.

The issue of repairs and funding is a constantly recurring item in the district's minutes. In 1829, $15 had been raised to build a "necessary" and to attend to some repairs. In 1840 a tax of $92 was levied for the purpose of repairing the schoolhouse. A new privy was built in 1852 at a cost of $8. Library money appears to have been an issue as well. Teacher salaries were a problem in 1850. Three different proposals were made to raise funds for wages, all of which were voted down. The district did provide, however, $60 for boarding teachers for forty-eight weeks. There were obviously other disagreements as well, because several times it was noted that elected officials refused to serve and had to be replaced.

Space had become a problem by 1843 and in 1844 Abishai Goodell was paid $12.50 for the rent of a school room. In 1844 instead of purchasing a site for a new schoolhouse, a $175 tax was raised to build an addition on the east side of the old schoolhouse. In 1852, however, it was decided to purchase the lot adjoining the schoolhouse (owned by Mrs. Bolen) for a new school, provided that it could be acquired for $450. In 1854 a plan for a two-story brick building, 36 feet by 50 feet, was approved despite considerable disagreement over the cost. James Van Buren stated that $3,000 was necessary for an adequate structure. His proposal was defeated. At a subsequent meeting the sum of $1,500 was proposed, lowered to $1,200, and approved. By 1855 it was obvious that $1,200 was insufficient for a two story building and another $1,000 had to be raised "for the purpose of adding and erecting a second story to the school house building already in process of erection." The new building had eight rooms with similar configurations on both floors, with a central stairway and coatrooms on either side of the center hall. Elementary students attended classes on the first floor and high school students on the second.

East Church Street School

District School #9 served village students until 1870 when the need for a more expanded high school curriculum led to the construction of a new building on West Church Street. Henry DeLand purchased the schoolhouse in 1873 and his sister Eliza Marring ran a boarding house there for teachers for ten years before it became a private residence. The Rightmire family purchased the house in 1905 and lived there for nearly fifty years. In 1951 the structure became the Fairport Gospel Center under the leadership of the Rev. Albert D'Annunzio. The remodeled building served as both church and residence for the D'Annunzio family. In 1970, a disastrous fire seriously damaged the building and it was razed later that year. The new building on the site is home to the Fairport Evangelical Church.

District School #10 - Turk Hill Road

The first District #10 School was in a log cabin that no longer exists on a road that also no longer exists. The road was Foley Road, which ran between Turk Hill and Moseley Roads in the vicinity of Casa Larga Vineyards. The log cabin schoolhouse was located down Foley Road to the west "in the hollow beyond the woods." In the early 1850's, when a new school house was built on Turk Hill Road at the corner of Foley Road on land donated by Anson Howard, the old building was moved to a nearby farm and used for storage.

School #10 first appears in the record in 1814 when the district was partly in Victor and partly in Perinton. By 1831 District #10 was wholly within the town limits, having been created from parts of Districts #3 and #1. Throughout those years, the school served a student population of between forty and fifty students and was apportioned public money in amounts ranging from $32.16 to $68.98. The school library, with an annual budget of between $2 and $8, and used by both the students and their families, was quite extensive for the times, including such titles as *The History of Greece, Plutarch's Lives, The Elephant as He Exists in the Wild State,* and *The Pursuit of Knowledge.*

During the last decades of the nineteenth century and into the early decades of the twentieth, the school usually served a population of about twenty-five students, ranging in age from six to fourteen in grades 1 through 8. Courses included the obligatory reading, writing, and arithmetic, as well as English, spelling, physiology, geography, drawing, nature study, and agriculture. Instruction was often geared to individual students, many of whom missed significant time due to family and farm needs. In 1920, for example, of thirty-one school-aged residents, twenty-three were registered, with an average attendance of only fourteen days. In the small one-room schoolhouse, however, they were able to make up lost work and progress at their own speed.

Certain family names occur frequently on the old rosters. Among them are Thayer, Bumpus, Copeland, Wood, Moseley, Baker, and Bulman. Edward Copeland, a Civil War veteran, whose sons Henry and Carl attended the school, taught there in 1877.

The School Commissioner's Reports of 1905 and 1906 show a school in generally good condition and in compliance with the standards and the statutes. Teachers Clara Gardner and Laura Carney were well-rated and paid $36.00 per month. The library contained 125 and 138 volumes respectively. In 1906, the only criticism was the need for a globe, a new dictionary, and a state map. A letter to the Commissioner was written requesting that the school be allowed to wait until the following year to comply since there was no money to purchase the items without levying a new tax. Unfortunately, there is no information on the outcome.

The school population steadily dwindled over the next several decades. In addition to fewer students overall, some chose to attend the larger village schools. In 1942-43 teacher Virginia Jordan had eight students, five boys and three girls aged 5 to 14, all from the Rodas, Bulman, and Smith families. At the end of that school year, the decision was made to close the school.

After centralization, #10 School was sold to Mr. and Mrs. Sidney Villere, who converted the school into a private residence, making a dining room from the woodshed, a kitchen from the coal bin, and a porch from the teacher's garage. Their daughter, Annabelle, continued the school connection as librarian at her alma mater, Fairport High School, for a number of years. The old schoolhouse remains a private residence today.

District School #11 - Whitebrook Academy, Wilkinson Road

"White Brook Academy" was formed in 1831 to serve children from the towns of Perinton, Macedon, Victor, and Farmington. It was located in the southeastern part of Perinton on the south side of Wilkinson Road near the South Perinton United Methodist Church. The one-room 25'x40' frame building had double doors which opened into the classroom, a belfry from which the bell called the children to class, and a woodshed on the east side. It was heated in the winter by a pot-bellied stove and cooled in the summer by breezes that came through the large double-hung windows. The two outhouses or "closets" were behind the building. Since there was no well, the students had to haul water in a bucket from the nearby Wilkinson farm.

White Brook served as a center for community activities. School events and other gatherings provided an opportunity for the Wilkinson, Pound, Northrup, Crosby, Bosworth, Cline, Nicholson, Ryan and Woolsey families to socialize. In addition, the Methodist Church congregation met in the school while awaiting the completion of their building, also on Wilkinson Road.

District #11 served a school population that grew from an average of forty to forty-two students to an average of sixty-two students and then back to about forty-five students by the 1860's. The library list from 1844 mentioned sixty-nine volumes, including *A Life of George Washington, Life of Black Hawk, History of Texas, Goldsmith's View of the World, Ship Wrecks and Disasters,* and *Sowing and Reaping.*

The 1850 report of the School District trustees has a wealth of information. That year the school was open for ten months and was allocated $38.64 from public funds, and an additional $6.75 for the library to purchase "a globe and books for the district library," which had 198 volumes. Of $40.62 raised in local tax money that year, $12.50 was used for fuel and $1.45 was used for repairs. $101.35 was also raised for wages. Eighty-two children were taught in the district that year, although many did not attend full time. The record shows that forty children attended between eight and twelve months, thirty-four for between two and eight months, and eight for less than two months. Two children were exempted from payment of teacher's wages "on account of indigence...." There were no "colored children."

Whitebrook school class

In 1906 the commissioner's report noted that the building was generally in good shape and was "well shaded." Agnes Dwyer taught the thirty-four enrolled students and earned $32.00 per month. She was well-rated, having the "confidence of pupils." Bessie Dryer, age eighteen, a graduate of Fairport High School and its teacher training class, taught at #11 school in 1909. Each day she took the

Rochester, Syracuse, and Eastern trolley to Egypt and then walked the two miles to the school. Her twenty-six students, in grades 1 through 8, were taught, mostly by the drill method, from basic texts that had been passed down from year to year. She remembered her students as well-behaved and interested. In addition to her teaching duties, Bessie served as janitor and was responsible for making out the district's tax lists.

The 1927 White Brook Academy reunion was attended by about 250, of which nine were former teachers: Bessie Dryer, Dora Bluhm, Celia Thayer, Mildred Hunt, Nellie Ryan, Charles Butler, Ella Blazey, William Harris, and Gertrude Ryan.

In 1951 when Fairport schools centralized, White Brook Academy was closed. Its contents were sold at auction, with the bell going to the Perinton Historical Society. In 1966 the structure was destroyed by fire.

The East Avenue or Northside School

Creating "Americans" out of a diverse and varied population has always been an important contribution of the public school. At the East Avenue School Fairport's immigrant children learned the language and customs of their new land that they then took home to their parents.

With the construction of the canal in 1825, many immigrants, mostly from Ireland, came to western New York. More Irish settlers arrived in the late 1850's and 60's to work as laborers on the New York Central Railroad. Those early arrivals lived in rooming houses and tenements built near the canal and the railroad on the north side of Fairport village. In the decades surrounding the turn of the twentieth century, many Italian and Greek families also settled in the village north of the canal where they had plentiful job opportunities with the railroad, the DeLand Chemical Company, and the Sanitary Can Company, among others.

1909 Northside school, 6th grade

Despite the growing population, up until the mid 1880's the only school in the village of Fairport was located on East Church Street. North side children attended that school and the #8 school on the corner of Turk Hill and Whitney Roads, while others attended classes in a former drying shed off East Avenue.

In October, 1883 $8,000 was appropriated for the building of a "handsome structure on East Avenue" on land purchased from C. G. DeWitt. The two story building, opened in 1886, was a "commodious brick structure of four rooms, admirably lighted and heated." The original building was later doubled in size.

The 1906-07 Fairport Public Schools directory lists four teachers and 133 students in grades one through six at the school. Stephanie Orford taught grades 7 and 8; Madge Vickery grades 5 and 6;

Minerva Devereaux grades 3 and 4; and Mary Jerrells grades 1 and 2. First grade students studied reading from *Ward's Primer and First Reader* and writing from *Natural Slant, Book 1.* Second grade saw the addition of the *American Word Book* for spelling. By the fourth grade, the curriculum also included language, arithmetic, geography, physiology, music, and drawing.

In 1921, Superintendent H. Claude Hardy concluded that they [the teachers] were a "fine lot…very much interested in their work and, on the whole, maintain high standards." Although the attendance record for the East Avenue school surpassed that of the other schools, the students there scored relatively poorly on standardized tests which he claimed was "accounted for in the fact that one third of the children tested were Italians, many of whom have not yet a sufficient knowledge of English to do themselves justice in a test of this sort." When schools were centralized in 1951, most of the small district schools were closed, but the Midvale and East Avenue schools remained open, providing extra classroom space during the transition.

After purchasing the school building for $5,000 in 1960, the Crosman Arms Company donated $10,000 and the old school building to the village of Fairport to be used as a recreational facility, because, in company president Philip Hahn's words, "We are indebted to the Fairport community for generating a good climate for doing business here. We want to show our appreciation for their kindness by guaranteeing good recreational facilities for youngsters and oldsters alike."

In 1962 a refurbished Crosman Community Center opened to the public. The center provided areas for elementary, junior and senior high school young people as well as a room for senior citizens. Activity rooms, a library, and an all-purpose room were located in the basement. The building served as a community recreational facility until the opening of the Turk Hill Road complex in 1997.

Between 1997 and 2002, the building's future was in question. In that year the Baldwin Real Estate Corporation under the leadership of Fairport resident Bill Durdel purchased the structure, planning to turn it into a senior housing complex, and saving it from demolition. An addition was constructed and "The Crosman's" 21 apartments were ready for occupancy in late 2002. An integral part of Fairport's north side history had been saved.

Fairport Union Free School

By 1870, as the student population increased, the need for a graded high school with more opportunities for advanced students became obvious. On February 26, 1870, the Fairport Union Free School District #9 was formed, land was subsequently purchased on West Church Street, and a building was erected at a cost of $20,000. Opened in 1872, it was a "fine, commodious structure, built of brick" with six classrooms, a nurse's office and the principal's office on the first floor, and three rooms in the cellar. Four more rooms were added in 1888.

The new school, accredited as a high school and chartered by the Board of Regents in 1874, provided preparatory and academic departments serving grades one through twelve and afforded "superior facilities to pupils of all grades of advancement." The academic department offered courses of study in English, the classics, and science, which prepared students for college. The three-year course of study was extended to four years in 1895 to conform to the requirements for a Regents diploma. In 1897 a Training Class was added for the preparation of teachers.

Nearly all of the teachers at the Union School had trained at state normal schools or were college graduates. Arthur C. Nute, high school principal in 1904, was a graduate of the University of Rochester, and Minerva DeLand, preceptress and classics teacher, was a graduate of Vassar College and Albany Normal School. Serving as role models for their students, teachers were to be in their classrooms fifteen to twenty minutes before the beginning of class and "were expected to be watchful for the interests of the children under all conditions." In turn, scholars were expected to "comply with all requirements made by their Teachers for the good of the school." They had to be "diligent in study, prompt in obedience, and *will avoid all social intercourse whatever during study hours."*

Fairport High School class of 1916

The first class was graduated from the Union School in 1876 and had four members: Mollie Hill, Ella Lewis, Charles Watson, and Charles Waldron. Faculty and class size increased steadily, rising to graduating classes of between twenty and thirty, with seventeen faculty members by the first decade of the twentieth century. The course of study included, at the minimum, English, mathematics, science, foreign languages, and history. In addition to a valedictorian and a salutatorian, by 1916 the Old English "F" was awarded to those who met the following requirements: 1. No illegal absence or tardiness. 2. A helpful effort and good conduct. 3. Good scholarship. 4. Representing the school in any interscholastic, debating or speaking contest. The best all around member of the class, as judged by the faculty, was to be awarded the Class Trophy Cup.

Despite the rules and academic requirements, there were diversions. In 1917 the senior class presented a play and a Shakespeare pageant. A glee club was established. The Sigma Alpha society for young men encouraged "debates, impromptus, and parliamentary practice." Alpha Gamma Sigma for young women was designed to make their "attainments broader" and required successful completion of at least one year of high school for admission. By the early twentieth century, the Athletic Association and the Gymnasium Association were managing a "vigorous foot ball team" and a baseball team. Team sports were considered important not only for the activity, but also for their "moral uplift." In order to play, a student had to maintain grade level work and pay a fee of fifty cents.

Between 1914 and 1923 the school district doubled in size, reflecting the ballooning growth of the community. The overcrowded school had to send some elementary students to the Northside School and hold half days sessions for others. The school trustees also had to purchase a house on West Avenue for additional classrooms.

Fairport High School building, Church St.

When a new high school on West Avenue was opened in 1924, the West Church Street School was remodeled and used as a grade school. It served elementary students for thirty-one years until the opening of Johanna Perrin School in 1955. Unfortunately, the building itself had been allowed to deteriorate. Having lost its cupola in 1939 due to ice and rain damage, the rest of the building was razed in 1955. The school district's central offices now occupy the site.

Fairport High School on West Avenue

"One of the finest high school buildings to be found in any town in the state" opened to Fairport students in September 1924. The state-of-the-art structure, designed by O.W. Harwood and B. Dryer, and located on West Avenue, had two stories and was built at a cost of less than $300,000. The Fairport School District had been growing rapidly, expanding from a total student population of 500 in 1914 to over 1,000 just ten years later, so the new school meant that for the first time in several years, all students could attend full time.

West Avenue school

The new Fairport High School had specific sites for its various courses of study. The basement provided six rooms for commercial courses such as typing, shop, mechanical drawing, and homemaking. The lunchroom was located there, as was the gym, which could accommodate about 600 for games and was also used for dances. Dressing rooms, showers, and lockers for both boys and girls were part of the gym complex as well. The furnace room, coal bins, janitor's office, and other storage rooms filled the remainder of the basement. The first floor housed the Superintendent's office, the Board of Education room, the principal's office, eight rooms for grades 7 and 8, the library, toilets, and an auditorium that could seat 725. The second floor accommodated the high school students. It had two study rooms and ten regular classrooms, including a biology lab and a chemistry/physics lab. The building was generally fireproof with reinforced concrete floors covered with maple. There was a master clock and bell system and, of course, each classroom had blackboards and bulletin boards. The two entrances (apparently the East for boys and the West for girls) led down to the gym and locker rooms, and up to the first floor library and junior high rooms. An east-west corridor connected the two sides and another staircase went from the basement to the second (senior high) floor.

Fairport High School faculty, 1929

Among those on the dais at the dedication of the building in December 1924, were Superintendent H. Claude Hardy, featured speaker Herbert Weet, Superintendent of the Rochester City School District, Principal Minerva DeLand, librarian Helen DeLand, and Board of Education president Yale Parce who "pledge[d] to every boy and girl in this community that we believe in them and are willing to pay the price to help them become good citizens by being better prepared to meet the problems of life when they leave school." The overflow crowd was entertained by "delightful music rendered by the excellent East High School Orchestra of Rochester…" Gifts from community groups and classes were presented, which included, among other things, bookcases, ten flags, sets of books, ferns for each classroom, and a statue of the Winged Victory. Over 1500 people participated in the ensuing open house, reception, and dance.

A 1927 newspaper article pointed out, "Ever since the opening of the new school, a splendid gift of the people of Fairport to their children and youth, there has been a deep interest shown in all the affairs of the school. This interest has so affected the efforts of the pupils as to bring out the best that they have." The best that year included three state scholarships, first prize at the Brockport Fair and the Rochester Exposition for the school exhibit, a basketball team that ranked among the best in the state, a football team that kept all opponents scoreless, and a "remarkable production of a modern American play."

As a 1927 *Fairport Herald-Mail* article noted, the interest of the community in its high school has helped students to achieve their best over the years. This interest manifested itself in support for sports teams and encouragement to excel academically.

The state basketball tournament of 1927 dominated the attention of many in Fairport. Over 400 fans were taken by a special train to Buffalo for that tournament. In the quarterfinal game against Oswego the lead changed a number of times, but Fairport came away with the win. Fans welcomed the team back to town at 3 a.m. with a blast on the fire whistle and a parade of cars around the village. The next day the team faced Yonkers in the semifinal. While the score was tied several times, Fairport came up short and lost 25 to 22. Nevertheless, the team was welcomed home by an impromptu parade of over 200 automobiles, hundreds of fans, and a band which accompanied the team from the Fullamtown bridge along West

Fairport High School baseball team, 1907

Church Street, to Main Street to West Avenue and up to the doors of the school. A footnote to the championship games was the participation of a female cheerleader for Fairport. The paper notes that "every eye was focused on [Helen Hart]." The record shows a continuing line of championship teams, particularly football, throughout the 1930's and 40's. The 1939 undefeated team had most of its starting lineup chosen for either the *Democrat & Chronicle* or the *Times-Union* all-county teams. Congressman Joseph J. O'Brien presented all the members of the team with gold plated footballs at the end of the season.

Academically, Fairport students were outstanding in science, winning top prizes at the New York State Science Congress over a number of years. Students also won awards at the Scholastic Art Competition. Many were awarded scholarships at local colleges including the University of Rochester and Nazareth College.

It is not difficult to conclude, from the photos and articles about Fairport graduates, how many of them have stayed in their hometown to raise their own families. For example, the class of 1931 included mayor and businessman Albert Knapp and Fairport teacher Florence Stolt. As of their 50th reunion, the majority of the class of 1934 lived in Fairport. Those members included Ken Dennis, Robert Dudley, Gordon and Louise Seaman, as well as many others. A reunion photo of the classes of 1935 and 1936 showed Fairport residents Bob and Meriel Bach, Bob and Natalie Mabry, Dorothy Tracy, Milt McMahon, Dick and Peg Ryon, Ed and Eunice Skeates, Perry Stolt, and "Hawk" and Charlie DiRisio. In addition, the first principal of the West Avenue School was Minerva DeLand, also a Fairport graduate.

By the late 1950's the Fairport School District was yet again in need of more space. In 1955 there were 600 students, grades 7-12, at West Avenue School, with a graduating class of 65. By 1959, there were 500 students in grades 9-12 with a graduating class of seventy-four students. The Class of 1960 would see the number of graduating seniors top 100. Consequently, in 1959, the new Minerva DeLand High School, named after the retiring principal of the West Avenue School, was opened. West Avenue's Fairport High School was renamed Martha Brown Junior High School, after another long-time teacher, and housed grades 6-8. In 1965, when the new Martha Brown Junior High School opened on Ayrault Road, the old building was renamed the West Avenue School. The structure was sold in 1983 and developed as condominiums. The still-elegant building is now known as "Packett's Glen."

The Fairport Central School District

The first central school law was passed in New York State in 1914, and the first central school district formed in 1925. Centralization would make the more modern educational facilities and programs already enjoyed by children in more densely settled areas available to rural children, and engender more uniformity in the subjects taught. By the late 1940's most of the school districts in New York State had been centralized and it was becoming increasingly obvious that Fairport needed to join them. Area population had been steadily increasing, existing school buildings were inadequate and overcrowded, and funding was becoming a problem. Many rural students finished their local school program and went on to attend the junior and senior high schools in Fairport for which they paid no fees. In addition, there was no uniformity of instruction among the small, independent local schools that were also responsible for maintaining their facilities and hiring their teachers.

In November of 1949 representatives of nine of Perinton's eleven area schools agreed "to consider making a survey on centralization in the Fairport Area." (District #1 had joined with Pittsford and District #11 had affiliated with Victor and Macedon.) In May 1950 the Fairport Centralization Committee, with William Vick as chairman and Helen Martin as secretary, agreed to send representatives to Albany to meet with representatives from the State Department of Education about the feasibility of centralization. Before the end of that year the decision was made to "approve the survey from the State Education Department as presented and . . . go on record as favoring a petition for centralization, and ... we recommend the dissemination of information on this subject." Franklyn

Hutchings, Lynn Holmes, Duane Hull, and Mrs. Parce Hannan were charged with the job of creating and distributing an informational booklet to the community.

The booklet described the process of centralization, beginning with the requirement that sixty percent of the voters in the outlying areas sign petitions requesting that the Commissioner of Education lay out a district for centralization. Only then would the process go forward and ultimately be presented to the voters for approval. The booklet also described the conditions in the Perinton-Fairport schools. The West Avenue School was overcrowded with students from outlying areas whose schools had closed. In some cases there were forty students in a class. At Midvale school most teachers taught two grades together, and there were schools where a single teacher handled six or seven grades. Centralization promised smaller class sizes, full-time physical education, remedial reading, art, and music teachers, as well as one teacher per grade level at the elementary level. At the secondary level there would be a wider choice of courses in the academic, commercial, and college entrance fields. More specialized training in homemaking and industrial arts would be available. The booklet also addressed issues of funding, state aid, building programs, and transportation.

1951 School Board

The information was mailed in January of 1951 and petitions were circulated to an estimated 1,274 voters, of which 825 or sixty-five percent expressed their approval to proceed with a plan for centralization. The Committee decided to approach local organizations like the PTA, Rotary, Lions, and the Grange, asking them to include speakers on centralization in their programs. The committee also agreed to run a series of question/answer columns in the Fairport *Herald-Mail.* Although many residents had fears about the new system, centralization passed on April 30, 1951, by a vote of 653 to 450 out of 3,600 eligible voters. Robert Dudley, Donald White, J. Gordon Ross, E. Duane Hull, Anne Hartigan, Lynn Holmes, and William Vick were elected to the school board. Frank A. Brokaw, who had been hired in February to replace the retiring Thomas Coffee, served as superintendent of the new Fairport Central School District.

Minerva DeLand and Robert Dudley

The newly consolidated Fairport Central School District opened in September 1951. Kindergarten classes were held at the East Avenue, West Church Street, and Midvale schools. Due to overcrowding, some of the first graders were moved from the West Church Street to the West Avenue school. The sixth grade rooms at West Avenue were needed for the junior high students, so the sixth graders were bused to Midvale School and District #3 on Turk Hill Road.

The problem of space did not improve. By 1952 the district was using seven school buildings, two churches, and the library basement to house its pupils. Some classrooms were partitioned to accommodate two classes; other classes were held in basements. At several of the small district schools, there was no hot water, and bricks were falling from the West Church Street school façade. Despite the poor conditions, the vote to build a new school on already-purchased land on Potter Place failed twice, with opponents citing high taxes and increased traffic as problems. The voters finally passed a third pared-down proposal in November 1953. The new school, named Johanna Perrin School after the first white woman to settle in Perinton, had forty-two rooms and housed all kindergarten through sixth grade students in the district. Grades seven through twelve attended the West Avenue School, and East Avenue and Midvale Schools were kept in reserve. The West Church School, which had been deteriorating, was razed in 1955.

By the mid 1950's the West Avenue School was severely overcrowded. In 1956, 140 students had to be sent to the East Avenue School due to the lack of space. Although the West Avenue School was built to accommodate only 500 students, projections estimated that by 1961 there would be 1,000 students in grades 7 –12. Since expansion was impossible at that facility, a proposal was made in 1955 to build a new $2.1 million structure on the former Filkins property south of Hulburt Road. Despite the significant increase in taxes of approximately $10 per thousand assessed valuation, the proposal was voted on and passed in June of 1956. As previously mentions, the new Minerva DeLand High School was opened in 1959. Miss DeLand was present at both the dedication and the first commencement exercises of the new high school.

Growth in the Fairport-Perinton community continued unabated during the 1960's and the early 1970's. Between 1961 and 1967 the school population doubled, and three more schools were built. Brooks Hill Primary School opened in 1962, the new Martha Brown Junior High School on Ayrault Road opened in 1965, and Jefferson Avenue Primary School opened in 1966. Building continued into the early 1970's, paralleling a constant increase in student population. In 1970 the district built a new high school on Ayrault Road on the site of the old Ayrault farm, and Minerva DeLand became a junior high school. The same year saw the opening of the Dudley-Northside complex with Dudley School housing grades 1-3 and Northside housing grades 4 – 6. At that point the district was running nine schools.

During the subsequent decade there was a small decline in the student population, leading to the closing and sale of the West Avenue School (and its conversion to condominiums). The 1990's brought a return to increasing enrollments, which was dealt with for several years by reconfiguring grade levels and constructing additions to the existing buildings.

In its third century, the Fairport district has continued to make additions and renovations to its current buildings and continues to work to meet the needs of the community and to provide students with a quality education appropriate for the new century.

The Little Brown Jug – A Football Tradition

While the Fairport school district sponsors many sports teams and has a long tradition in many of them, the "Little Brown Jug" football rivalry ranks among the most well-known and is therefore featured here.

Sometime early in the first decade of the twentieth century, Fairport fielded its first high school football team. A newspaper notation in the fall of 1903 noted that Ellis E. Lawton of Syracuse "has been engaged to coach the football team for a week, and they will be given their first real hard work." Norman Bedell (1904 graduate) was the captain of that team and the principal, A.C. Nute, was the manager.

In supporting an athletic program, Fairport was following the popular late nineteenth century trend that touted athletics as beneficial not only physically but also mentally and socially. Being on a team engendered discipline, order, obedience, and cooperation and mitigated against crime and delinquency. It also encouraged school loyalty and community involvement. Since those beginnings, Fairport's football program has enjoyed over 100 years of success and popularity. Perhaps one of the most lasting traditions over those years was the "Little Brown Jug" rivalry with East Rochester, which began with the 1939 game between the two teams.

1939 Fairport High School football team

The communities of Fairport and East Rochester are interconnected in a number of ways. The village of East Rochester was founded by Fairport native Walter Parce and before becoming an independent town/village was partly within the town of Perinton. Perinton and Fairport residents have worked in East Rochester and East Rochester residents have worked in Fairport. People in both communities have parents or relatives that live in the other town or village. Because the names of important football players became as well known to community members as they were to the student body and faculty, the football rivalry extended well beyond the schools and engulfed the two communities. When Don Santini returned to his alma mater as football coach in 1975, he notes that he was overwhelmed the week prior to the game with the hype, not only from community members but from the local press as well. This was a rivalry that was known not only in the area, but also throughout the state. Proof of the widespread popularity of the game was evident in the large number of community members and former players and their families that regularly attended the Big Game. For example in 1978 not only did 10,000 people attend the game, but many more followed the game on Channel 10 WHEC-TV.

The "Little Brown Jug" rivalry actually began in February of 1940, when the Perinton Republican Club sponsored a victory dance for Fairport and East Rochester athletic teams. Perinton supervisor Ken Courtney, recalling the rivalry between the University of Minnesota and the University of Wisconsin from his undergraduate days, purchased a jug for $.20, painted it with the letters ERS and FHS, and recorded the 1939 game score (Fairport 24, ER 0). Before the dancing began, Courtney and the principals of both schools, Thomas Coffee of Fairport and Willis Potter of East Rochester, welcomed the guests, which included students and other residents of both communities. The East Rochester band played, and Congressman Joseph O'Brien spoke on "Sportsmanship in the Game of Life" and presented each player with a gold football. Finally, Courtney presented the jug to Louis Masciangelo, President of the Fairport Student Association, expressing the hope that the game and the awarding of the jug would become tradition. Needless to say, for the next forty-nine years, the Fairport-East Rochester game was the game of the year.

For many of those forty-nine years, East Rochester and Fairport High Schools were approximately the same size and the "won" and "lost" columns were close. As Fairport grew in size and new schools were built, the game in Fairport was played at different fields, moving from the West Avenue High School field, to the Minerva DeLand High School field, to the Fairport High School field on Ayrault Road. When playing on the West Avenue field, long time coach Joe Cummings reported that "you always wanted to win the coin toss there so you could go downhill in the 4th quarter." The field differed in elevation from one end to the other by four feet. In East Rochester, games were first played in Eyer Park and then at the school's Fairport Road location.

Because the "Little Brown Jug" game was THE GAME for both students and townsfolk in both communities, a series of traditions developed. Since the game was always the last one of the season, enthusiasm had time to build. In the early days of the rivalry, the week's preparation culminated in the Friday pep rally and bonfire, which was attended by students, faculty, and townsfolk. The first bonfires were held on the West Avenue School field, later moving to the area behind the Village Hall and then eventually to Fairport High School on Ayrault Road. After the rally, which included an inspirational talk by the coach, fans would snake dance through the streets of the village, usually ending up at the coach's house where they were treated with yet another inspirational talk by either Coach Joe Cummings, Paul Lopez, Pete Logan, or Don Santini. By the late 1960's and developing and expanding during the subsequent two decades, the schools celebrated "Spirit Week" prior to the game. Each day was assigned a different costume, ending with red, blue, and white day on Friday in Fairport and brown in East Rochester. Signs were everywhere. In Fairport "BDR" (beat ER) was a very popular one. Former head coach and Fairport High graduate Don Santini remembers singing "We are from Fairport, the best are we; Piano Town, East Rochester, all off key." East Rochester had their song which went something like "Ricky coax, coax, coax, Give 'em the ax, the ax, the ax, Who can, we can, Tin Can Fairport." Of course, "piano town" and "tin can Fairport" referred to the major industries in each town: the East Rochester Piano Works and Fairport's American Can Company.

The teams created special plays and special effects just for the Big Game. Coach Santini recalled an "ER Special" and the "Hey, wait a minute" play among many others. Former head coach Joe Cummings noted that the players often became overzealous during practice and he had to call off contact drills or "the kids would have killed themselves from hitting each other so hard." Former Coach Paul Lopez noted that sometimes the ER teams knew just as much about the trick plays as Fairport did. In 1976 Coach Santini had his team march from Martha Brown School, through the Brambleridge East subdivision, and down the hill in a long line to the Minerva DeLand field. According to Santini, Fairport was ahead "on psyche" at halftime, but ended up losing the game. Coach Santini also remembers when he, as a player on Fairport's 1956 team, put a snap over the punter's head giving ER its only points in the 33-2 game of 1956.

Another well-known tradition was the wheelbarrow ride given by the loser to the winner. In the 1950 game, Fairport, under the leadership of Coach Joe Cummings, intercepted a pass in the end zone with eight seconds to go, holding on to win. Al "Hawk" DiRisio, President of the Lions Club, got a ride in a wheelbarrow from ER Lions Club President August Corea all around the field to West Church, to South Main, and back to West Avenue. The following year the tradition changed to involve the towns' mayors. Over the years the ride got shorter and shorter until it was just a ride across the field at halftime. This particular tradition eventually died out.

The presentation of the jug to the winning school at the end of each season was the defining event of the rivalry. The losing coach and team captains presented the jug to the student body at a following Monday morning assembly. Former Fairport Coach Joe Cummings remembered it as the hardest part of losing and former Coach Don Santini noted that it was an unforgettable event.

Growth and change would eventually doom the Brown Jug tradition. Between the 1960's and the 1980's the town of Perinton, which includes Fairport village, underwent tremendous growth, more than doubling its population. East Rochester, on the other hand, had limited potential for growth, maintaining a population of about 7,000. By 1987 the Fairport School District was one of the largest in the county and East Rochester was one of the smallest. For years ER had fielded a strong football team, despite its small size, but by the end of the 1980's the size discrepancy had become too great and the decision was made to end the Jug contest.

In 1988, after forty-nine years of Little Brown Jug rivalry and sixty years of interscholastic play, the contests came to an end. A duplicate of the jug was made so that each school could have one on display, showing twenty-six wins for East Rochester, twenty-two wins for Fairport, and one tie (0-0 in 1951). While fans understood the decision, there was widespread disappointment. Former Fairport Mayor Vincent Kennelley was quoted in a 1988 newspaper article noting that "This was the finest rivalry in the country…we looked forward to it all year. No one made plans for that Saturday." Former East Rochester Coach Don Quinn commented that "The townspeople – they've had more fun than anybody. The crowds were phenomenal. Many of these people will talk about these games for years to come." And they have.

Post Offices in Perinton and Fairport

It is hard to imagine waiting six to eight weeks for an answer to a letter, but in 1672 that is how long it took to get an answer back from a letter sent, for example, from Boston to New York. Mail was sent via Route 1, known as the Boston Post Road, and took three to four weeks each way. By the 1770's, Benjamin Franklin, who was serving as postmaster, had improved service to a three times per week delivery between New York and Philadelphia. Changes came swiftly in the nineteenth century. The first adhesive stamps were introduced in the 1840's, street letter boxes in the 1850's, and free mail delivery in forty-nine cities along with railway mail service by the 1860's. The twentieth century brought Parcel Post in 1913, airmail in 1918, and the ZIP code in 1963. The twenty-first century has also brought increasing amounts of junk mail and of course e-mail, Facebook, blogs, texting, and Twitter.

Originally, postage was paid on delivery, often resulting in unclaimed letters due to lack of cash. Delivery was more certain when the item was pre-paid. No envelopes were used; single sheets of paper were folded and sealed with sealing wax. In the early 1800's, the cost for mailing a single sheet went from $.08 for one sheet up to 40 miles to $.25 for over 500 miles.

In Western New York, by the end of the eighteenth century, there were only four post offices: in Canandaigua, Geneva, Bath, and Williamsburg, (a town that was located to the south on the Genesee River). By 1811 a post office had been established in Boyle (Pittsford) to serve what is now Monroe County, and the Postmaster General had authorized setting up additional post offices north of the Buffalo Road. In general, mail was delivered once a week until 1820.

On April 8, 1822 the Perinton Post Office was established. It was located at Fullam's Basin where the bridge crosses the canal (today's Perinton Park). John Hartwell was appointed as the first Perinton Postmaster, followed in the same year by Elisha Fullam. Egypt opened its own post office in 1826 and Bushnell's Basin followed suit in 1838. The village of Fairport continued to grow due to the Erie Canal and the post office moved into the village in 1829. It was common practice for the postmaster to house the post office either in his house or his place of business, so when Abishai Goodell became postmaster in 1829, he located the post office in his store, Aiken & Goodell's. Since there were nine postmasters between 1841 and 1897, it is possible that the post office had nine homes during that time. In 1853, when a Chemung County post office named Fairport closed, the merchants of the village of Fairport were successful in getting the local post office redesignated as the Fairport Post Office, noting that it would be better for business.

George Bown became postmaster in 1897 and moved the post office to his large building on South Main Street (current Village Landing location) where it remained until 1916.

In 1892 rural free delivery had been authorized by the Congress and funds were appropriated in 1896; however, by the turn of the century Perinton/Fairport had yet to establish a rural service. A Danish immigrant farmer named Hans Hansen was about to change that. Rebuffed by the local postmaster, Hansen surveyed local farmers about possible service. Determining their interest, he drew up a proposed route and submitted the survey results and his plan to the postal inspector. Upon acceptance of his plan, Hanson began to prepare for the civil service exam. After passing the exam (placing third on the list), he was named the first rural route carrier in Perinton. He began his route in 1902 and continued to deliver in his two-wheel horse-drawn gig until 1918 when the high cost of a

Bown Block Post Office

delivery automobile led to his retirement. A second rural route was quickly established, and partly due to the new rural routes, both the Egypt and the Bushnell's Basin post offices were closed by 1902. Rural mail carriers performed many functions in addition to delivering the mail. They applied first aid when needed, notified patrons when their cows were out, delivered doctors to outlying areas, carried surplus milk to the needy, did minor chores when asked, and, of course, conveyed any local news or gossip. 1913 saw the institution of the first home delivery of mail in the village of Fairport. Three routes were established and the first carriers included Loren and Gerald Filkins, Alvin Kinsella, and George Emerich. In 1916 the post office was moved from the Bown Block to a building on the other side of the street just north of the Municipal Building.

Growth of the town and village by the 1930's necessitated larger quarters and in 1936, the U.S. government selected a site on South Main Street for a new Fairport Post Office. The Treasury Department purchased land from Eugene T. Peacock and the County of Monroe in 1937 for around $8,000. The new brick $60,000 post office building at 121 South Main Street was opened and dedicated in July, 1938. Mayor Irving Neiss presided at the dedication where Congressman George B. Kelly presented the keys to Postmaster John J. Finnegan. Music was provided by the WPA Band from Rochester. The building was then opened to the public for inspection. Later that day, a dinner was held at the Green Lantern Inn, attended by over one hundred invitees. It was indeed a festive occasion.

Postal workers

A year later the US government presented the Fairport Post Office with a hammered bronze relief entitled "Harvest" to hang in the lobby over the postmaster's office door. The art deco style sculpture of hammered eighteen gauge bronze is approximately six feet by five feet. Sculptor Henry Van Wolf of Brooklyn, who was chosen to do the work after entering a competition, was paid $700 and worked under the auspices of the Treasury Department's Section of Fine Arts. According to a 1939 news article, the bronze is "intended to express the joy and happiness of the American farmer and his family, bringing in the fruits of the fields and celebrating the harvest festival, the life of the farmer, his devotion to his family and his love toward animals." Before it arrived in Fairport the sculpture was on exhibit at the American Salon, 110 East 59th Street, New York.

The 1938 facility was used by the post office until 1976 when the move was made to a new and larger location on the corner of Ayrault and Moseley Roads. In 2001, the Fairport Post Office opened a new office in Perinton Square (in a building formerly occupied by "Perkins") for all transactions and business except mail sorting, processing, and pickup, which continue to be done at the Ayrault Road facility. The 1938 bronze sculpture was eventually moved to the current facility where is hangs behind the customer desk.

Fairport's Newspapers

Stating in his opening editorial words to the effect that "It isn't much of a town that can't support its own newspaper and that only with a local newspaper can one be guarded from the misbehavior of the elected, and only with their own newspaper can the chaff of rumor be flailed into fact," George C. Taylor published the premier issue of Fairport's first paper, the *Fairport Herald*, on February 15, 1873. Taylor had moved to Fairport in 1866 and was the manufacturer of a popular patent medicine, *Taylor's Oil of Life*. He believed that a local paper would stimulate interest in local affairs and industry.

The paper was to be published every Friday at a yearly subscription rate of $1.25. The first issue was a double sheet of four unnumbered pages with five columns of small print containing numerous advertisements. Taylor himself advertised his *Oil of Life,* "good for man or beast," Howe & McFarland and C.J. DeLand advertised groceries, Mrs. William Bly and Mrs. L.M. Shaw advertised themselves as "fashionable milliners," and W.H. Vance advertised "monumental marble work." Local events that made that first issue included a report on a group of "much to be admired" young men bent on forming a chapter of the Sons of Temperance, the fact that the canning company was about to begin construction, and an announcement that Fairport Nurseries (Parce and Solly) had added ornamental shrubs to their line. The "Home Matters" column included plugs for various businesses: J.& P. Cronin were "good paper hangers," William Todd promised to "clothe you cheaply – call and be convinced," Green & McAuliffe sold "first class lumber," and W.A. Trescott was "an artist – he draws teeth, - if you want a good set of false teeth, or any filling, call him."

There were a number of changes in the paper during its first few years of existence. In April of 1873 the paper made the following announcement: "Owing to the time occupied in moving our office we are late in issuing this week's paper. Our patrons must bear patiently with us for a few weeks until we get settled in our new quarters, when we shall endeavor to be prompt on publication day." The new quarters were probably in the DeLand building just north of the canal on Main Street. In February of 1874, Mr. Taylor wrote, "Some two weeks since, the *Herald* office passed out of our hands, having sold the establishment to George T. Frost of Rochester and Jared Newman of this village. Mr. Frost has 35 years experience as a practical printer." The price of the paper was raised to $1.50 per year and the pages were two inches longer and wider. New equipment included a steam engine, a cylinder press, a paper cutter and type, totaling an outlay of about $3,000. In September of 1874, Mr. Frost bought out Mr. Newman and increased the paper from five to six columns.

Andrew Deal, with prior experience in publishing at the *Lima Recorder*, the *Canandaigua Times*, and the *Mt. Morris Enterprise*, purchased the *Fairport Herald* in 1876 and would guide the paper for the next thirty years. His goals were to "furnish a paper which shall encourage the business interests of Fairport [and] supply the citizens of Fairport, the villages and surrounding country with the local news

Andrew Deal

Will O. Greene

Floyd Miner

and 'seem like a letter from home' to those who formerly resided in this vicinity." In addition he hoped to "get an honest living." While the paper "would be Republican," Deal promised that local news would be the "leading feature." Over the next several years, Deal moved operations twice, first to the second floor of the Chadwick block on the corner of Main Street and West Avenue and then to a new building at 32 North Main Street, the Deal block. The facility was large enough to house the paper and its offices, as well as rental space. In addition the paper's page size increased, although the number of pages remained at four.

By 1881 the *Fairport Herald* was strongly ensconced as Fairport's local paper, but that year a second newspaper, the *Monroe County Mail*, started publication. The *Mail*, under the direction of S.D. Palmer and headquartered on West Avenue in the Butler block, was a "radical prohibition" paper. It was apparently quite successful, as steam power and a new large Campbell press were quickly added. The cost of a weekly subscription was $1.

Will O. Greene, who had moved to Fairport from Onondaga, New York, purchased the *Mail* in 1886 and made the following statement: "The policy of the paper will be entire independence on political and social questions. Though a believer in temperance, the field does not seem large enough to support a Prohibition paper. Much space will be given to local news." The paper appeared to thrive under Greene's leadership, moving several times to increasingly larger quarters. In 1890 the paper made a final move, this time to a building on West Avenue that had a "first class printing office." The lower floor was divided into an editorial, a composing, and a press room. The space had heat, electric lights, and telephone service. An 1898 *Business Directory* entry described it as being "equipped with modern and up-to-date printing material ...the power supplied by water." Greene himself not only published a popular paper, but also was known in the area as an expert printer.

Meanwhile, the *Fairport Herald* was purchased by Floyd Miner in 1906. Both papers continued to serve the citizens of Fairport and Perinton in a spirit of friendly rivalry until the 1920's when some significant changes were made. Will Greene sold the *Mail* to Edwin Hurd in 1921 and Floyd Miner sold the *Herald* to Fletcher Elliot in 1925. In the latter year a group of local businessmen with $25,000 to invest formed the Fairport Publishing Company and purchased both papers with the goal of consolidating and publishing one paper from the *Mail's* facility at 36 West Avenue. Floyd Miner was named President and Editor with Fletcher Elliot as the superintendent. The merger continued to

Monroe County Mail office

provide everyone with the news, and also had a lower cost for advertising. The last issue of the *Mail*, which had the largest circulation of any weekly publication in the county outside of Rochester, was printed on April 30, 1925. The first two issues of the combined papers, May 7 and 14, 1925, had both names on the masthead. After that date the paper was known as the *Fairport Herald-Mail*, cost subscribers $1.50 per year, and had a circulation of over 3,000.

1945 was an important year for the local newspaper. Curt Gerling, who was the President of the *Rochester Sun* Corporation, publishers of the *Rochester Sun,* purchased the *Fairport Herald-Mail.* He appointed Glenn Gazley as Publisher and Carrie Williams Buss as Editor. Glenn Gazley was a Fairport native who was active in local affairs and the proprietor of his own printing business. He had served as a reporter for the Rochester papers during the 1920's and had published a Fairport weekly magazine in 1941 and 1942. He not only published the paper, but he also composed and sold advertisements and continued to do reporting. Carrie Buss was, for thirty-five years, not only the *Herald-Mail*'s authority on the mechanics of publishing, spelling and grammar, but also on hundreds of Fairport families.

Gerling was interested in the business end of the newspaper. He increased its circulation and advertising base, and while he did write editorials and some articles on politics, he generally left the reporting to others. Eventually he owned nine suburban papers under the aegis of Empire State Weeklies. The *Fairport Herald-Mail* was published and printed in Fairport from the West Avenue office until 1957 when printing operations were moved to Webster. Although Gerling sold Empire State Weeklies in 1977, he remained with the paper as publisher and columnist until 1988.

The *Fairport Herald-Mail* continued to be published by Empire State Weeklies until 1992, when it was purchased by A&P Publications of Pittsford. Unfortunately, the company was unable to support the paper as its costs were rising and its readership declining. Consequently, what was probably the oldest continuously published newspaper in Monroe County printed its last issue on February 10, 1993.

Upon the demise of the *Fairport Herald-Mail,* the job of reporting local Fairport and Perinton news fell to Wolfe Publications' *Perinton-Fairport Post.* Wolfe Publications, owned by Andrew Wolfe, merged with Canandaigua Messenger Inc. in 1996. The organization publishes nine weekly papers, mostly in Monroe County, as well as the Daily/Sunday Messenger that serves Ontario County and parts of Yates and Wayne Counties.

Since 1993, the *Perinton-Fairport Post*, now the *Fairport-East Rochester Post* has been the "official" town and village paper and continues to build on a long heritage of local papers and local reporting.

The Telephone Comes to Fairport and Perinton

Answering machines, call waiting, caller ID, call forwarding, voice mail, cordless phones, cell phones, speed dialing. Telephone service has changed drastically since Alexander Graham Bell received his patent for the telephone in 1876 and Fairport's first phone was installed in Levi DeLand's home in 1877.

That first telephone line ran from the DeLand Chemical Works at the canal up to the DeLand home on the corner of Whitney and North Main Street, making it possible for Mr. DeLand to be on call 24 hours a day in case of any emergency. An article in the November 23, 1877, issue of the *Fairport Herald* noted that "Few people have heard the telephone but who has not heard of it? For some time the paragraphist has mentioned it, the interviewer has ferreted it out, the professor has discoursed about it and all have read, thought, and talked about it. The telephone in all its purity has reached Fairport, and is domiciled where its beauty will be appreciated and its utility thoroughly tested." The article concludes with an invitation from Mr. DeLand to "all of his friends who are interested in the wonder to call at his office at any time and he will take great pleasure in showing them how it works."

The first public phone appeared in Fairport village in the early 1880's and was located in Hodskin's & Peacock's Drug Store. It was the only available phone in town, and manager Charles Peacock, who lived over the store, was obliging and courteous enough to take messages and even have them delivered, often at night.

The popularity of the new invention was evident by 1896, as two telephone companies were in business and a switchboard had been installed in the village. The two companies were the Home Company, managed by Frederick Best, and the Bell Telephone Company, located over Bramer's Drug Store on the corner of West Avenue and South Main Street. While residential customers would have one line or the other, most businesses had lines from both companies and consequently had two numbers. Early advertisements might state "both phones" or in some cases give both numbers like "Bell Telephone 2232" and "Home Telephone 3A."

By the first decade of the twentieth century, telephone service had begun to expand beyond the village to the outlying farms. A party line on Watson Road at that time cost $12 per year, not including tolls. In most cases, rural subscribers were served by party lines, with a different ring for each subscriber. Nationwide, 1914 saw the first transcontinental phone hookup with a call from New York to San Francisco costing $20.70 for twenty-three minutes. The first dial phone came into service in 1919.

In Fairport, the original two telephone companies merged sometime between 1910 and 1920 and called themselves the New York Telephone Company. They, in turn, were bought out by Rochester Telephone Company in 1921. The company rented space for a magneto-operated switchboard which was run by a single operator. Customers made a call by cranking their phone to reach the operator and then giving her the number they wanted. In 1928, Mary Gimble of 69 East Church Street became the thousandth telephone subscriber in town.

In 1930 the telephone company built a new central exchange at 48 West Avenue, where the battery-powered switchboard had room for seven operators. Now customers could simply pick up the receiver and give the operator the number they wanted to call. Telephone numbers were usually three digits and a letter: 178R or 596W. It was a relatively efficient system, but had basically been the same for fifty years.

The late 1950's brought a number of significant changes to the telephone system. Rochester Telephone built a new facility on Fairport Road and began switching Fairport, Pittsford and East Rochester to dial systems. The last group of operators, Anne Kenney, Freda Schrader, Mildred Malone, Estelle McGuire, Dorothy King, Virginia Buck, Mary Dodson, Alice Hendricks, and Muriel Deleguardis, prepared to retire. On August 18, 1957, Pittsford, East Rochester, and Fairport began using their new dialing exchanges: LUdlow and FRontier, followed by five numbers. Pamphlets were available to explain such things as how a dial worked, what a dial tone sounded like, how to use a pay phone, and the proper etiquette on a party line.

Further changes took place in the 1960's. Fairport was included in the Rochester area toll-free zone, letter exchanges were replaced with straight number sequences, area codes were added and direct long-distance dialing and touch tone phones became available. Subsequently in the early 1970's, a new facility was planned for Pittsford-Palmyra Road as the number of customers continued to grow.

Developments and changes in communications continue to accelerate. Companies merge and change, and new services are added, giving the customer not only an incredible list of choices, but also the ability to be connected 24 hours a day, 7 days a week via a cell phone. Today it is not unusual to use that phone to take photos (and send them), to send messages, to surf the internet, and occasionally to actually make telephone calls.

The Library in Fairport

In 1839 the record for District School #9, which was located on East Church Street, showed a tax levy of $10 for "the purchase of a library." This was the first reported evidence of public funding for a library in the Fairport community. Records also show that maps and a globe were added in 1844 and that, by 1848, patrons were using the library on Saturday from 3 to 6 p.m. These events were common practice, as during most of the nineteenth century, libraries were located in the schools, but were open to both students and the public. Rental libraries did exist, however, and there were two of them in Fairport. One was run by John Hardick, proprietor of Hardick's Stationery and Book Store, and the other by the Dickinson sisters.

The Dickinson "subscription library," as it was known, lent books for about twenty years until it closed in 1894. It apparently was quite popular, outgrowing its first home in the upper hall of 10 East Church Street, and having to move around the corner to Thomas Dickinson's house (site of today's Shaheen Paints). Julia and Emma Dickinson and their friend Elizabeth Dowd ran the library at 10 East Church and Mrs. Buckland and Mr. and Mrs. Case were in charge after the move to South Main Street. Fees for borrowing books were $.50 for six months or $1.00 for one year. While there were no fines, the local paper listed missing books and requested that they be returned at once. New titles were also listed in the paper. Despite the move to larger quarters and the apparent popularity of the books, according to some sources there was a general indifference and even hostility toward the Dickinson library, leading to its abrupt closing in 1894. A small notice in the local paper read, "It having been decided to close the Public Library permanently, subscribers who have books will confer a favor by returning them promptly, and any amounts due on unexpired subscriptions will be refunded at the library on application."

Well before the closing of the Dickinson library there had been talk about establishing a public library that was "free, or nearly so." A *Fairport Herald* article dated July 21, 1876, published an appeal stating, "A public library for Fairport is really a thing to be desired and a thing very easily attainable too. It will not cost so very much but will prove of priceless value to our people who will start such a movement by a gift of money or books - good books ... that can come within reach of all." In an open letter published in the November 7, 1895 issue of the *Monroe County Mail*, attention was called to a new state law that permitted the transfer of school libraries to a public committee, thus making the books available to the general public. The letter ended with a plea to every family to donate books and contribute a "dollar or a dime" in order that a free library could be open to all in Fairport. The Board of Education subsequently named a library committee including Dr. E. D. Pratt, Charles D. Case, Arthur B. Newman, Mrs. Augusta Beardsley, and Mrs. L. M. Shaw, and a state charter was received soon thereafter on November 21, 1895. The committee purchased books costing about $200 and was hoping that some "public spirited citizen will eventually put up a library building and donate it to the village." Unfortunately, it would be some forty years before that would happen, and in the meantime the Fairport Public Library had a number of homes.

The first home of the Fairport Public Library was in the Hawkins Block on South Main Street in a second floor room overlooking the canal. Dr. Pratt lent the library a bookcase, two chairs, and a small table for the librarian. Books were donated by a number of people, including the school trustees, and Mabel Dobbin took on the job of classifying the approximately 1000 books and established a charging system. The library, under the direction of Mrs. Frank Howard, was open on Tuesdays and Thursdays from 3:30 to 4:30 p.m. and on Saturdays from 2:30 to 5:30 p.m. In 1901 the library moved across the street to somewhat larger quarters in the Bown Block. The move cost $10. Nettie Reynolds, librarian from 1901 to 1906, issued the first catalog in 1903, listing 1300 volumes, of which about 300 were for young people, but very few reference titles. After a 1906 move to larger rooms in the Bown Block, the reference section was expanded and a reading room was provided. In addition, the library charter was finally made permanent in that same year. By 1908, with a children's room added, the library grew in popularity and expanded its weekly hours from eight to thirty to accommodate the demand.

Space continued to be an issue for the Fairport Library during the second decade of the twentieth century. By 1912, the library had over 5,000 users and by 1914 the limitations of the Bown Block location were quite evident. The Rev. Charles Stetzle, who did a village survey in 1914, reported that "the entire space is overcrowded and books and pamphlets have to be stored outside[in the hall] for lack of shelf room," and there was "no auditorium nor adequate reading room … " The Chamber of Commerce responded by appointing a committee to study the possibilities for expansion. Discussion with the Carnegie Foundation resulted in the promise of an $11,000 grant, provided that $1100 in yearly maintenance funds and a site for the building were guaranteed by the community. The committee submitted a plan to the School Board recommending that the new building be constructed on a site owned by the Fairport School District at 18 Perrin Street. The School Board accepted the proposal and approved $1200 per year for maintenance. The package was presented to the voters in June of 1914 who rejected it. Subsequently, Ella Higbie offered a free site on the corner of North Main Street and East Avenue which was also turned down. A site at 40 South Main Street suffered the same fate. The squabbling resulted in the loss of the $11,000 Carnegie Grant and the library was still left with a space problem.

Finally in 1917, with an acute space problem, something had to be done. Reluctantly, the decision was made to move into the building at 18 Perrin Street that belonged to the school district. It was a small dwelling, with a low ceiling and small windows, but it did have a second story that could be used for storage purposes. In addition, the location was convenient for the high school whose pupils were entirely dependent on the public library for reference work. The librarian, Ida Cheesbrough, arranged the twenty-five or so bookcases, created a reference corner, added a large reading table with chairs and a children's section with a child-sized table and chairs, and placed her desk in the center with a typewriter and table by the window. It all appeared quite warm and inviting and would remain the library's home for the next fifteen to twenty years.

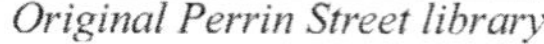

Original Perrin Street library

1938 Perrin Street library

During the administrations of Ida Cheesbrough (1906-1921) and Helen DeLand (1923-1933) the library became not only a reading room but also a social center. Boys' Story Night at the library led directly to the formation of troops of Boy Scouts. Fairport's Italian community made use of the library's Italian language collection as well as its children's story hour. The local papers gave generous space for library publicity and patrons made more and more use of the reference volumes. The collection was augmented during these years by gifts from the W.C.T.U., the Chautauqua Circle, the Red Men, and the Fairport Historical Club, among others. The Historical Club's contributions averaged over $100 per year for some twenty years.

As the new high school on West Avenue was being completed in 1924, it was decided to combine the public library and the high school library under single management. Since the librarian's salary would be shared by both, it could become a living wage. The two libraries coordinated book purchases and information on how to use either library. Helen DeLand held both positions until 1933, when she found it impossible to handle both libraries. She continued as high school librarian while Elma Gaffney took over as public librarian. A former library page remembered Ms. DeLand as being "quite deaf and rather shy," but also notes that she became a librarian largely due to Helen DeLand's influence.

The 1930's would be a significant decade for the library. The little building that had been housing the library since 1917, while remembered by some as a cozy place to tuck away in a corner of the stacks to read undisturbed, was growing steadily more decrepit. Mrs. Gaffney noted that "the little old building was bulging…mice were running around under the desk … walls were growing dingier … cracks in the floor were widening … the front steps tilted further southward … and bricks were dropping intermittently from the chimney." Clearly something had to be done. Over the years the library had received a number of gifts, the most generous of which was 500 shares of stock in the Douglas Packing Company given by Robert Douglas. This gift, along with one from the Perinton Patriotic League, made it possible to hire architect Henry Martin to design a new building. Construction, however, had to wait several years because the value of the stock had declined as a result of the Depression. Finally, in 1936, WPA labor and funding became available and the old building was razed and construction began on the new one. The library, meanwhile, had moved to an interim location on West Avenue. At long last the Fairport Library was to have its own home.

On Saturday March 5, 1938, Fairport's new library building at 18 Perrin Street formally opened. It had taken forty-three years from the granting of its original charter for Fairport's library to find a permanent home. The building, designed by the firm of Wiard & Martin, is in the Greek Revival style with a brick façade, a white-columned porch entrance flanked by large windows, and gutters that are hidden in the cornices.

Old library reading room

The interior was designed specifically for the needs of the library. The main floor accommodated the library proper, and included a children's area, a large central area for the librarian's desk, the card catalog and display cases, a spacious reading room, and a reference area. The basement area, in addition to the heating plant, included a large meeting room capable of seating about 100 people, a small kitchen, and an area devoted to the receiving, unpacking, and repairing of books. The second floor provided a place for smaller meetings and also storage areas. The foyer and a good part of the interior of the first floor were paneled and a large mural by local artist Carl Peters depicting the development of Fairport as a canal village, was painted on the 20 foot by 4 ½ foot wall above the librarian's desk.

The new library had space for more books and immediately the library organized a drive to raise $5,000 to purchase new books. According to newspaper accounts, many people participated by going door to door to solicit funds. The number of volumes in the library increased from 9,829 in 1938 to 10,243 in 1940 to 11,234 in 1942 and 12,048 by 1943. Apparently the book drive was successful. Library usage went from 21,000 in 1932 to 35,000 by 1939, and then declined somewhat during the war years.

The post World War II years brought significant changes to the local library. By 1946 the library was handling about 1,500 people per week and librarian Elma Gaffney knew most of their reading habits and guided their selections. For many, she embodied the spirit of the library. In 1951 she founded the Library Guild, which met once a month to help with filing, shelving and book repair. Also in the early 1950's she became involved with the formation of the Monroe County Library System. The system, while allowing each library to remain independent, would benefit members through mass purchasing, rotating collections, and inter-library loans. According to Harold Hacker, Director of the Monroe County Library System, Elma Gaffney was "part of the missionary team that spread the gospel of library systems throughout New York State, speaking to all interested groups and the New York Library Association about the benefits to be derived when a group of libraries banded together to share resources." Fairport joined the system in 1953.

The library grew along with the community during the 1950's and 1960's. The number of volumes increased to approximately 30,000 and the number of patrons increased along with the community's population. The children's room was moved downstairs to the former meeting room. And Elma Gaffney retired in 1969 after thirty-six years as librarian.

Changes were coming. The library was beginning to expand its concept of circulation, lending paintings, sculptures and audio tapes as well as books. The computer, which would revolutionize the availability of information, was on the horizon and space was again an issue.

Addressing that issue, in 1971 voters approved the purchase of property on East Church Street, then the site of the Perinton Community Church, for a new library. Plans were drawn up for a 20,600 square foot one-story building and a vote to pass a bond issue was presented to the voters. After two rejections by the voters, the library expansion was put on hold. Meanwhile, the proposed urban renewal project for the village of Fairport was underway and it appeared that an adequate space could be leased for the library in the new Village Landing. After a vigorous campaign by library trustees and the Friends of the Library Association, voters approved the leasing of space in the Village Landing in May of 1976.

Moving the library - 1975

In March of 1978 the new 18,000 square foot facility in Fairport's Village Landing was opened. On March 11, 1978 nearly 400 Perinton citizens moved all the books, periodicals, catalogs, and related materials to the new library. The line of volunteers snaked between 18 Perrin Street and the village landing, each one carrying a box, which was unloaded in its designated place. The new library opened to the public on March 20, 1978. The facility was one of the largest community libraries in the area and within months of the move its circulation nearly doubled. By 1982 Fairport was the busiest individual library in Monroe County.

The library has not restricted itself to lending books and periodicals and providing a place to do research. It offers programming for pre-schoolers, school aged children, the disabled, and the community in general. In cooperation with Perinton Recreation & Parks, the library sponsors a very popular summer music series in the gazebo by the canal. The Perinton Historian leads a series of history-based walking tours. Local artists and authors are recognized as well. Flanking the large window in the reading area are two paintings by Fairport artist Carl Peters, and outside near the gazebo, is a sculpture based on the children's book *Mousepaint,* by local author Ellen Stoll Walsh.

Because the Fairport Library is a school district library, the two entities work closely together to meet student needs. The community has given back as well, fielding a strong volunteer force that provides clerical help and coordinates such events as the annual used-book sale.

Over the last twenty years the library has changed considerably, as technology has revolutionized the way people access information. In the mid-1990's the traditional card catalog was replaced by CARL, an on-line catalog that links over 500 terminals in the county, allowing libraries to share information and patrons to find materials throughout the county. At the beginning, Fairport had seven computer terminals. It now has several dozen with a variety of purposes such as internet access, card catalog, and paid data bases, which have in many cases supplanted encyclopedias as resources for research.

As demand increased not only for books and research but also for video tapes, CDs, DVD's, and internet access, space again became a problem. As the library celebrated its 100th birthday in 1995, plans were underway to increase the library area by about 6700 square feet, a project that was completed in 1997. The new space made it possible for the library to enhance its computer retrieval systems, provide public internet access, increase its collection of books and audio-visual materials, and also provide more space for patrons. These changes occurred under the leadership of librarian Raymond Buchanan, who retired in 2000 after thirty-one years as director.

As the Fairport Library moves into its second century, under director Elizabeth Gilbert and her staff of fifty, it has evolved into a multimedia clearing house providing patrons the ability to access information on a world-wide scale. Not only have collections increased, but the number of programs, especially for children and young adults, has expanded. Reading and book groups for everyone from infants and their parents to junior high school students to adults are offered as are programs about wild animals and creating artistic t-shirts. Many participate in holiday sing-a-longs and Red Cross babysitting classes. The Fairport Library also provides a program (and a research area) for small business entrepreneurs and educates patrons in the use of new on-line resources.

For the library to continue to be a comfortable community place to be in the twenty-first century, it will have to increase its square footage. Meeting rooms are at a premium and there is little room to expand except at the expense of quiet reading or study areas. Librarian Elizabeth Gilbert would like to see a library that not only is able to expand its regular collections, but one that can also provide a variety of spaces for meetings, programs, education, local art displays, and just comfortable reading areas. She would like to see the library continue to be the welcoming, inviting place that it is, while maintaining its place as the library with the highest single-building circulation level in Monroe County.

- IX -
CHURCHES AND CEMETERIES

Among the earliest institutions that pioneers established were the church and a burial ground. Perinton's first burial ground was established in 1820, and its first congregation in 1824. Over the town's 200 year history, those institutions have continued to grow, evolve, and change.

First Congregational Church

In 1824 nine people met in the home of Jesse Perrin just south of the village of Fairport. This meeting was the genesis of today's Congregational Church on East Church Street in Fairport, the first church to be organized in Perinton. Huldah Wight, Lemuel Wight, Nancy Perrin Blackmon, Leah Packard, Lucy Eaton, Lettice Norton, Lucy Bristol, Captain Simeon Bristol, and William Stebbins met with the Rev. John Taylor of Penfield and the Rev. Asa Carpenter of Macedon on December 18, and the church was formally initiated with the signing of a Covenant and nine Articles of Faith. At the time, having no designated building, the group met in area homes and schools. Although the first pastor was a Mr. Morgan, records show that services were conducted by a variety of individuals. Little activity was recorded from 1824 to 1828, when there was some question as to whether the group would merge with Presbyterians from Bushnell's Basin. As envisaged by its New England Congregational ancestors, however, the group decided to remain independent.

The early years in Fairport showed only small growth and minimal activity, including occasional celebrations of the Lord's Supper. Ezra Whittlesey was selected as deacon. Two resolutions were passed stating that "female members of this church may, if they wish, have a vote in all matters that come before the church" and "every person uniting with this church shall be required to give their pledge to this church that they will abstain entirely from the use of ardent spirits except as medicine." The first baptism, that of George Bristol, took place in 1826. In the 1830's, under the leadership of the Rev. Mr. Brooks, and inspired by increased religious fervor as a result of the Second Great Awakening, the congregation was able to erect its first house of worship. Apparently the revival also inspired stricter discipline because, in 1835, Diantha Blackmon was excluded from the church fellowship for "Sabbath breaking" and a committee of two was created to remonstrate with Brother Daniel Willson for having worked his harvest the previous July on the Sabbath. He was the subject of special prayers for two weeks, but there was no subsequent record of whether or not either of these two mended their ways.

The first building on the present site was completed in 1833. The church continued to expand and in 1844 the first building was moved just west of the First Baptist Church and a new building was constructed on the site. As Fairport continued to thrive due to the railroad and the canal, so did the church. In 1868 the main portion of the present building was built by a Rochester firm at a cost of under $18,000 and the 1844 building was moved to West Avenue, where it was remodeled into Shaw's Hall. An early Sunday School building was moved to 9 Filkins Street in the early 1900's to make room for an addition. In 1922 a primary department was completed thanks to the generosity of Mr. and Mrs. Joseph Snow, Dr. and Mrs. Wesley Clapp, and others. Further additions followed to

house the expanding congregation and active Sunday School, the most recent one in 1971. More recently, the congregation restored and renovated both the interior and the exterior of the building and added a memorial garden.

The church has had many pastors, most of whom only served one or two years. The longest serving pastors include the Rev. Jeremiah Butler, the Rev. Lee Fletcher, and the Rev. James Doellefeld. They all served for more than ten years. The pastor as of 2010, the Rev. John Cedarleaf, has been in Fairport since 1984.

The First Congregational Church has been active in the community since its inception. The church has provided a number of opportunities for service and social activity as well as for spiritual renewal. As late as the 1920's, church was an all-day affair. Morning services would be held at 10:30 a.m., followed by Sunday school at noon and a second service and sometimes a second Sunday school following that. Many brought their dinners to eat between the services. They also may have brought fire pans or foot warmers in the colder weather. The first funeral (for Gilbert Benedict) was held in 1869, but the early practice of tolling the bell when a member died was soon discontinued to avoid disturbing the peaceful rest of neighbors.

Congregational Church Choir in 1924 with Mr. Brown

While a Sunday school had met as early as 1820 in local school houses, a regular church school was started in 1835. By the 1920's, there were nearly 300 names on the registry. One man recalls of his class that "we had the highest average collections nearly every Sunday for two years, and there were five pairs of brothers in the class." Sunday School, however, wasn't just for children. One hundred fifty men were part of a mid-nineteenth century Bible Class which studied the whole Bible verse by verse. There was also an elderly men's class referred to as "The Saints of Rest." In the 1880's a "Christian Endeavor Society" was formed to broaden the social and religious life of young people.

The very first church choir was started shortly after 1833. Apparently, during the sermon, the leader of those early choirs would hunt for an appropriate anthem to fit the theme of the sermon and the choir would then sing it (without any rehearsal), "scarcely ever beginning or finishing all at the same time." Until 1850, at which time a melodeon, a small reed organ, was purchased, a tuning fork and an occasional bass were the only instruments used. The first pipe organ was installed in 1874 and needed a "blow boy" to pump the bellows from the dark organ chamber. In the 1950's when a new organ was installed, there were three choirs for adults, youth, and younger children, all of whom performed after rehearsing.

From the early days the church has been involved in outreach programs. The Women's Foreign Missionary Society, formed in 1874, supported foreign missions, and the Home Mission Society, formed in 1882, supported domestic missions with money and materials. The Ladies' Aid Society, formed in 1909, raised money through food sales and cafeteria suppers, which they used to fund new furnishings or building repairs, as well as worthy causes like various war efforts and the local Welfare Association. For over forty-five years the Women's Fellowship Committee organized and ran an annual antique show and sale, which became known as one of the finest in the area and was a major fund raiser for the Church. The church has sponsored a Boy Scout troop for many years as well as an active youth group whose activities have included participation in programs like Habitat for Humanity and "Reach Camps" which rehab homes in places like West Virginia, Ohio, and New York. Over the years this congregation has supported such community endeavors as the Fairport Apartments, the Perinton Lay-Clergy Council, Advent House, Meals on Wheels, and the Bertha Agor Memorial Nursery School has also extended its outreach to include involvement with the Joy Community Church of Rochester, Bethany House in Rochester, and Water for Sudan, Inc. This latter project raised $10,000 during the 2009 Lenten season for a well in the Darfur region of Sudan.

This venerable congregation, which, in 1961, became part of the national United Church of Christ, when the Congregational Church merged with the Evangelical and Reformed Churches, has been an important and integral part of the Fairport-Perinton community for over 185 years.

First Baptist Church

In the Joy School on Macedon Center Road on January 8, 1842, a small group of "brethren and sisters"adopted Articles of Faith and Practice and resolved themselves into a Baptist conference. Elder Charles Howe was chosen as the moderator and Justus Beardsley as clerk. The brethren and sisters included John Budlong, John and Hannah Walker, Sylvia Curtis, and Cynthia and Ursula Noyes. The first baptismal candidates were immersed in a running stream on January 30; they were Joel DeLand, Lucinda DeLand, Bleeker Webb, and Louisa Smith. The first regular church meeting of the First Baptist Church and Society of Perinton took place on February 2, 1842, with twenty-eight members. In May of 1842 the first pastor, Franklin Woodward, arrived and stayed for three years at a salary of $300. This active beginning, however, was not the first time that Baptists had attempted to organize in the Perinton area. There is evidence of a Baptist Society as early as 1816. A Certificate of Organization for a Baptist Society was drawn up at School #3 in 1832, but it was dissolved in 1836 and nothing more is noted until the 1842 meetings.

The Articles of Faith that the group adopted included Baptist principles of belief as laid down in the Scriptures. They also laid out strict rules for everyday life, declaring that "church members are not ordinarily to sue each other at law", that "alms are to be bestowed upon the needy members of the church...", and that heads of families are "to give their children religious instruction and restrain them from balls and other vicious courses." Although they adhered to the resolution that "believing the cause of temperance to be the cause of truth, we feel it our duty to require our members to practice according to the principle of total abstinence," it was never formally added to their Articles of Faith and Practice. An initial resolution about slavery was proposed in 1842, but not acted upon. In 1846, however, it was resolved that "slavery was the sin of the nation and the church and that we have no fellowship in it." Over the years there is evidence that these rules of life were not merely statements. In the 1840's records show a number of members from whom "the hand of fellowship was withdrawn"

First Baptist Church postcard

for various infractions, such as intemperance, neglecting to fill one's place in church, neglect of family, and even one for attending dancing school. On the other hand, members were restored after confession and amendment.

These early Perinton Baptists first met in the East Church Street Schoolhouse and also in the Universalist (later the Episcopal) Church on East Church Street, but very quickly purchased land for their own building. In 1842 the lot on the corner of Church and Main Street was bought from Lyman and Eleanor Hall for $500. Apparently the construction of the small wooden building was quite a festive event. As the walls were raised, the children watched and the women brought hampers of food and prepared a meal. To insure the building a tax was levied on the pews, or "slips." This proved to be such an easy and convenient way of raising money that it was used for a variety of other purposes and evolved into pew or slip "rental." By the 1860's, Pew Rental Day had become quite a social event with a free supper. While several pews were set aside for the poor or for strangers, by the 1890's, pews were assigned to each member for life, which caused some problems as the only way to get a seat was for someone to die. Eventually the pew rental system was replaced by the pledge system of raising money and all seats were free and unassigned.

Baptisms had traditionally been by total immersion in a running stream. They were usually done in Irondequoit Creek or Curtis Pond on Macedon Center Road. Winter did not deter the faithful. In February of 1863, it was noted in the records that "although it was a very cold day many persons witnessed the ordinance (of baptism) which was solemn and impressive and all the converts went away rejoicing and happy." Later that year, however, in a second round of building improvements, an inside baptistry was added, although as late as the 1870's, some still preferred to go to the stream to be baptized.

First Baptist Church Sunday school

Between the 1840's and the early 1900's a number of revivals helped add to the growth of the congregation. Revival meetings were often held in January and sometimes before Christmas. In 1899 four leaders of the church called on many residents of the community, which resulted in sixty-five members being received and twelve being baptized. In 1914 the Burgess and Butts revival campaign drew over one hundred new members. This growth led to the need for a new larger church. An additional piece of land on West Church Street was purchased from the Chadwick family. The pastor's house was moved to 48 E. Church Street. The session house was advertised for sale in the local paper and was purchased for $100 and moved to 11 Filkins Street. The original meeting house was moved to the back of the lot and eventually made into a home by Harrison Wooden. It burned in 1890.

The new brick building, built at a cost of $35,000, was an imposing and elegant addition to Fairport village and the ninety-foot spire served as a significant landmark. The brick work was highlighted with trim of Berea sandstone and the front doors were flanked by Scotch granite columns. The lovely rose window was given by the Henry DeLand family, who also gave $12,000 to the building fund. The auditorium of the church was finished in oiled chestnut and included a thirty foot long baptistry. The church was dedicated on Oct. 30-Nov. 1, 1877. Immediately, a drive began to raise money for a pipe organ, which was dedicated in 1881. It was described as "very tasty in appearance as well as adapted to fill the large audience room with the harmony of music." The first choir seems to have been formed in the 1850's under the direction of Mr. Scofield. Emma Bortle served as organist for forty-four years, retiring in 1917. It is recorded that there was often a male quartet who sang regularly and on special occasions there was a four to six piece orchestra added.

Soon after the organ was installed, plaster moldings fell from the ceiling and damaged some of the pews. It was decided to remove the plaster and install a wooden ceiling. This second ceiling proved to have such poor acoustics that a third and lower ceiling was finally installed. Twice in the history of this building the spire was struck by lightning. Despite some discussion as to whether or not to remove the spire, both times it was repaired. In the 1950's the church considered moving out of the village, but with the purchase and remodeling of the Hupp automobile dealership next door for much needed classroom and fellowship space, it was decided to stay in the village. The new building was named the DeLand Center after the family that had contributed so much to the church over the years.

First Baptist Church has a history of social involvement and religious education. In the early years of the church, prayer meetings were regularly held on Saturday afternoons and Wednesday evenings, but eventually, people abandoned the custom of weekly prayer meetings and attended only the Sunday service. The Sunday School was organized along with the church itself in 1842, and included adult classes as well as Bible study groups. Social events included an annual Christmas supper, complete with fresh oranges sent from Florida by Henry DeLand, and a midsummer picnic, which was a grand event with lots of food, a band, and singing. An active youth group met regularly on Mondays and was variously known as the Covenant Band, the Young Peoples' Union, and the Christian Endeavor Society, among others. There was great interest and concern for the missions, both foreign and domestic. The Women's Baptist Foreign Missionary Society, formed in 1871, met and supported those who worked in overseas missions. In 1911 the first missionaries sent by the church, Mr. and Mrs. David Graham, were given a gala farewell before they left for China. Several women served as teachers with the Home Mission Society, doing Bible School and Americanization work with newly-arrived immigrants. All were supported with funds and goods by the Missionary Society. In addition, the group also contributed to the upkeep of the church itself. The King's Daughters Circle, the Fruitful Circle, the Scattergood Circle, and the Whatsoever Class, (named after their motto, "Whatsoever Thy Hand findeth to do, do with Thy Might.") raised money and collected goods for the needy and for the upkeep of the church.

The First Baptist Church of Fairport continues to have a dedicated congregation and to be active in the community as supporters of the Perinton Food Shelf and the Fairport Baptist Homes, among others. The church building has been added to the National Register of Historic Places and is also a designated Fairport landmark, insuring that this elegant structure will continue to stand and welcome people into the village of Fairport and to the church itself.

Fairport Community Baptist Church

Many of Perinton's pioneers settled in the hamlet of Egypt and one of the first institutions they created was a church. In 1840 a group of nineteen people met to form the Free Baptist Church and called D. G. Holmes as their first pastor. They probably met in either the Methodist meeting house, or the Egypt schoolhouse, both on Pittsford-Palmyra Road.

In 1848, after changing its name to Fairport Free Will Baptist Church, the congregation decided to move into the village of Fairport. After holding their first meetings in a house on Church Street just east of number 38, they erected a Greek Revival building on the present site. It cost $3,000, which was paid in full upon completion. Like many churches of the period, yearly income for the church was raised through the use of pew rents. A church history piques interest by stating that "Nothing of great importance shows on the records of the next few years although the covenant meetings were held very regularly. The language used and disposition of certain cases would certainly bring a smile to the faces of the present day folks."

The 1880's and 1890's were significant decades in the life of this congregation. The name was again changed to First Free Baptist Church of Fairport; the first mention was made of an organist when Mrs. Bilby was voted in as church organist; and the Rev. L.W. Raymond was called to the church as pastor. In 1889, on a lot just west of the church, ground was broken for a new parsonage, which was dedicated the following year when the keys were transferred from C. L. Peacock, Chairman of the Trustees, to Deacon O.C. Adams, and finally to Pastor Raymond and his family, who were then welcomed to their new home.

Interior of the Free Will Baptist Church

A subscription committee was formed in the early 1890's to consider construction of a new church building. Members O. C. Adams, J.C. Spear, Mrs. W. B. Bly, and Mrs. W. A. Trescott, and the trustees agreed that the sum of $5,500 had to be on hand before work could begin. Among other significant gifts, Mrs. Maria Wood gave $1,000 for the purchase of Warsaw Blue Stone for the wall facings. On May 20, 1892 a resolution was adopted which stated in part: "Resolved that we accept the offer of Mr. O. C. Adams of $50.00 for the old building. The same to be removed by him without delay. ... Also resolved that subscriptions and pledges are sufficient and available to warrant the trustees to proceed with the building." Mr. Adams moved the building to 154-156 South Main Street where it remains today, serving as apartments; however, due to the impossibility of turning the building around, the rear of the building faces on the street.

Three days after the passing of the above resolution, ground was broken for the new church building. The first shovelfuls of dirt were removed by Pastor Raymond, Mrs. Wood (the oldest church member), and Clarence Ellsworth (the youngest member), among others. Frank Longley contracted with the church to build the walls for $1,220 and an Elmira contractor was awarded the contract for the slate roof at a cost of $7 per square. The Warsaw Blue stone for the wall facing was shipped in by boat and unloaded on East Church Street. Church members also contributed their time and talent. Among them, Charles Knapp hauled in a load of stone for the walls each time he came to town and Mr. Bly offered to put up a roof ready for the laying of the slate tiles. No mention is made of the cost of any lumber for the building and no help was employed that cost more than $2.00 per day. In August of 1892 the cornerstone was laid, which contained, among other items, a Bible, denominational papers and periodicals, the Free Baptist Treatise, village papers, and the names of the pastor, officers of the church and Sunday School, and those who had donated. Shortly after the installation of a furnace, which cost $109.68, the completed church was finally dedicated on February 7, 1895.

Raymond Memorial/ Fairport Community Baptist Church

In 1903 Fairport Free Baptist Church bade goodbye to the Rev. Raymond and welcomed the Rev. W. R. Wood. During the Rev. Wood's tenure, the church accepted a gift from Andrew Carnegie that paid half the cost of a new pipe organ, and a number of repairs were done on both the church and the parsonage, including the installation of electric lights and new furnaces in both the church and the parsonage. In 1915 the church again changed its name, this time to Raymond Baptist, in honor of the pastor who had overseen the extensive building program of the 1880's and 90's. In 1918, committees were formed at both of Fairport's Baptist churches, First Baptist and Raymond Baptist to look into the possibility of unification; however, the move was not successful and the committees disbanded.

Throughout its history, the congregation of this church has had active Sunday School classes and youth and adult groups of various kinds. No written records have been found regarding the establishment of a Sunday School, but it would seem from recollections that the Sunday school is probably one of the oldest of the church's organizations. For most of the early part of the twentieth century, the practice was to give the various classes names like the "Golden Rule", "Sunshine Class", "Willing Workers", and "Pioneers." For the women there were the Women's Missionary Society, who supported missions, both domestic and foreign, as well as the Fairport Baptist Home, and the Ladies Guild, who provided social activities such as regular monthly suppers and financial support for the purchase of items like pew cushions and carpeting. From the 1880's to the early twentieth century the young people's group called themselves the "Advocates of Christian Fidelity," holding socials and raising money for the needs of their church as well as for missions. The group also was part of the Monroe County Christian Endeavor Union, and in the 1930's was known as the Baptist Young People's Union.

Newspaper records from the 1920's and 1930's indicate a very active church with numerous groups meeting for Bible study throughout the week. Prayer meetings were held every Wednesday at

7:30 p.m. The Spear Bible Class met regularly at homes of parishioners, as did several other study groups. Social gatherings were also popular. One excerpt notes that "About 50 members of the Spear class and members of the families held a most enjoyable social in the church Friday evening. A bountiful picnic supper was served at six...." Obviously members of the church studied, but they also enjoyed themselves - they referred to themselves as the "cheerful church."

Sometime between 1940 and the 1970's the church changed its name once again. Apparently, the name Raymond Baptist led many to think that the church was located in a place called Raymond, New York. In order to avoid confusion the name was changed to Raymond Memorial Baptist.

In 1992 Raymond Memorial celebrated its centennial anniversary in its stone church. Among other activities, they opened the cornerstone that had been buried in 1892 and added items from 1992 before reburying for, it is hoped, another 100 years. Under the leadership of Pastor William Kerr, who was pastor from 1975-97, the church continued its activity in the community, being instrumental in the creation of the successful and necessary Perinton Food Shelf.

In 1998, after the retirement of William Kerr, John Tuff arrived to take over the job of pastor. Under his leadership, the church saw strong growth in its ministry to young people with its "Kid's Club," as well as in its music program. A mid-week Bible study has proved to be quite popular as are the monthly community pancake breakfasts. In 2005 the church changed its name to Fairport Community Baptist Church.

Along with many of the other local churches, the Fairport Community Baptist Church is involved in support for Advent House, the Perinton Food Shelf, and the Perinton Clergy-Lay Council. Clearly, this active village congregation is very much a part of the community.

First United Methodist Church

The Methodists arrived early to the Perinton area. Methodist circuit riders in their stove pipe hats were a familiar sight as they came to hold services, to which all were invited, and to baptize and marry lonely and isolated settlers. There is evidence that meetings were held as early as 1808 at Bennett Joy's home on Macedon Center Road, and a Methodist Society was organized in Egypt in 1810, meeting in a large two-story hall on Pittsford-Palmyra Road.

The first Methodist Society in Fairport village was formed in 1825 and this group built a small frame church on North Main Street. Among those early members were Jacob Sperbeck, Warren Caulkins, Martin Sperbeck, and Eban Sherman. There are few records of this early group and they did not prosper, succumbing to the dissension created by the Millerites, who, in the 1830's, predicted that the world was going to end in 1843. The society disbanded in 1838 and the church building was sold to Jeremiah Chadwick, who used it as a carriage and wagon shop.

By 1881 the Free Methodist Society, led by the Rev. Mr. B. T. Roberts, was meeting in Fairport village at 14 Cole Street. Mr. Roberts had been "read out of meeting" in 1860 for his "strong and different opinions" and had, as a result, started his own version of Methodism. His more conservative and dramatic and exuberant style attracted some and repelled others, but the sect was short-lived. By 1910 most had rejoined the regular Methodist Church. The house had various owners until it was razed in 1939, but the back lot was still used for Free Methodist revival meetings.

Another Methodist society formed in the southeast portion of Perinton in the 1830's and met in the schoolhouse there before building and dedicating a church structure in 1837. That building is home today to the South Perinton United Methodist Church.

Methodist Church 1879 building

The current Methodist church in Fairport village was formed with twelve members in the home of Dr. and Mrs. C. H. Greene on South Main Street in 1876. The group met for three years in the former Universalist Church on East Church Street. A "....weak, struggling band at first, but being composed of earnest leaders and wide awake workers, the church soon obtained a substantial foothold, and in 1879 the original brick structure [on West Church Street] was erected....." Much of the labor on the building was performed by church members themselves, and the society moved into the church long before it was completed. Old seats, pulpit, and windows from the First Baptist Church were donated, as was the first communion set consisting of two glass goblets and an earthenware pitcher. Levi DeLand gave the first gas lighting plant and set of fixtures. For several years there were no carpets on the floor, and "the ladies of the society used to get together at regular intervals and mop and scrub the large floor, occasionally the work falling on two or three of the most faithful members, who would sometimes labor until the midnight hour, in order to have the church bright and clean for Sunday morning services." To secure children for the Sunday School the women of the church "literally went out into the highways and byways to bring in those who were out of touch with the religion of Jesus." They also brought in the nearly destitute, and organized sewing circles to provide them with needed clothing. As one recorder noted, "this was heroic missionary work right here in our own village...."

Of the early pastors, The Rev. Porter McKinstry stayed only four months. The Rev. Benjamin Copeland stayed a mere two weeks, saying that the society could not support a church. The Rev. John Cline came in from South Perinton every Sunday for six months to hold services, and few subsequent pastors stayed more than two years. The Greenes, who were original members, often housed short-term pastors in their home, leading some to refer to their house as "Greene's Methodist Hotel."

The Fairport Methodist Church entered a period of growth and prominence as the twentieth century began. Under the pastorate of the Rev. Mark Kelley, who came in 1899, the church building was finally dedicated on September 20, 1901, after sufficient funds had been raised to pay off all indebtedness, including a $4,000 mortgage. The building was remodeled in 1904 after the Akron Plan, which provided for circular seating on a graduated floor, and a new heating plant was installed. In the early teens, Miss Para Woolsey donated a new organ, which enhanced the already strong tradition of music in the church. A distinguishing characteristic of the early Methodists was their singing, and after all, Methodist founder Charles Wesley had written over 6500 hymns and songs for all occasions and all times of the day.

The church was a center of social as well as religious activity. There were church suppers and picnics. Bible study and prayer groups as well as various other organizations met regularly. The Women's Missionary Society raised money for the foreign and domestic missions and also had speakers from places like Japan. Goods for the needy at home and abroad were collected by the Ladies' Aid Society, who also raised funds for outside needs, as well as those of the church itself. In 1921 there is a record of "Rally Day," where the congregation, using all autos and carriages available to them, reached out into the community and "compelled the people to come in." Rockers were provided for the elderly, infirm, and mothers with babies, and a special Sunday School program was held. As with most Methodist churches, the Christian education and youth programs were always vital and active.

Methodist Church 2008

The church continued to grow with the Perinton-Fairport community during the second half of the twentieth century. In 1955, the first part of a major renovation occurred. A large church school addition was built to the west of the sanctuary, which was at that time located at the corner of South Avenue and West Church Street. The second phase of the renovation was completed when, after purchasing the remaining lots between Filkins and South Avenues in the early 1960's, the old sanctuary was demolished and a new one built on the corner of West Church and Filkins Streets. Two windows from the old church, the Good Shepherd window and the window of Christ knocking at the door, were preserved and incorporated into the new building.

In 1968 another kind of growth and change occurred when the Methodists and the Evangelical United Brethren merged to become the United Methodists.

The First Methodist Church is a dominant landmark on West Church Street and continues its outreach and concern in the community by supporting endeavors like Advent House and the Perinton Food Shelf, as well as holding a once-a-month Sunday dinner for those in need in the community. The church's outreach extends as far as the Democratic Republic of the Congo where they are working with other groups on economic development. The church's active youth groups plan regular services and volunteer in a variety of ways in the community. They also take part in a yearly mission work camp trip, offering their skills and enthusiasm to those in need.

St. Luke's Episcopal Church

The first Episcopal services in Perinton probably were held in 1828 or 1829 by the Rev. Ezekiel Gear from West Avon and there is mention of sporadic services being held in the 1860's. By 1886 a small congregation of about forty-five people had leased the former Universalist Church on East Church Street, organized a choir, a Ladies' Aid Society, a Sunday School and was holding regular services. The Rev. George Thomas LeBouillier, who came from Pittsford on a railroad handcart (which had been lent to him by the railroad), celebrated the first of those regular services on Sunday morning, September 12, 1886.

In 1887, for $2300, the group purchased the land and building that they had been leasing and incorporated themselves as St. Luke's Episcopal Church. The first vestry members were Theron Pritchard, John Robinson, C. L. Dunbar, B. L. Thompson, R. M. Swift, and A. G. Odell. The church was furnished with an altar and lectern built by Henry Suter and given by Mrs. Swift's Sunday School class and the Sunday School of Christ Church, Pittsford, respectively. Otherwise the interior furnishings were sparse, lacking carpets or any means of heating. Although congregations numbered more than 100 in the early days, by 1897 records list only twenty communicants. In 1907 Bishop Walker described the Fairport church as "moribund"; however, since the Fairport community was growing rapidly, the pastor at the time, Archdeacon William Davis, was not willing to give up. He is quoted in a history of the diocese as saying: "Last fall I decided that the best thing to do was to take down the old building and from the debris erect, as far as possible, a new one on more churchly lines. When I announced my purpose to the people, it was received with incredulous looks. They had been dead so long and were so happy in their grave clothes, that they resented even the thought of a resurrection ... When I started out with a subscription paper, one man offered me fifty cents. In two days, I had a little over one hundred dollars subscribed and one dollar paid in. With this small financial backing, I sent for two carpenters who had worked for me before, and much to the consternation of the people, we began the work of tearing down. Each week I collected the money to pay the men, and by the last of the month, we had, from the old materials, reconstructed and enclosed what promises to be a neat Gothic building, at an expenditure of a little over $400. We need about $400 more to complete the structure ... I am my own architect, and, as occasion may require, my own builder ... The people of the town have already had a vision of a man in clerical garb upon the roof of the church laying shingles." Apparently, Fr. Davis inspired the small congregation because by 1924 the mortgage was paid off, and the church had received a number of memorial gifts, including a baptismal font, given in 1907, which is still in use. In 1927, under the leadership of the Rev. Ridgley Lytle, a parish house addition was built which contained a kitchen, an assembly hall, and a heating plant for both the parish hall and the church.

St. Luke's Church on East Church Street

The parish declined during the years of the Depression. In 1936, for example, there were only twenty-five pledges. The congregation held services in the parish hall because they lacked money to repair the furnace that heated the church itself, and there was a stove in the parish hall. The church, however, managed to survive and begin to grow again. Women were given voting rights in parish elections, and as a result of post World War II growth, a house on West Church Street was purchased for the rectory, and, in 1952, St. Luke's became a self-sustaining parish under the leadership of the Rev. Elwyn Brown.

By 1955 St. Luke's had grown to about 200 households and there was talk of building a new and larger church. One plan proposed building a central church for the communities of Perinton, Penfield, and East Rochester; however, a survey indicted that the majority of church members were opposed. Subsequently, the Church of the Incarnation was established in Penfield and St. Luke's plans for expansion were tabled.

The decade of the 1960's was a tumultuous one for the Church. In 1962, under the leadership of its rector, the Reverend Dustin Ordway, the parish sold the village property to the Fairport Public Library (who subsequently sold it to the village as the site for the fire hall), and purchased sixteen acres of land on a hill off Ayrault Road on what would become Country Corner Lane in the Brambleridge East subdivision. With the growth in Perinton, the church would now have a more central location in the town. As a result of several bequests, St. Luke's already had about $91,000 in a capital fund. The proposed new church, designed by noted architect Marcel Breuer, was to be a large, modern, concrete structure. Mr. Breuer declined to work within a budget and the proposed cost of his plan came to well over $400,000. Issues surrounding the building plans caused significant dissension within the congregation, and eventually the plan was discarded, primarily due to lack of sufficient funding. A smaller, prefabricated structure was built and opened in 1968 with the hope that it would eventually become a parish hall when and if the Breuer design was ever built. Despite the fact that the town population was growing in the late 60's and early 70's, St. Luke's did not see significant expansion, perhaps due to the social stresses of that period, changes in the prayer book, issues like the ordination of women, and disagreements over the role the church should play in commenting on social, political, or national issues.

St. Lukes Church on Country Corner Lane

During the 1980's, however, the parish enjoyed significant growth which led to a space crunch in the small church building, and some minor remodeling was done to expand the space. At the same time, several generous gifts made it possible to purchase a pipe organ to enhance St. Luke's tradition of excellent music. The congregation has been fortunate in its music directors, which have included two American Guild of Organists national competition winners.

Space problems continued to plague St. Luke's throughout the 1980's, and in 1988, when the Reverend Hugh Stevenson was rector, a "Second Century Fund" was established to raise money for a new church building. This time the building project was successful and a more traditional stone building was erected and dedicated in 1990. In addition to a larger worship space, the building includes meeting rooms and Sunday School rooms as well as a columbarium, an area that houses niches for funerary urns.

Today, St. Luke's describes itself as "an open, Christ-centered community, caring for each other, and doing God's work in the world." In addition to church school, adult education, youth programs, and social events, the parish also has an active outreach program that supports a number of local organizations, including Advent House, Perinton Lay-Clergy Council, Fairport Community Vacation Bible School, a Meal and More, and Safe Journey. Parishioners also are involved in tutoring programs at several Rochester city elementary schools. And St. Luke's Hill Nursery School has met at the church for over thirty years. In 2009 the congregation began working to develop a relationship with a Dalit congregation in India.

St. Luke's remains committed to fulfilling its goal of "doing God's work in the world" as the twenty-first century moves forward.

Roman Catholic Churches

It was 1849 when Father Michael Guilbride, an upstate missionary, celebrated the first Roman Catholic mass in Fairport. Smith Brennan, an immigrant Irish blacksmith who lived along the towpath on what would become State Street, opened his home for the services. Brennan was one of the many Irish Catholics who had immigrated to the United States in the 1840's to escape the first of the potato famines. Between 1852 and 1856 mass was celebrated in various homes by Father John Tuohy, who came in from Palmyra to serve this new mission of St. Anne's of Palmyra.

Church of the Assumption 1883

The fledgling parish moved into its first home in 1856. Father William Casey oversaw the building of a 30 foot by 35 foot frame building on High Street. The building, enlarged in 1866, still stands and has been used over the years as a feed store and a grocery store. When masses were first held there, the building served as a produce market during the week. Bishop Bernard McQuaid held the first confirmation on June 20, 1864. The first baptism, that of Mary White, was held on August 26, 1866, and the first wedding, that of Martin O'Neal and Anna Quirk, was celebrated on September 9, 1866.

By 1866, the new congregation had doubled in size and under Father Lewis Miller, Assumption of Our Lady Church became a self-sustaining parish. A house was purchased as a rectory and moved east of the present church. In 1872, growth led to the purchase of three lots on East Avenue for $1500, where, within ten years, a new church would be built.

Father John Codyre, born and educated in Galway County, Ireland, came to Fairport in 1878 and in the subsequent fifty years witnessed great change and growth. In 1883 he presided over the dedication of a $15,000 brick church building on East Avenue. During the period of his pastorship, Fairport developed as an industrial center, home to the DeLand Chemical Company and the Sanitary Can Company, among others, and the population of Perinton more than doubled from under 4,000 people to over 9,000.

Father Codyre was a strict priest, but one who was both respected and loved. He cared for families, literally from the cradle to the grave, as he baptized them, married them, and buried them. Fairport became his home, even after retirement and a trip to Ireland. Since he was so much a part of so many lives for so long, there are numerous anecdotes that feature his wit and personality. Many of Assumption's parishioners came by the Rochester, Syracuse, and Eastern Trolley to the village of Fairport and would often sneak out of Mass early in order to catch the trolley home. "Father Codyre would whip around from the altar and scream at them, 'Come back here, you Egyptians.'" There was a man who used to go through the church refuse checking the wine bottles, raising them and peeking in to see if anything was left. "Around the fifth or sixth bottle, with it still in the air and him looking up at it - he hears, much to his embarrassment, a voice from behind coming from Father Codyre saying, 'Sorry, but them's all dead soldiers.'" Dr. Willis Trescott, who owned the Trescott Company on Railroad and North Main Street, and Father Codrye were friends, even though Trescott never attended church. One evening, during his walk, Father Codyre passed Dr. Trescott, who was watching his workers remodel the front of his building. He stopped and looked and said to Dr. Trescott, "Whatcha doin?" Trescott, puffing on his cigar and not turning around said, "I'm building me a new church." Father Codyre took a couple of steps, stopped, turned around and said in his Irish brogue, "It's not churches we need, it's Christians!"

Assumption of Our Lady Church

Following Father Codyre, two priests served Fairport's Assumption parish for the next fifty years, from 1925-1975, years of challenge, growth, and change. Father James Wood's pastorate weathered the Depression, World War II, and the beginning of suburban growth. A new rectory was built, the church was remodeled and redecorated twice, and a new heating system and a new pipe organ were installed. Under Father Leonard Kelly, the church implemented the changes in form and practice called for by the Vatican II Council, which included the celebration of the Mass in English. The church building itself underwent a $100,000 renovation which included new exits, a new basement hall, and an expanded parking lot. Father Kelly's brainchild, the Assumption School for Religious Training, said to be unique in the nation, opened in September, 1956. Under a released-time program, all Catholic children received religious instruction for one hour each week. The school and convent were located on Baumer Place in Fairport village and were originally staffed by lay volunteers and four Sister-teachers, who were Mission Helpers of the Sacred Heart from Baltimore.

Perinton and Assumption parish continued to grow through the 1970's and into the 1980's, serving more than 2,000 families. The parish clearly needed more space, and Father Joseph Beatini started an appeal for a building fund and began planning for a new church building. In 1983, the old church, which had stood for 100 years, was demolished and replaced with a modern and much larger facility. Father John Norris presided over the building and the subsequent move. In recent years Assumption Church has seen the completion of a new parish life center, the creation of new offices, and the relocation of the rectory to High Street, near the original church building.

St. John of Rochester Church

Between 1960 and 1973 two other Roman Catholic parishes were established in Perinton, reflecting the tremendous growth, not only of the town itself, but also its faith community. St. John of Rochester was established in 1961 and the Church of the Resurrection in 1973.

Church of the Resurrection

Worshippers had been attending mass at the mission Chapel of the Immaculate Heart of Mary at the corner of Pittsford-Victor and Thornell Roads in Bushnell's Basin since 1948. By 1961 there were enough members to form an independent parish, and in 1962, Bishop James Kearney formally established the parish of St. John of Rochester, named after St. John Fisher, who was Bishop of Rochester, England, during the reign of King Henry VIII. In 1963 a combined church and school building was built on the corner of Wickford Way and Pittsford-Palmyra Road and was opened by Father John LeVeque, its first pastor, in September of that year. Over the next twenty years, St. John of Rochester continued to grow and expand, eventually necessitating a new church building which was dedicated in 1983. St. John's school served students until its closing in 2008 when the Rochester diocese shuttered thirteen suburban parish schools.

The Church of the Resurrection was originally founded at the request of Bishop Joseph Hogan of Rochester in 1973. The first daily masses were celebrated by Father Robert Kreckel in the basement of the rectory on Hamilton Road and the first Sunday masses were held in the building next to Martha Brown School (now a Montessori School). The congregation moved into a contemporary building on Mason Road in 1976. During the subsequent twenty years the community continued to expand, and in 1998 completed an ambitious expansion of its worship area.

These three parishes continue to be active and vibrant contributors to the spiritual life of the Perinton/Fairport community.

Lutheran Churches

It was on August 7, 1921, that ninety-five people, including a Sunday school group of twenty, held Fairport's first Lutheran service in the Town Hall with Pastor W. G.Hoffmann presiding. At a business meeting held the same month in the Grange Hall, Henry Schumacher, A.W. Fett, and Fred Schoolmaster were selected as trustees, Fred Schmidt was elected secretary, and James Peck was elected treasurer. A constitution was adopted by the congregation and the name Bethlehem Evangelical Lutheran Church of Fairport, New York, was chosen as the official name. The church is part of the Evangelical Lutheran Church of America Synod. In September a resolution was passed instructing the Mission Committee of the Buffalo Synod to call the Rev. H. D. Schultz as pastor.

Bethlehem Lutheran Church in the 1960's

The next several years were busy ones for the new congregation. The early months of 1922 saw the first annual congregational meeting where the first elders, Charles Steffen and Charles W. Steubing, were selected, and E. F. Bandhold and Fred Schoolmaster were chosen as Deacons. Pastor Schultz was installed and the congregation incorporated. It was also decided to purchase the Jacobson property on West Church Street for $1150.00 as the site for the proposed church building. In February the congregation selected a building committee whose members were E. F.

Bandhold, Charles Steffen, and Charles Steubing. Excavation was begun in May and on Sunday, August 20, 1922, "a goodly conger- gation gathered to witness the cornerstone laying ceremonies." During the construction the congregation held services in the Bown block on South Main Street. The group did not have long to wait, however. A church history notes that "steady progress was made in the erection of the building. The great part of the work was contributed by members. The desire for a temple of worship provided the incentive and a spirit of cooperation made the goal possible." The new building and its furnishings were consecrated "to the service of the Triune God on Sunday, March 11, 1923." Donations included pews from the Ladies Aid Society, windows from individual members and the Sunday School class, a baptismal font from the Rev. and Mrs. Beutler, and a pipe organ from the Concordia Lutheran Church of Rochester. By that time the congregation had also purchased 40 Perrin Street as a parsonage for Pastor Schultz.

Bethlehem Lutheran Church

The church continued to grow and prosper, necessitating a remodeling in the early 1930's. As the people worshipped in the basement, a new arched chancel with three art glass windows donated by Karl Stroh was installed, as were a new electric organ and choir loft. The latter were gifts of the Ladies Aid Society. The church was rededicated and reconsecrated upon completion of the new additions and a complete redecoration. In 1937 the church became self-supporting.

The 1940's and 1950's brought steady growth, the establishment of a memorial fund, and the purchase of more property. In 1953 42 Perrin Street was purchased as a new parsonage, replacing #40. In 1955 the former Brooks property on the corner of West Church and Perrin Streets was purchased for a parish house. Nine of the twelve rooms in the house were remodeled to serve as Sunday School classrooms. Other rooms were used as church offices and meeting rooms.

The church marked its thirtieth anniversary in 1953 with a gala celebration. A dinner and several services attended by three former pastors marked the occasion. Donations given in honor of the event included a missal stand, a credence table, hymnals, and a new carpet, among others. Pastor Donald Rehkoph presided at the events that included the welcoming of thirty new parishioners. At that point in its history, the congregation numbered 440 baptized members with an average Sunday attendance of 150 persons. The Sunday school had an average of eighty-five children each week.

Bethlehem Lutheran has always provided many activities for parishioners in addition to regular Sunday worship The church instituted a Vacation Bible School in the mid-1950's that was very well attended. Youth groups and men's and women's groups were popular as well. The youth group of around forty contributed to the church by holding bake sales and suppers. The men's group met regularly for dinner and to hear speakers on current issues. The women's group was concerned with aiding the domestic and foreign missionary work of the church, particularly the support of the Rev. Paul Schultz (the son of the first pastor) who was working in New Guinea. In 1959 the church ordained one of its lifelong members, Richard Hembrock, who joined another church member, Kenneth Sharp, in the ministry.

In the 1960's and 1970's it was evident that the church plant would have to expand to accommodate growth. Under the leadership of the Rev. H. E. Jorgensen, the church consolidated the Perrin Street properties in anticipation of building. Plans were drawn up for a new education and office wing, and in 1970, the former parish house and parsonage were demolished and an addition to the church building was erected on the corner of West Church and Perrin Streets. A gift of $25,000 from the estate of Charles Stroh greatly enhanced the building fund. The new parish center was dedicated in September, 1971. At that time the number of baptized members had reached 669 and the budget had increased more than tenfold from the 1930 figure of $2,470 to the 1971 figure of $28,360.

In the 1990's Bethlehem Lutheran had a total congregation of about 800 with an average weekly attendance of about 350. The Rev. Kent Garner, who was pastor from 1977 (when the weekly attendance was about 100) until his retirement in 2008, saw the parish grow to nearly 1,000 members. That growth led to the remodeling of both the sanctuary and the parish center. The congregation is proud of its excellent music and educational programs and is also very involved in the community. Bethlehem Lutheran was the birthplace of the idea for Advent House, Perinton's hospice, as well as for Sojourner House, a refuge for battered women. The church is a member of the Perinton Clergy-Lay Council and the Fairport Housing Council, which has and continues to be instrumental in the creation of affordable housing for seniors. The church completed an extensive expansion in 2001, which included a 6,000 square foot addition as well the incorporation of stained glass windows and an altar and communion rail from the original 1921 church. Bethlehem Lutheran is committed to being a village church and to growing and changing with the needs of community while maintaining its roots.

Bethlehem Lutheran has been joined in Perinton by two other Lutheran churches: Risen Christ Lutheran on Moseley Road, which was built in the 1980's, and Prince of Peace Lutheran on Pittsford-Palmyra Road, which was dedicated in 1993. Risen Christ, part of the Missouri Synod, has experienced rapid expansion. The church offers both traditional and contemporary worship services. The contemporary service, which features a "praise band," video clips, and dramatic presentations, appeals to younger families. Prince of Peace Lutheran, part of the Wisconsin Evangelical Lutheran Synod, has been in Perinton since 1988, building a permanent home on Pittsford-Palmyra Road in 1992. The church has been described by its pastor as a mission church with the goal of carrying the Biblical message of God's grace in Christ to those who are without a church. Emphasis is on children's programs including, for example, a popular Vacation Bible School program, open to the community. All three Lutheran churches head into the coming decades with a strong commitment to young families and to growth as part of the Perinton community.

Risen Christ Lutheran Church

Prince of Peace Lutheran Church

Newer Churches

As the town of Perinton grew as a suburb starting in the 1950's, existing churches grew and new ones organized to meet the demand. The first to organize after the end of World War II was the Fairport Gospel Center (later known as the Evangel Church). This group was followed by the Jehovah's Witnesses, the Perinton Community Church, the Latter Day Saints, the United Church of Christ's Mountain Rise Church in the 1960's, and the Presbyterian Church in the 1980's. During this time as well, two more Roman Catholic parishes and two more Lutheran parishes were established in the community.

The Gospel Center/Evangel Church began with Bible study meetings in the Bown Block on South Main Street in 1946 under the leadership of the Rev. Albert D'Annunzio. By 1948 the congregation had grown enough to incorporate and in 1951 they purchased the former East Church Street School. The 1855 building was extensively remodeled by the congregation and served as their home until it was destroyed by fire in 1971. Subsequently, the parish built the structure that now stands at 38 East Church Street. The congregation eventually changed its name to the Evangelical Church of Fairport in order that people might better understand its mission of spreading the good news of the Gospel.

Evangelical Church

The Jehovah's Witnesses have been a presence in Perinton since the early 1960's. Their first church was located on High Street Extension. Currently, they are located on Moseley Road.

The United Church of Christ established a mission church on Mountain Rise off Pittsford-Palmyra Road in 1962. While awaiting the building of their church, the group had a temporary home in a building on Ayrault Road between Kreag Road and the canal led by their first pastor, the Rev. Charles B. Higgins. The organization was formalized in June 1963 when 110 charter members signed the roll. The new church building was completed in 1966 and the parish became self-sustaining in 1969. The congregation presents itself as an "open & affirming" church, meaning that we welcome all to full participation..." The Mountain Rise Church building also serves as the Etz Chaim Congregation's synagogue. The two groups not only share facilities, but also have cooperated in such area outreach programs as "Make a Difference Day."

Perinton Community Church had its beginnings in 1968 when five couples met on a Sunday for fellowship and to seek guidance concerning the establishment of an organized group dedicated to the spreading of the Gospel. After close to a year of meetings and the addition of more people, the group rented the former St. Luke's Episcopal Church (the present site of the Fire Department) for $150 per month. After the first formal meeting on December 31, 1968, regular worship and Bible classes began in January 1969. The church was incorporated in February 1969 and in June of that year, the Rev. Robert Barr came as pastor. The congregation continued to grow,

Mountain Rise Church

and property on High Street Extension was purchased in 1970. The facility was completed in December of 1972. Mr. Barr continued as pastor until 1989, when illness forced his retirement. This non-denominational church is closely aligned with the National Association of Evangelicals.

Perinton Community Church

A new ward of the Church of Jesus Christ of the Latter Day Saints was formed in Perinton in 1969 with 350 people from the Rochester ward. In the Mormon Church, when a ward numbers between 700 and 800, a new one splits off. The congregation met at the Forman Center while raising money for a building of their own. The facility at 460 Kreag Road was completed in 1971 and also includes a Family History Center.

The Presbyterian Church in Perinton was officially organized in 1983 at a service held in the Fairport Masonic Hall on South Main Street. This followed two years of study by the Presbytery of Genesee Valley who conducted a random survey in 1981 that found thirty-three families interested in establishing a congregation in Perinton. The Rev. David Gellert was called as pastor to the fledgling group. By 1985 the congregation numbered sixty-six families and purchased land on Pittsford-Palmyra Road for a church building which opened in 1988. By their 25th anniversary in 2008, the church had nearly 600 members and had completed an addition that tripled the size of the original building.

Because religion, like the society of which it is a part, is dynamic and diverse, new congregations and groups are always meeting and organizing. Because these groups have yet to establish a "history," they have not been included here. Nonetheless, they are an important part of the vibrant Perinton community.

Perinton Presbyterian Church

Mormon (LDS) Church

South Perinton United Methodist Church and Cemetery

Responding to the religious fervor of the "Second Great Awakening" and Methodist circuit riders, a group of residents in the vicinity of Wilkinson Road met to hold religious services in the local schoolhouse, where two of them, John and William Wells, also established a church school. Two Baptist ministers, John Rose and James Woolsey, reportedly officiated at these early meetings. The group called themselves the "South Perinton Methodist Episcopal Society" and formally organized in February 1837. The church membership book records that Susan Wilkinson, age fifteen, was the first person to join on that February date. She was joined by Mary Wilkinson, John and Joseph Wilkinson, Mary, wife of Joseph, and Lorenzo and Martha Woolsey. Other charter members included the Wells, Snedeker, Rose, Wing, Mosher, and Cline families, all of whom lived in the area.

South Perinton United Methodist Church in the snow

In 1839 Nicholas Mosher transferred a parcel of land on Wilkinson Road to church trustees George Wing, Isaac Snedeker, John Cline, and Nathan Comstock. They built a small Greek Revival building in front of the South Perinton Cemetery, and dedicated it on October 19, 1837. The church itself was but a single room, sparsely furnished and heated by a box stove. Early trustees included John Rose, William Potter, Lorenzo Woolsey, and John and James Wilkinson. In 1839, Joseph Wilkinson paid off a remaining mortgage balance of $1,000. The church shared a pastor with a Methodist church in Victor until 1859, when it affiliated with Macedon Center, a connection which continues today.

The church experienced significant growth in the late 1860's as a result of another religious revival. Forty-five new members joined the church when they were baptized in nearby White Brook, "four preferring the rite of baptism by immersion, two by pouring, and the balance by sprinkling." To accommodate the larger congregation, a two-story Italianate addition to the front of the building provided a vestibule, a bell tower, and an upper room for the Sunday School. In 1894 an organ was purchased at a cost of somewhat over $100, a sum raised by the Epworth League through such fund raisers as lawn parties and ice cream socials. Pliny Sexton donated a piece of property which was used to build "a fine row of sheds" for horses and buggies. The sheds were built and dedicated in 1896. In 1909 new concrete steps were added.

This is a picture of the choir of the South Perinton Methodist church of 45 years ago. Standing: Mr. and Mrs. Henry Cline. Seated, left to right: Mitchell Wilson, deceased; Bertha Bowerman Stevens, deceased; Minnie Wilkinson Wilson, now living at Arcadia, Calif.; and Cora Pannell, now living at 555 Averill Avenue, Rochester. FHM 2/7

Continued growth led to the addition of a kitchen and dining annex in 1915. A bell for the tower was given by

John Woolsey in memory of his parents around the same time. Memorial stained glass windows were added in 1936 and dedicated to Lorenzo and Martha Woolsey; Robert and Helen Wilson; Mitchell, Sara, and Lewis Wilson; Earl and Eliza Marquis; E. Augusta Woolsey; Charles and Catherine Blazey; and Charles J. Blazey. A carillon was dedicated in 1961. Another addition was built in 2001 to accommodate the increasing size of the congregation. Old oil lamps (now electrified), original benches, and an embossed tin ceiling in the entrance hall as well as in the sanctuary, serve as reminders of the past. Despite many updates and on-going maintenance, however, the church has managed to retain many of its original features as well as its historic ambiance.

South Perinton Methodist Church on Wilkinson Road was a center of community life in the nineteenth century, providing not only religious services, but also Sunday School classes, choir, youth groups, lectures, ice cream socials, and even meetings to scrape lint for Civil War bandages. Evidently, the church also had an influence on other area activities, as Lorenzo Woolsey's diary states that "There was horse racing, ball playing and card playing in front of where the church service was held, but through the efforts of a few zealous Christian families and the Rev. T. J. Champion, a Methodist minister from Victor, a revival was the result of changing these conditions."

South Perinton Cemetery

Over the years the parish has been led by many dedicated pastors. Jonathan Benson served as the first minister. William R. Benham was pastor during the revivals of the 1840's when the church gained a number of new members. The Rev. John Cline, who was born in Victor and was married to Phebe Wilkinson, daughter of charter members Joseph and Mary, was the Sunday School Superintendent and an assistant minister for over fifty years, from the 1850's to the end of the century and had a significant impact on Methodism in the area. He served not only the South Perinton church, but was instrumental in the formation of Fairport's First Methodist Church. For three years in the 1870's he rode into the village of Fairport to minister to that new congregation. Most pastors served for a period of two to three years; however, the Rev. John MacGuidwin served for fourteen years, from 1917 to 1931 and the Rev. Donald Turk was with the parish for nine years.

This church also has the distinction of being the only church in Perinton to have an adjacent cemetery. One of first people to be buried there was Thomas Richardson, a Revolutionary War veteran, who died in 1813. War of 1812 burials include Jeremiah Richardson and Aldophus Aldrich. Civil War veterans include Stephen Austin, killed at Winchester, Virginia; Lewis Smith, wounded at the Wilderness; Egbert Hart and John Harrison, both of the 33rd New York; and Reuben Crosby, a prisoner at Andersonville. John Pannell, after whom nearby Pannell Road is named, is buried there, as is the Rev. John Cline. Members of a number of the founding families of the church, including the Wilkinson, Snedeker, Woolsey, and Mosher families, also have plots in the cemetery.

The South Perinton Historic District preserves a church and a cemetery in a lovely and unique rural setting which is central to the history of Perinton as an agricultural community and to the social history of this part of the country. The church is also a vital part of twenty-first century Perinton as it continues to be an active and thriving congregation.

Perinton Center Cemetery

The earliest burial plots in the Perinton area were probably along the canal or the overland routes or on the family farm. Most of these early areas have been lost, their wooden or stone markers rotted or crumbled and the land built over. They were referred to as "God's Acre" or the "Church Yard" or the "Burial Ground" long before they were termed cemeteries (which means "sleeping place"). According to former Perinton historian Helen Butler, there were three early burial grounds in Perinton of which there is no longer any trace. One was located on the southwest corner of Ayrault and Turk Hill Roads on land that was originally owned by the Slocum family. Tradition has it that they buried five of their children there. After the Ellsworth family acquired the property, another source referred to it as the "slave cemetery," because apparently some slaves had been buried there. As late as the 1920's there were around sixteen stones still left at the site. Another site was reportedly located on Roselawn Avenue in the Village of Fairport. It was called "Peter's Burying Ground." A third lost site was located at Furman and County Line Roads.

Perinton Center Cemetery

One of the earliest of Perinton's extant pioneer cemeteries, Perinton Center Cemetery, is located on Ayrault Road (formerly Wapping Road) high on a knoll across from Martha Brown School. The land, approximately one acre, was deeded by Lyman Barker in 1813 to the cemetery trustees, among them Jesse Perrin, Samuel Bennett, and Abner Wight. Local legend says that Jesse Perrin helped clear the land. The cemetery is still active, so it is possible to see gravestones that reflect over 200 years of burial customs as well as Perinton history. The stones are of various materials, some very eroded and unreadable, some very clear with long inscriptions, and others inscribed with symbols that were popular during the Victorian Era such as the willow tree, a dove, or a hand pointing to heaven. There are graves of those who fought in the Revolution, the Civil War, and the two World Wars.

The earliest gravestone in the cemetery is that of Hollister Perrin, son of Jesse and Abigail, who died as an infant in 1797. The body probably was moved from the family farm on Moseley Road to the cemetery sometime after 1813. Both of Hollister's parents, Jesse and Abigail, are buried with their son. Charles Arnold, one of Perinton's pioneer Quaker settlers, is buried there. One of his family members, Isaac, owned and ran Arnold's Tavern still standing on the northwest corner of Ayrault and Turk Hill Roads.

Members of the Eaton family who moved to Perinton in 1810 and bought the Glover Perrin farm are buried there. Stephen was Postmaster, Overseer of Highways, a juror, and a Revolutionary War veteran. Lucy, his wife, was one of the founders of the Congregational Church. They are joined by Ransom, their son, who died at the age of twenty-one.

The view south from the cemetery looks out over land that was owned by the Ellsworth and Hannan families, a number of whom are buried in this place. The most impressive stone in the Ellsworth plot is that of Lincoln Byron Ellsworth (1862-1941) which is engraved with information not only about him, but also about his family. Lincoln was a farmer and an inventor who built one of the town's first steam engines and who was well known for his work on the development of the bicycle. Lincoln's grandfather, William Pratt, clan patriarch, industrialist and banker, grandmother Irena Cady, teacher and designer of early water power mills, and his father, James, and mother Mary Theresa Yale are also in the family plot. Among the many other Ellsworths is Deva (1895-1925), a musician who toured with several bands and also served in World War I as a member of America's Ladies Military Band.

The Ellsworth and Hannan families are related through marriage. Lincoln's wife was Jessie Julia MacMillan, daughter of James and Susan Ann Hannan MacMillan. Susan's parents were James and Lucretia Packard Hannan. Lucretia was known as an excellent horsewoman who taught school before her marriage and move from Egypt to a farm at the intersection of Route 31 and 250. Lucretia's father, Cyrus, was an innkeeper in Egypt before becoming Perinton's first Supervisor. Their son, Jesse, was a Perinton Supervisor, Chairman of the Monroe County Board of Supervisors, and ran the family farm. All their graves may be found in Center Cemetery.

Visitors to this still-active cemetery should be sure to read the gravestone inscriptions and note the ages, enjoy the view south, and try to imagine what is was like nearly 200 years ago when this "God's Acre" was cleared.

Egypt's Mason Road Cemetery

On Mason Road near the center of the hamlet of Egypt is a small old cemetery fronted by a white fence. Although many of the stones are still readable, others are worn, some are broken, and judging from the empty areas, many are missing. Land for the cemetery was given by the Ramsdell family who were among the first settlers to come to Egypt in the early 1800's because of its fertile and well watered land. In 1816, the year "without a summer," the fertility of the land was proven when, alone among many areas, Egypt's corn crop was plentiful. According to some sources, that was how Egypt acquired its name – after the land to which the Old Testament Hebrews had gone for food.

Not only was Egypt an area of fertile farms, but it was also halfway between Canandaigua and Rochester on the main east-west stage route, and as such was a logical place for taverns, inns, stores, and liveries to be built. Of the three well-known taverns in the hamlet, Cyrus Packard's was the site of Perinton's first town meetings, Oliver Loud's served as a polling place, a post office and a courtroom, and Olney Staples' was the largest, providing a stable and a change of horses. The thriving community included a number of businesses, a school, a church, and by 1828, the Mason Road Cemetery.

Thomas Ramsdell and his family, Quakers who had moved to the area in 1802 and donated land for the cemetery, had homes and farms on both Pittsford-Palmyra and Mason Roads. Both houses are still standing, and the Mason Road house is said to have been a stop on the Underground Railroad. Although they gave the land for the cemetery and many of their relatives are buried there, many of the Ramsdells themselves are buried in the Friends' Cemetery in Farmington.

Mason Road Cemetery

The first burial at the Mason Road Cemetery was that of Lucy Ramsdell Lapham, Thomas's daughter, who died in childbirth at the age of thirty-four in 1827. Her husband, Fayette Lapham, worked as a millwright on the Rochester Erie Canal aqueduct and ran a foundry in Egypt that manufactured the popular "Egypt plow." He also owned extensive land in the hamlet and was a leading citizen, active as a member of the Board of Trustees of Fairport's Methodist Church and a charter member of the Fairport Masonic Lodge. Fayette and their son (La)Fayette are buried with Lucy.

Nine members of the Bortle family rest in Mason Road Cemetery. They are descendants of Lucy Lapham Bortle (Lucy and Fayette's daughter). Their gravestones hint of several tragic stories over the years. Leonard died as an infant in

1926; Gordon died in 1942 at age thirteen, apparently as a result of a bicycle accident. According to sources, Robert was killed in an auto accident in 1966, and his son Jonathan was killed in Vietnam in 1969.

The graves of Oliver Loud, the well-known innkeeper, and his family can be found on Mason Road. He ran a sawmill and a store in the hamlet and served his community as a School Inspector and Commissioner, a Fence Viewer, and Overseer of Highways. In addition he published a popular weather almanac. His wife, Charlotte, and his children Charles, Cullen, and Susan are buried with him.

Solomon Aldrich, a local landowner, community activist, and patriarch of the Aldrich clan, is buried on Mason Road along with his wife Susan, his son George's wife Mary, his grandson Josiah, and his wife Samantha. The family farmed a large area of land around what is today Aldrich Road.

Eight members of the Wood family are interred in this country cemetery. David Wood moved to Perinton after fleeing from the British in Niagara County during the War of 1812. He purchased land from the Ramsdell family, built a log cabin, cleared land, and left his family a "good farm" when he died in 1844. His wife Margaret, sons David and Jonathan, and their wives Emily and Sarah are buried with him, as are his grandsons Byron and George.

Mason Road Cemetery is unique among Perinton's cemeteries because it includes a "Potter's Field." Usually in the nineteenth century a community would set aside an area in one of the local cemeteries for the burial of transients, vagrants, and the poor. This area is along the eastern boundary of the Mason Road Cemetery. The most recent example of the use of the Potter's Field occurred in 1985 when unidentified skeletal remains, which had been unearthed at an excavation site, were reinterred at Mason Road in an unmarked grave.

On this quiet parcel of land, overlooking both farmland and subdivision, visitors might reflect on how the past and the present, as well as the known and the unknown, have been brought together in this small country cemetery.

Schummers' Cemetery

On Fairport Road, west of Island Valley golf course, on the corner of Dell Road, set off by a split rail fence, is another of Perinton's pioneer burial grounds: Schummers' Cemetery. This is a one-acre tract of land that was given to the Town of Perinton by the Northrup family. According to sources, around 1810 Isaiah Northrup and his brother Andrew, settled on a large tract of land west of Fairport, built a house and a sawmill on Thomas Creek, and opened for business. His land extended from Baird Road at Thomas Creek down to Fairport Road. Although Andrew married and moved further west, and another brother died soon after arriving in Fairport, other Northrups came and settled, including a Dr. E. Northrup who apparently served the community as a physician for twenty years. Six members of the Northrup family are buried in the cemetery: Isaiah (1817, aged 74), Isaiah (1819, aged 40), Lewis (1853, aged 72), Mary (1817, aged 71), Rebecca (1863, aged 80), and Sally (1823, aged 14). The burial plot was subsequently named Schummers after the Fred Schummers family who farmed an extensive area around the cemetery at the turn of the twentieth century. Curiously, there are no Schummers buried in the cemetery.

Schummers' Cemetery

Schummers' Cemetery records burials from 1817 to 1928. Over that period of time, and continuing to the present, burial practices have changed significantly. In early times, there were no funeral directors or undertakers. Often a local woman would take charge of preparing the body while the family dug the grave. The body was washed, wrapped in a shroud, a linen sheet dipped in wax, and lowered into the grave, which was probably not more than two or three feet deep. With the advent of sawmills came the regular use of caskets or coffins. Local furniture makers would often serve as undertakers, providing caskets, as did livery stable owners who could also furnish a hearse. In the 1868 Fairport directory, Jared Newman, Ed Kellogg and C. Howe are listed as manufacturers of furniture and also as undertakers. The widespread use of embalming, which developed after the Civil War, made possible the practice of having the body lie in state in the home or the church. The front parlor, often reserved for events like funerals and weddings, would have been decorated with much black crepe. With the increase in smaller homes without a convenient room to set aside for funerals, the need arose for funeral parlors. In the 1908 Fairport Old Home Week booklet, Henry Relyea advertised as undertaker, and George Esten and the Worden Brothers advertised their monument businesses. In 1929 Clinton Emery Sr. and Flor Malone purchased Henry Steiger's funeral business, which he had run from his home, and the Van Alst home on South Main Street, and established the first recognized funeral parlor in Fairport. David Doser runs the establishment today. In 1930 Dr. Fox sold his home next to the Town Hall to Victor J. Tischer and H. F. VanHorn for a funeral home. That business is continued today by Richard Keenan.

There are about seventy-two identifiable stones in Schummers' cemetery, but the site has many open spaces, most likely due to missing stones, as the last recorded burial, that of Sybil Hazen, was in 1928. According to one source, at least ten stones that were there in the 1930's are missing today. In some cases, the stones are decorated with symbols that were popular during the mid to late nineteenth century and early twentieth century or with a brief verse; however, in this cemetery, most have only the names and dates. Graves of the early settlers in the area, the Northrups, Turrells, and Rowells, can be found in Schummers. The six Northrup graves are easily readable. One of the two Isaiahs, Mary, and Rebecca lived into their seventies and eighties, while Sally's grave serves as a reminder that people were often struck down in their youth. Mary Northrup is the earliest recorded burial in the cemetery. Her stone also refers to her as the "consort," or spouse, of Isaiah. Similarly a stone might refer to a woman as a "relict" which is an obsolete term for widow or one who has been left behind. Two of the four Turrell/Turrill graves are damaged or missing. The two Rowell graves are set together with the names and dates and the notation "Mother" and "Father."

The Treadwell family came from Connecticut and had several members who served in the Civil War. Delia's grave notes that she was born in Connecticut in 1805. David served with the Connecticut militia and Orson with the 8th New York Cavalry. G. E. Treadwell's grave merely states "War 1861-65" while Isaiah, David and Delia's son, "died at Chattanooga in the service of his country."

Throughout the cemetery the stones of Civil War Veterans are often marked with a small bronze star with "G.A.R" on it. Veterans of all wars usually are marked with a small flag. Of poignant note in most old cemeteries are the gravesites of children and young people. The stone of Nellie Louise Babcock, who died at the age of five is engraved with the verse "Sleep on sweet baby...." Engraved on eleven month old Laura Aldrich's grave is "We miss thee" and a spray of flowers. Another grave says simply "Our Baby." On Josiah Ashley's grave is the phrase "Gone but not forgotten." He died at the age of twenty-three. In family plots, there will often be a stone that says simply "Mother" or "Father," and in the case of the Bucher plot, "Ellen" and "Emily."

Imagine this cemetery, which is one of Perinton's designated landmarks, in an earlier time with no busy main road and just the big trees and the surrounding farmland. The graves hold many silent stories.

Bushnell's Basin Cemetery

Linking the present to the past in one of Perinton's early hamlets, Bushnell's Basin, is the small pioneer cemetery on Route 96 just east of Garnsey Road. This early burial ground, along with the school that stood between it and the road, and the white frame church that still stands in the Basin, formed the nucleus of this community. Bushnell's Basin, first settled in 1812, boomed with the construction of the Erie Canal.

The peaceful burial spot, once shaded by many trees, is the resting place for over two hundred Perinton residents, many of them war veterans and prominent contributors to the development of Perinton. The cemetery has a Victorian flavor. Although some stones are missing, most of the remaining ones are of marble and many have high quality carving. Carvings of a willow tree, a finger pointing to heaven, a dove, an urn, or a grieving figure were commonly used gravestone symbols of Victorian era mourning. The willow tree, first used in ancient times as a sign of mourning, signifies nature's lament. A severed tree branch indicates mortality, while a sprouting branch promises life everlasting. A finger pointing upward means heavenly reward, faith, and the promise of ascension to heaven. Angels also signify ascension. The dove, often found on children's graves, represents Christian constancy, devotion, and purity, and can be related to the Noah's ark story. A lamb, also found on children's graves, means innocence. Various fruits such as figs and pineapples, mean prosperity and eternal life, while flowers refer to the frailty of life and mortality. On the other hand, a garland symbolizes victory. The anchor is an ancient Christian symbol and also signifies hope. Doors or columns signify heavenly entrance. A skull, sometimes with wings, often found on early New England gravestones, symbolizes mortality, the wings indicating the flight of the soul from mortal mankind. All the symbols, however simple or elaborate, are attempts to express a range of human emotions from grief to the certainty of eternal rewards.

Bushnell's Basin Cemetery, as is true of many older community burial grounds, is a place where the story of the area unfolds. The first burial was that of Clarissa Richardson, who died in 1827 at the age of twenty-five. Although the written records end with 1937, the most recent gravestone is that of George Dickens, who died in 1956. Veterans' graves include those of Amos Woodin, who fought in the Revolution, Jared Frisbee, who fought in the War of 1812, and a number of Civil War soldiers: Otis Rosebrook, George Hill, Robert Hill, and Captain David Hill. George, Robert and David were brothers.

Twenty-one members of the Collins family are listed in the cemetery record. They owned property to the east on Route 96, once called Ketchum Road, and built the elegant Greek Revival house at number 1041. When Harskeline Collins owned the house, there is some evidence that it operated as a stop on the Underground Railway.

The Ketchums, after whom Route 96 was once named, lived down the road from the Collins family, and owned three hundred acres. Around 1850 they built the farmhouse that is now #1433. Four Ketchums are buried in the cemetery, including Joseph, who originally purchased the property.

Bushnell's Basin Cemetery

Gould and Elias Richardson managed and then probably owned the tavern that was built in 1818 and eventually took their name. Elias, his daughter Susan, and Gould's wife Clarissa, mentioned above, are all interred at Bushnell's Basin.

The Joseph McCoord family moved to the Basin area in the 1860's and settled on a seventy-five acre farm just north of Garnsey Road. The McCoords raised oats and rye, but their main crop was apples that they processed in a cider mill near the site of today's Hess service station. By 1902 the family owned property in the central Basin, both where Hitching Post Plaza is and across the street, as well as one hundred eight acres on Austin Road in the vicinity of Garnsey Road. McCoord burials are indicative of the fragility of life. Joseph G. was three days old when he died, Malachi was two, and Joseph F. drowned in the Colorado River at age twenty-one.

Fifteen members of the VanNess family are listed in the burial records. The family owned several hundred acres in the area along Ketchum Road /Route 96. One of Perinton's designated landmarks, 24 LaSalle Parkway, was built in the late 1850's or early 1860's by either John or Calvin VanNess. The VanNess family had ties to both the Ketchums and Hannans, two of Perinton's significant pioneer families.

A cemetery can reveal family stories. Illness may take more than one family member at a time, like Emily Collins who died in March 1835 at the age of one, and her brother Hiram who died in April at age three. Three or four members of one family may go off to the same war like the Hill brothers. The closeness (or size) of families is evident when fifteen or more of its members are buried in the same cemetery. Not only are there numerous graves of children, but there are also those of people like Louise Dickens and John Lash who managed to survive childhood and childbirth and disease and war to live into their nineties.

A little imagination and bit of quiet time to reflect on the lives of those who are buried at Bushnell's Basin not only helps to link the past to the present, but also makes real the stories that are told there.

Elmwood Cemetery

In the northeast quadrant of Perinton, at the corner of Carter and Furman Roads is a neatly laid out burial ground that once was graced by towering elm trees, and thus was named Elmwood Cemetery. Farmers first settled the area in the early nineteenth century, but settlement really boomed with the coming of the Erie Canal. Carter Road, Fellows Road and Fairport-Webster Road became the main north-south arteries for farmers bringing their produce to market in the growing canal town of Fairport.

Unlike other populated areas in Perinton, this northeast section had no "center," but settlement did bring additional houses, farms, a school, and the cemetery. Elmwood is a neighborhood burial ground where the settlers and farmers of the area are interred. The cemetery was laid out around 1820 when the Conklin family dedicated an acre of land on the corner of Carter and Furman Roads for that purpose. In 1843 it was expanded by a land grant of 2.62 acres from the Carter family. Elmwood was originally surrounded by a wrought-iron fence, which together with the trees and plantings, was typical of a Victorian cemetery of the period. Among the over 700 gravesites can be found those of early area families such as the Woolseys, Furmans, Estens, Carters, and Talmans.

Elmwood Cemetery

The Woolsey family were early residents of Carter Road. Richard moved to Perinton in 1817 or 1818. He served his community as an Overseer of Highways and a Fence Viewer and was one of the first to be buried in Elmwood after he was killed in 1821 by a falling log in the process of "raising" a distillery on Carter Road. Richard, Jr., his mother, his wife, and several other Woolseys are buried with Richard, Sr.

The owner of "Pleasant View Farm," George W. Esten, and his family are buried in Elmwood. The Esten family built their farmhouse at 4394 Carter Road, also a Perinton designated landmark.

Both the Carter and Furman families have members in Elmwood Cemetery. Miles and Elizabeth Carter came to Perinton in 1830 and built a farm on the west side of Carter Road just south of Furman Road. The Furmans came in 1835 and began farming an eighty acre parcel on what would become known as Furman Road. In 1953 the family was honored as "Century Farmers," as they had worked the same farm for over one hundred years.

A number of Talmans came to Perinton in the early 1800's, settling along Whitney, Wakeman, and Budlong Roads. They built substantial houses, raised oats, barley, corn, and potatoes, and supported herds of dairy cows and sheep on their 350 acres, while also serving their community as Town Supervisors, School Trustees, Overseers of Highways, and Fence Viewers. Both Darius and Isaac, as well as many members of their families, are buried in the local cemetery.

Elmwood is still an active cemetery with over seven hundred gravesites that are maintained by the members of its cemetery association. The setting and the familiar community names among the markers, like Knapp, Huber, Fellows, Plumb, and Warner, along with Talman, Carter, and Esten, are lasting reminders of Perinton's history and its rural past.

St. Mary's Cemetery

The first Roman Catholic masses in Fairport were celebrated in 1849 and by the 1860's the congregation of the Church of the Assumption of Our Lady was worshipping in a large wooden building on High Street. In another ten years, the growing congregation had built a substantial brick structure on the same street. This thriving community was in need of a consecrated burial ground. An area Catholic cemetery on Pinnacle Road had opened in 1839, and some of the German Catholic churches had their own cemeteries, but the need for more space was apparent not only in the wider diocese, but also locally. In 1870 Bishop McQuaid purchased land for a "well arranged and properly conducted cemetery" on Charlotte Boulevard in Rochester, which was consecrated in 1871 as Holy Sepulchre Cemetery. The next year a Catholic cemetery was established on a secluded hillside off of Turk Hill Road in Perinton.

St. Mary's Cemetery, run by Assumption of Our Lady Parish in the Village of Fairport, was dedicated in 1872 by Bishop McQuaid. The land for the cemetery lay between farms owned by Frank Traw (Trau) and J. R. Murphy, and may have been donated by the former. The cemetery has always been cared for by dedicated members of the parish. One gentleman, Peter Doyle, spent countless hours mowing, trimming, and developing the site for over thirty years.

The first burials in the cemetery were members of the Brennan family, three of whom died in 1872: Maria who was twenty-three, Sarah, forty-eight, and Anna Marie, ten weeks. Multiple deaths in a year and the deaths of infants and children are but two of the observations that can be made from reading through the cemetery lists and reading gravestones. In the Biracree family, five of nine plots are those of infants and children. On the other hand, there is no lack of gravestones showing ages well into the 70's and 80's. Guiseppe LaPietra died at age eighty and Bridget Lucas lived to eighty-eight. If one could survive childhood, childbirth, and workplace accidents, the chances of a long life increased.

A large majority of the families in St. Mary's are Irish or Italian, reflecting the immigration pattern of the United States as a whole during the nineteenth century. The Irish came first with the canal and the subsequent expansion of the area. By the latter part of the century, the factories of the newly industrialized towns and cities were attracting more and more people from eastern and southern Europe. A number of St. Mary's burial records note births in County Kilkenny while others simply

St. Mary's Roman Catholic Cemetery

note Ireland or Italy or Germany. Many of the families are large, sometimes having fifteen or twenty burials in a family plot. The Burns, Murphy, and Kennedy family plots have over twenty graves each. Many of the Irish and Italian surnames, such as Ryan and Kennelly and Finnigan; DiRisio and Fiandacca and Pomponio are familiar in the town and village. Although first names differ from generation to generation, a core of names seem to last, like Catherine, Michael, Thomas, Mary, Joseph, and John; others, like Antonio or Giovanni, have been Anglicized; others are rarely seen today, like Aloysius or Agatha or Erasmo. At least one surname was changed form Pidnikowski to Pierce.

Visits to Perinton cemeteries are travels in history. Pioneers and immigrants, veterans from our wars, founders of businesses and community activists, educators and politicians, children and the very old – they are all there. St. Mary's, a quiet, secluded hilltop cemetery, is one stop on the journey.

Greenvale Cemetery

In 1825 Oliver and Ann Tomlinson sold John Peters, Abisha Goodell, and Solomon Ralph land for a "burying ground." The cost was $40. The new burial ground was located on East Church Street between the road and the canal and was the first one in the growing village of Fairport. Over the next several decades, Allen Ayrault and the Thomas Slocum family added to Greenvale Cemetery until it reached its present size of over two acres.

The stones in Greenvale are of many kinds, reflecting the nearly 200 years of the burial ground's existence. Throughout the 1800's, grave markers, which from the 1820's were made of rectangular pieces of marble, limestone, or sandstone, with a variety of top designs, gradually become more elaborate, often including relatively long inscriptions describing the person's character or position in the community. By 1850 Fairport had its own marble worker. W. H. Vance had his marble works near Main Street and did many stones of that period. Between the Civil War and the turn of the century, the use of obelisks increased. The Sears catalog offered a metal "stone", at least one of which, that of Omer Wilcox, can be found in Greenvale. The post-1920 stones are usually of a lower profile and may be polished. Gravestone lettering is usually either incised or raised, and a picture or a symbol is usually included. Due to erosion, weathering, and pollution, many of the older stones are unreadable.

Greenvale Cemetery

Greenvale Cemetery, having opened in 1825, reflects the life of the town and the village over nearly 200 years. The first burial was that of Salmon Mallett who died April 7, 1825. He was one of the village's original settlers and one of the first trustees of the cemetery. Also buried at that time were three of Peter Ripley's children, who died between 1813 and 1822, and were originally buried in a family plot near Ripley's Mill on North Main Street. Another early burial was that of Col. John Peters, one the nine men who owned all the land that would become Fairport Village. Col. Peters owned a tavern near the present Turk Hill Road Bridge and probably owned a fleet of canal boats. After speculating in the grain market, and losing his fortune in the panic of 1839, Peters drowned himself in his well.

Among the over 1,000 men, women, and children buried in Greenvale Cemetery are farmers, public servants, veterans, and entrepreneurs who contributed significantly to the life and growth of Perinton and Fairport. Farmers include Jeremiah Baker, who owned a farm at the intersection of Turk Hill and East Church Streets and for whom Baker Road (now Turk Hill Road) was named for a time. Allen Ayrault and his family, after whom Ayrault Road is named, owned a large stock farm at the present location of Fairport High School. A member of his family also owned a home on East Church Street. Milton and Clarissa Budlong were prominent farmers in the southeast portion of Perinton, hence Budlong Road (now Perinton Parkway). They were also among the founders of Raymond Memorial Baptist Church (today's Fairport Community Baptist Church).

Among the veterans buried at Greenvale is Col. Simeon Howard, who fought in the Civil War and returned to Fairport as a businessman. Larry Wilcox was an early settler and a veteran of the War of 1812. Dr. George Price, a prominent local physician for over sixty years, served as a director of an army hospital during World War I.

Fletcher Defendorf, Charlotte Clapp, Elizabeth Price, and Charles Dickinson all served the community in a variety of ways. Defendorf served as President of the Village of Fairport, Town Supervisor, New York State Assemblyman, and delegate to the 1890 Democratic Convention. He was also a member of the Fairport School Board, the first Water Board and the first Municipal Commission. Charlotte Clapp, active in business and professional areas, was the Town Clerk for thirty-one years and the Town Historian for thirty-four years. Elizabeth Price, a member of the Albany Library College's first class to graduate women, was a school board member and library board member for thirty-five years. Charles Dickinson, who moved his house from Fullamtown to 10 East Church Street, served as Town Clerk, Supervisor, and Highway Commissioner, in addition to running a successful mercantile business. Both of his daughters, Julia and Emma, who were missionaries, and who also started Fairport's first library, a subscription library, are buried there as well.

George Taylor, Thomas Hulburt, and George Filkins contributed to Fairport's growth and development. George Taylor, who died in 1909, ran a patent medicine business on North Main Street. He developed and sold "Taylor's Oil of Life," which was designed to cure any and all ills of both man and beast. Apparently Buffalo Bill Cody used it on his horses. Taylor also is responsible for starting the first Fairport newspaper. Both Thomas Hulburt and George Filkins were developers. Hulbert developed the land bordered by West Church Street, Hulburt Avenue, and Potter Place. Filkins developed George and Filkins Streets and South Avenue. He also built three charming Italianate homes on South Main Street.

This large village cemetery, with its variety of markers and numbers of town and village "movers and shakers," offers a significant look into the history and heritage of our community.

Mt. Pleasant Cemetery

"A few of the enterprising men of Fairport have been much interested for a few months past in grading and laying into lots a most lovely plot of ground, a little south of the village, for a new cemetery....The grounds are on an elevation that overlooks the village and surrounding country, and even some parts of the city of Rochester are seen from the summit." – *Union and Advertiser, September 13, 1865.* In such a way was Fairport's Mt. Pleasant Cemetery founded in 1865. The 250 lots were available at a cost of $22 each.

By the middle of the nineteenth century, burial customs were changing. With the advent of new embalming techniques, which arose out of the needs of the Civil War, it was no longer crucial to have a rapid burial. New wealth, the rise of a significant middle class with more leisure time, and concerns over health, coupled with the new standard of mourning set by Queen Victoria all played roles in the changes. Many more people could now afford grave markers and even mausoleums, all with the requisite symbolic carving, and were looking for a more rural, quiet, and peaceful resting place for their loved ones to replace the often crowded, noisy, and unsanitary burial sites found in town.

The new Victorian cemeteries were laid out as gardens; beauty was intentionally planned with curved roads and pathways, trees, flowers and other plantings. When possible, they were located on a hill with a view and with knolls and valleys that were conducive to Sunday strolls and picnics, as well as quiet mourning.

Etching of the DeLand plot in Mt. Pleasant Cemetery

Mt. Pleasant is clearly in the Victorian mode. It is set on a hill, and was originally accessible by a curving road from East Church Street. The entrance was through a wrought iron gate complemented by a similar fence that surrounded the area. The pathways still wind through the plots and there are lots of trees, which provide shady spots to be quiet or to mourn. When the cemetery was dedicated in September of 1865, a plea was also made for "two thousand dollars to erect a monument in the memory of the men of this town who have given their lives in their country's struggle...this seems to be just and fitting." By the following November, the granite column, carved with the names of those who had died, had been erected and dedicated. It still stands.

There are a number of family plots with ten to fifteen members. One of the most significant is that of the DeLand family. Marked by an obelisk and individual stones are twenty-one members of the family, including Daniel and Minerva, the founders of the DeLand Chemical Co., and Henry, builder of the Green Lantern Inn and founder of DeLand, Florida and his wife Sarah. The Benedict family plot has sixteen identified stones and five unknown ones. Gould Benedict, who fought in the Civil War, Elmer, who was active in local politics, and Hannah, who served the sick, the poor and the needy for most of her sixty-five years are among those buried here. The Bown family plot has ten sites. George Bown was a carriage maker who built one of the major commercial blocks in the old village.

Familiar names can be found among the many interred at Mt. Pleasant. Andrew Deal, a former publisher of the *Fairport Herald*, is buried there, as are Byron and Bedent Baird, who owned large amounts of property in the Baird Road area, and Smith Morey, who owned a clothing establishment on Main Street. George L. C. Seeley, another Fairport businessman and builder, is interred here, as are members of the DeNise, Knapp, and Sperbeck families.

Space does not permit listing more names, but the cemetery with its hilltop location, trees, and winding paths is a quiet place to walk and to remember those who were here before – just as the Victorians had planned.

- X -
Recreation & Leisure

Recreation and leisure in Perinton and Fairport encompass a variety of activities. Service and educational groups include Rotary, Masons, Lions, Grange, Scout groups, and groups interested in researching history. The community's many parks provide opportunities to play baseball, hike, picnic, swim, or go kayaking or canoeing. And at one time there was the opportunity to attend either of two movie theaters.

Fairport Historical Club

On Thursday evening, October 23, 1884, a group of women met at the home of Miss Lena Newman and elected officers for a club whose aim would be to educate and to entertain. That club would eventually be known as the Fairport Historical Club. During the latter part of the nineteenth century, educated women were seeking outlets for their knowledge and for their desire to participate in the life of their communities. As a result there was an increase in the growth of women's clubs, among them our Fairport Historical Club, one of the oldest in the state. This club is distinct from the Perinton Historical Society which was formed in 1935 and runs the Fairport Historical Museum.

Originally, regular weekly meetings were originally held on Wednesdays from 7 to 9:30 p.m. and were to be both "entertaining and instructive." Within a couple of years, however, the meetings were moved to 4 p.m. on Thursdays. Dues were $.25. At their first few meetings, the members discussed possible names for the group choosing "Roundabout Club" or the "RAC" and rejecting "Yellow Plush" and "Butterfly" Club. The first officers included Miss Newman as President, Mrs. Birdsey as 1st Vice President, Mrs. Parce as 2nd Vice President, Miss Stella DeLand as Secretary/Treasurer, and Miss Nellie Jane as Librarian. New members were nominated and voted on by the membership and members were required to attend at least half the meetings or face being dropped. Husbands and brothers could be "associate members," and their names first appeared in the 1902-03 program booklet. In 1887 membership was limited to twenty-five, a constitution was written, and committees were established to deal with money and with programs. In the 1920's terms of office were limited to two years, a change that occurred after Helen DeLand had served as President for nineteen years. The name of the group was changed several times, becoming the Ladies' Historical Club in 1887 and finally the Fairport Historical Club in 1904.

Four Fairport Historical Club members, 1914
left to right: Mrs. George Mulliner, Helen DeLand, Mabel (Mrs. Yale) Parce, Charlotte Clapp

As the purpose of the club was both educational and recreational, much effort went into planning not only study programs, but also entertainment and social events. Programs in those early years were demanding and serious and were usually presented by the members themselves. From the outset, music was very important and regularly played a role in the meetings. Emphasis was also placed on having at least one gala event per season. Study topics during those early years included a series of papers given on English history, including the Druids, the Roman invasion, and the Saxon and Plantagenet kings. The group studied painters such as Rembrandt and Rubens, and composers such as Haydn and Handel. Some of the topics from the turn of the twentieth century included British and American literature, German literature and history, Italian art and history, and a "Comparative Study of the Novel." The programs were quite extensive; for example, the program for October 15, 1896, included papers on the Anglo-Saxons, Beowulf, Caedmon, Bede, King Alfred, and the Saxon Chroniclers. The study of the novel included Walter Scott, Johann Goethe, Victor Hugo, Charlotte Bronte, and Leo Tolstoy, among others. The topics turned to domestic issues as the twentieth century progressed. The programs for 1911-12 focused on "Home Life and Town Housekeeping" while those for the following year dealt with "Industrial Problems."

It could be that the programs were at times a bit too deep and strenuous because the attendance record for the early 1890's in particular was not very good. It could also be due in part to the early practice of critiquing a member's presentation. Early minutes note the existence of a critic's report whose job it was to critique the papers from the standpoint of grammar or pronunciation. That rather uncomfortable custom was soon abandoned. In any case, by the end of the 1890's attendance had improved.

Occasionally a new idea or gimmick was introduced, but the record indicates that most did not last. For example at one point everyone was to be identified by a mythological name. The only one recorded is Miss Higbie's choice of Mercury. Another time members were required to respond to roll call with an item of interest about one of the chosen topics, which included anecdotes of Abraham Lincoln, quotations from *Uncle Tom's Cabin*, Irish jokes, birds, religion, and current events. At another time, members were asked to guess the author of a quotation.

After much discussion during that first year, it was decided to hold a more informal event at the end of the season in March of 1885. It was to be a "candy-pull" and each member could invite an associate member. In 1897 the gala event was a presentation of Shakespeare's "As You Like It" by a Miss Williams from New York City. It was held in a hall on the second floor of the Bown Block on South Main Street and realized $25. The 1906 event of the season was a dinner and program. The menu included fruit salad, chicken salad, bread, tutti frutti ice cream, assorted cakes, bonbons, and coffee, while the program included toasts by members to the associate members, old friends, club work, fads, music, and civic improvement.

During the early decades of the twentieth century, the club worked to find ways to raise money that could be donated to the library and other needy organizations. In 1912 or 1913 a "Loan Exhibit" was held in the Ives' house next door to the Municipal Building. Eight rooms were furnished in the colonial manner with articles loaned by community residents. An International Bazaar held in November of 1917 was run in cooperation with the Fairport Welfare Association and was held in the Grange Hall, which was located in the Osburn House, just north of the railroad tracks. The proceeds of approximately $250 were divided between the library and the Red Cross. Other fund raisers in the 1920's, which included the publication of a club cookbook in 1929, brought in amounts ranging from $75 to $500 for library books and the library building fund.

Musical programs were regularly sponsored by the club and there was often a musical component to the regular meetings. A vocal solo by Mrs. Snow is mentioned in an 1888 program and a mandolin and guitar duet in an 1895 program. In 1902 there is a record of Smith Morey and Bruner Bown entertaining the group with a mandolin duet. The club was entertained at other times by the Susan Tompkins Orchestra from Rochester as well as the University of Rochester and Elmira glee clubs. In more recent years, the group attended a yearly musical program sponsored by the Fairport Musicale and were entertained by a Fairport High School string quartet at a Christmas tea.

The Fairport Historical Club is one of the oldest, if not the oldest continuing women's club in New York and in its over 125 years of existence has undergone a number of changes while maintaining its basic goal of educating and entertaining. Although the membership has fluctuated, the number has remained fairly stable at around thirty-five since the turn of the twentieth century. Programs are presented by the members and also by outside speakers. While the programs may not be as rigorous as those from the turn of the last century, the members continue to maintain a high level of intellectual curiosity and interest in the world at large. The club continues its interest in and support of the library and also the Fairport Historical Museum, giving yearly gifts, and follows the custom of donating a book to the library in memory of members who have died.

As the club continues in the twenty-first century, it is striving to adapt to a world quite different from that of its founders, but one that still depends on an educated and aware population.

Fairport Historical Club 2010

Pictured in photo: Jean Keplinger, Jean Whitney, Caren Hess, Doris Davis-Fritsch, Helen Edelman, Holly Wolf, Catherine Angevine, Pat Knapp, Liz Boorsma, Christine Fredette, Pat Wilcox, Jean Lauder, Mary Ann Cady, Priscilla Petersen, Joanne Fisher, Thelma Hammerton, Jane McComb, Nancy Slaybaugh, Helen Matthews, Kay Pearson, Wanda Ahrendsen

The Perinton Historical Society

The Perinton Historical Society was formed in 1935 "to collect and preserve relics and documents relating to the early history of the town of Perinton and its environs and to promote interest in the early history of Perinton." The initial idea was proposed at a meeting in Mrs. Clarence Moore's home. Charter members included Mrs. Clarence Moore, Mrs. Gardner Bown, Miss Charlotte Clapp, Mrs. Marjorie Merriman, Mrs. Henry Martin, Mrs. DeEtte Maurhofer, Mrs. Gertrude Miller, Mrs. George Price, and Mrs. Lucille Redhead. Marjorie Merriman was elected President.

Prospective members had to be residents of Perinton, nominated in writing, and elected by a majority of members present at any meeting of the Board of Managers. In 1936, thirteen people were invited to be members and eleven accepted the invitation. Soon, however, membership was opened to any man or woman who expressed interest in the purpose of the Society. Monthly meetings from September through May were held early on in the homes of members and subsequently at the Fairport Public Library. Dues were one dollar per year.

Every other meeting generally featured a speaker and was open to the public. In 1941, for example, the group heard Walter Vogel of Rochester speak on "How to tell Old Furniture from New," and J. S. Villere give a "very interesting lecture on the history of playing cards." In 1947 Town Historian Charlotte Clapp talked about Perinton, World War II, and Mary Jemison. In that same year, Fred Soden of Rochester presented a program on his collection of mechanical banks. Programs from the 1950's include such topics as the archeology, geology, and folklore of this region of New York, the Korean War, and Perinton's Century Farms. Over the years the Underground Railroad, the Erie Canal, the Rochester, Syracuse and Eastern Railway, early Perinton roads, Perinton landmarks and pioneers, and even urban renewal were all explored in programs presented to the Society. Alternate monthly meetings were devoted to discussing the research that Society members were engaged in. Each member worked on a committee that compiled such information as cemetery lists, land use records, family histories of early settlers, and more.

The Society offered other opportunities as well. In 1936 it held its first historical tour, which included Perinton Center Cemetery on Ayrault Road, the Ellsworth property on the corner of Turk Hill and Ayrault Roads, the Mason Road house of Gideon Ramsdell, and Staples Tavern, which stood on Pittsford-Palmyra Road in the current location of Town Centre Plaza. The tour concluded at the home of Marjorie Merriman where the participants heard a talk by Mrs. James Davis about the geology and geography of Perinton. Another tour included the DeLand Chemical Works, Mallett's Tavern (both on North Main Street), the Dickinson house at 10 East Church, the Beers house at 39 East Church Street, the Perrin homes on South Main Street, the Bushnell's Basin area, and Powder Mills Park. Members have enjoyed, at various times, displays of early American prints, a three-day exhibit of antique china and glassware, and a showing of Carl Peters' paintings. Trips to the Campbell-Whittlesey House, the Eastman House, and the Granger Homestead, and one of the earliest Erie Canal excursions were also sponsored by the Society.

In 1950 the Perinton Historical Society was formally incorporated and given a provisional charter by the Board of Regents, which empowered the Society to own property. The incorporators or Board of Trustees included Marjorie Snow Merriman, Ethel V. Mosher, Adelaide Clarke, Addis V. Adams, and J. Sheldon Fisher.

The biggest difficulty faced by the Society was finding a place to house a growing collection of artifacts and documents. Large items were stored in A.B. Hupp's barn while the rest of the collection was kept in the library loft. Meetings were moved from the library to the Potter Community Center after it was opened in 1944, but there was still no place for storage or on-going displays. It was not until 1950 that the Society seriously began to seek out a permanent home. It appeared that perhaps the recently vacated Bushnell's Basin School was going to fit the bill; however, plans to lease the building fell though and the old schoolhouse became a community center. Finally, in 1962 the Society was able to secure a small permanent home in the Crosman Community Center, which opened that year in the old East Avenue School.

Curator Dr. James Welch, along with Clayton Bridges, both long-time Perinton Historical Society members, spent the next seventeen years storing, cataloging, and exhibiting Perinton documents and artifacts in a small room on the second floor of the Crosman Building. Despite the cramped quarters, the Society continued to have meetings and exhibits and also to publish *The Perinton Papers* (1971) and *A Walking Tour of Fairport Village (1976).*

A fine opportunity presented itself to the Perinton Historical Society in 1978 when the Fairport Library moved from Perrin Street to the Village Landing. The library building, which was owned by the school district, was loaned to the village who in turn leased it to the Society. The new venture was strongly supported by Mayor Peter McDonough and Fairport Historian Bernadette McDonough, both active members of the Society.

Fairport Museum interior

After thirty-four years, the Perinton Historical Society finally had an adequate home with space to display its artifacts and books, store its documents, and hold meetings, workshops, and classes. The grand opening took place in June of 1979 with Robert Smith of West Avenue as Director; Warren Stevens as Curator, and Matson Ewell as President of the Society. Members were excited to have a place to display their collection, which they had been unable to do in the small room that they previously occupied in the Crosman Building. Artifacts that are on display include diaries, period clothing and home furnishings illustrating nineteenth century life. Other exhibits feature area businesses, schools, families, and local inventions. In addition the former library shelves hold, among many other things, land records that list the names of nearly every person who ever owned land in Perinton or Fairport.

The village of Fairport owns the building and maintains the exterior. The Society maintains the interior and pays for the utilities. In order to maintain the facility and the collection, the Society collects dues, runs a gift shop in the museum, and has held craft sales and auctions. The Society continues to sponsor a very popular house tour in the fall, which, because it is open only to dues-paying members, has been a good source of income.

In addition to house tours, the Society reaches out to the community in a variety of ways. Many of Fairport's fourth graders enjoy a program at the museum each spring where they investigate pictures, maps, and artifacts illustrating Perinton and Fairport history and hear stories about early settlers. The Peter McDonough Memorial Scholarship, requiring applicants to write an essay about local history, encourages young citizens to explore the history of the town and village. The Society publishes a newsletter which Ruth Ewell edited for over thirty years. Both Ruth and her husband, Matson, have given countless volunteer hours to the museum, helping in more ways than can be enumerated. In addition to its newsletter, the Society has published three very popular books about Perinton and Fairport history entitled *Perinton, Fairport, and the Erie Canal*, *Perinton and Fairport in the 20th Century*, and *Then & Now: Fairport and Perinton.* All of the publications have been written and compiled by Society members. A website is also available.

The museum is a natural destination for tourists interested in area history. The building itself is charming. It is in the Greek Revival style with a brick façade and a white-columned porch entrance flanked by large windows, and has gutters that are hidden in the cornices. The foyer features a mural by local artist Carl Peters depicting the development of Fairport as a canal village. The first floor houses displays, books, and files; the second floor is storage, and the basement has a meeting room. Members of the Society provide volunteer staffing. Imogene Blum was one who for many years not only was on hand to greet visitors, but also did much of the cataloging of the museum's collection.

More members than it is possible to name give generously of their time and talent to keep up the museum and its collection. Others offer help to those searching for information about homes, families, and past events.

The Society, which boasts between 200 and 300 members and its museum, is continually looking at future programs and plans that will make the museum attractive and accessible to more people. Overall, the Society members are looking toward a future that is more active and creates a higher profile for this significant and essential repository of Perinton and Fairport history.

The Elite Club

In the first decade of the twentieth century, a group of Fairport men calling themselves the "Elite Club" regularly met over F. F. Schummer's Hardware Store, which used to be located on West Avenue more or less on the site of today's Gazebo Park. Virtually nothing is known about the group except their meeting place and their names. In the photo below, they are left to right: Edward R. Brown, Sabin C. Schummers, George S. Holman, D. B. Howard, and George A. Fellows.

Elite Club, 1907

The Improved Order of Redmen

The Improved Order of Redmen, a patriotic, fraternal, and benevolent association, was established in 1834 in Baltimore to inspire "a greater love for the United States of American and the principles of American Liberty." Tracing their origins to early patriotic societies like the Sons of Liberty and the Sons of St. Tammany, they pledged to aid each other in sickness and distress and to stand together against all hazards. An early bit of verse summarizes their aims:

> "Freedom our motto,
> Toleration our aim,
> Friendship our watch word
> And Red Men our name."

The Redmen's rituals and regalia are modeled after those used by Native Americans. The Ka-Ne-Hoot Tribe No. 366 of Fairport was instituted October 4, 1897 with a membership of thirty-three which by 1908 had increase to 107 members. The Tribe met every Monday night in the Bown Block on South Main Street (site of the Village Landing).

DEPUTY GREAT SACHEM J. W. McLOUGHLIN AND STAFF
1908

Back row, left to right:—Chas. Slocum, Great Sachem; R. S. Rocheville, Great Keeper of Wampum; J. T. McCarthy, Great Mishmewa; F. M. Hyde, Great Collector of Wampum; Wm. Groat, Great Chief of Records. Front row:—John Finnegan, Great Sr. Sagamore; J. M. Bahler, Great Prophet; J. W. McLoughlin, Deputy Great Sachem; Frank Borden, Great Jr. Sagamore.

The National Grange of the Order of Patrons of Husbandry

"The Grange" was organized in 1867 as a result of Oliver Hudson Kelley's trip through the South to assess the agricultural situation after the Civil War. Seeing the need for both an economic and social organization to improve the lot of farmers, Kelley and six others formed the organization. They took the name "grange" from the Latin word for "grain," which is also related to the word "granary." Early meetings were patterned after popular fraternal groups of the times such as the Masons. The organization soon became an advocacy group for farmers, growing to over 800,000 members all over the nation by 1875. This growth was in part spurred by the economic crisis of 1873, but also because farmers were subject to the whims of the big railroad monopolies who had grown powerful with the construction of the transcontinental railroad and who were arbitrarily setting shipping rates and controlling track-side warehouses.

The concerns of the Grange, however, were not limited to railroad rates. They supported a number of Progressive Era initiatives and goals, including women's suffrage and direct election of senators. The Grange, in fact, treated both women and youth equally, requiring that four of the sixteen elected positions be held by women. In addition, the Grange had active Youth or Juvenile Granges. Over the decades, the organization lent its support to the establishment of Rural Free Delivery (of mail), the establishment of the Cooperative Extension Service, and the Farm Credit system.

Membership has vacillated over the 150 years of Grange existence. Since the turn of the twentieth century, the numbers have dropped by about forty percent and as of 2003 totaled about 300,000. The drop in numbers is in large part due to the fact that just two percent of the US population are farmers.

The Fairport Grange, 2000
Front row: (l.to r.) Marcy Ellsworth, Iona Diedrich, Fannie DeMuth, Esther Michelson
Back row: Charles McCarthy, Mary McCarthy, Harold Michelson, Jim Smith (Perinton Supervisor), Beverly Marvin, Letitia Pickering

The Fairport-Perinton Grange #467 was founded in 1883 with twelve charter members: John Zollman, Fred Warner, Addie Perkins, George Bahler, Edgar Phelps, George Slegehl, H. S. Dickens, A. F. Perkins, George March, Amelia Zollman, Eva Warner, and Amanda Dickens. At their first meeting on February 24th of that year, it was decided to meet on alternate Saturdays. They voted to "meet at Brother Warner's for the purpose of sawing wood for the hall stove" and to "pay twenty-five dollars a year for use of room." In August 1883 it was noted that they had "rented rooms from Mr. Hawkins for five years; for fifty dollars per year, the grange to fit up the rooms at their own expense." They also established a committee to look into forming an organization for the "apprehension of, and protection against, horse thieves." They were obviously successful, because such a group was indeed established.

The local grange has drawn members from not only the farming population, but also from business people and village residents. Some families have been active grangers for four generations. Family names of members that have been part of Perinton for generations include Pickering, Bown, Ellsworth, Osburn, and Marvin. Both the 50th and the 100th anniversary celebrations drew over 150 participants. They met regularly in various places in Perinton and Fairport, including the Potter house and the Osburn Hotel, until they purchased the old Egypt schoolhouse on Pittsford-Palmyra Road in 1955.

While the Grange Hall on Pittsford-Palmyra Road was sold in 1997 due to declining Grange membership, twelve to fourteen members continue to meet regularly in a restaurant once a month. The organization donates to many area charities from the Grange Hall sale proceeds. Among their many recipients are Advent House, Dollars for Scholars, the Senior Bash, and other Grange groups, including the museum in Cortland, junior Grange programs, and founder Oliver Kelley's farm in Minnesota. Each year the group gives five hundred dictionaries to Fairport's third graders. The knitting group supplies baby hats and chemo hats to both Thompson and Unity Hospitals. Although small in numbers, the Fairport Grange is anything but small in its dedication to the community.

Boy Scouting in Perinton and Fairport

Perinton and Fairport have a long history of strong involvement with the Boy Scouts. Scouting came to the United States in 1910 from England where General Robert Baden-Powell had organized an outdoor youth program for boys in 1907-08. The U.S. version was started by Chicago publisher William Boyce on February 8, 1910. At that time in the US, several other loosely-structured outdoor-oriented youth organizations were using the name "Boy Scout" and a number of other groups were using some variation of the British Scout program. Boyce's key contribution was to organize the BSA as a business. He incorporated the organization (in Washington, DC, rather than Chicago), recruited key youth professionals to design and operate the program, and provided key funding for the infant organization.

The first troop in Fairport, #1, was well-organized by 1917 as the scouts contributed significantly to the World War I home front effort. While that first troop was discontinued in 1922, it was immediately followed by Troop #2 under the leadership of Amos Sullivan, who remained as leader until 1929. The troop's three patrols met in the Brooks-Shepherd American Legion Post. Charles White was the leader of the Flying Eagle Patrol, Harold VanNorman of the Beaver Patrol, and Elmer Bills of the Pine Tree Patrol.

A May 1923 news article describes Scout activities. A "Mentally Awake" hike was scheduled where the Scout who observed the most objects on the hike would be considered "mentally awake." The schedule for "Patriotic Night" was listed and included among other items the following:

The Star Spangled Banner: sung by the Troop
The American Revolution: a brief history by Allen Steffen
America the Beautiful: sung by the Troop Quartet
Military Life: a poem by Donald Park
A tribute to Frank Marion Beaumont, a charter member of the Fairport Boy Scouts, who made the supreme sacrifice for America during the late World War (I). Scoutmaster Amos C. Sullivan
Violin Solo: Harold VanNorman
Allegiance to the American Flag: Troop

A September 1923 *Scout News* article thanked the American Legion for the use of their facility and described a meeting. "Bandaging" was the subject for instruction, where the boys learned about the uses of the roller, spiral, and spiral reverse bandages, and were given a demonstration by Charles White about the application of the "triangular bandage to the head, hands and feet." The Scout Master then gave a "blackboard talk" on The History and Composition of the American Flag which was followed by a four minute talk from Stuart Walling about the 5th Scout Law, "A Scout is Courteous." The Beaver Patrol was in charge of recreation, promising a "program that is different." Finally a letter from President Calvin Coolidge was read, noting that he regarded scouting as "… an ideal mode of citizenship development and character construction."

In 1929 the Fairport troop joined the Rochester Council and was renamed Troop 118. A news article dated October 25, 1934, noted that 147 Scouts were to be honored at the Court of Honor, among them a number from Fairport's Troop 118. The troop, under the leadership of Scoutmaster C. L. Ackley, was awarded six First Class badges, four Star badges, one Silver Eagle, one Gold Palm, and thirty Merit badges. The number of boys involved in Scouting increased rapidly and by the late 1930's, the troop had to be divided into three parts, becoming Troops 207,208, and 209. The roster of boys, who had to choose which of the three troops to join, included, among others, Stewart Pierce, Warren DeLand, Dewey Jackson, and Charles Barranco.

Boy Scout group, 1930's. *Photo: Stewart Pierce*

Boy Scouting in Perinton and Fairport in the 1940's and 1950's continued to grow and thrive. This interest resulted in the introduction of the first Cub Scout Pack in 1944. The First Congregational Church organized and sponsored the first Cub Pack after two mothers had to take their boys to Pittsford in order for them to be Cub Scouts. Howard McFarland served as Cubmaster with Frank Reese as assistant and Mrs. Willis Allen, Mrs. Howard McFarland, Mrs. Clarence Newcomb, and Mrs. Howard Salmon as den mothers. By 1950 Pack 789 had about seventy boys in eight dens, with a waiting list. Troops 207, 208, and 209, each of which had been formed in 1937, continued to flourish and add to their impressive numbers of Eagle awards, and celebrated their fiftieth anniversaries in 1987.

Troop 207 was sponsored by the First Congregational Church. Warren DeLand was the group's first Eagle Scout, and in 1942, eight boys and two leaders received that award. The boys aided in the war effort by organizing an "Air Scout Patrol" Explorer Post which spotted planes from a cabin near the village water tank (probably on Summit Street). John D. Ward recalled that Troop 207 sent ten scouts to the New York World's Fair in 1939 as part of a "Service Troop." He also recalled that many of his fellow scouts served in the military (as he did) and then went on to productive and active professional lives. He noted that "Bob Wagner went into law and later became the Honorable Judge Wagner of the New York State Supreme Court" and that "Ed Ryder became Dr. Ed Ryder" and that "Bob Abbott went into the Army Air Force [and subsequently] earned a Ph.D. from Harvard." During the forties and the fifties the troop continued to participate in camp-outs, camporees, and trips to Massawepie in the Adirondacks and to contribute to numerous service projects. Troops 208 and 209 have followed the same path. Troop 208, sponsored by the Fairport Methodist Church, worked with Alta Fisher (Perinton Historian from 1956 to 1966) to identify a number of historic sites in Fairport and Perinton. In 1950, Troop 209, sponsored by the Raymond Baptist and First Baptist Churches, had the second largest registration in the district.

Both Cubs and Scouts have continued to enjoy camping and canoe trips, attendance at jamborees and participation in various service projects such as the construction of a bridge along a hiking path in Beechwoods Park, the cleaning up of Mt. Pleasant Cemetery, refurbishing of toys for needy children, clothing and paper drives, and food collections for area food shelf programs. Cub Scouts continue to enjoy such activities as soapbox racing contests (otherwise known as the "Pinewood Derby"), competitive turtle races, Christmas caroling, craft and service projects, visits to local businesses, a

"Cub Olympics," and a very popular popcorn sale. Older scouts continue to work toward and earn the prestigious Eagle Scout award.

Scouting has grown along with Perinton's population. The average troop size in the 1950's was about thirty-five, but began to grow during the 1960's, resulting in the creation of a new troop, number 307. At the same time, Cub Pack 789 was followed by others. As of 2010 nearly 900 boys are members of twelve Cub Packs and eleven Boy Scout troops in Perinton and Fairport. High school aged young people, both boys and girls, take part in the scout Venture Program, which gives them opportunities for leadership training, high activity outdoor adventures, community service, and hobby-based programs. Many of the community's churches as well as the Rotary and Lion's Clubs and several PTSA groups serve as sponsors and many, many parents serve as volunteers. Reaching probably one-third of boys in grades one through five, and twenty percent of boys in grades six through twelve, Boy Scouting is clearly a strong force in the life of the community.

Girl Scouting in Perinton and Fairport

Beginning with eighteen members in Savannah, Georgia, on March 12, 1912, Juliette "Daisy" Low's Girl Scouts now number about 2.6 million members in the United States and ninety other countries (through USA Girl Scouts Overseas). Low's goal was to create a girl-centered organization that would engage young women in the life of the community, help them to develop to their full potential, and instill in them love of the outdoors. By all measures over 50 million alumnae would agree that the organization was and continues to be successful.

The first Perinton Girl Scout troop was formed in 1930 by Marion Dodge and Norma Quinlan. A number of local organizations served as sponsors, among them the Memorial Post VFW, First Congregational Church, Raymond Baptist Church (Fairport Community Baptist), Ayrault Road PTA, Central PTA, and the Dorothy Laird Group from the Methodist Church. From the 1940's, groups also met at the Nook at Potter Memorial, the American Legion room in the Town Hall and in the old schoolhouse on West Church Street. The number of girls involved in scouting increased rapidly. Within twenty years there were eleven troops, with over 250 girls.

While the general goal of scouting has remained the same, the details have changed. This is evident in the types of skill badges that the scouts work to earn. Badge requirements have changed significantly over the past 100 years as evidenced by the following comparison:

Circa 1915

<u>Telegrapher</u>
-Send 22 words per minute
using a sounder & Morse Code
-Receive 25 words per minute
and write out in longhand

<u>Economist</u>
-Keep clothing in good repair
-Spend allowance on good quality
stockings, shoes, and gloves

<u>Health Winner</u>
-Go to bed by 9:30 pm
-Not go to late parties or any
other late entertainment on nights
before school or work
-Eat no sweets except for dessert

Circa 2000

<u>Computer Smarts</u>
-Open an Internet Browser
and visit links
-Learn how computers work
in today's job market
-Learn the difference
between .com, .org, and .net

<u>Penny Power</u>
For Brownies:
-Keep track of how much is spent on
lunch, toys, and phone calls

<u>Healthy Habits</u>
-Exercise
-Brush twice a day
-not smoke
-Learn to deal with various feelings

1915	***2000***
Matron Housekeeper	Ms. Fix-It
-Use a vacuum cleaner or stain and polish hardwood floors	-Replace a broken windowpane
-Store fur and flannels	-Show how to repair a leaky toilet
-Clean glass, kitchen utensils, brass and silverware	-Help with painting, wallpapering or other repair work to walls
-Know three cuts of meat & prices of each	-Find out what changes could be made to a home that would help save water

Volunteers make all of the Girl Scout projects happen. By 2006, over 600 adults volunteered for the seventy-two troops in Perinton and Fairport. They follow in the footsteps of people like Marion Dodge, Norma Quinlan, Alberta Cleveland, Jean Flannigan, Louise Seaman, Harriett Knapp, Louise Dean, Alta Hutchings, and Betty Steffen, who saw scouting grow from one troop in 1930 to twenty-three in 1960.

Girl Scouts at Camp Beech-Wood

Girl Scouting is open to all girls between the ages of five and seventeen. Five and six olds can join the Daisy Girl Scouts while seven and eight year olds become Brownie Scouts. Girl Scouts Juniors are in grades 4 and 5 and Girl Scout Cadettes in grades 6-8. Teens in grades 9 and 10 are Girl Scout Seniors while those in grades 11 and 12 are known as Girl Scout Ambassadors. Scouts can choose from a variety of programs and opportunities including STUDIO 2B, an internet site especially for teen girls.

From the beginning Fairport's Girl Scouts have been very involved with community projects and outdoor activities. They have learned Native American crafts and history, worked on homemaking and health and safety skills, and developed an appreciation for international issues. At various times groups have prepared Easter baskets for the Fairport Baptist Home, rolled bandages for the Cancer Society, "Caroled for Cans" to benefit the Perinton Food Shelf, collected pencils for needy children overseas, made Halloween favors for local hospitals, and entertained senior groups. Local Girl Scouts have been involved with a tutoring program at the Pines of Perinton housing project, service projects for their many sponsors, a food drive together with the Boy Scouts in the spring, and various school festivals. Community service is also the main component of the Girl Scout Bronze, Silver, and Gold

Awards, which require between twenty to sixty hours of service. There is no question that a primary focus of Girl Scouting is doing for others.

Outdoor activities have always been very important to Girl Scouting. There are several area camps, the first of which, Camp Beechwood on Lake Ontario, was started in 1929. In 1951 Whispering Willow Day Camp was built at Powder Mills Park. The camp was proposed by Fairport's Louise Dean and named by her daughter Barbara. It operated for two weeks each summer and provided training in outdoor cooking, crafts such as whittling, hiking, fishing, survival living techniques, nature lore, and general camping skills. Camp Pinewood in Dansville was opened in 1960, joining Camp Beechwood as an overnight camp. Camp Cutler, a "day and stay" camp, opened in 1967, providing both day camp and overnight experiences. As of 2010 both Camp Pinewood and Camp Culter are still in use.

In 1970 Ann Piper gave the area Girl Scouts sixty acres of land off Turk Hill Road in Perinton. She also donated $1,400,000 to build a lodge and otherwise endow the camp. Since its dedication in 1979, the camp, which can accommodate eighty girls, has been used for troop camping and environmental as well as leadership training. In addition, Camp Piper Woods offers three weeks of day and overnight camping during the summer.

No discussion of the Girl Scouts would be complete without mention of *COOKIES*. The earliest mention of Girl Scout cookie sales was in 1917 in Oklahoma. In the 20's and 30's Girl Scouts in different parts of the country baked and sold simple sugar cookies packed in wax paper bags for about 25 to 35 cents a dozen. By the 1950's, there were three varieties of cookies: sandwich, shortbread, and chocolate mints. In 1978 four bakeries supplied cookies for the annual sale and for the first time all the cookie boxes featured the same designs and scenes. By the 1990's, two bakeries supplied the eight varieties which now included low-fat and sugar-free choices. Cookie sales generally take place in October and sale proceeds, which are second only to those of Nabisco, go to programs and a scholarship fund.

Certainly for the girls of Perinton and Fairport's seventy-five troops, the Girl Scout Law emphasizing honesty, responsibility, and respect epitomizes their character and commitment.

San Sebastian Society

The final decades of the nineteenth century and the first several decades of the twentieth century saw a spike in immigration into the United States, particularly from southern and eastern Europe. In the village of Fairport that meant an increase in the Italian population. Most settled on the north side of the Erie Canal and often worked at the American Can Company or in the car shops of East Rochester. A number ran small businesses. Immigrants faced the challenges of customs, language, and assimilation in addition to the basic issues of food and shelter. On February 23, 1915, a group of Fairport's Italian immigrants met in the Fiandach building on North Main Street to form the San Sebastian Society with the goal of trying to deal with some of the many issues facing their members.

Most of the adult males of Italian ancestry in Fairport became members of the San Sebastian Society. Charter members of the group included Salvatore Bartolotta, Crocie and Anthony Fiandach, Frank Stolt, Anthony Carlomusto, Anthony Pace, Carmen Pignato, Camillo and Dominic Pomponio, John and Salvatore Rinaldo, Joseph Mollura, Roy Saporito, Peter Prinzivalli, John Masciangelo, Francisco Basile, Biago Aparo, Joseph Fiorenzo, and Joseph DiRisio, among others. John Sebaste of Rochester and East Rochester served as advisor. The main purpose of the group was to provide mutual aid benefits for members and their families as well as to provide a venue for sharing ideas and concerns and for socializing and communicating in their native tongue.

A mutual aid group acts as an insurance company seeing that its members do not go without food, shelter, or medical care. To raise money members paid monthly dues and ran fundraisers including dances in the old Osburn Hotel/ Fairport Gas and Oil building, and summertime pig roasts.

Throughout the decades of the 1920's, 30's, and 40's, members received medical benefits including doctors' and dentists' fees, hospital costs, and weekly financial help.

Minute books that exist from the 1950's through 1981 provide a look into the activities of the group. Meetings were held in various places including LaRosa's Hall on State Street, Bown's Hall on South Main, and eventually in the "new church hall." Discussions in the 1950's appeared to have centered around finances, picnic and spaghetti dinner fundraisers, the annual banquet, membership drives, donations, and doctor payments. The society would not pay for tooth extractions, but did pay $15 per day for hospital care for a maximum of ten days. However, the Society would not pay for a second hospitalization for the same illness. Payments for doctors' visits were set at $3 for an office call and $4 for a house call with no payments for check-ups. Death benefits of $100 and eventually $500 were also paid. The treasury was to be kept at $4,000, and if it dropped below that, members were to make an additional contribution. Fundraisers were organized and held and the 1956 annual banquet was held at the Green Lantern Inn.

During the 1960's there were many discussions about the Society's property on Mill Street, which was finally sold to Charlie Kopp. Financially, a member embezzled over $5,000 from the Society treasury leading to a six-month suspension of member benefits. The offender was arrested, paroled, and had to repay the debt in the amount of $10 per week. (It was repaid by the middle of the decade.) Several meetings were devoted to plans for participation in the Perinton 1962 Sesquicentennial as well as annual Memorial Day parades.

The last entries in the minute books are concerned with membership and plans for disbanding the Society. Membership had consistently dwindled over the years and by the 1970's only about nine members regularly attended meetings. The first mention of disbanding occurred as early as 1969 with a proposal to turn the San Sebastian Society into a social club. It was finally decided in 1981 to give a special benefit of $500 to each member and formally end dues and benefits as of December 31, 1981. The last entry in the minute books is dated January 12, 1982; however, it does mention a meeting to be held in June, 1982. Apparently, dinners or banquets were held in subsequent years, according to a note dated 1983 stating that a motion was made and passed to continue having banquets until the money was gone.

The San Sebastian Society clearly fulfilled its purpose of caring for its members and provided a venue for discussion and camaraderie.

Fairport Masonic Lodge

The Masons are perhaps the oldest of the commonly known American service and fraternal organizations. Although their real origins are more or less shrouded in mystery, 1717 is often given as date when the first Grand Lodge was established in England. It is believed that Masonic groups might have developed from the guilds of masons that existed in the Middle Ages, stonemasons being the elite craftsmen responsible for much of the glories of Gothic architecture. Not only were guilds organizations of craftsmen, but they also played a significant role in social welfare, protecting and caring for artisans and their families.

Masonry existed in the American colonies by the 1730's and tended to attract the professional and the well-educated. Many of our revolutionary leaders, including George Washington claimed membership in the Masons.

Rochester's first Grand Lodge was formed in Gates in 1815, but the growth of Masonry in the area was slowed by the apparent abduction and murder of one William Morgan, who felt strongly that the secret rituals and rites of the organization should be revealed to the public. His death (or disappearance) influenced the rise of the Anti-Masonic Party beginning in 1831. In addition, the Roman Catholic Church was essentially anti-Mason. The party fielded unsuccessful presidential candidates in 1832 and 1836, running on a platform in opposition to "abuses of democracy" (defined as secret societies).

As anti-masonic feeling was waning, a group of Fairport gentlemen met in April of 1859 to form the first local Masonic Lodge. They were Joshua C. Easton, T. V. B. Durand, H. H. Van Buren, James Burlingame, Remsen Vanderhoof, O. B. Fullum, Seymour G. Palmer, John G. Palmer, Elisha Marlett, Ortis C. Easton, W.K. Goodrich, W.M. Wilcox, Samuel Noyes, Jacob Chase, Lafayette Lapham, and Asa Wight. Within three months Daniel DeLand, C. J. DeLand, and Jarvis Eddy joined the group. Fairport Lodge #476 was officially chartered on July 5, 1859.

The first decade of the Fairport Lodge was very successful as the new lodge "drew to itself men, who not only labored for the success of the Lodge, but have also been identified with the success and prosperity of the town." While the subsequent two decades were less successful, "Brother L. H. Powers, ... turned the tide that has since led to success, and each succeeding year has added interest, enthusiasm and accession...." By 1890 the Lodge had 113 members and a full treasury. As was the common practice in all Masonic Lodges, members had to be voted in.

Fairport Lodge members served their country and their community. A number served in the Spanish-American War and the First and Second World Wars. George Kelsey and Howard Shepard gave their lives. The Lodge also strongly supported the efforts on the homefront through the Red Cross, the purchase of war bonds, and relief fund drives.

Meetings in those early years were held in the Henry Block on South Main Street. In 1916 the Lodge purchased the building at 11 West Avenue. It served as their meeting hall, surviving the Depression, two world wars and a fire, until the Lodge outgrew it in 1947, having at that time over 300 members. Herman Steffen and George Pruitt headed a building committee and proceeded to raise funds for new facilities by presenting minstrel shows, dances, and card parties, among other events. By 1958 the Lodge had raised $23,000 and purchased, in that year, the Temple Theater Building on South Main Street for $30,000. The Lodge rented out the two stores flanking the theater and renovated the theater itself for their use. The renovated Lodge was dedicated on October 3, 1959 as part of the Lodge's 100th Anniversary Celebration.

Over the last several decades Lodge membership has fluctuated. A decline in membership led to the merger in 2001 of the Fairport Lodge and Rochester's Flower City Lodge #910 to create the Fairport-Flower City Lodge #476. More recently, however, the Fairport Lodge has seen an increase in new, younger members.

The Fairport Lodge has a history of supporting not only Masonic charities such as the Shriner's Childrens' Hospitals and the Masonic Medical Research Center in Utica, New York, but also a number of local charities. The group regularly donates to the Perinton Food Shelf and Dollars for Scholars program, supports a Little League team, and takes part in Fairport's Canal Days festivities.

This oldest of fraternal organizations is very much a part of the community.

Fairport Rotary Club

A "gold thread in the fabric of the community" was how Perinton Supervisor Jim Smith described Fairport's Rotary Club on its 70th anniversary in 1996. Over those 70 years the club has clearly lived up to its motto of "service over self."

The first Rotary Club was founded in 1905 in Chicago by Paul Harris, who envisioned a service club that also would embody the friendliness of a small town that he had known as a child. Twenty-one years later, in 1926, Harry Tinney, a Fairport resident who belonged to the Rochester Rotary Club, decided that Fairport should have its own club. Joined by nineteen others, among them Herman Steffen, Samuel Arms, Edward McGinnis, John Bahler, and James Welch, Harry Tinney called an organizational meeting to order on October 22, 1926 all filled out application cards and turned them in with the $20 initiation fee. Sam Arms was elected President; James Welch, Vice-President; Ed McGinnis, Treasurer; and Lynn Dodge, Secretary. The first regular meeting was held on November 7th, and Charter Night, when the new club received its formal charter, was held in the

Fairport High School gym on February 8, 1927. Women of the local PTA prepared and served "an excellent dinner" to the 350 area Rotarians who were present.

As a service club, Rotary is dedicated to community service and donates both time and money to those organizations that show need. It is also a social group that participates in community affairs. Both these aspects are well represented in the Fairport club.

Even before its charter meeting, the new club began its community service by sponsoring a Christmas party at the Baptist Home. A chicken dinner and entertainment were provided, culminating in a sightseeing drive around Fairport and Perinton to view the Christmas lights and decorations. This activity was followed by the club's first service project, which helped members of the Fairport High School band purchase uniforms and instruments. Each club member signed a $200 note to raise the necessary $3,000, and a Mardi Gras gala was held to raise money to help pay off the debt.

In 1955 charter member Dr. James Welch recalled some of the projects involving early members. He remembered that the Club was one of the first organizations to come to the aid of the needy after the Crash of 1929, providing Christmas baskets of toys, food, and clothing. The aid continued for the duration of the Depression. Rotarians also supplied local young men with seed potatoes that not only were planted for food, but also taught the recipients something about farming. Money was also loaned for college tuition.

Many of the Rotarians' projects and events have centered around children and young people. Rotary sponsored a kite-flying contest on "Health and Recreation Day" (May 1, 1948). Kites had to be built by the contestants, and ten $3 prizes were awarded. Dances were recurring events as well. Further, the Rotary Club was actively involved in the development of the Fairport Little League, with Rotarian Tod Malcolm serving as its first president. Rotarians were responsible for the warming shed at Potter ice rink, a building for clubs and scout meetings at the Foreman Center, and more recently, aid to the Fairport Crew Club. The group has also donated to the Lion's Den Teen Center. Young people too have been involved in service through the Interact Club, a youth organization sponsored by Rotary.

Rotarian interests and concerns have not been exclusive to Fairport. Members are involved both on the regional, national and international level with a variety of projects. In 1956 Fairport Rotarians were instrumental, along with a number of other area Rotary Clubs, in establishing Camp Haccamo for physically handicapped children of Monroe County. Dave Jordan and Warren Shaddock were Fairport's representatives. The first camp was held in 1957 at the rifle range used by the Culver Road Armory in Rush, NY. In 1960, the camp moved to a new site near Panorama Plaza on land donated by Emil Muller, the developer of the plaza. Cabins were constructed, each supported by a different Rotary Club from around the Rochester area. Monroe County campers with disabilities ranging from cancer to Downs Syndrome can enjoy a one week stay free of charge.

Rotary projects have also gone international. Rotarians participated in the "Polio Plus" campaign, begun in 1986, whose goal was to eradicate polio by providing vaccines to developing countries and also to work against other serious diseases like tuberculosis, diphtheria, and whooping cough. One benefit dinner raised $14,500. Rotarians also sponsor international student exchanges as well as group study program exchanges, which provide travel grants for groups of five people to study in different corporate settings and cultures. For example, in 1998 a Swedish group visited Fairport and Rochester. In 1999 Rotarian Jean Wells, along with members from Penfield, East Rochester, and Wheaton, Illinois, traveled to Peru as part of a medical mission. Among other endeavors, India has received hospital equipment, funding has supported a project to dig water wells in the Sudan, solar ovens were sent to Nicaragua, and aid was sent to Zimbabwe.

Obviously there have to be ways to raise money for all the projects. Dues and fines alone would not suffice. The Club has held dances, auctions, and raffles to accumulate funds, but several large events raise the bulk of the money. The popular and long-running Antique Show and Sale in early June was a major source of income for over fifty years. A new fundraiser, "Savor the Flavor of Fairport" was initiated in 2007. Within two years, 350 people enjoyed tastings from fourteen area restaurants and twenty-one area wineries. The annual fall pancake breakfast is another widely attended event. Since the early 1980's, Rotary has worked to make the LPGA tournament a successful event and in the process has made it a lucrative source of income for Camp Haccamo and Rochester's

Sunshine Camp, both of which serve the area's disabled children. In the late 1990's the Club initiated the "Polar Bear Open," a winter golfing event whose proceeds go the Cerebral Palsy Foundation of Rochester and other Rotary charities. In its first four years, the tournament raised over $170,000. In October of 2006 Rotary and its youth arm, Interact, served food to the night shift at the Sheriff's Department, Perinton ambulance, Advent house, and the Fairport Fire and Police Departments; sponsored a Halloween parade; painted the Perinton food shelf; and served a spaghetti dinner at the VFW in honor of "Make a Difference Day." Each year since, Rotary has partnered with different charities and conducted different service projects in continuing to "make a difference."

Since 2000, Fairport's Rotarians have donated money to Upstate Guide Dogs, student exchange programs, and the Fairport School District "Robotics" team in addition to providing ongoing support to Camp Haccamo, the Lion's Den teen center, the Crew Club, and the Little League among others. In 2004 Rotarians gave $30,000 toward the renovation of Columbus Commons from a parking lot into a festival site, with a pavilion which was named after longtime Rotarian Albert Knapp. Rotarians support School 3 in Rochester with dictionaries and field trips and also by serving as classroom mentors and volunteer readers. The group regularly supports the Perinton Food Shelf and the Toys for Tots program among many others.

With a healthy membership, the Fairport Rotary Club continues to be one of the community's premier service organizations.

photo by the Rev. Albert D'Annunzio

Rotary members 50th Anniversary (l. to r.: Dr. James Welch, J. Sidney Villere, Art Roberts, Hal Scoby)

The Fairport Lions Club

On September 19, 1949 President Albert DiRisio accepted the charter of Fairport's Lions Club, "emblem of unselfish community service," on behalf of its membership. At the ensuing celebration over 200 Lions, their wives, and guests enjoyed a full-course dinner, a baton-twirling demonstration by Fairport High School drum majorettes, singing by the Sodus Central School Girls' Trio and Art Steffen, and after-dinner dancing. The first officers of the club were Albert DiRisio, president; William Brewerton, First Vice-President; Joseph Mamrock, Second Vice-President; Louis DiRisio, Secretary; Robert Smith, Treasurer; and Don Malcolm, Tail Twister.

Albert DiRisio decided to start the Club when after speaking to the Victor Lions Club about his experiences in World War II, an organizer from the International Lions Club suggested that he start a club in Fairport. "He told me to get 10 merchants together at $10 each and he'd be back in touch with me." DiRisio had twenty members when he was subsequently contacted and the group had its first meeting in August of 1949.

The International Association of Lions Clubs began as the dream of Chicago businessman Melvin Jones. He believed that local business clubs should expand their horizons from purely professional concerns to the betterment of their communities and the world at large. Jones' group, the Business Circle of Chicago, agreed. After contacting similar groups around the United States, an organizational meeting was held on June 7, 1917 in Chicago, Illinois. The new group took the name of one of the invited groups, the "Association of Lions Clubs," and a national convention was held in Dallas, Texas in October of that year. A constitution, by-laws and a code of ethics were approved. Among the objects adopted in those early years was one that read, "No club shall hold out the financial betterment of its members as its object." This call for unselfish service to others remains one of the association's main tenets.

Fairport's newly formed Lions Club, approximately fifty in number, wasted no time in getting involved in community service projects. From the outset, the Club was instrumental in supporting the Buffalo Eye Bank, the collection of eye glasses for re-use by the needy, and the creation of the Rochester Eye Bank and Research Society. Concern with eye health has been an on-going project for the Club, having been encouraged by Helen Keller to become "knights of the blind in the crusade against darkness."

Lions Club 25th Anniversary at Island Valley, November 3, 1973

(l. to r.: Mr. and Mrs. George Aklin, Tom Reynolds, Albert DiRisio, Margaret Reynolds, Mr. and Mrs. Edward Boyce, Mr. and Mrs. William Brewerton, Mr. and Mrs. Allan G. Stranford)

In other areas of health, the Club donated resuscitators to both the police and fire departments, and was instrumental in the formation and organization of the Perinton Volunteer Ambulance Corps. The Red Cross and Easter Seals receive annual donations as well.

The Lions Club has been involved in youth activities too numerous to list. They have sponsored Scout troops (including a Special Boy Scout troop), Little League and bowling teams, organized bicycle safety campaigns and Christmas parties. They donated basketball courts and a skating rink at Potter Park, tennis courts at Perinton Park, bus shelters, and an electronic scoreboard at Fairport High School. They have given aid to CARE, and the Al Sigl Center, and have underwritten scholarship programs at Fairport High School. One of the Club's major projects was the Lions Den Teen Center, which opened in 1990. The Lions Club raised over $175,000 from a variety of local sources and received grants from the Lions Club International and New York State. In addition they oversaw the construction of the building that sits behind the old carriage house of the Potter Mansion on West Church Street. In recent years the Club has sponsored the creation of a youth division, the Leo Club, which like its parent organization is committed to community service.

For all their many contributions to the community, the Perinton Chamber of Commerce presented the Club with their Community Appreciation Award for 1990. On their 40th anniversary in 1989, the Town of Perinton also recognized the club for its "strength and commitment to the Fairport-Perinton community."

The Lions Club continues to be deeply involved in community service, supporting such groups as Mercy Flight, Fairport Baptist Homes, and Ronald McDonald House, as well as continuing its commitment to improved eye sight and youth programs. Specifically, among other projects, the local Club provides vision screening for pre-schoolers and eye glasses for needy children. The Lions Club is also known for regularly providing food at events such as the annual 4th of July celebration in Perinton Park.

Fairport's Lions Club is part of the Lions Clubs International which has grown to include 1.3 million men and women in approximately 45,000 clubs located in 200 countries and geographic areas. The groups work to improve the environment, build homes for the disabled, support diabetes education, conduct hearing and vision programs, provide services for youth and, through their foundation, provide disaster relief around the world.

West Avenue's Shaw's Hall

Attend a meeting, vote, see a movie or an amateur theater production, buy groceries or hardware or a beer, have old furniture reupholstered. A Fairport resident could do any one of these things at one time or another at 23 West Avenue in a building known for much of its life as Shaw's Hall.

The original single-story building was moved from a location north of the canal in 1854. It was enlarged when the old meeting house belonging to the Congregational Society was moved from East Church Street and built into the structure. Subsequently a second story and balcony were added and the building was faced with brick. The ground floor housed at various times Billy Kershaw's Harness Shop, Hollender & Scoville's Grocery Store, a dressmaker, L. M. Shaw's "undertaking parlor," an auto parts store, Mrs. Chadwick's and Miss Lee's hat shop, and Jensen's (later Gerald Williams') Hardware Store. The second story added a large meeting room capable of holding up to 450 people. It was the largest meeting place in the village and consequently was the place for revival meetings, lectures on prohibition and temperance, dances, vaudeville shows, other public meetings and voting. Two early vaudeville productions were "Uncle Tom's Cabin," and "True Blue," a Civil War drama put on by the members of E. A. Slocum Post 211. The productions were necessarily small ones as the stage could accommodate no more than a four-person act. One account of village elections notes that the "Republican leaders and the Democratic 'Big Four' lined up the patriotic voters and marched them to the ballot box where they made sure they voted the right ticket and deposited it before they were given a card, which when presented to the pay-off man, drew $1 or $2 depending on the real need of additional votes."

Shaw's Hall, also known as Shaw's Opera House, The Bijou, The Bijou Dream, and the Rivoli, was perhaps best remembered as Fairport's first movie house. Silent movies arrived in town about 1906 when the theater was run by Charles Aldrich and Hollis Shilling. Tickets were eleven cents for adults, six cents for children, and could be purchased from the box office at the entrance. By the 1920's the fee had risen to 15 cents for adults. After buying tickets, patrons had to climb the one set of stairs to the theater and often had to wait while the patrons from an earlier show exited via the same stairs. Charles Clark, manager of the theater from 1921 to 1925, recalled that there were movies six days a week and an occasional vaudeville act.

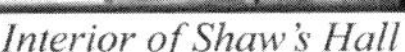

Interior of Shaw's Hall

Front view

Shaw's Hall curtain

An old piano provided background music for the movies, at first to cover the noise of the projector and later to set the mood: soft for love scenes, louder for war scenes. The piano was located in a small pit in front of the screen so the accompanist could watch the film. Pianist Grace Drew said the goal was to "keep the music in the background – you were the accompanist, not the main attraction." The projection booth was suspended from the ceiling near the street end of the building. The projectionist climbed a steel ladder to reach his perch from which he could see the entire hall with its cloth covered panels and gold woodwork, its two-light candelabra, the rows of seats, the stage, the pianist, the customers, and the curtain. Movies continued to be shown there probably until the mid-1930's.

The gold hand-painted curtain had a pastoral scene in the center and was surrounded by advertisements paid for by local merchants. For $15 advertisers could tell patrons waiting for the movie to "Call on Percy & Clark for your hardware needs," or to "Come in for a bite at C. W. Lathrop's." A. G. Filkins promoted his automobile supplies and The Sugar Bowl offered choice confections and ice cream. George Slocum touted insurance and John D. Webb promised pure food in his market.

After over 100 years of continuous use, Shaw's Hall was razed in 1975 as part of Fairport's urban renewal projects, leaving behind its long history.

Schine's Temple Theater

In less than thirty years, the motion picture industry went from its first twelve minute narrative film, "The Great Train Robbery," (produced in 1903), to an industry that was showing films lasting several hours in thousands of "movie palaces." Entrepreneurs looking to prosper from the new industry developed chains of movie theaters. Two of the most successful were Myer and Louis Schine, sons of Latvian immigrants whose initial investment in a theater in Gloversville, New York, grew into a nationwide chain of theaters that included one in Fairport, the chain's 105th addition. The Schine brothers believed that the public should be pleased at all times, and that all dealings should be open, courteous, clean and above board. Service was to be the watchword and all employees were to "radiate with a no trouble to assist you spirit."

Schine's Temple Theater (showing Don Juan starring John Barrymore)

The Fairport embodiment of the Schine philosophy was built in 1927 at 85 South Main Street at a cost of $175,000. The 60 by 150 foot building with a 15 by 30 foot stage was of Italianate design and was advertised as "absolutely fireproof." Patrons entered a tiled lobby, passed through massive doors in the foyer, which was separated from the auditorium by a glass screen, and could head up stairs to the balcony from either end. The 1,000 seat auditorium's handsomely decorated wall panels and rounded ceiling were enhanced by the indirect lighting. The pitched floor made it possible for every patron to see the screen from the large mahogany-backed leather seats. Five emergency exits, leading from the sides and rear, in addition to the main entrance, afforded movie-goers a quick and safe way to empty the house in event of any emergency.

A Wurlitzer organ was made especially for the theater. It was said to be able to produce "almost any kind of noise needed to make the pictures more realistic, excepting of course, the human voice." The Schine Company promised to get one of the best organists available in order to evoke the multitude of sounds available from the massive instrument, which had stops that replicated almost an entire orchestra and others that produced the sounds of an auto horn, a fire gong, horses' hooves, a moving train, and the whirr of an airplane, among many others. The equipment for projecting the pictures was of the very latest and most modern design, and patrons were promised that there would be no eye strain.

The Schine Temple Theater opened with a flourish in August of 1927. Charles Clark of Fairport was the manager and promised the public "to serve quietly and efficiently; to be at all times solicitous of your comfort; to present a program of motion pictures representing the highest art of great producers; to give you a theater to which you may point with pride; to maintain a standard to which adverse criticism cannot be directed …" Opening night featured Richard Betts, the singing organist from New York City, presenting "A Trip Throughout the Organ, a stage presentation featuring Neil O'Brien and his orchestra, and of course a feature picture, considered by critics to be one of the funniest comedies ever made, Syd Chaplin in "The Better 'Ole."

Schine Theater policy allowed the showing of only the latest and cleanest type of pictures that would satisfy movie lovers and continue to make them patrons. Programs tried to offer something artistic, novel, instructive, and amusing. Movies usually changed four times a week, with adult features offered every day with a children's matinee added on Saturday. Some of those early films included "The Night of Love" with Ronald Coleman, and "Love of Sunya" with Gloria Swanson. Saturday matinee times were for children with shows like "Bigger than Barnum's," a circus picture, and Rin-Tin-Tin in "While London Sleeps."

It was not long before the theater switched to talking films, the first of which, "The Jazz Singer," was produced in 1927. Since those films were of longer duration, the daily program came to include two features separated by a newsreel. Saturday matinees ran cartoons, often a serial, and a feature film. Despite the Depression, movie houses flourished with 1939 being a key year with the release of "Gone with the Wind" and "The Wizard of Oz" among many others. During those difficult years, the Temple Theater would offer incentives such as a certificate that along with $.15 would buy a volume of an encyclopedia, or a "dish night" when patrons would receive a piece of glassware with their admission ticket.

In the decade of the 1940's, shows changed three times a week. Sunday and Monday might feature a Judy Garland film, "The Harvey Girls" paired with a thriller "Fatal Witness." Tuesday through Thursday might highlight Errol Flynn in "Northern Pursuit" and Olivia DeHaviland in "Princess O'Rourke." Friday and Saturday night completed the cycle which of course was rounded out with a Saturday matinee including Mickey Mouse, Donald Duck, and Bugs Bunny cartoons.

Schine theaters celebrated their 25th anniversary in 1946 with a "Why I Like to Attend a Schine Theater" contest. Prizes were boxes of Silver Jubilee Candy. In that post-war period, the theater chain also actively recruited young men between the ages of twenty-one and thirty-one to learn theater management. A "good salary" was offered to the "right man" and the Schine theaters looked to another twenty-five years of growth.

Unfortunately movie going habits changed in the 1950's with the advent of television and the local theaters could not compete. The Schine organization sold the Temple Theater to the Fairport Masonic Lodge in 1958 for $30,000. The Lodge still owns the structure, which stands at 85 South Main Street.

Powder Mills Park

In the southeastern part of Perinton there lies a hilly wooded tract near Irondequoit Creek, which was once the bed of an arm of the old Genesee River delta. The hills were covered with a heavy growth of oak, maple, walnut, beech and ash and abundant willows bordered the streams. Stone implements and spear and arrow points have been found near a spring there, leading historians to believe that the area was probably a favorite stopping place on the trail from the Seneca villages near Canandaigua and Victor to Indian Landing at the head of Irondequoit Bay.

This hilly, secluded, and somewhat mysterious tract of land was perfect for the business that Daniel C. Rand and Mortimer Wadhams wanted to develop. Rand was born and educated in New Hampshire and about 1820 went to Middletown, Connecticut to learn the black powder making business at a mill owned by his Aunt Lucia Rand. Several years later he came to Honeoye Falls looking to start his own business. It was there that he met Mortimer Wadhams, the owner of a saw and grist mill business, who was acquainted with the area. Investigating the land together, in 1853 the two men decided to locate their new business on about 175 acres in southeastern Perinton, which would become known as the Powder Mills tract. The seclusion of the area, the availability of water and willow trees as well as maples, and the hilly topography made it ideal for the creation of a safe black powder manufacturing business. On the other hand it was close enough to the Erie Canal to allow for materials to be shipped in and the finished product to be shipped out.

Rand and Wadhams built a number of buildings, including a mill. They also built a dam about ¾ of a mile from the mill and brought the water in via a mill race. A nine-foot fall supplied water to the mill wheels. The site provided ample wood for the charcoal, especially willow, which was said to give the powder "quickness and polish," and maple, which was said to give the powder "heft." The charcoal was burned in a large kiln. The other two ingredients in black powder, saltpeter and sulfur, were brought to Bushnell's Basin via the Erie Canal and carried to the mill site by horse and wagon. The buildings for completing the manufacturing process were widely spaced so as to avoid explosions, but were connected by a crude wooden railway, over which push carts carried the powder through its various stages of manufacture. The finished product was packed in wooden kegs sealed with tar and shipped out on the Erie Canal, primarily to Pennsylvania coal mines and quarries around Holley and Medina. Contrary to some stories, the local powder was not used for munitions; it was not ground finely enough. Proving the attention that Rand and Wadhams paid to safety, there were few explosions. A reported 1899 explosion in the mill scattered planks, embedding one in an old elm tree. Otherwise the only injury reports were of several bad burns.

Near a water mill in Powder Mills Park

The business was quite successful and truly became a family affair when Daniel married Stella, Mortimer Wadham's daughter. The couple subsequently had four daughters and three sons and lived in a large twenty-five room home on a hilltop near the mill. Two of the sons maintained the business after the death of Daniel in 1883 and Mortimer in 1887, but in 1910 decided to move operations to Uniontown, Pennsylvania, to be nearer the mines they supplied. In 1929 the Rand Powder Company was sold to DuPont.

Between 1910 and 1930 the old Rand Company buildings and equipment rotted away and became overgrown as the woodland reclaimed the land. In 1930, as part of a larger plan for open spaces, Monroe County purchased the former Powder Mills land, which along with part of the former Woolston farm, became the 286 acre Powder Mills Park. The purchase price was $56,000. Aside from building a new access road, cleaning up debris and brush, providing a few picnic tables and hiking trails, the county planned to make few changes, leaving the natural beauty of the park to speak for itself.

The new park provided many recreational opportunities for county residents. One of the earliest was fishing. The fish hatchery was in operation in the early 1930's and reared and released brook, rainbow, and brown trout for sport fishing. There were additional facilities for baseball, tennis, horseshoes, and archery, and trails for horseback riding and hiking. For many years the park featured a toboggan run and a ski area that included a ski jump and a rope tow.

Today the park continues to draw those who love the outdoors, offering fishing, hiking, and picnicking in the summer, cross-country skiing and snowshoeing in the winter. And thanks to a number of volunteers, the fish hatchery continues to provide fish for the angler and amusement for the younger people.

Powder Mills Park, with its hills, woods, streams, and history is a beautiful place to visit and enjoy and is just one more asset to the Town of Perinton.

Baseball Teams

Baseball, traditionally known as the "National Pastime," apparently was quite popular in Perinton and Fairport in the early years of the twentieth century. There are photos of several teams including a Y.M.C.A. group, a team from Egypt and Fairport, one of a semi-pro league team, and one with C.P.F. on their shirts, but lacking any other information.

Fairport Athletic Club (Y.M.C.A.) 1892 Baseball Team

The 1892 Fairport Athletic Club Y.M.C.A. baseball team players are identified as follows. **Top row** (left to right): J. Calihan, 2nd base; J.B. Crippen, center field; **second row**: W. Milton Dixon, left field; Clarence Greene, 1st base; George Cobb, manager; T. Cashman, shortstop; Dennis Doherty, left field. **Front row**: Frank Southworth, catcher and George Mulliner, pitcher.

Egypt-Fairport Baseball Team

The 1930-31 Egypt-Fairport Baseball Team played on a field located in the vicinity of today's Perinton Square, which, in addition to being well-kept and frequently used, also had bleachers for the fans. The players can be identified as follows: **Front Row** (L to R): Tut Morgan (from Rochester), George Long, Howard Footer, Ed Bortle, Harry Rainbow, Jr., Sid Delano, Ernie Burns, Carl Nelson, and mascot Bobbie Burns. **Second Row**: Louie O'Leary, Jay Staley, Bill Kodweis (sponsor), George Rainbow, Harry Rainbow, Sr., Purrell Hitchcock (manager), (-?-), and Corny Crowley.

Western New York Semi-Pro league

The above photo, probably dating from the early twentieth century, is of a Fairport semi-pro baseball team in the Western New York League. Identifications are as follows: **Back row** (left to right): A.N. Clark, Edwin Jordan, Denby Waud, F.A. Terpening, Bert Stuben, Carl Rapp, (-?-), and Charles Carpenter. In the **front row**: Al Lippincott sits third from the left and Frank Wood (also known as "Mr. Athlete") is fourth from the right.

C.P.F. Baseball Team

This local team photo has no dates or identifications on the photo, and no hint as to what C.P.F. stands for.

Fairport Little League

Little League baseball was founded in 1939 by Carl Stotz in Williamsport, Pennsylvania, and has been a part of the Perinton and Fairport scene since 1951. In 1950 the Fairport Rotary Club asked several of its members to investigate the possibility of bringing Little League to the community. East Rochester already had four teams. It was hoped that teams could be organized to play a short season in the spring and summer of 1950. Sponsors pledged $200 each to supply uniforms and equipment, and a local builder offered to level an area in Potter Park for a diamond. However, residents of Potter Place were not happy with the prospect of screaming children and heavy traffic three to four nights each week and complained to the Village Board. The Board ruled that village property could not be used by any outside organization and since Little League was headquartered in Pennsylvania, they could not use Potter Park. Little League was on hold, but not for long.

The next year, 1951, four organizations, Lions, Masons, Rotary, and the Fairport Fire Department formulated plans for bringing baseball to Perinton and Fairport youngsters. The executive committee included Tod Malcolm, Napoleon Mancuso, Gene Malcolm, and Hugh Stevely. The fields would be located in the then unused Fairport Park (today's Perinton Park). Frank Wood, a local contractor, volunteered to bulldoze the area and volunteers from the sponsoring organization completed the preparation. That year, Little League began its first season in Fairport/Perinton with four teams and forty-eight players.

The games were popular and had many fans, among them a young man who was, because of crippling rheumatoid arthritis, unable to play. David Marsh was often asked to throw out the first pitch of the season and in 1953 was named Honorary League President. In that same year, the field was named David Marsh Field. Marsh died in 1964, and in 1988 an historic marker in his memory was erected at the site of those first Little League fields.

Within ten years, the number of teams had doubled to eight and there were opportunities for boys younger than eight to participate. Donations provided money for baseball and grounds keeping equipment, a P.A system, and a snack bar. By the end of the 1960's there were 700 boys playing on fifty teams, and games took place not only at David Marsh Field but also on school fields. It was obvious that the League needed more space.

Little League opening Day

In 1969 ground breaking for new state-of-the-art ball fields took place at a twenty-acre site on Lyndon Road just north of the Erie Canal. Present were Gerald Zornow, Kodak president; Cal Ripken, Red Wings manager; Chico Fernandez, Red Wings coach; and George Sisler, President of the International Baseball League. Within ten years the Lyndon Road complex opened with eight fields, a snack bar, and a storage building. It was the largest Little League complex in the state.

Local participation continued to grow with seventy-eight teams and over 1,000 participants in 1978 and eighty-four teams and 1300 players by the late 1980's. To accommodate the growth, the Lyndon Road complex was renovated and expanded to include eleven fields and three new fields were constructed on High Acres land in 1994-5. A new concession stand was opened in 2004 at the Lyndon Road site.

Little League has grown and changed since its inception. In addition to leagues in every state, by 1951 the league went international with teams in Canada and Panama and is now represented in eighty nations around the world. By the middle 1950's the Little League World Series was being televised. In 1974 the first Little League girls' teams were started, and in 1990 the Challenger Division was created for those with physical and mental disabilities. Little League also sponsors softball teams.

Fairport Little League celebrates its 60th year in 2011 by welcoming over 1400 players in baseball and softball. The Challenger Division enters its twenty-first year with over forty players. Fairport Little League is also offering fall ball for baseball players, following the success of girls' softball last fall with over 85 players.

Little League depends on dedicated volunteers and sponsors. Over the years literally thousands of parents and baseball fans and local businesses have made it possible for youngsters between the ages of five and eighteen to participate in a game that is traditionally known as the "National Pastime."

The Crescent Trail Association

In the early 1970's as Perinton was undergoing significant growth, a number of people were concerned that the agricultural and environmental heritage of Perinton would be lost to suburban sprawl. The town took several measures to prevent this from happening, among them the creation of a Conservation Board, the passage of Conservation Easement and Limited Development District ordinances, and the development of an open space master plan. At the same time there was some discussion about constructing a trail system in the town that would link several town parks and would be more or less crescent-shaped. However, there was little interest at the time and the idea lay dormant.

In 1980, David Schaeffer, a member of the Conservation Board in the early 1970's and at one time its chairman, along with Allen Donk and Christine Fredette of that board, and Beverly Jones of the Perinton Recreation and Parks Commission decided to try to revive the trail proposal. This time the idea gained legs. With the backing of Pete and Judy Logan and about ten to fifteen others who met in the Logans' family room on Little Spring Run, the Crescent Trail Association was born. Judy Logan was named Chairman, Allen Donk, Vice-Chairman, Dave Schaeffer, Trail Master, Nancy Whitcombe, Treasurer, and Bruce Nellis, Trail Crew Leader. Desmond Murray helped with legal issues, Paul Lopez and Pete Logan handled publicity, and Tom Dinse managed programs.

The Crescent Trail Association, as a community-based non-profit, planned to work with the town to create the trail system. It would obtain authorization for access primarily through permits and easements, build and maintain the trails, and sponsor educational programs related to uses of the trail. Initially the group hoped to create a crescent-shaped trail starting at Kreag Road park, heading south past Garnsey Road, east across Moseley and Turk Hill Roads, north near the Victor-Egypt Road, crossing Route 31 east of Aldrich Road, and finally joining the Erie Canal towpath near Lyndon Road.

During the summer of 1980 the sixty-one members of the Crescent Trail Association began marking, clearing, and blazing the first section of the trail. In the fall, the public was invited to join in the Association's first "Grand Hike" and 110 people showed up. By 1982 trails included a loop incorporating Kreag Road Park and the area behind Little Spring Run, a section from Garnsey to Moseley Road, and a loop on Horizon Hill. The trails were explored on regularly scheduled Sunday afternoon hikes. Over the next ten years the trail system grew, as did interest in the Association itself, with membership expansion, (a total of 164 families by 1990), and the inclusion of the Association master plan in the Town's Master Plan. In addition, a quarterly newsletter containing trail and environmental information and upcoming events was published and distributed to members.

By 1990 there were twenty-two miles of paths, mostly in the southern part of Perinton including the Kreag Road Park, Horizon Hill and Indian Hill areas. In 1995, with the availability of a new parcel of open space, the southern portions of the trail were connected, bringing the total number of miles to approximately twenty-six. The trails were marked with blazes: orange for the main trail, blue for return routes, red for connecting routes, white for local access paths, and yellow for branch trails.

Creating and maintaining Perinton trails are obviously the primary functions of the Crescent Trail Association. Essentially the trails are single-file footpaths that follow lot lines, hedgerows, old farm and logging roads, contours of wooded slopes and uplands, and the edges of wetlands, streams, and the Erie Canal. Charter member Doug Stinson noted that there was "a lot of art and science involved in planning a trail. You have to watch out for erosion patterns, and you want to make sure that it follows the contour of the land." Annual maintenance begins in April with a "trail sweep" and continues with monthly volunteer work parties under the leadership of a trail boss. A men's group and a women's group named the "Silver Foxes" and the "Foxy Lady Clippers and Loppers" (a.k.a. CLIPs) respectively, work constantly to keep the trails in good condition. They mow, cut away fallen trees and vines, clip back honeysuckle and rose bushes, and even build bridges across streams and swampy areas. Boy Scout candidates for Eagle rank have often helped by planning, organizing, and conducting service projects on the trails. In a normal year trail maintenance takes time, but the ice storm of 1991 caused so much damage that trail boss Howie Newton lamented that it was "almost like rebuilding the entire twenty-six mile trail system from scratch." The wind storms of 1998 and the ice storm of 2003 caused yet more challenges to the volunteers who maintain the trails.

On the Trail

Crescent Trail Association trails are not the only walking/hiking trails in Perinton. In the early 1990's, when the canal came under the aegis of the Thruway Authority, a newly-formed Canal Recreationway Commission began to look at ways to further use the canal as a recreational resource, and part of that plan included expanding and developing the tow path. The resulting "Erie Canal Heritage Trail" has added nine miles to Perinton's available trails. In addition, about the time that the Crescent Trail was being conceived, the first moves toward developing the old Rochester, Syracuse, and Eastern Trolley bed into a hikeway-bikeway were being taken. The project took off with the transfer of ownership of the right-of-way to Perinton in 1994 and by 1996 a Rails to Trails Conservancy guide book listed the trolley trail as one of "40 great rail trails in New York and New England." Overall these developments have provided over forty miles of trails in Perinton. The trails are not only for hiking and walking. They provide wonderful places to cross-country ski or snowshoe in the winter.

Realizing that there was something unique and special about Perinton's trail system, in 1996 the Crescent Trail Association nominated Perinton for *Trail Town USA* status, as determined by the American Hiking Society. David Lillard of the AHS explained that they "asked for nominations from places that went beyond using trails purely for recreational purposes. Recreation is one important aspect of a healthy trail system, but we were also looking for areas where trails promote non-motorized transportation, bring added economic benefits to the area, and connect to other trail systems, adding to the ongoing effort to create a nationwide system of trails and greenways." Perinton was subsequently named as one of the top ten trail towns of 1996. The others included Jefferson County, Colorado; Anchorage, Alaska; Pinetop-Lakeside, Arizona; Manchester, Connecticut; Xenia, Ohio; Los Angeles County, California; Lincoln, Nebraska; Orinda, California; and Raleigh, North Carolina.

Becoming "Trail Town, USA" has not meant the end of trail development. Since that time, the Association has added a number of "connectors" – small sections of trail that join older, longer sections. One of those joins the hikeway-bikeway (old trolley bed) path to the trail that heads up Thayer Hill, another connects Mason Valley, Carmel Estates, and the White Brook Nature Area, and yet another completes the Indian Hill-Thayer Hill loop. Larger areas that have been added to the list of trails include Howell Road Park and the White Brook Nature Area. As of 2010, the Association has completed its original plan to create a crescent-shaped trail system in Perinton from the Bushnell's Basin area in the southwest to the Howell Road area in the northeast except for a small segment near the High Acres landfill.

The Crescent Trail would not have been possible without the dedication of many people: Dave Schaeffer, one of the founders and a continuing guiding force; Allan Donk, often referred to as the "soul of the CTA"; Doug Stinson and Joy Barnitz, former Chairs; Nancy Whitcombe, another original member; Judy and Pete Logan in whose house the Association took form; Howie Newton, longtime Trail Boss; Jeannie Cole and Jim Unckless, longtime members; all the "Silver Foxes," "CLIPs," and every one of the dedicated members who have loved and cared for the trails.

While the trail system is available any time using the available maps, the Association offers monthly Sunday afternoon guided hikes over its more than thirty-five miles of trails. The members of the Association are dedicated to managing and maintaining those many miles for the benefit of the community, helping to make Perinton truly "Trail Town USA."

Perinton's Parks and Recreation Programs

Perinton may be known as "Trail Town, USA," but to its residents it might also be called "park town," as it has more open space and parks than any other community in the area. It has not, however, always been that way. The existence of community parks is a relatively new phenomenon. The first park in the village of Fairport was opened in 1932 and the first town park wasn't established until the 1960's. Today, Perinton has over 700 acres of open space and parkland that appeal to a wide variety of users of all ages, from walkers to cyclists to soccer players to cross-country runners.

Fairport Village Park, which is known today as Perinton Park, was the community's first. In 1920, Perinton acquired twelve acres of land on the west side of the canal north of the Rochester Road. It had been used as a dump for dirt dredged from the canal widening of 1912-13 and, according to one source, had also been at one time a campsite for gypsies and a "jungle where the youngsters used to trap muskrats."

In 1932 the town of Perinton turned those twelve acres over to the village of Fairport. At the time Addis Adams and his group of tennis enthusiasts were looking for a suitable site for tennis courts. The Rotary Club and the American Legion supported the project and plans were drawn up and submitted to the village, proposing to build the courts for about $500. Adams assured the Village Board that his group would be able to find ways to fund the project. Within a year the land was cleaned up and landscaped, the lower level drained in preparation for the building of a baseball field, a picnic area prepared, and the tennis courts constructed. The park indeed was a model for surrounding communities. Although the park was much used, the Depression took its toll and by the 1940's the area was in decline, and the park closed in 1948.

With the growth of industry and the availability of more leisure time during the latter decades of the nineteenth century, there developed an interest in recreational programs, especially for youth, "to keep young men off the streets." The earliest of those programs were run by the Y.M.C.A., which had a Fairport branch for about six years in the 1890's. Programs included Scout activities, musical entertainment, lectures, and other recreation for young people. In the 1920's the Fairport Community League was started to supervise youth activities. 109 "original members" contributed $5 a year to support baseball teams, volleyball, basketball, a summer picnic, sledding on South Main Street hill, skiing, and social dinners. In 1936, Joe Cummings, Fairport's new football coach that year, was hired as the part time Director of Recreation by Anne Hartigan, Chair of the Fairport-Perinton Youth Committee. Cummings' ties to the school district meant that recreational programs were often held in school facilities. In addition to Fairport Village Park, programs were held at schools in Egypt, and on Baird Road, Ayrault Road, East Avenue, and West Church Street. Although suggestions for the development of a community center appeared in both 1934 and 1941, nothing materialized until the Potter bequest of 1943.

Playground at West Church School - 1943

Fred Potter, who died in 1943, left his home at 53 West Church Street, five acres of land, and a sum of money for their care to the village of Fairport in a "nicely drawn will." The house was developed as a community center with the help of volunteers from scouts to seniors. During the war the land was used as a victory garden, and afterward, with the help of Joe Cummings and Ellen Hawver, both teachers, it was developed as a playground including ball fields. Cummings was also instrumental in getting the carriage house remodeled as the "Nook," a teen center with a game room and a place for dances. During the late 1940's programs included dances, game nights, a softball league, painting lessons, afternoon movies in the summer, and ice skating on the canal in winter. In addition, with the help of volunteer Louise Dean, Hawver opened a playground behind the West Church Street School. Equipment consisted of donated soccer balls. All the programs were so successful that there appeared to be a need for a full time recreation director to replace Joe Cummings, who had been the part time director since 1936. The Fairport-Perinton Recreation Council (formerly the Fairport-Perinton Youth Committee) named Frank Dearborn to the position in 1953. Adding to the work of Cummings, Dearborn continued to expand programs, which by 1956 included riflery, bowling, junior and senior high dances, bridge classes, square dancing at the Potter Community Center, tumbling, wrestling, ballet and tap lessons. He did all of this with the help of volunteers, eighteen summer helpers, and a part-time secretary. A 1956 newspaper noted that Perinton's recreation program was the most extensive in the Rochester area. Charles Heidelberger, who became Recreation Director in 1957, added the first softball team for men and also was active in starting programs for women such as softball and physical fitness training.

The recreation program for 1955 included nearly 100 dances for sixth through twelfth graders, tennis, dance and swimming instruction, 112 afternoons at the Nook for fifth through eighth graders, thirty-five days of summer supervised playground, eight days of skating, a girls' softball league, and eighteen afternoons for ninety members of the Golden Age Club. It should be noted that students who attended functions at The Nook had to adhere to a dress code: "No dungarees! No Levis! and No Bermuda shorts"; girls were required to wear skirts and it was "all right for boys to wear khakis."

Special events that drew over 100 participants that year included a Halloween Party, a Christmas Party, a rodeo, a playground circus, and a family night.

However, despite the nearly fifty increase in population during the 1950's, in 1959 there were only two parks in Perinton, Potter Park and Perinton Park, known at that time as the Fairport Village Park and which was unused at the time. Responding to this lack as well as to the increasing number of housing developments, in 1959 the town appointed a five-member Recreation Commission to work with developers to preserve land for open space and for parks.

In 1960 the town bought the then-unused Fairport Village Park by the canal at Fairport Road and constructed rest rooms, a picnic shelter, new tennis courts, and a playground. At the same time Fairport village converted the old East Avenue School building into a community recreation center. The building had been donated to the village by the Crosman Arms Company. After $10,000 worth of remodeling, it was opened in 1962 with a room for dances and movies, a pellet-gun range, a hobby room, a crafts room, a body-building room, a games room, and a senior citizens' room. One of the most popular programs was rifle shooting, which was enthusiastically backed by local Police Chief Thomas Aldrich. In addition, the playground was improved for use in the summer recreation program. Further, in 1961, the old Bushnell's Basin Schoolhouse was opened, providing additional meeting space for scout troops, senior citizens, and community groups from the southwest part of town.

Perinton Park

The years between 1959 and 1975 would see the creation of eight parks in the town and the allocation of a total of 550 acres of land to parks and open space. Egypt, Spring Lake, Kreag, and Fellows Road Parks, in addition to the Beechwood Nature area and the Garnsey Arboretum joined the reopened Perinton Park (formerly Fairport Village Park) and Potter Park as recreation areas for Perinton and Fairport residents. Perinton came to be known as having "more parkland per capita and more developed park recreation programs than virtually any other [town] in the state."

During the 1960's and 1970's, under the leadership of directors Oakes, Kennedy and Pearson, not only was there a dramatic increase in the number of parks and the amount of open space available, but also a tremendous increase in the number of programs available for citizens of all ages. Sports offerings for youth made use of various school gyms. For example, there were over 300 enrolled in the gymnastics program at West Avenue School in the late 1970's. In addition to summer playground programs like Little League and soccer, a number of drop-in programs were offered at school gyms and pools. In the winter, ski instruction was available for all age groups, and four skating rinks were open at Potter, Spring Lake, Fellows Road, and Kreag Road Parks. There was also a rink exclusively for hockey at Potter.

As the community continued to grow during the 1980's, so did the offerings of the Recreation Department. Two teen centers existed, one in the Potter Community Center's carriage barn, the "Tiger and Toe," and another at the Crosman Center. Instruction was available in tennis, soccer, basketball, field hockey, lacrosse, and wrestling. In addition there were tennis, soccer, and softball leagues for both boys and girls. Arts and crafts programs were developed and offered as were a number of family programs. One of these, the pizza contest where residents sample and choose the best pizza in town, is still an anticipated annual event. Opportunities for seniors included the Golden Age Club, the Retired Men's Club and the Retired & Senior Citizens Drop-in Program. The Recreation Department also began to develop a town hiking/biking trail along the old Rochester, Syracuse, and Eastern trolley bed. Other programs included Friends 'n' Fun, a program for mentally challenged youth, physical fitness programs for all ages, and the popular Thursday night gazebo concerts. Of benefit to the overall operation of the Recreation Department was the move of the offices from the Crosman Center to the Turk Hill Town Hall in 1980.

During the last decade of the twentieth century and at the beginning of the twenty-first, the number of programs and opportunities for recreation would expand dramatically. The 1990's brought significant additions to Perinton's recreation programs under the leadership of Ken Zeller, Superintendent of Parks and Recreation, Jim Donahue, Director of Recreation, and Dave Morgan, Director of Parks. In 1990 a new teen center, the Lion's Den, built by the Lions Club, opened behind Potter Memorial. Perinton Park received a major facelift in the mid 1990's. O'Connor Road was realigned to the west side of the park, new boat docks and a canoe launch were constructed, and a new picnic pavilion built, among other upgrades. In 1997, after many years of work and planning, the new Perinton Community Center opened on Turk Hill Road. The facility boasts an inviting senior center, two rooms for pre-schoolers, a large banquet facility, a number of meeting rooms, a cardio center, a weight room, and a room for fitness classes. Since the availability of school gym time for the public decreased about eighty-percent between the 1970's and the 1990's, the new community center with its gym, track, and other fitness areas, opened at the optimum time.

The 1990's also saw the largest growth in programs, reflecting not only demand but also the opening of the Community Center. In 1990 there were somewhat over 100 different programs to choose from, and by 2002 there were just over 700. In 2010 registration for over 1,200 classes numbered just under 16,000. This number does not include the many programs for seniors or the numbers of people who use the fitness equipment. Offerings are open to all age groups from pre-school to seniors; programs range from baby sitting to safety, from dancing to yoga, from basketball to exercise with rock music (for teens), from cooking to holiday crafts, from fencing to ceramics. In addition, the town has taken over the summer swim program from the Fairport Central School District. Reflecting the tremendous increase in usage since 1994, the number of full-time recreation staff and the revenue from programs, as well as the budget, have increased.

Aquatic center

In 2001 Center Stage opened behind the community center offering theater and musical programs. The first summer featured an evening of jazz, *Nunsense,* several country groups, the RPO Brass Quintet, the Fairport Fire Department Band, and the Perinton Concert Band. The subsequent seasons have featured jazz, swing, country, R & B, and folk music programs and often end with a patriotic celebration. The park also has an extensive playground for children and has recently opened a cross-country course in conjunction with the Fairport schools.

The next addition to the Perinton community center complex, the aquatic center, with a lap pool, a recreational pool with water slides and play area, and a whirlpool opened in 2004. Programs include Red Cross swim courses along with aquatic fitness programs and general open swim. There are also opportunities for parties and special events. At the same time some additions were made to the fitness area and to the locker rooms.

Perinton's Parks and Recreation programs are as successful as they are because of excellent leadership, and also because of strong community support and an atmosphere of cooperation among the town, the school district, and the many other community sports and arts groups.

Somewhere in a park or recreational facility in Perinton, one can work out, go boating or hiking, go swimming, have a gathering in one of the park pavilions, take classes, drop off children for day care or classes, take part in team sports in the gym, have lunch in the Nut 'n' Fancy Café at the Perinton Community Center, or simply enjoy walking or biking along the canal, hiking on the Crescent Trail, or snowshoeing on the old Rochester, Syracuse, and Eastern trolley bed. Without a doubt Perinton's parks and recreation programs are the best.

Concert at Center Stage

Summer playground group

Summer Lacrosse camp

Concert crowd at Center Stage

- INDEX -

-W-

Jean Keplinger

Jean Tower Keplinger was born and grew up in northern New Jersey. She received a B.A. in European History and French, *summa cum laude*, from William Smith College, and a M.S. in Education from Nazareth College of Rochester. She taught Social Studies in the Fairport Schools for many years, and upon her retirement in 1997, she became Perinton Town Historian. Jean, a Perinton resident since 1969, lives in the hamlet of Egypt with her husband Bill, also a retired Fairport teacher. They have two children and five grandchildren.